Prisoners of War and the German High Command

Prisoners of War and the German High Command

The British and American Experience

Vasilis Vourkoutiotis
University of Ottawa
Canada

© Vasilis Vourkoutiotis 2003

All rights reserved. No reproduction, copy or transmission of this publication may be made without written permission.

No paragraph of this publication may be reproduced, copied or transmitted save with written permission or in accordance with the provisions of the Copyright, Designs and Patents Act 1988, or under the terms of any licence permitting limited copying issued by the Copyright Licensing Agency, 90 Tottenham Court Road, London W1T 4LP.

Any person who does any unauthorised act in relation to this publication may be liable to criminal prosecution and civil claims for damages.

The author has asserted his right to be identified as the author of this work in accordance with the Copyright, Designs and Patents Act 1988.

First published 2003 by
PALGRAVE MACMILLAN
Houndmills, Basingstoke, Hampshire RG21 6XS and
175 Fifth Avenue, New York, N.Y. 10010
Companies and representatives throughout the world

PALGRAVE MACMILLAN is the global academic imprint of the Palgrave Macmillan division of St. Martin's Press, LLC and of Palgrave Macmillan Ltd. Macmillan® is a registered trademark in the United States, United Kingdom and other countries. Palgrave is a registered trademark in the European Union and other countries.

ISBN 1–4039–1169–X

This book is printed on paper suitable for recycling and made from fully managed and sustained forest sources.

A catalogue record for this book is available from the British Library

Library of Congress Cataloging-in-Publication Data
Vourkoutiotis, Vasilis, 1970–
   Prisoners of War and the German High Command: the British and American experience / by Vasilis Vourkoutiotis.
       p. cm.
   Includes bibliographical references and index.
       ISBN 1–4039–1169–X
   1. World War, 1939–1945–Prisoners and prisons, German. 2. Prisoners of war–United States–History–20th century. 3. Prisoners of war–Great Britain–History–20th century. I. Title.

D805.G3V648 2003
940.54'7243–dc21
                                                                2002044801

10 9 8 7 6 5 4 3 2 1
12 11 10 09 08 07 06 05 04 03

Printed and bound in Great Britain by
Antony Rowe Ltd, Chippenham, Wiltshire

Contents

List of Figures	vi
Foreword	vii
List of Abbreviations and Terms	viii

1 Introduction ... 1

2 Background Information ... 11
   2.1 Historical Background ... 11
   2.2 The Geneva Convention, and the National Prisoner-of-war Policies of Britain, Canada, the United States, and Germany, 1939 ... 25
   2.3 The Structure of Prisoner-of-war Affairs in Germany ... 29

3 General Issues on Policy and Prisoner-of-war Camps ... 37
   3.1 Identification and Status of Prisoners of War ... 37
   3.2 Early Days: Issues surrounding Capture and Captivity ... 43
   3.3 General Camp Infrastructure ... 48

4 Crimes and Punishment of Prisoners of War ... 75
   4.1 Basic Issues ... 75
   4.2 Matters of Discipline ... 76
   4.3 Justice Matters ... 87
   4.4 Related Security Issues ... 94

5 Economics and External Relations of Prisoners of War ... 109
   5.1 Labor and Finance ... 109
   5.2 External Relations of Prisoners of War ... 133

6 Final Assessments ... 165
   6.1 What the Inspectors Saw ... 165
   6.2 Policy versus Evidence ... 183
   6.3 Conclusions ... 185

Notes ... 203

Bibliography ... 256

Index ... 265

List of Figures

1	Organizational chart of Germany's prisoner-of-war administration, Oct. 1, 1944	ix
2	*Wehrkreise* – German military districts, with regional headquarters	x
3	Total number of reports of visits, by ICRC or Protecting Power	166
4	Material conditions in the camps	167
5	Material conditions in the camps (as a percentage of total reports of visits)	168
6	Visits made to each type of camp (as a percentage of total visits)	177
7	Material conditions (as a percentage of all visits to each type of camp)	177
8	Geneva Convention violations	178
9	Geneva Convention violations (as a percentage of total reports of visits)	178
10	Geneva Convention violations (as a percentage of all visits to each type of camp)	183

Foreword

There are many people to whom, over the course of the preparation of this study, first as a doctoral dissertation and then as a manuscript, I owe a debt of gratitude.

I was fortunate to work under the supervision of Professor Peter Hoffmann at McGill University, without whose expert guidance and understanding this project would never have reached completion; I also thank my Ph.D. minor-field supervisors, Professor Valentin Boss and the late but not forgotten Professor Robert Vogel. The archivists and staff at the Bundesarchiv-Militärarchiv in Freiburg im Breisgau, the Public Record Office in London, the Imperial War Museum in London, the International Committee of the Red Cross in Geneva, the German Red Cross Committee, the National Archives and Records Administration in Washington DC and College Park Maryland, the Air Force Historical Research Agency at Maxwell Air Force Base (Montgomery, Alabama), the National Archives of Canada, the Canadian Armed Forces Directorate of History and Heritage, Cornell University Library, the Inter-Library Loan department at McGill University, and the staff of McGill's History Department all made researching this field a pleasure. While these individuals saved me time and from errors, any mistakes which remain are, of course, my own.

During the period of revising the dissertation into a manuscript, I was given the opportunity by Civic Education Project to lecture at two Russian universities, and offer a special thanks to the Russia Country Director Irina Zorina and her staff, as well as to my colleagues and friends at the Faculty of International Relations at Ural State University, and Smolny College, St. Petersburg State University. A warm thanks, as well, to Luciana O' Flaherty and the staff at Palgrave Macmillan, who patiently oversaw the transformation of a revised dissertation into a manuscript.

Personally, many friends assisted me in ways I can never begin to repay, except by publicly acknowledging their help: J. Black, G. Bruce, A. Duplessis, M. Howard, A. Izzo, M. Kleinberg, W. Klemperer, K. Reynolds, S. Robinson, K. Sams, J. Stubbs, R. Vakil, L. van Boxel, and J. and A. Zander. And last, but not least, the project would never have been possible without the support of the Vourkoutiotis and Sato families, and especially my wife Takako and daughter Siaki-chan.

List of Abbreviations and Terms

BA-MA	Bundesarchiv-Militärarchiv
BAB	Bau- und Arbeits-Bataillone: prisoner-of-war labor battalions
Dulag (Luft)	Prisoner-of-war transit camp (airforce)
ICRC	International Committee of the Red Cross
IMT	International Military Tribunal, *Trial of the Major War Criminals before the International Military Tribunal*, 42 vols. Nuremburg, 1947–9.
Kgf	*Kriegsgefangenen*, prisoner of war
Marlag	Navy prisoner-of-war camp
MMC	Mixed Medical Commission
MOC	Man of Confidence
NAC	National Archives of Canada
NARA	National Archives and Records Administration, Washington DC
Oflag	Prisoner-of-war camp for commissioned officers
OKH	Oberkommando der Heer (German Army High Command)
OKL	Oberkommando der Luftwaffe (German Air Force High Command)
OKM	Oberkommando der Kriegsmarine (German Navy High Command)
OKW	Oberkommando der Wehrmacht (German Armed Forces High Command)
PRO	Public Record Office of the UK
RM	Reichsmark, the former standard monetary unit of Germany
SAO/SBO	Senior American Officer/Senior British Officer
Stalag (Luft)	Prisoner-of-war camp for soldiers (airforce personnel)
WASt	Wehrmacht-Auskunftsstelle (Armed Forces Information Office for prisoners of war)
WK	Wehrkreis (Military District)
WUSt	Wehrmacht-Untersuchungsstelle (Armed Forces War Crimes Office)

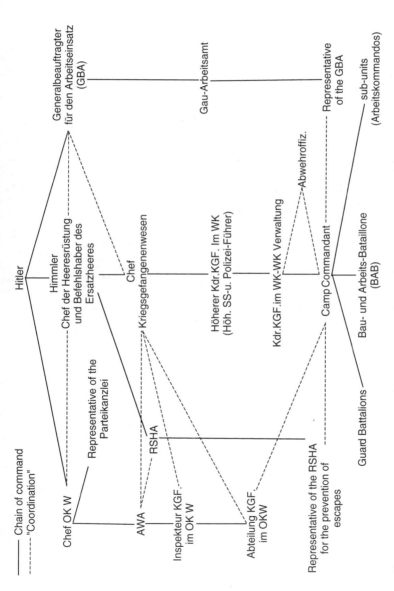

Figure 1   Organizational chart of Germany's prisoner-of-war administration, Oct. 1, 1944

Figure 2 Wehrkreise – German military districts, with regional headquarters

" ... What I want to understand is this. You were a Field Marshal, standing in the boots of Blücher, Gneisenau, and Moltke. How did you tolerate all these young men being murdered, one after the other without making any protest? ... You were a Field Marshal, Kesselring was a Field Marshal, Milch was a Field Marshal, all, I gather, with military training behind them and all having their influence if not their command, among the Armed Forces of Germany. How was it that there was not one man of your rank, of your military tradition, with the courage to stand up and oppose cold-blooded murder [of captured Allied commandos]? That is what I want to know." – *British Prosecutor at Nuremberg, Sir David Maxwell-Fyfe*

"I did not do it; I made no further objection to these things. I can say no more and I cannot speak for others." – *the Defendant, Field Marshal Wilhelm Keitel* (IMT, vol. 10, pp. 643–4)

1
Introduction

At first glance, the field of prisoner-of-war history, especially with regard to the Second World War, may strike one as cluttered with innumerable writings. Many articles and memoirs await the interested reader. Likewise, in the area of popular culture, many films and television programs and series were produced after the close of hostilities in 1945; the plight of the prisoner-of-war has been raised to heroic levels, as in Stalag 13, as well as lowered to the level of farce, as in Hogan's Heroes.

Perhaps reflecting the public's interest in daring escapes and supposed cat-and-mouse outwitting of evil Nazi jailers, many of the printed works which appeared soon after the war can also be classified as "light," or unscholarly, history. Often these works pay no attention to academic traditions (let alone the inclusion of source references), but some are nonetheless interesting to read for their own sake, and should be thought of less as attempts at writing "history" (whatever the claims of the dust-jacket promoters) than as efforts to provide a popular literary equivalent to what was appearing on the screens of cinemas and televisions. Straddling the boundary with more scholastic history are the many memoirs by former prisoners of war; these present a challenge for the historian. A distinction needs to be made between diaries, which provided a contemporary record of fact, albeit from the limited perspective of the person writing, and memoirs which appeared several years after the war was over, when recall of many details receded.[1] The issue of their utility is a quandary until one determines precisely what one is interested in. For the purposes of this study, as will be seen, they are not of direct relevance, and their consultation should be considered complementary to this work, rather than a prerequisite.[2] The first major task of the student of Second

World War prisoner-of-war history, on the whole, then, is to separate the popular works from the far fewer attempts to apply more rigorous historical assessments of the period. Once this is accomplished, the field becomes much more manageable, in a historiographical sense.

The historiography

One of the first things noticeable about the academic works is that they tend to approach the topic from the perspective of nationality. Thus, the plight of French prisoners of war is covered by such authors as Yves Durand[3] and Jean-Marie d'Hoop[4], as well as the editors of *Revue d'histoire de la deuxième guerre mondiale*.[5] Durand, especially, provides a complete and thorough examination of most aspects of the French experience, which was more complicated than others by the capitulation and subsequent agreements concerning prisoners of war between the postcapitulation French government located at Vichy, and Germany. Likewise, the histories of most other countries of occupied Europe have included examinations of their prisoner-of-war experiences.[6] The barbarity and cruelty of German policy toward the east Europeans (especially the Poles and Russians) have been the subject of many detailed academic studies.[7] In most cases, these studies begin with the initial German decisions to exempt themselves from the obligations of the Geneva Convention on the Treatment of Prisoners of War of July 1929[8] – in the Polish case, because a Polish "state" no longer existed, and in the case of the Soviet Union, because it was not a signatory to the Convention (which seems inconsistent with Article 82).

German historians, too, approach the field from a national perspective, covering the plight of German prisoners of war, especially in Russia,[9] leaving the study of German treatment of British and American prisoners of war to their counterparts in those countries. Occasionally, case-studies of the wartime experiences in German local regions, or "Heimats," include references to the treatment of the Allied prisoners of war in the relevant districts,[10] but not in a meaningful way that would contribute to the examination of overall military policy.

Of the powers involved in the European theatre of the war, the case of the Americans and the British (a term which, in keeping with its use at the time, should be taken to include servicemen of the British Commonwealth as well as Great Britain) were unique in several ways.

First, their countries (with the exception of the Channel Islands) were unoccupied by Germany. Second, the United States, Great Britain, and Canada were the three countries which held a vast number of German servicemen in captivity, ensuring, as will later be seen, the attention of the German government. And lastly, their status as "legitimate" signatories to the Geneva Conventions was not called into doubt by the German government. For both the Americans and the British, studies of various aspects of prisoner-of-war history have been written. Specifically, David Rolf[11] and David Foy[12] both made fairly recent contributions.

Rolf's book, in fact, covers much of the same ground as this study, but with a notable difference: his account of the experiences and life inside the camps for prisoners of war is written from the perspective of the prisoners themselves, relying for the most part on memoirs, private papers, and correspondence. He made full use of the records available at the Public Record Office in London, but his use of German archival material is significantly deficient: he wrote, for example,[13] that only fragmentary evidence remains of the nature of the German command structure for prisoners of war, and that papers of the Chef Kriegsgefangenenwesen did not survive the war. However, in files of several series which he apparently did not consult,[14] clear pictures emerge of both the German command structure[15] as well as the orders and policy changes made by the Chef Kriegsgefangenenwesen.[16] Rolf's "bottom–top" historical approach, a detailed history of how the prisoners viewed their captivity, is also his weakness.

David Foy wrote the only other notable recently published work purporting to provide comprehensive coverage of Germany's treatment of American prisoners of war. Based largely on his dissertation on prisoners of war from the US Army and Army Air Corps,[17] Foy's work is more thoroughly grounded in archival research. Like Rolf, however, Foy focuses his attention on the perspectives and experiences of the prisoners of war themselves. He used the extensive archival holdings in the United States and correspondences with former prisoners of war, but he made no direct use of German archival material.[18] Given that his aim was to produce a "national" history of prisoner-of-war experience, this is perhaps understandable. However, it does not further the understanding of precisely what German policy *was* at the start of the war and how it evolved subsequently. Like Rolf's work for mostly British prisoners of war, Foy's dissertation and book give the reader an understanding only of what daily life was like for many of the American prisoners of war in Germany, often in their own words.

Andrew Hasselbring's doctoral dissertation[19] also suffers from some of the same weaknesses. He makes almost no use of original German source material, relying instead on the Red Cross/Protecting Power reports, and reports produced by the American Armed Forces during the war. His strengths lie in a section of his work titled "Daily Life as a Prisoner of War," which is as thorough for its topic as Foy's work. His failure to use German material, however, leads him to make many questionable, sweeping generalizations without suitable evidence.[20] At other times, he makes completely erroneous statements.[21] Hasselbring is on much firmer ground when he stays close to the daily lives of the prisoners themselves.

The issue for Canada, which had large numbers of German prisoners of war as well as their own in German captivity, has been best examined by Jonathan Vance's thorough work.[22] But like the authors of the American histories, his is a national study, and as such the scope is of more limited value for the reader trying to understand the nature and evolution of overall German military policy.[23] A relatively recent study of the experiences of Australian prisoners of war was written by Patsy Adam-Smith; her use of interviews with former prisoners of war provides interesting anecdotes and examples of life as a prisoner, but does little beyond this to further the understanding of the greater picture of prisoner-of-war history in the Second World War.[24]

In addition to these authors' largely national studies of Second World War prisoners of war, there are studies of specific camps.[25] The most notable of these were often also popular-history style works, surrounding the escapades of the "incorrigibles" in Oflag IV C Colditz.[26] There are also other, more scholarly works, as for the Naval Internment camp attached to Stalag X B Sandbostel.[27] The benefit of this book is that it provides a detailed examination of all facets of life, from German commands down to the Red Cross reports on their visits, of an important internment camp. However, its very focus is also its undoing, as experiences varied greatly between camps, depending, as will be seen below, on many factors, from the temperament of the commandant to the physical location and climate of the camp. Arthur Durand's examination of life at Stalag Luft III Sagan belies its somewhat sensationalist title.[28] Based upon his doctoral dissertation, this camp study is a thorough evaluation of conditions at the camp which became well-known after the mass escape of 75 British airmen and the murderous reprisals against most of the recaptured escapees. Like Rolf and Foy, Arthur Durand's story is also told largely from the perspective of the prisoners of war themselves. But unlike the other two authors, Durand moves beyond the personal recollections of the prisoners to examine in some detail, based on extensive use of archival holdings in the United States, changes in the conditions experienced over the course of the war years. Although the book approaches the topic from the prisoners' point of view, its main weakness is that the analysis of Germany's military policy is often uninformed.[29] For example, in the discussion of German food rations given to the prisoners of war,[30] Durand notes that the German rations were far below the levels envisioned by the Geneva Convention, and concludes in part that "the prisoners could not have survived for extended periods of time on either the German rations or the Red Cross food, but the combination provided an adequate, though by no means tasty, diet."[31] While literally correct, this does not acknowledge the fact that the low levels of rations issued by the German authorities were the result of a formal policy decision made by the OKW, who realized early in the war that the Allies could and would provide generous supplements through the Red Cross, and saw in this an opportunity to reduce the cost of maintaining the prisoners of war (thus causing the Allies to subsidize, indirectly, the German war effort).[32] Further, given the implementation of food rationing for the civilian population as well as the prisoners, the threat of an Allied reprisal with reductions in food rations against the German prisoners of war in the British Commonwealth and, later, the United States, was judged small, and the German policy remained in force. In other words, what at first seems like simply a capricious policy of near-starvation with regard to American and British prisoners was, in fact, part of the general German policy of avoiding as much of their treaty obligations as possible without provoking a direct reprisal against their own prisoners in British–American captivity, in order to save material resources for the main war effort. As with many other aspects of prisoner-of-war life, Arthur Durand, like Foy and Rolf before him, concentrates on the ultimate reality for the prisoners, without examining the German policy directives which caused it.

Statistical studies concerning Allied prisoners of war are, surprisingly, rare. The official American history of the Second World War[33] does not contain monthly breakdowns of the numbers of Americans in German captivity. Not particularly useful statistics concerning the servicemen of Great Britain are found in the Surgeon General's volume of the British series.[34] The Canadian official history of the war[35] provides monthly breakdowns by service branch, but this is the exception rather than the rule among such official national histories of the war. The International Committee of the Red Cross (ICRC), in their official history,[36] or in their *Revue Internationale de la Croix-Rouge*[37] published monthly during the war years, or even in the quasi-official studies published since then,[38] did not provide much statistical information that could be of use to the researcher in this field. Likewise, among German sources, no statistical compilation for the western prisoners of war has been published. Useful studies, including statistical information, do exist for the German prisoners of war in American captivity,[39] but one has to look to archival sources to find comparative data concerning British and American prisoners of war in German captivity.[40] In general, the dearth of statistical information forms one of the more puzzling gaps in this field. A recent attempt by John Ellis[41] to rectify the situation met with decidedly ambivalent success.

One of the few measures of the numbers of prisoners of war in German captivity comes from the reports made by Red Cross and Protecting Power. Under the terms of the Geneva Convention, delegates from the International Red Cross and a Protecting Power (the USA on behalf of the British prisoners of war until December 1941; thereafter the Swiss looked after both American and British interests) were permitted to visit the prisoner-of-war camps, examine conditions, speak unhindered with the prisoners' senior officer representative or Man of Confidence (MOC, the elected representative[42] of the other-ranks), and write a report to be sent to the governments whose soldiers were held captive. These reports are one of the few places where one will find the effective strength, broken down by nationality, for a prisoner-of-war camp at a given time. If there are few statistical compilations of information concerning prisoners of war, the same cannot be said of general archival information.

As Jonathan Vance demonstrates in his study of Canadian prisoners of war,[43] the National Archives of Canada,[44] as well as special library collections, contain much information concerning the home government's bureaucratic response to issues concerning their soldiers in German captivity, as well as responses to the Red Cross and Protecting Power reports made of visits to the camps. The same can be said of both the American[45] and British[46] national archives. The German military archives contain a wealth of information about the implementation of policies and directives dealing with the treatment of the prisoners of war in their care. These four archives provide the main sources of information for this study.

For all the previous publications and primary source material available, then, one significant gap in the historiography emerges in this field: there are no studies which trace the evolution of the German High Command's overall military policy toward British and American prisoners of war over the course of the war years. The few writings which purport to be general examinations of Germany's treatment of British or American prisoners of war approach the topic from the bottom – that is, they reconstruct what life was like for the individual prisoners of war, usually through interviews and memoirs, and tend to make use of archival resources in a more limited fashion, to support their observations. Another gap in the historiography is the lack of any attempt to examine the full picture, or an assessment of how conditions changed over the course of the war by referring to all the camp reports available in the national archives of the relevant countries.

This study is an attempt, then, to fill in these gaps: to examine the nature of German military policy toward the British and American prisoners of war at the outbreak of the war and to compare it to their obligations under the 1929 Geneva Convention, to see how the policy changed as the war progressed, and to see the impact of German military policy on the conditions endured by the prisoners of war during the course of the war, as described by Red Cross and Protecting Power inspection reports.[47]

By way of background, this examination will begin with an overview of the evolution of prisoner-of-war history in general terms, followed by a focus on modern Germany in particular, and will then examine the state of German military policy on prisoners of war at the outbreak of war in 1939. This background section will draw mostly on secondary publications and dissertations. It will also examine both the Geneva Convention of 1929, and the Germany military writings in place at the start of hostilities. For comparative purposes, a brief description of the initial British, Canadian, and American policies will be provided, as well as more specialized analysis in the appropriate sections.

A significant portion of this study will consist of chronicling and commenting upon developments in German policy as the war progressed. The focus here is not on the debates surrounding various issues on prisoner-of-war policy in Hitler's headquarters (of which there were few, except surrounding the issues of mass escapes and the Allied Commandos, which will be examined below, separately), but on the final decisions made by the OKW. The main source of information for this examination are the orders, policy outlines, and clarifications sent by the OKW down the chain of command to the various levels of the prisoner-of-war administration, culled from the German military archives.

To independently assess the impact of these decisions, this study relied upon every single ICRC or Protecting Power report of a visit to prisoner-of-war main camps and major work detachments which could be found in the national archives of the United States, Great Britain, and Canada: these three countries accounted for the majority of Anglo-American prisoners of war in German captivity, and likewise held large numbers of German prisoners taken by the United States' and the British Commonwealth countries' forces. Reports concerning other Commonwealth troops (from Australia, New Zealand, South Africa, and India) were sent through the British government in London, which retained copies now held at the Public Record Office, and were thus among those consulted. As the reports ran well into the hundreds, they have been categorized by time, the quality of material conditions, and incidents of violations of the prisoners' rights under the Geneva Convention; further, many of the reports on visits to very small work detachments (from a handful to a few dozen prisoners) were noted only if their findings presented an exception from the remainder of the work groups attached to their main camp. Given the types of problems and difficulties noted in the reports themselves, the basic unit of time which seemed to make the most sense for this study was the calendar season (autumn [22 September to 21 December], winter [22 December to 21 March], spring [22 March to 21 June], and summer [22 June to 21 September]), and it was in this way that camp reports were grouped for further assessment.

The Protecting Power delegates reported in a set format on the following subjects during their visits: General Description, Capacity and Present Personnel, Interior Arrangements, Bathing and Washing Facilities, Toilet Facilities, Food and Cooking, Medical Attention and Sickness, Clothing, Laundry, Money and Pay, Canteen, Religious Activity, Recreation and Exercise, Mail, Welfare Work, Complaints, General Impression. The ICRC delegates, likewise, tended to follow a set format in reporting the conditions they found: Camp Leaders, Strength, Accommodation, Food, Clothing, Canteen, Leisure and Intellectual and Religious Needs, Hygiene, Discipline, Collective Parcels, Correspondence, Work and Pay, Interview with the Camp Leaders, Conclusion. While these formats were generally adhered to, expediency often led to many reports offering observations only if the delegates found conditions either exceptionally good or very poor, or very short summaries to be telexed to the home countries.

In assessing trends in the material conditions of the camps from these reports, some clarification of terminology is needed, *as well as some caution*. From the start of the war to the end, the definitions, of "excellent," "very good," "satisfactory," "unsatisfactory," and "wholly inadequate," and their synonyms, used by the inspectors, changed. As can be seen by comparing the specific examples given in each season, what was "unsatisfactory" in a camp in the summer of 1940 may well have been considered "good" in the winter of 1944/5. One must therefore keep in mind that the standards to which the inspectors held the Detaining Power accountable slid downwards as the war continued, to the point where the existence of subsistence conditions, with shelter and freedom from life-threatening health problems, were welcomed, regardless of how closely they conformed to the ideal standards of the Depot troops demanded in the Geneva Convention. Likewise, if an inspector noted that food rations were "standard," that often referred to the standards set by the Germans (which, as will be seen, slid significantly over the course of the war), and not necessarily the standard set out by the Convention. Overall, then, the below-average conditions reported in the spring of 1945 were certainly far worse than those noted in the spring of 1940.

No sources of information are, of course, entirely impartial or infallible, and the same must be said of these reports. Pressures of both travel and other sorts (from either the Home Power or the Detaining Power, or even their own organizations) may have weighed on the minds of the inspectors when they were visiting the camps. There were also many instances (documented in the reports themselves) in which a German Commandant, when being informed of an upcoming visit, would do his best to effect immediate if often minor changes, in the hopes of staving off criticisms. In short, the inspectors were human, and so the reports they wrote were subject to the normal frailties of the species. Despite this, however, one thing remains clear after examing all the existing archival evidence: no other source of information exists which provides as comprehensive a coverage of the camps over the course of the war year. For all the possible failings, then, the Protecting Power and ICRC reports are still the best available source of information open to the historical researcher who is attempting to gauge the overall picture.

After an overview of both the specifics of German military policy as well as conditions at the camps as revealed in the Red Cross and Protecting Power reports, it will be seen that German military policy toward, and treatment of, British and American prisoners of war was initially fairly consistent with the terms of the Geneva Convention. Shortly after the war began, however, unilateral actions were taken (such as the reduction of food rations with national Red Cross parcels expected to take up the slack) whenever it seemed that no retaliation was likely against German prisoners of war in Anglo-American captivity. For the most part, these actions were limited to questions of logistical supplies, aimed at reducing the demands upon resources born by Germany for maintaining the prisoners of war. As the war progressed, and material shortages combined with military defeats, incidents of Nazi Party influence on the military's responsibility increased, culminating in the appointment of Himmler in September 1944 as the head of the OKW's prisoner-of-war administration. Acts of outright atrocity against British and American prisoners of war occurred against few of the total prisoners of war held by Germany – most significantly as concerns the capture of Allied Commandos, and the reprisal murders of 50 recaptured prisoners of war following the mass escape from the Luftwaffe camp for Allied airmen at Sagan. But for the most part, atrocities were not common once prisoners of war were accepted as such and taken into formal captivity. As is clear from the German records themselves, one of the prime motivations for this was fear of reprisals against German prisoners. In several instances, German camp Commandants chose to ignore orders they found distasteful, or applied them in a fashion which rendered them ineffective, such as during the shackling of Canadian and other British prisoners of war in 1942/3. Orders from the OKW were often applied unevenly, and the temper, character, and professionalism of the German military staff seemed of significant importance in determining the quality of life experienced by the prisoners of war, at least until the German economy as a whole fell into chaos toward the end of the conflict, at which point no amount of good will could procure supplies which didn't exist.

An examination of the Nuremberg proceedings verifies that the main complaints against the OKW with regard to British and American prisoners of war (as opposed to violations against the Soviet, French, and others) revolved around the denial of prisoner-of-war status to, and execution of, captured Allied Commandos; there were few mass reprisals and atrocities.

2
Background Information

2.1 Historical background

The 1929 Geneva Convention on the Treatment of Prisoners of War[1] was the first codification of rules regarding prisoners of war independent from general rules of conduct during war. Until then, prisoner-of-war policy had been subsumed under general military behavior. The evolution of attitudes toward prisoners of war is, in the first instance, the evolution of moderation in general warfare, from pre-Christian times to the present, and it appears worthwhile to examine this evolution, to set the rules in place in 1939 within their overall historical context.

The early days

In the Old Testament, moderation seemed to depend upon the extent of a threat which the nations in question posed to the Israelites, either spiritually or territorially. "Now go and smite Amalak, and utterly destroy all that they have, and spare them not; but slay both man and woman, infant and suckling, ox and sheep, camel and ass,"[2] and "thou shalt utterly destroy ... the Hittites, and the Amorites, the Canaanites, and the Perizzites, the Hivites, and the Jebusites; as the Lord thy God hath commanded thee: That they teach you not to do after all their abominations, which they have done unto their gods; [lest] ye sin against the Lord your God."[3] In the event that an offer of peace from the Israelites was rejected by peoples whose city did not form part of the Israelites' divine inheritance, a relative amount of moderation was to be shown:

> And if it [the city] will make no peace with thee, but will make war against thee, then thou shalt beseige it: And when the Lord thy God

hath delivered it into thine hands, thou shalt smite every male thereof with the edge of the sword: But the women, and the little ones, and the cattle, and all that is in the city, even all the spoil thereof, shalt thou take unto thyself; and thou shalt eat the spoil of thine enemies, which the Lord thy God hath given thee. Thus shalt thou do unto all the cities which are very far off from thee, which are not of the cities of these nations. But of the cities of these people, which the Lord thy God doth give thee for an inheritance, thou shalt save alive nothing that breatheth ...[4]

From almost the other side of the world, Sun Tzu, writing in 500 BC in China, encouraged the taking of prisoners instead of the killing of the enemy where possible, but for utilitarian rather than humanitarian reasons: "Generally in war the best policy is to take a state intact; to ruin it is inferior to this.... To capture the enemy's army is better than to destroy it; to take intact a battalion, a company or a five-man squad is better than to destroy them. For to win one hundred victories in one hundred battles is not the acme of skill. To subdue the enemy without fighting is the acme of skill. Thus, what is of supreme importance in war is to attack the enemy's strategy."[5] How prisoners were treated in early Chinese history was also commented upon repeatedly in the *Tso-chuan*, a series of texts written around the turn of the first century BC, covering the political history of the Eastern Chou period (770–403 BC).[6] After a battle, prisoners would either be slaughtered (with some of their blood being ceremonially smeared on the victors' drums), held for ransom (with the left ear cut off), or used as slaves.[7] Slaughter was rarely indiscriminate during the Ch'un-ch'iu period (722–481 BC); enslavement or ransoming was more likely.[8] During the Warring States period (403–221 BC), slaughter of captured prisoners occurred more frequently, but usually with the disclaimer that it was logistically necessary. By the Ch'u Han times (209–202 BC), however, it was more common: the entire surrendered army of Ch'in was executed at the order of Hsiang Yü during this period.[9] The surrender of a foreign king and his subjects was, on the other hand, usually met with the conferral of honors and noble titles, to ensure future loyalty. Thus, when the Hun-hsieh king surrendered to Han with a large number of his followers in 121 BC, 10,000 households were granted varying rights of nobility.[10]

As noted by Thucydides, treaties between Athens and Sparta in Ancient Greece provided for prisoner exchanges. During the Peloponnesian War, Demosthenes eventually surrendered to Gylippus in Sicily under the following terms: "[all the troops serving under him] were to lay down their arms on the condition that no one was to be put to death either summarily, or by imprisonment, or by lack of the necessities of life." Nicias, surrounded by Gylippus shortly thereafter, would only surrender on the condition that his army be free to go, and that Athens would pay to Syracuse all the money that they had spent on the war, with Athenian hostages being given (at a rate of one hostage per talent owed) until the full amount was paid. This offer was refused, Nicias continued to fight, and the remainder of the Athenian army in Sicily was thus slaughtered, with Nicias being captured. When Demosthenes surrendered he only secured the lives of those who served under him, and not his own; he and Nicias, against Gylippus's protests to the Syracusans, were later put to death.[11]

Socrates also believed that, as the superior race, it did not behove Greeks to enslave other Greeks; the enslavement of prisoners could only be justified if they were captured barbarians. To pillage and destroy the lands of other Greeks was also not justifiable: at most, a conquering army should burn the current year's harvest of crops.[12]

Generally, the Romans were considered to be more lenient toward the prisoners than the Greeks; only those who had carried weapons against Rome were to be enslaved. Captives could be killed when they became an encumbrance, or when their killing was useful in terrifying their enemies and glorifying Rome.[13] Thus, magnanimity was entirely a luxury, to be dispensed with when no longer expedient.[14] Romans taken prisoner by barbarians could be kept for ransom, but were more often enslaved, leading the Romans, when concluding peace treaties, to generally demand as a condition the release of compatriots captured in earlier raids.[15] Prisoners could also be a source of information for new technology: Romans who had been taken prisoner built the siege engines used by barbarians at the siege of Vetera, AD 70.

A common use by Romans of barbarians who were captured in war was to colonize parts of the empire.[16] Colonies of prisoners of war were governed by precise regulations: they paid taxes, were not placed in border territories close to their homes, and were not required to offer recruits for the army for a period of 20 years, so that their agricultural system had time to develop.[17] Though evidence concerning the treatment of eventual recruits from these settlements is tenuous, it generally appears that they were treated in the same manner as recruits from elsewhere in the empire.[18]

In the fourth century AD, barbarian prisoners were also often recruited by Romans for service in the army immediately upon capture. They were usually split up into small groups and dispersed among

Romans, though on one occasion (the defeat of Radagaisus in 406) 12,000 prisoners were recruited to serve wholesale (possibly as an emergency measure, as Alaric was threatening Italy at the time).[19] Also, individual prisoners of war of some repute, such as King Vadomarius who had been kidnapped in Gaul, might be pressed into service in another part of the empire. Generally, whether immediately after a battle or eventually from a colony, the Romans made use of prisoners of war as soldiers within their own army. They were also used to obtain topographic and strategic information about the main enemy bodies.[20]

Of knights and men

In central Europe, the Thuringians, after being defeated at Chalons, murdered all hostages and captives. The Avars cut the throats of all their captives to demonstrate their view of them as useless merchandise, having had their price for them refused by Maurice of Saxony, in the late sixth century.[21] The Magyar invaders of German territories, from 899 to 955, always attempted to recapture those of their comrades who had been made prisoners in the course of a battle. Otto the Great, at the battle of Augsburg of August 10, 955, ordered that all captured Magyar chieftains be slaughtered rather than taken prisoner, to discourage future raids.[22]

From the end of the Middle Ages, the slaughter or enslavement of prisoners of war among the Christian nations in Europe abated significantly. Though the admonitions of the Church can certainly be supposed to have had an impact in this development, the fortunes which could be had by ransoming played none too small a part in establishing the tradition of mercy on the battlefield. Indeed, as Keen points out, the final stages of battles in this time were often highly chaotic, almost comedic, scenes, with the victors and their servants rushing about to receive the right-hand gauntlets of as many men as they could; in the confusion, prisoners could even be made of one's allies, with the profiteering captains loath to give up their captives until a court judgment could be obtained.[23] This state of affairs was also noted in some detail by a nineteenth-century chronicler of the evolution of international rules, Robert Ward.[24] The December 1120 peace between King Henry I of England and King Louis VI of France called, among other things, for the freeing of prisoners, as well as the restitution of castles.[25]

It was common practice during the Middle Ages for the rights to obtain prisoners of war and hold them for ransom to be detailed in formal contracts called "indentures of war," concluded before the actual campaign. For example, an indenture concluded at Savoy in 1369 between John of Gaunt, Duke of Lancaster, and Sir John de Neville, Lord of Raby, stated that bounty and prisoners were to be shared by the two of them.[26] A 1475 indenture of war, between the Duke of Gloucester and Esquire Edmund Paston, stated that Paston had to inform the duke within six days of the name, rank, state, condition, number, and value of any prisoners captured in battle. In keeping with the tradition that captives of high rank had to be turned over to the commander, Paston could keep for ransom any prisoners he caught with the exception of: the King of France, his sons, dukes, counts, lieutenants, or captains in chief. These men were to be turned over to the duke or the King of England, in exchange for an appropriate compensation.[27]

Throughout this time, Christianity was interpreted as allowing for the slaughter of infidels and the enslavement of other Christians; and despite the admonishment of the Lateran Council of 1179, the enslavement of Christians after battle continued to be practiced beyond this date.[28]

Froissart noted, regarding the 1369 battle between the Frisians and Holland, France, and England: "As for taking any prisoners, one can hardly get any of them nor will they surrender but they fight to the death saying that it is better to die a free Frisian than to be subject to a lord or prince. And as for the prisoners that have been taken, hardly any ransoms can be exacted, nor will their friends and relatives redeem them, but they leave them to die one after another in prison, nor otherwise will they ransom their people unless, having taken some of their enemies, they exchange them man for man. Yet if they think that none of their men are prisoners, they will certainly put all their prisoners to death."[29] As surrender for ransom was by no means guaranteed, gentlemen often took care, even in the course of a defeat, to avoid surrendering to commoners, from whom they expected no mercy.[30]

St. Thomas Aquinas's 1273 contribution to the issue of rules in warfare, in *Summa Theologica*, had more to do with general notions of justice, than with specific prescriptions concerning prisoners of war. However, insofar as it forms a component in the link of the evolution of thought on the limits of war, they are worth noting. Question XL, "On War,"[31] argued that the waging of war was not necessarily a sin, and that three things were required for a war to be a just war: that it be waged on the authority of the sovereign, with a just cause, and that the belligerents had "a right intention" in waging the war. As St. Thomas Aquinas quoted from St. Augustine, "[t]rue religion does not [consider] sinful those wars that are waged not for motives of aggrandisement, or cruelty, but with the object of securing peace, of punishing evildoers, and of uplifting the good ... The passion for inflicting harm, the cruel thirst for vengeance, an unpacific and relentless spirit, the fever of revolt, the lust of power, and such things, all these are rightly condemned in war."[32] Left unstated, however, was whether the enemy soldiers were candidates for punishment as "evildoers," and therefore whether it was necessary to spare them if peace had already been secured.

By the late Byzantine period, Turkish prisoners of war could be taken as slaves. After a series of victories by Philanthropenos over Turks in the Meander valley in 1294 and 1295, for instance, so many prisoners were taken that the price of a Turkish slave fell below the price of a sheep.[33] This represented the exception rather than the rule by Europeans; slaves were not made of captured Europeans, such as Serbs and Bulgars. Turkish allied troops, however, continued to enslave captured European enemies, which was spoken of with disapproval by the Byzantines.[34] Throughout the period, the practice continued of recruiting prisoners of war, some from as far from Constantinople as northern France, for service in the Byzantine army or navy.[35] The fate which awaited the Byzantines who were taken captive by the Turks at the fall of Constantinople in 1453 was variable. Though 50,000 captives were taken by the Turks, and many were later ransomed, many of those who were military leaders or otherwise famous were executed.[36]

Thoughts on prisoners of war in Asia during this time generally maintained a link with the thoughts of Sun Tzu. For example, Timur, the Mongol warrior who began his successful campaign westwards in 1380, believed in taking prisoners, arguing that "a living dog is of more use than a dead lion."[37]

Moving into modernity

According to a study by Dr. Ernst Gurlt,[38] 291 agreements concerning treatment of sick, wounded, and prisoners of war were concluded between 1581 and 1864. Of these, 44 concerned the exchange and ransom of prisoners. Some early treaties with provisions for mass exchange of prisoners without ransom included: Treaty of the Pyrenees, 1659, between France and Spain (articles 106, 107); Treaty of Utrecht, 1713, between France and England (article 23); Treaty of Belgrade, 1739, between Austria and Turkey (article 6); Treaty of Bâle, 1795, between France and Prussia (article 9), and between France and Spain (article 12).

Despite his reputation for being the father of modern (and hence "humane") international law, Hugo Grotius, in *De Jure Belli ac Pacis* (1645), set very few limits on what could be done to prisoners of war obtained in a just war. Beginning with an overview of various Roman writers, he traced the evolution of the customs of war with regard to prisoners to his conclusion that, quoting Euripides: "The laws permit harming a foe, wherever he is taken."[39] How far the rule could be extended, Grotius noted, "may be gathered from the fact that the slaughter of infants and women too is committed with impunity and sanctioned by the same law of war."[40] If prisoners were held for ransom, it was at the discretion of the captors; at no time did the captors relinquish the right to kill them. Despite Grotius's arguments, the Treaty of Westphalia of 1648 required, in part, that all prisoners be released without ransom upon the cessation of hostilities. This marked the first formal departure from the practice of ransoming, though it would continue, as in the Cartel of 1673 between France and the United Provinces, which provided for either ransom or exchange of prisoners. A century later, the 1748 Treaty of Aachen between England, France, and the Netherlands, called for the simple and direct exchange of all prisoners of war to begin after the ratification of the Treaty.

In 1748, Montesquieu, in *L'Esprit des Lois* (Bk. X, ch. III), made the first major break from the previous ancient traditions concerning the right of conquerors to dispose of their enemies as they saw fit. One of the greatest errors of law, he argued, was the arbitrary right it gave the participants in war to murder. In keeping with his view that war in general was justified only to preserve the state from destruction, and that war between states was qualitatively different from conflict between individuals, he posited that, once the conquest was completed, the conqueror had no right to murder those enemies in his power except in the case of self-defence. Enslavement, likewise, should be prohibited, as it came about as an accident of conquest, and not as a derived right.[41]

David Hume, in 1751,[42] took issue with Montesquieu on several counts.[43] He made an important caveat concerning the applicability of the laws of war. The laws existed, as did the basic notion of justice, only insofar as they were based on their advantage and utility to the state, and not on higher, philosophical notions of reason. Therefore, "were a civilised nation engaged with barbarians, who observed no rules even of war, the former must also suspend their observance of them, where they no longer serve to any purpose; and must render every action of encounter as bloody and pernicious as possible to the first aggressors."[44] Rules of war, then, existed only when both sides agreed on them; "justice" was subordinate to context.[45] Agreeing with Grotius and earlier writers, Hume pronounced that "[t]hese conclusions are so natural and obvious, that they have not escaped even the poets."[46] Rules of war were desirable insofar as they served the mutual advantage of all the belligerents.

It fell to Rousseau, in 1762,[47] to carry Montesquieu's arguments further and reply to what he saw as the errors of Grotius and Hume, claiming that his own principles "are not Grotius's principles; they are not based on the authority of poets, but derive from the nature of things, and are based on reason."[48] Specifically, Rousseau took issue with Grotius's defence of enslavement as based on the conqueror's right to kill his enemies. Rousseau argued that the "right" to kill the conquered did not derive in any way from the state of war: men were not naturally enemies, and if they existed in a state of war between themselves it was through an accident of political conditions. War was a relationship between states, not men, and conquest was the destruction of another state. Men were institutions of the state while they performed for the state, but once the conquest was complete and they were defeated, they reverted to their normal status of private citizens, against whom no quarrel could be had; the only justifiable thing to do to them, therefore, was to deprive them of the ability of becoming once again instruments of their state (i.e. to intern and disarm them). Offering Cato as a historical justification, he noted that oaths taken by Roman citizens who served as soldiers were valid for a specific enemy only; if that enemy was conquered and military action was required against a new enemy, a new oath had to be taken. In the end, "[enemies] may rightfully be killed so long as they are carrying arms; but as soon as they lay them down and surrender, ceasing to be enemies or agents of the enemy, they become simply men again, and there is no longer any right over their lives. On occasion it is possible to kill the state without killing any of its members; war confers no rights that are not necessary to its purpose."[49]

Principles into practice

The first practical application of Montesquieu's and Rousseau's principles was the Treaty of Amity and Commerce of 1785, between Prussia and the United States (article 24); the treaty was renewed without time limit in 1799. As noted in an American Red Cross paper produced in 1942,[50] the provisions for prisoners of war in this early treaty were even more complete and humane than those later provided by the

Hague Conventions of 1899 and 1907. In case of war between the two countries, prisoners of war were to be imprisoned under wholesome conditions in Europe or America; not to be sent to distant and unhealthy spots in Africa or Asia nor to be held in dungeons in irons; their use of limbs was not to be restricted in any way; officers were to be paroled; soldiers were to be held in barracks of the same quality as those enjoyed by the Home Army, and to receive the same kind of meals, the costs to be settled after the war; there were to be inspections of prisoners' facilities by their own countrymen, who were to be allowed to distribute comforts from home and make reports to their respective governments on the conditions found; officers who broke parole or soldiers who escaped, and were recaptured, were to be confined – their punishment was that they were not eligible for another parole and nor could they be left at large within the camp.

A few years later, on 23 May, 1793, the French government took European society one step further away from the practices of the previous centuries as regards prisoners of war, by passing a law forbidding payment of ransom.[51] The 1801 Treaty of Lunéville (article 20) between France and the Holy Roman Empire also provided for the repatriation of prisoners of war to occur immediately after the signature of the treaty. In 1805, recognizing that unequal costs might arise in maintaining unequal numbers of prisoners of war, the United States and the governor of Tripoli agreed to exchange prisoners rank for rank in case of war between them;[52] further, $500 for each captain and $200 for each seaman would be paid if there were no prisoners of equal rank being held by the other side. And the Treaty of Paris of 1815 stated that prisoners were to be returned "in the shortest time possible."[53]

Henry Wheaton, in his comprehensive 1845 study of the evolution of international law, noted that since the Treaty of Westphalia, the main progress in the treatment of prisoners of war concerned the replacement of private ransoming with simple, complete exchanges.[54] The process was far from uniform, however, and public, as opposed to private, ransoming persisted: as recently as 1780, he noted, France and Great Britain affixed monetary values to different ranks, to be paid if at the end of hostilities not enough prisoners existed on one side to be exchanged with the other.[55]

On February 26, 1842, US Secretary of State Daniel Webster wrote that a prisoner of war was an unfortunate human being, but not a criminal; the rights of the captor brought also certain duties, and did not include the right to dispose of a prisoner as the captor saw fit: to provide the captive with the necessities of life, to feed him plain but wholesome food, to treat him humanely, and to abstain from punishment of the captive not merited by an offence against the captor's laws after the date of the capture.[56] In an 1856 treaty between the United States and Morocco, prisoners of equal ranks were to be exchanged. No mention was made of ransom, though enslavement of prisoners was expressly prohibited.[57]

The last mass exchange of prisoners of war during war appears to have occurred during the early stages of the American Civil War; later appeals for an exchange during that war were turned down by President Lincoln and General Grant. In 1863, President Lincoln asked Dr. Francis Lieber, a prominent New York lawyer, to draft a codification of the international laws pertinent to the conduct of war on land. This became the Lieber Code, known officially as "Instructions for the Government of Armies of the United States in the Field." The parts dealing with prisoners of war were articles 48 to 146.[58] A prisoner of war was defined as a public enemy, armed or attached to the hostile army for active aid, who had fallen into the hands of the captor by surrender or capture, wounded or fighting; citizens who arose in a *levée-en-masse* to face an advancing army and who were captured were also to be considered prisoners of war. Prisoners of war could expect to suffer the "inconveniences" as well as the privileges of their detention. They were considered public, and not private, enemies; ransoms were prohibited, and only the detaining government could release them. A command of "no quarter" to the enemy could only be given if a commanding officer was in such dire straits that it was impossible for him to encumber himself with prisoners of war. Even for troops given "no quarter," it was prohibited to kill the wounded; a captive given quarter (i.e. spared) could be killed if it was discovered within three days that he belonged to a corps which in turn gave no quarter while fighting. Article 76 of the "Instructions" stated that prisoners of war would be treated with humanity; no differentiation in the general treatment of prisoners of war was permissible, and no distinctions with regard to "color" (race) could be made. Without outlining consequences, article 107 stated that prisoners of war were obliged to give their ranks, or face punishment. Article 80, however, prohibited the use of violence against a prisoner of war who refused to divulge information about his own army, and stated further that he could not be punished for giving false information. Any soldier convicted of giving additional wounds to, or killing, a prisoner of war would be executed; wounded prisoners of war were to be given treatment to the best ability of the medical staff present. Small sums of money, extra clothing, and other valuables were the private property of the prisoner of war, and could not be appropriated. Prisoners of war could be confined as far as was necessary for their own safety, but could not be subject to any other "intentional indignity." They could be required to work for the benefit of the captor's government, according to rank and medical condition, but had to be fed sufficient and wholesome food. Medical personnel and clergy were generally to be sent back to their home armies, unless a local commander had a good reason to keep them with the other prisoners. While crimes committed by a prisoner of war during the course of his soldiering would only be punished if he had not already faced prosecution by his Home Army, all prisoners of war were nonetheless subject to retaliatory measures. Individual prisoners of war were to be protected from acts of revenge, such as personal disgrace, withholding food, or mutilation or killing. Individual prisoners who escaped but were recaptured could not be punished for their escape. They could be killed in flight, however, and conspirators plotting a mass escape could face vigorous punishment, and even death. Commissioned officers taken prisoner could be paroled at their request, but the punishment for breaking the parole was death. The details of exchanges of prisoners of war were left largely to the local commanders, with the general rule that equity in numbers, or other formulas decided by both sides, be followed. And lastly, civilians accompanying an army could be made prisoners of war if captured, while diplomatic and civic officials of the enemy who had not received a prior guarantee of safe conduct were definitely to be made prisoners of war.

At the same time as Dr. Lieber's "Instructions" appeared, Henri Dunant in Switzerland was organizing the Red Cross; the envoys of 12 powers gathered at Geneva and on August 22, 1864, signed the Convention of Geneva "For the Amelioration of the Condition of Sick and Wounded of Armies in the Field." Though the primary focus of the convention was for the medical treatment of the wounded on the battlefield, the signatories were also obliged to take care of them regardless of nationalities (i.e. of prisoners of war), according to article 6.[59] This was made explicit in the 1906 Geneva Convention on the Sick and Wounded. Thus, it was in the middle of the nineteenth century that attempts were made to move beyond simple bilateral or multilateral treaties, and to enshrine codes of behavior in a more general convention.

By June 1868, the International Committee of the Red Cross proposed the creation of a central agency to function in times of war, between belligerents; it was approved at the International Conference of Berlin, April 22–7, 1869. This central agency was put into practice soon thereafter, during the Franco-Prussian war. It was established on July 18, 1870, at Basle, one day before the French declaration of war. Similar agencies were set up at Trieste (1877), Laurenço Marques (1900), Belgrade (1912), and Geneva (1914).[60]

The never-ratified Treaty of Petrograd was also concluded in 1868. At the invitation of the Czar, the signatories to the 1864 Geneva Treaty were invited to clarify and modify that treaty, and extend it to cover war at sea. Article 7 exempted clergy and medical personnel from becoming prisoners of war, article 6 clarified the conditions for repatriation of the wounded except for officers, and article 8 stated that clergy and medical personnel could be released at a time decided upon by the commanding officer, upon completion of their duties of caring for the sick and wounded.[61]

In 1874, based primarily on the Lieber Code, a conference of the "Association to Ameliorate Prisoner of War Conditions" was held in Paris, resulting in a draft of a code of 146 articles. After approaching diplomatic representatives of the major powers, it was discovered that Russia had also been working on such a code; the association combined their efforts with those of the Russians, and there followed the diplomatic Conference of Brussels. On August 27, 1874, 56 articles were agreed to and signed, by 15 states. Though these governments did not eventually ratify the articles, Russia declared, during the Russo-Turkish War in 1877, that it would nonetheless abide by them.[62]

Russia again took the initiative in trying to prod the other powers into a binding Convention, when Count Mouravieff, the Minister of Foreign Affairs, sent out notes in August 1898 to the diplomatic representatives accredited to the Russian court, proposing a peace conference to consider "a possible reduction of the excessive armaments which weigh upon all nations." After positive replies were received, another note was sent out on December 30, 1898, leading to the Hague Conference of 1899. Though no agreement could be reached on the issue of arms reductions, there was interest in dealing with the customs of war on land, drawing heavily on the unratified Brussels Conference, with articles 4 through 20 dealing with prisoners of war.

Interest had been shown in continuing negotiations on the ratified 1899 Hague Convention, but work on it had to wait until after the conclusion of the Russo-Japanese War. In 1906, a Geneva Conference led to revisions of the 1864 Treaty relating to the care of sick and wounded soldiers, making specific reference to the fact that captured wounded were prisoners of war, and that therefore they were entitled to the provisions of international treaties on their status. After the Russo-Japanese war was concluded, another Hague Convention was signed, in 1907. The new convention, however, made few alterations to the conditions for prisoners of war stipulated in 1899: it prohibited the employment of officers, and made pay for officers mandatory instead of optional. As Bulgaria, Greece, Italy, Serbia, Persia, and Turkey did not ratify the agreement, it was not legally in force among all the belligerents of the First World War (article 2: the Convention was in force only between signatories).[63]

During the First World War, bilateral and multilateral agreements were concluded between many of the signatories of the Hague Convention, usually based on the articles of the convention,[64] and sometimes with the aim of clarifying and in some cases improving the terms of captivity.[65] The United States was of the opinion that the rules of the 1907 Hague Convention, despite the fact that it was not legally binding in the sense of a fully ratified contract, nonetheless should be thought of as an expression of the evolution of general customs and laws among nations, and that it thus formed international law. In 1917, US General Pershing instructed the Provost Marshall General "to follow the principles of the Hague and Geneva Conventions in the treatment of prisoners."[66]

The British Manual of Military Law and the German Kriegsbrauch, in place during the First World War, had similar interpretations of the requirements of the Hague Conventions.[67] Both guidelines took the requirements of the Convention to mean that the prisoners of war were entitled to the same rations as the Detaining Power's peacetime troops, but neither country actually gave their prisoners of war these rations. The British came close to the required rations before cutting them in January 1916 and again in June 1918, along with the civilian population's rations.[68] The German rations for the prisoners of war were significantly worse, leading in some cases to near-starvation and disease among the British prisoners; almost mirroring the case a quarter of a century later, parcels arriving through the intermediary offices of the International Committee of the Red Cross made a significant difference for the British prisoners, as by 1918, because of the complete British blockade of all items, Germany no longer had the resources to meet the needs of its own armed forces, let alone the prisoners of war.[69] With regard to the treatment of the prisoners of war by guards, again the British provided a better standard of conduct, in part because the German prisoners were often left to organize themselves within their camps, creating, in the words of one American inspector (before the US entry into the war), their "own little republic under their non-commissioned officers, who were responsible to the British military authorities."[70] German guards' treatment of the British prisoners varied greatly from camp to camp, but often included verbal abuse, blows, and kicks.[71]

Although reprisals against prisoners of war were not forbidden by the Hague Conventions, the number of such major measures was low during the First World War: a decision by Winston Churchill to intern all U-boat prisoners in Royal Navy detention barracks even before the declaration of unrestricted U-boat warfare was met with a German decision to intern a similar number of British officers in arrest barracks; the issue was defused only when Churchill's replacement, Arthur Balfour, rescinded the previous order.[72] Germany began a process of moving British prisoners to the centers of towns (starting with Freiburg im Breisgau after May 1917), in the hopes of rendering the town centers safe from enemy bombardment.[73] Despite sensationalist agitation from the British press to place German prisoners in British towns as early as February 1916, the British government did not do so until it was clear that the Germans were endangering (if cities were to be bombed) British prisoners in this manner; German prisoners were placed in the center of Ramsgate, Margate, and Southend in May 1918.[74] With regard to the implementation of disciplinary punishments, both the British and Germans generally sentenced each other's prisoners to longer terms of confinement without hard labor, rather than short terms with hard labor (the preferred mode of punishment of the French).[75]

Both sides took in sudden influxes of prisoners of war in 1918: Germany as the result of their spring offences, and Britain with the subsequent counteroffences. By this time, however, the material resources of Germany were so stretched that the almost 100,000 British prisoners suffered far greater material privations than the quarter of a million Germans in British captivity in October 1918.[76] The role of the United States in the prisoner-of-war history of the First World War was, comparatively, much smaller: American troops had only engaged German soldiers in large numbers in 1918, and by November 1918, little more than 2,000 American soldiers had been taken captive; given the Armistice, there was almost no time in which to see how the comparative treatment of prisoners of war between the United States and Germany could have developed.[77] On the whole, then, the intentions of the Hague Conventions on prisoners of war were not met during the

First World War, mainly due to a lack of specificity within the text of the Conventions themselves.

After the First World War, the Grotius Society, in 1919, prepared a list of improvements to the Hague Convention, based on the experiences of the war. This list was taken to heart by the International Committee of the Red Cross, which in turn set the wheels in motion to create a more standard set of rules based on the 1864 Geneva Treaty as well as the 1907 Hague Convention. Working with the Swiss Federal Council, the diplomacy moved with such deliberate speed that it was not until 1928 that most countries who were signatories to these agreements agreed to meet for a new conference. The result was the Convention Relating to Prisoners of War which was signed on July 26, 1929.[78] On July 27, 1929, a revision of the 1906 Geneva Convention called "The Amelioration of the Condition of the Sick and Wounded of Armies in the Field" was also signed, which also included points on prisoners of war.

2.2 The Geneva Convention, and the national prisoner-of-war policies of Britain, Canada, the United States, and Germany, 1939

Indicative of how seriously many countries had come to regard the issue, the 1929 Convention, as stated earlier, was the first separate international treaty on the treatment of prisoners of war; all previous references to them were within the context of general conventions on laws of war. Further, it was to come into force as soon as two signatories had deposited formal ratifications with the Swiss Federal Council (article 92). The Soviet Union was not a signatory, and the Convention was signed but never ratified by Japan and Finland. The other belligerents of the Second World War had both signed and ratified the Convention.[79]

The Convention was broken down into eight major parts:[80] (1) the "General provisions" (articles 1–4) identified who was entitled to be treated as a prisoner of war and affirmed that they were prisoners of the Detaining Power, and not the individuals who had captured them; (2) "Capture" (articles 5–6) provided basic outlines on how prisoners were to be treated immediately after they were caught, including what possessions they could retain; (3) the 60 articles of "Captivity" dealt with the details of life for the prisoners of war – their evacuation from the war zone (articles 7–8), the establishment of prisoner-of-war camps (article 10), the food and clothing requirements (articles 11–12), hygiene in the camps (articles 13–15), the intellectual and moral needs of prisoners of war (articles 16–17), the internal discipline of camps (articles 18–20), special provisions concerning officers (articles 21–2), the pecuniary resources of prisoners of war (articles 23–4), transfers of the prisoners (articles 25–6), general provisions regarding work (article 27), the organization of work (articles 28–30), prohibited work (articles 31–2), the creation of labor detachments (article 33), pay (article 34), the relations of prisoners of war with the exterior (articles 35–41), complaints of prisoners of war regarding the conditions of captivity (article 42); prisoner-of-war representatives (articles 43–4), general provisions regarding penal sanctions against prisoners (articles 45–53), disciplinary punishments (articles 54–9), and judicial proceedings against prisoners of war (articles 60–7); (4) "End of captivity" (articles 68–75), elaborated on repatriation due to serious injury or illness and liberation at the end of hostilities; (5) the section on "Deaths of prisoners of war" (article 76) provided the instructions on dealing with that issue; (6) "Bureaux of relief and information" (articles 77–80) indicated the terms by which the International Committee of the Red Cross, and others, could contribute to ameliorating the conditions of life for the prisoners; (7) article 81 served as a stand-alone part of the Convention on applying its provisions to "certain categories of civilians"; and (8) "Execution of the convention" (articles 82–97), provided the administrative instructions and details for the signatories of the Convention.

Anglo-Americans, 1939

Given the sweeping applicability of the Convention, and the advances it made to previous efforts to codify rules of conduct toward prisoners of war, it is not surprising that the national military regulations of Canada, Great Britain, the United States, and Germany (at the start of the war, at least) followed the text and terms of the Convention very closely.

The Canadian regulations[81] for dealing with prisoners of war in force during the Second World War mirrored those of Great Britain,[82] and followed the terms and phraseology of the Geneva Convention closely. General measures announce to the reader that: the regulations are in accordance with the Geneva Convention of 1929; the text of the Convention will be posted whenever possible in the language of the prisoners, or at least be explained to them; all orders to them must be given in a language which they understand; and that the prisoners are subject to the military laws in force in the country.[83] With regard to orders for the prisoners of war, the regulations state: the prisoners have to comply with all regulations for the maintenance of discipline and good order; the prisoners must obey commands from those placed in authority over them; any prisoner guilty of disobedience will be punished; mutiny will be met with force of arms if necessary; prisoners will be fired upon if they attempt to escape or otherwise leave the posted boundaries without authority; they will not communicate with people other than other prisoners of war or camp staff without permission; officer prisoners of war will salute other officers of equal or higher rank; the prisoners are permitted to wear badges of rank and decorations; they are free to perform their religious duties; they will not have liquor or consume it without permission given for medical reasons; and all gambling or betting is illegal.[84]

The section on officer prisoners of war essentially restated the terms of the Geneva Convention,[85] while the right of the other prisoners of war to appoint a representative was also confirmed.[86] The medical and employment terms likewise reiterated the text of the Convention.[87] For the conditions under which the Protecting Power or other visitors could visit the camp, the reader is referred directly to article 86 of the Convention. Postal rights, such as free postage, and the right of the Detaining Power to censor outgoing mail were referred to in terms of the Convention, without departure from the text of the treaty.[88] The disciplinary regulations[89] likewise did not depart from the terms outlined in the Convention, to which it referred. The final and by far largest section of the regulations outlines the rules for judicial complaints[90] and the precise procedures to be followed for courts martial;[91] as with the earlier sections, this essentially reprints the terms of the Geneva Convention, and places them in the context of existing British or Canadian regulations. The British Commonwealth regulations, then, aimed at providing a framework for treating prisoners of war based solidly on the terms of the Geneva Convention, with future, more precise instructions to be issued as necessary by the various Commonwealth militaries.[92]

The military regulations in force for the United States military with regard to prisoners of war during the Second World War were written by the War Department in 1940, and, like their British and Canadian counterparts, closely followed the Geneva Convention.[93] Chapter 4 of the American regulations, encompassing sections 70–172, covered rules regarding prisoners of war, while chapter 5, sections 173–201, dealt with caring for the sick and wounded in the field. Both of these chapters essentially repeat the Geneva Conventions. The first sections of each chapter state that the rules to be followed were the articles of the two

Conventions, and from there the remaining sections merely paraphrase the Conventions, without substantive alteration. At the end of each section, in parentheses, the reader is informed of the relevant section of the Conventions from which the preceding information was drawn.

Given the later German practice of defining Allied Commandos as spies, and thus not under the protection of the Geneva Conventions, it is worth examining the American regulations concerning espionage and treason, as outlined in chapter 6 of the same military manual. Specifically excluded from the definition of spies, outlined in section 202, were "soldiers not wearing a disguise who have penetrated into the zone of operations of the hostile army for the purpose of obtaining information." The key prerequisite for identifying spies was the use of a disguise in an attempt to gather information. Lastly, "[a] spy who, after rejoining the army to which he belongs, is subsequently captured by the enemy, is treated as a prisoner of war, and incurs no responsibility for his previous acts of espionage" (section 212).[94]

Germany, 1939

As with the Canadians, British, and Americans, German military policy, at the start of the war, regarding the treatment of prisoners of war was entirely in keeping with the Geneva Convention of 1929. Indeed, one of the first military manuals produced by the OKW concerning prisoner-of-war affairs for distribution to the Kriegsmarine (navy), Luftwaffe (airforce), and Heer (army) was simply a complete reprint of the entire 1929 Convention.[95] This was followed by a series of manuals on all aspects of running Dulags (*Durchgangslager* – transit camps to which prisoners of war were first brought for sorting), Stalags (*Mannschafts-Stammlager* – prisoner-of-war camps for noncommissioned officers and other-ranks), and Oflags (*Offizierlager* – prisoner-of-war camps for officers).[96]

Each of the manuals outlined the fundamental rules by which the commandants were to be governed in their behavior toward the prisoners of war under their charge.[97] The objectives of the commandant of a camp were: protection of the German Reich against enemy personnel; firm, but correct, application of the Geneva Convention; and the immediate redress of any type of abuse;[98] even small deviations from a firm but correct application of the Geneva Convention would reflect poorly on the honor of the German soldier.[99] From the experiences of the Great War, it was evident, wrote the OKW, that the enemy's personnel, even if unarmed, remained constant and active enemies of Germany, until they were transported back home.[100] Prisoners of war could be expected to carry on, whenever possible, their fight through espionage and sabotage.[101] Making the direct reference to fear of reprisals and the general principle of reciprocity, the OKW directed the Commandants to carefully note that any violations of the Geneva Convention could affect German prisoners of war held in the enemy's captivity.[102]

In general terms, the German regulations followed the same pattern as the British, Canadian, and American regulations: reprinting and using the Geneva Convention as a template upon which to later add more specific orders.[103] Thus, at the start of the war, all of these parties appeared ready to follow the terms of the Convention, as vague or as precise as they were in the actual text.

2.3 The structure of prisoner-of-war affairs in Germany

Administration

The process by which newly captured prisoners of war were sent back to the permanent camps remained constant over the course of the war years, as did the administrative superstructure above it. The administrative structure under which the permanent prisoner-of-war camps were controlled in Germany, on the other hand, was somewhat complicated at the beginning of the war, and became even more confusing as the war progressed and further reorganizations occurred.

Newly captured soldier prisoners of war were to be sent back from the combat units to Kriegsgefangenenstellen, Frontstalags, and finally Dulags – increasingly large gathering centers for prisoners of war leading finally to the main transit camps.[104] The various offices to which these branches of prisoner-of-war units reported came under the ultimate authority of the High Command of the German Army (Oberkommando des Heeres, or OKH): they initially reported to the Armeeoberkommando (AOK), which reported to the Befehlshaber Heeresgebiet, which reported to the Generalquartiermeister, which finally reported to the OKH.[105] Allied airmen were held by either the capturing military body or the local police, until they could be transferred to Dulag Luft for the initial interrogations.[106] At that point, they entered into the captivity of the Luftwaffe, whose structure for permanent camps mirrored those of the army, described below. Naval personnel, after interrogation at a Kriegsmarine transit camp, were eventually transferred to Marlag/Milag Nord, the permanent camp which grew out of Stalag X B Sandbostel.[107] The permanent prisoner-of-war units and installations to which prisoners of war were eventually sent – the Stalags and Oflags – came under a different chain of command from that which existed for the capturing process.

The prisoner-of-war administration for Germany was under the authority of the Reserve Army Command, and spread out over the various military districts (*Wehrkreis*, or WK) in Germany. The prisoner-of-war camp names themselves indicated their jurisdiction: Stalag I A was the first (hence "A") men's camp located in Wehrkreis I; Oflag IX B was the second (thus "B") officers' camp located in Wehrkreis IX, and so forth; occasionally, prisoner-of-war camps were given Arabic numeral designation, if they had been upgraded to "Stalag" from a previously lower designation, such as "Arbeitskommando" or "Bau- und Arbeitsbataillon," if they were created later in the war years near the Eastern Front, or if a camp was renamed before accepting prisoners of war of a new nationality.[108]

From top to bottom, the chain of command over the prisoners of war in the Stalags or Oflags was: Hitler, "Chef OKW," "Allgemeines Wehrmachtamt" (AWA), "Abteilung für Kriegsgefangenenwesen" ("Abt.Kgf.Wesen.," reporting to the AWA), OKH (or, for airforce and naval prisoners, the OKL and OKM), "Wehrkreiskommando" (for the army only), "Kommandeur der Kriegsgefangenen im Wehrkreis" (or "Luftgau"), and lastly the commandants of the prisoner-of-war camp. From the beginning of the war until 1942, there was also an "Inspekteur für das Kriegsgefangenenwesen im OKW," reporting to the AWA, who had the authority to examine standards and inspect all levels of the prisoner-of-war command structure, including the camps.

In the beginning of 1942, a new post, "Chef der Kriegsgefangenen im OKW," was created, reporting to the AWA. The existing "Abteilung für Kriegsgefangenenwesen im OKW" and a new "Organisationsabteilung für Kriegsgefangenenwesen im OKW" reported to this new office. This change was offered for reasons of "clarity," and as it took place above the level of the Abt.Kgf.Wesen, it did not affect the military districts.

On 1 October 1944, a new organizational scheme was introduced for managing prisoner-of-war affairs, right down to the camp commandant level. As it is substantially more complicated than the previous schemes, it is best viewed as a chart (see Figure 1 on p. ix, above).

These late-1944 changes were prompted by the implication of the Head of the Reserve Army, General Fromm, and many of his staff in the July 20 plot to kill Hitler. Hitler was also frustrated over the inability of the OKW to lower the number of escapes occurring in the camps; and giving Himmler a military command title, Head of the Reserve Army (thus in charge of the military districts), allowed Himmler the ability to increase "coordination" between the camp commandants and the RSHA.[109]

Although the changes in the administrative structures for prisoner-of-war affairs became increasingly more bureaucratic and complicated as the war went on, the ultimate reality for the commandants of the camps was the same from the beginning of the war: they received orders on how to run their camps and on official changes to the military policy in place at the start of the war from the OKW. The changes in the administrative hierarchy which occurred as the war progressed came at a high enough level (above the military districts, for the most part) as not to affect the day-to-day running of the camps.

Distribution and opening dates of camps (see fig. 2, p. x)

The preparations of the OKW for the creation of prisoner-of-war camps in Germany had begun before the outbreak of the war,[110] and after one month of war, 31 camps had already been established for prisoners of all nationalities.[111] As can be noted by examining the camp names, the northern and central military districts had the most camps, while the military districts in the southwest had the fewest, and some of the districts (X, XVIII, Bohemia-Moravia, XX, and XXI) had no camps initially: 6 camps were located in Wehrkreis II;[112] 4 each were in Wehrkreise VI and XI;[113] 3 were in Wehrkreis VIII;[114] 2 each were in Wehrkreise I, IV, VII, and XVII;[115] and one camp was located in each of Wehrkreise V, IX, XII, and XIII.[116]

By the war's end, 248 prisoner-of-war camps had been operated by Germany, of which 134 had contained, at one point or another, either British or American prisoners of war.[117] These tended to be spread evenly through the military districts; the camps created later in the war (bearing Arabic numerical designation) contained many fewer British or American prisoners of war than the main ones (bearing Roman numerical names) located in the military districts.[118]

In the eastern Wehrkreise (I, XX, XXI, and VIII), the camps containing British or American prisoners of war at some points in the war included: Stalag I A (Stablack, 06/09/39 to 26/01/45); Stalag XX A Thorn (16/12/39 to 01/01/45), Stalag XX B (Recklinghausen, Littschen-Marienwerder, Marienburg, 14/08/41 to 24/01/45); Oflag XXI A (Schokken, 15/08/40 to 17/04/42), Oflag XXI B (Schubin/Altburgund, 18/09/40 to 01/09/43), Stalag XXI A (Schildberg/Wartheland, 05/10/39 to 01/06/43), Stalag XXI B (Schubin, 01/12/39 to 28/04/42), Stalag XXI C (Wollstein, 12/06/40 to 01/03/43), Stalag XXI D (Posen, 01/08/40 to 01/01/45), Stalag XXI E (Grätz, 21/06/41 to 10/03/42); Oflag VIII A (Kreuzburg/Oberschlesien,

14/12/39 to 11/05/42), Oflag VIII C (Juliusburg, 25/05/40 to 01/12/42), Oflag VIII E (Johannisbrunn/Troppau, 28/07/40 to 01/07/42), Oflag VIII F (Wahlstatt bei Liegnitz, Mährisch-Trübau, 24/07/40 to 09/06/44), Oflag VIII G (Weidenau, 01/08/40 to 22/09/42), Oflag VIII H (Oberlangendorf, 01/08/40 to 18/08/43), Stalag VIII A (Görlizt, 25/08/39 to 01/01/45), Stalag VIII B (Lamsdorf, 26/08/39 to 01/03/45), Stalag VIII C (Kunau, Sagan, 26/08/39 to 01/01/45), Stalag VIII D (Teschen, 05/05/41 to 16/09/42), and Stalag VIII E (Neuhammer/Quais, 14/08/41 to 01/07/42). Also located in Wehrkreise XX and XXI were the Bau- und Arbeitsbataillone containing thousands of mostly British prisoners of war: BAB 20 (Heydebreck, Breslau, 5/09/40 to 23/08/43), BAB 21 (ollstein, Breslau, Blechhammer bei Heydebreck, 15/09/40 to 23/08/43), BAB 40 (Heydebreck/Oberschlesien, 29/11/40 to 10/03/43), and BAB 48 (Blechhammer bei Heydebreck/Oberschlesien, 16/12/40 to 10/03/43). BAB 51 was located in Wehrkreis XI (Hannover, Fallingbostel, 16/12/40 to 01/03/45), and briefly contained some British prisoners of war.

The military districts located in the north-central area of Germany (Wehrkreise II, III, X, and XI) contained camps holding British and American prisoners of war at: Oflag II E (Neubrandenburg, 23/09/40 to 22/03/44), Stalag II A (Neubrandenburg/Meckl., 01/09/39 to 01/02/45), Stalag II B (Westfalennof, Hammerstein/Kreis Schlochau, 15/09/39 to 27/01/45), Stalag II D (Stargard/Pommern, 13/09/39 to 01/01/45); and Oflag III A (Luckenwalde, 03/11/39 to 31/12/41), Oflag III C (Lübben, 01/08/40 to 01/06/43), Stalag III A (Luckenwalde, 28/08/39 to 31/12/41), Stalag III B (Amtitz, Fürstenberg/Oder, Luckenwalde, Stettin, 26/08/39 to 28/04/45), Stalag III C (Alt Drewitz über Küstrin, 12/06/40 to 01/01/45), Stalag III D (Berlin-Lichterfelde, 14/08/40 to 01/05/45), Stalag III E (Kirchhain, 01/02/41 to 04/06/42); Oflag X B (Nienburg/Weser, 01/02/41 to 01/01/45), Oflag X C (Lübeck, 01/06/40 to 02/05/45), Stalag X B (Sandbostel, 02/08/40 to 29/04/45), Stalag X C (Nienburg/Weser, 17/02/41 to 01/01/45); Stalag XI A (Altengrabow, 01/12/39 to 01/01/45), Stalag XI B (Fallingbostel, 24/09/39 to 01/01/45), Stalag XI C (Bergen-Belsen, 14/08/41 to 10/06/43), and Stalag XI D (Oberbke über Walsrode, 14/08/41 to 21/03/43). Also located in Wehrkreis X was the main camp for British and American naval personnel, Marlag-Milag (Sandbostel, 28/02/41 to 01/01/45).

Within the three military districts located in the west part of the country (Wehrkreise VI, XII, and V), the British and Americans were detained at: Oflag VI B (Dössel bei Warburg, 09/07/40 to 01/01/45), Oflag VI D (Münster, Soest, 01/02/41 to 01/10/44), Oflag VI E (Dorsten, 15/11/39 to 01/02/42), Stalag VI A (Hemer, 10/10/39 to 01/01/45), Stalag

VI B (Neu Versen, 29/09/39 to 13/05/42), Stalag VI C (Oberlangen, Münster, 25/09/39 to 01/10/44), Stalag VI D (Dortmund, 21/09/39 to 01/01/45), Stalag VI F (Bocholt, Münster, 03/10/39 to 01/01/45), Stalag VI F/Z (Dorsten, 01/10/42 to 01/02/42), Stalag VI G (Bergisch-Gladbach, Bonn-Duisdorf, Bergneustadt, 28/02/41 to 01/01/45), Stalag VI H (Arnoldsweiler bei Düren, Borissow, 28/03/40 to 29/04/42), Stalag VI J (Krefeld, 17/02/41 to 01/01/45); Oflag V A (Weinsberg/Heilbron, 15/12/39 to 11/02/44), Oflag V B (Biberach/Riß, 28/08/40 to n/a), Oflag V D (Offenburg, Biberach/Riß, Wurzach, 01/07/41 to n/a), Stalag V A (Ludwigsburg, 26/08/39 to 21/04/45), Stalag V B (Villingen/Schwarwald, 28/03/40 to 01/01/45), Stalag V C (Offenburg, 28/03/40 to 14/12/44), Stalag V E (Mülhausen, 01/12/40 to 19/03/42); Oflag XII A (Hadamar, 16/11/39 to 27/05/42), Oflag XII B (Mainz, Hadamar, 01/09/41 to 14/12/44), Stalag XII A (Limburg, 26/08/39 to 01/01/45), Stalag XII D (Trier-Petrisberg, Waldbreitbach bei Newied, 17/02/41 to 01/01/45), and Stalag XII F (Saarburg, Forbach, 07/08/40 to 01/01/45).

Wehrkreise IV, IX, and XIII, located in central Germany, contained British and American prisoners of war at: Oflag IV B (Königstein/Kreis Pirna auf der Festung, 14/10/39 to 01/02/45), Oflag IV C (Colditz, 30/10/39 to 15/04/45), Oflag IV D (Annaburg/Kreis Torgau, 09/04/41 to 31/05/42), Oflag IV E (Elsterhorst bei Hoyerswerda, 05/06/40 to 01/02/45), Stalag IV A (Hoyerswerda, Elsterhorst, Hohnstein über Bad Schandau, 26/08/39 to 01/03/45), Stalag IV B (Mühlberg/Elbe, 29/09/39 to 19/02/45), Stalag IV C (Wistriz bei Teplitz-Schönau, 01/08/40 to 01/01/45), Stalag IV D (Torgau/Elbe, 05/08/40 to 05/04/45), Stalag IV D/Z (Annaburg, 01/06/42 to 05/04/45), Stalag IV F (Hartmannsdorf, 01/02/41 to 01/03/45), Stalag IV G (Oschatz/Sachsen, 01/02/41 to 01/01/45); Oflag IX A (Spangenberg, 02/10/39 to 03/06/40), Oflag IX A/H (Spangenberg, Rothenburg/Fulda, 03/06/40 to 01/01/45), Oflag IX A/Z (Rothenburg/Fulda, 03/06/40 to 01/09/43), Stalag IX A (Ziegenhain/Kassel, 26/09/39 to 21/06/45), Stalag IX B (Bad Orb, 01/12/39 to 01/01/45), Stalag IX C (Bad Sulza/Thüringen, 06/02/40 to 11/04/45); Oflag XIII B (Nürnberg, Marsfeld, Hammelburg, 30/05/41 to 30/04/45), Stalag XIII B (Weiden, 17/07/40 to 01/01/45), Stalag XIII C (Hammelburg, 11/07/40 to 01/01/45), Stalag XIII D (Nürnberg-Langwasser, 01/11/42 to 01/01/45).

In the southern German military districts (Wehrkreise VII, XVII, and XVIII), the American and British prisoners were held captive at: Oflag VII A (Murnau, 25/09/39 to 01/01/45), Oflag VII B (Eichstätt/Bayern, 18/10/39 to 01/01/45), Oflag VII C (Laufen, 03/12/39 to 28/01/42), Oflag VII C/H (Laufen, 09/07/40 to 03/01/41), Oflag VII C/Z (Laufen, 25/07/40 to 23/01/41), Oflag VII D (Laufen, 23/01/41 to 17/04/42),

Stalag VII A (Moosburg/Oberbayern, 25/09/39 to 29/04/45), Stalag VII B (Memmingen, 11/08/40 to 01/01/45); Stalag XVII A (Kaisersteinbruch bei Wien, 29/08/39 to 01/01/45), Stalag XVII B (Krems-Gneixendorf, 25/09/39 to 05/05/45); Stalag XVIII A (Wolfsberg/Kärnten, 01/03/41 to 08/05/45), Stalag XVIII A/Z (Spittal/Drau, 01/03/41 to 25/09/44), Stalag XVIII B (Spittal, Pupping/Efferding, 07/04/41 to 27/02/43), Stalag XVIII C (Markt Pongau, 01/06/41 to 08/05/45), and Stalag XVIII D (Marburg/Drau, 07/12/39 to 01/11/42).

The remaining camps which held British and American prisoners of war were those issued Arabic numbers:[119] Oflag 6 (Tost, Oberlangen, 26/11/43 to 01/10/44), Oflag 54 (Annaburg bei Torgau, 09/04/41 to 31/05/42), Oflag 55 (Biberach, Offenburg, Biberach, 01/04/41 to 19/12/42), Oflag 64 (Wahlstatt/Schlesien, Schubin, 06/03/43 to 22/01/45), Oflag 78 (Grossmain/Salzburg, Eichstätt, Hohenfels, Nürnberg, 30/04/41 to 01/08/44), Oflag 79 (Querum bei Braunschweig, 01/12/43 to n/a), Stalag 133 (Chartres-Morances, 22/02/43 to 01/10/43), Stalag 194 (Nancy, 01/09/43 to 01/10/43), Stalag 221 (Rennes, 01/09/43 to 01/10/43), Stalag 222 (Bayonne, 01/09/43 to 01/10/43), Stalag 308 (Neuhammer, Ssumy, Bathorn, 08/04/41 to 01/01/45), Stalag 317 (Markt Pongau, 07/04/41 to n/a), Stalag 319 (Chelm, Skierniewice, 10/04/41 to 01/08/44), Stalag 344 (Eydkau/Ostpr., Wilna, Lamsdorf, 28/08/41 to 01/01/45), Stalag 356 (Roen, Compiègne, Oerbke, 20/04/41 to 09/06/44), Stalag 383 (Hohenfels/Oberbayern, 15/12/43 to 14/12/44), and Stalag 398 (Pupping, 27/02/43 to 01/01/45).

As the prisoner-of-war camps for British and American airmen were administered by the Luftwaffe and not the OKW, their names did not reflect their location in a military district. The permanent camps were generally located in the eastern districts (Wehrkreise I, II, and VIII) to make escape difficult for pilots (the most valuable of servicemen to the enemy, after all): Dulag Luft (Oberursel/Taunus, Frankfurt am Main, Wetzlar-Klosterwald, 01/01/40 to 06/09/44), Stalag Luft I (Barth, 26/08/40 to 01/05/45), Stalag Luft II (Litzmannstadt, Königsberg/Neumark, 15/09/41 to 01/01/45), Stalag Luft III (Sagan, 01/05/42 to 27/01/45), Stalag Luft IV (Sagan, Gross Tychan/Pommern, 01/03/43 to 01/02/45), Stalag Luft VI (Heydekrug, St Wendel/Saarland, Königsberg/Neumark, 01/08/43 to 14/12/44), and Stalag Luft VII (Moritzfelde bei Wehlau, Borzau bei Kreuzburg/Oberschlesien, 01/06/43 to 01/01/45).

Numbers of prisoners of war

The OKW first compiled a comprehensive list of the numbers of prisoners of war in its custody in September 1940, thus incorporating those British troops captured after the initial campaigns in the west, the retreat at Dunkirk, and the final capitulation of Denmark, Norway, and then France that summer.[120] Of the 37,693 British prisoners of war, 1,522 were officers; the total number of prisoners of all nationalities held by Germany at this time was almost 1.5 million. All of the British prisoners were in Oflags, Stalags, and BABs – none were yet listed in the OKW's compilations as being in the custody of the Luftwaffe or the Kriegsmarine.[121] By January 10, 1941, Germany held 39,956 British prisoners, of whom 1,725 were officers;[122] by comparison, less than one month previous, the total number of German prisoners of war in British hands were only 3,594.[123]

By July 1941, several significant events in the war had occurred: the German Africa Corps had been formed under Rommel, and fought at Benghazi, El Gazal, and El Alamein; Germany had marched southwards through Europe to finish the job started by Italy, and conquered Greece; and Germany's invasion of the Soviet Union had begun. At the start of July 1941, the total number of British prisoners held by Germany had risen to 50,717 (of whom 1,959 were officers).[124] The ratio of 10 British soldiers held by Germany for every one German soldier held by Britain continued: at the end of July 1941, only 5,010 German prisoners of war were in British captivity (of whom 693 were officers).[125]

By December 1941, with the United States just entering the war, the most significant encounters between Germany and Britain occurred in north Africa, with General Montgomery's counteroffensives of October and November. At this point, Britain held only 6,245 German prisoners of war (of whom 763 were officers).[126] Germany continued to hold more than 10 times that number of British soldiers in its captivity: 3,430 officers out of a total 67,643 British prisoners of war.[127] The total number of prisoners of war of all nationalities in German captivity by this time, according to the OKW's official count, was 1,886,264.[128]

In December 1942, one year after the entry of the United States into the war and one month after the Allied landings in north Africa (Operation Torch), the numbers of British and American prisoners of war had not increased considerably: Germany held 74,318 Britishers (4,083 were officers) and 67 Americans (46 of whom were officers),[129] out of a total of 2,480,974 prisoners of war of all nationalities.[130] In contrast, the number of German prisoners of war held by both the British Commonwealth and the United States increased considerably: 25,190 (1,376 were officers) were in British hands, while the United States held just 468 German prisoners of war (of whom 28 were officers).[131]

In late September/early October 1943, many changes had occurred in the war situation between the Americans and British, and Germany; Germany had capitulated in north Africa in mid-May, and the Allies landed and established themselves in Sicily by August. The encounters were reflected in the increased numbers of prisoners of war held by both sides. The British and Americans, as of September 30, held 79,372 German prisoners of war (of whom 4,051 were officers).[132] Germany, as of October 1, 1943, held a total of 130,205 Anglo-Americans: 121,725 British prisoners of war (6,542 were officers) and 8,489 Americans (1,697 officers).[133]

By July 1944, Rome had fallen to the Allies, and the fight at Normandy was ongoing, with the increased level of military engagement between Germany and the American/British forces leading to increased levels of captivity on both sides. Germany had 176,688 British and American prisoners of war at this point.[134] The United States held 142,881 German prisoners of war (4,340 were officers), while Britain held 43,243 (2,075 were officers), for a total of 186,375 German prisoners of war in American and British captivity: more, for the first time in the war, than the number of their soldiers held by Germany.

The last point at which total numbers of prisoners of war held by Germany can be accurately assessed is January 1, 1945; at that point, Germany held 225,996 American and British prisoners of war, out of a total of 2,393,322 prisoners of all nationalities.[135] At the end of January 1945, the British held 109,363 German prisoners (of whom 5,331 were officers), and the United States had 193,637 German prisoners (of whom 5,530 were officers); the total for the British and Americans, then, was 303,000 Germans. In the remaining months until the war's end, with the crossing of the Rhine in March 1945 and the final capitulation of Berlin occurring in May, the advancing armies liberated many of the prisoner-of-war camps. Given the increased chaos and continuous movements of both prisoners of war and the German Army itself, accurate records are no longer available.

3
General Issues on Policy and Prisoner-of-war Camps

3.1 Identification and status of prisoners of war

The first task of the Geneva Convention was to identify who was entitled to be classified as a prisoner of war: article 1 began by referring directly to those individuals identified in articles 1, 2, and 3 of the Fourth Hague Convention of October 1907. The first of these articles set out the requirements which had to be fulfilled by any army or militia/volunteer corps whose soldiers wished, in case of capture by enemy forces, to be considered prisoners of war: "1. They must be commanded by a person responsible for his subordinates. 2. They must have a fixed distinctive sign recognisable at a distance. 3. They must carry arms openly. 4. They must conduct their operations in accordance with the laws and customs of war. In countries where militia or volunteer corps constitute the army, or form part of it, they are included under the denomination 'army.'" The second article of the 1907 Hague Convention added that "[t]he inhabitants of a territory not under occupation, who, on the approach of the enemy, spontaneously take up arms to resist the invading troops without having had time to organise themselves in accordance with article 1, shall be regarded as belligerents if they carry arms openly and if they respect the laws and customs of war." The third article reminded the signatories that the armed forces of the belligerents could consist of "combatants" and "noncombatants," and that, in the case of capture by the enemy, both had the right to be treated as prisoners of war.

The Geneva Convention of 1929 went on to include naval and airforce personnel, by extending the definition of prisoner of war and the rights of the Convention to "all persons belonging to the armed forces of belligerents who are captured by the enemy in the course of operations of maritime or aerial war, subject to such exceptions (derogations) as the conditions of such capture render inevitable. Nevertheless these exceptions shall not infringe the fundamental principles of the present Convention; they shall cease from the moment when the captured persons shall have reached a prisoners of war camp."

The German military manuals of 1939 did not stray from the text of the Convention in describing who could claim to be a prisoner of war; they referred the reader, in fact, directly to article 1 of the 1929 Geneva Convention.[1] Enemy medical personnel or field clergy, however, were not prisoners of war; until their transport home could be organized in coordination with the OKW, they were to be employed in looking after their own soldiers. However, even though they were not prisoners of war, they still, for reasons of state security, had to have their movements restricted.[2] In accordance with the Convention, the German manuals stated that all prisoners of war were to be separated by nationality, race, and sex.[3] The main indicators of a prisoner of war's status (rank) were his insignia and his paybook, both of which were not to be taken away from him.[4]

Concerning the definition of a prisoner of war, Dr. Waltzog's 1942 update to German regulations[5] also stayed close to the text of the Convention. But as the issue of citizenship had not been specifically addressed in the Convention, Waltzog offered his own guidelines for the possibility of dealing with a German national caught fighting against Germany in a foreign army: they did not have claim to being treated as prisoners of war; the only exception was for those with dual citizenship, who did have the right to the protections offered prisoners of war. In case of doubt, the individual was to be treated as a prisoner of war pending final clarification of his citizenship. If German citizenship did not exist, the individual's personal citizenship was utterly irrelevant – he was to be treated as a prisoner of war of the country in whose uniform he fought: a Polish citizen caught while fighting in the French Army was not a Polish prisoner of war, but a French one.[6]

The uniform makes the man

One of the most obvious factors affecting the treatment a prisoner of war could expect to receive was his nationality; Soviet prisoners were treated entirely differently from Americans. However, the distinction between nationality and ethnicity seemed to have confused the issue for many Germans. The basic rule of thumb that the uniform determined the nationality of the prisoner of war, for the purposes of his captivity, was confirmed in the middle of June 1941, when the OKW began sending fortnightly compilations of orders concerning prisoners of war (*Befehlsammlungen*), in addition to occasional individual orders.

The first of these, after establishing the administrative mechanism for future collective orders, clarified and cofirmed the important issue regarding the determination of a prisoner of war's nationality: the uniform in which an enemy soldier was captured indeed determined his prisoner-of-war nationality. Thus, captured Poles serving in British uniforms would be treated as British prisoners of war.[7]

That the issue was not clear-cut in the minds of some within the German military was evident by the fact that, in mid-May 1942, the issue of prisoner-of-war nationality again arose, and the OKW felt the need to reconfirm that the uniform being worn by the prisoner at the time of capture indicated his nationality. In cases of doubt the hometown in which the prisoner lived before the war, or in which his relatives currently lived, could be used as an indicator.[8] In January 1944, the OKW again stated to its subordinate branches that the uniform a prisoner of war was captured in determined his nationality for purposes of captivity. The order further stated that American citizens who were captured in Canadian uniform were to be regarded as British prisoners of war if they were in the Canadian military before or up to the American entrance into the war.[9]

At the start of August 1944, the OKW stated that Poles captured serving in British uniforms in Italy or North Africa were to be treated as British prisoners of war; even if the unit was a "Polish unit" of the British Army, the soldiers were still classified, according to well-known guidelines, as British prisoners of war and were to be treated accordingly. It was stressed as important that these prisoners of war be separated from other Polish prisoners of war or workers who had been in German captivity since 1939.[10]

Once the prisoners' nationality had been determined, the next step was to separate them from each other. The fundamental rule used by the OKW was established in early September 1942, when camp commandants to were directed to separate into different compounds, whenever possible, prisoners of war of different nationalities when their number reached more than 50.[11]

In late October 1942, the OKW ordered that members of the Royal Army Service Corps who had been captured along with British land, naval, or air forces, were to be considered military personnel and treated in captivity as prisoners of war, rather than civilian internees or protected personnel.[12]

A question of class

As early as the end of January 1940, the OKW issued instructions that prisoner-of-war officers to be considered inferior in rank to the German staff working in the camps, thus preventing the possibility of guards being ordered to unlock the gates by enemy officers. This initial order was reiterated by Waltzog in March 1942, and then reconfirmed by special order of the Führer, on June 26, 1942.[13] Though this order made perfect sense from the standpoint of disciplinary authority, it was also taken in practice by many Germans to mean that prisoner-of-war officers had to salute lower-ranking German soldiers; this interpretation led to heated differences of opinion between the prisoners of war on the one hand, and their captors on the other, and was eventually dropped by the OKW.

As a prisoner's basic status (officer, noncommissioned officer, or other rank) would directly affect the uses to which he could be put, the interpretation by the OKW of British and American ranks which did not exist in the German military was a matter of some significance. The OKW gave up on trying to reconcile the British Army rank of Warrant-Officer with German ranks, and ordered that British Army Warrant-Officer prisoners of war be treated as noncommissioned officers, and Royal Navy Warrant-Officers be treated as officers. Royal Air Force commissioned Warrant-Officers were deemed officers, while RAF noncommissioned Warrant-Officers were not. British Aspirant Officers, Ensigns, Midshipmen, and Senior Ensigns were to be treated as officers, as were Acting Pilots, while Corporals and Bombardiers were viewed as noncommissioned officers.[14] The Royal Navy ranks of Leading Seaman and Leading Stocker were, in mid-January 1944, recognized by the OKW as noncommissioned officers, and prisoners of war with these ranks were to be treated as such.[15]

By the middle of August 1944, the OKW stated that in cases in which a British prisoner-of-war soldier claimed to be a noncommissioned officer, the appropriate indication in his paybook could serve as proof. If there was any suspicion of forgery, however, the prisoner of war's status as a noncommissioned officer would only be acknowledged upon receipt of a "Confirmation of Rank," which could be requested from the home army by the chief Man of Confidence through the Protecting Power. Until this certificate arrived, the prisoner of war was to be treated as a simple soldier.[16]

In addition to the basic classifications for prisoners of war, a special category, *Kriegsgefangenen-Geheimnisträger*, was created by the OKW for "especially important prisoners of war." No mention was made of which office within the OKW would decide upon such a designation, or the criteria which would be used.[17]

Toward the end of December 1944, the OKW issued its orders concerning the treatment of partisans as prisoners of war,[18] something of significance for the Anglo-Americans, given the nature of British and American "Military Missions" in southeast Europe. According to the orders, men caught fighting during partisan activity were to be treated as prisoners of war of their respective nationality, and were to be accommodated in prisoner-of-war camps within Germany. A decision as to whether or not the individual was a partisan was to be made where he was captured; conversely, the individual himself could offer the requisite proof. When possible, partisans were to be segregated away from other prisoners of war in the camps. For employment purposes, they were to be treated as other-ranks and employed in general groups.[19] Before their first use as laborers, they were to undergo a background check by the secret police. The nearest Gestapo section was to conduct this check as soon as the prisoner of war arrived in the camp. Recognizably untrustworthy or unreliable ones were to be dismissed from captivity and turned over to the secret police. Regardless of whether they were captured in civilian-style clothing or uniforms, a large dot and the letters "Kgf"[20] were to be painted on the back, so they could be recognized as prisoners of war from a distance. Further classifications and reports concerning them were to be made using the same procedures as for other prisoners of war. They were considered exclusively as members of the partisan band in which they fought, and were not to receive consideration for ranks they previously might have held with a regular army, unless they could offer unequivocal proof of the rank themselves.

In one of the few directives issued during the war concerning Jewish prisoners of war, the OKW stated, on March 11, 1942, that the Jewish star was a measure of the German government for identification on the streets and in business, and that Jewish prisoners of war were not to wear such a star. Whenever possible, though, they were, as permitted by the Geneva Convention to be isolated from other prisoners of war within the camps.[21] British prisoners of war of Irish descent were another group specifically designated by the OKW to be separated from other prisoners of war.[22]

Trimmings

The basic uniform of the prisoner of war could be supplemented by additional identification markings issued by the German camp staff. The OKW forbade prisoners, however, from wearing any insignia which were not part of their national military uniforms except for those issued by German military authorities.[23]

In May 1942, the OKW decreed that all personal identification held by prisoners of war, with the exception of those of a purely military nature (protected under article 6 of the Geneva Convention), were to be taken away and placed in storage with the prisoner-of-war's other valuables.[24] If a prisoner lost his prisoner-of-war identification, he was to be issued a new one, and not one with the old number, so as to prevent any confusion. WASt was to be informed of each new issue.[25] At the start of August 1944, the OKW decided that this order was proving administratively troublesome; prisoners of war were to be given new identifications with their old numbers, after all.[26] Due to problems identifying dead prisoners of war after air-raids, the OKW ordered the military districts and camp commandants to more closely enforce previous orders which required prisoners of war to carry their identification cards with them at all times, and for the work detachment leaders or guards to carry a current list of each work detachment, with a master list to be kept in the main camp, and a copy to be sent to the military district headquarters.[27]

Lists of lists

The maintenance of lists to keep all sides informed of precisely who was a prisoner of war in the Detaining Power's captivity was required by article 77 of the Geneva Convention. In early March 1940, the OKW, through the OKM, ordered that the names of Allied prisoners of war captured at sea be broadcast over the radio.[28] That this was for the purpose of getting foreign radio listeners to tune into German radio propaganda is clear from another OKW order issued on April 19, 1940. All units were ordered to send triplicate lists of captured/rescued Allied personnel to OKW in Berlin. Care was to be taken that: the captured prisoner-of-war had already sent off his first postcard, notifying his family of his capture;[29] the names were not announced to the ICRC in Geneva by telegram until the broadcast was finished; and that the camp commandant did not allow visits to the prisoners of war by foreign reporters before the names were released.[30]

For reasons of reciprocity with the British Commonwealth and American governments, the OKW ordered that the name, rank, birthday, and birthplace of newly captured British and American prisoners of war be transmitted by telegraph to their respective governments. Therefore, camp commandants were to ensure that lists with this information were sent up the chain of command for every new prisoner of war.[31] The OKW also ordered that monthly lists of all British and American prisoners of war be prepared for sending to their Protecting Power, the Swiss government. These lists had to be broken down by rank, camp, specific nationality, number in hospital, and total number.[32] For administrative purposes, the notification cards sent by newly captured British prisoners of war to the ICRC were to be slightly altered; instead of "Rank and Unit," the British prisoners of war should fill in "Rank and Serial Number."[33]

In early July 1940, a request went out to all prisoner-of-war camps to send in to the OKW a list of Indian prisoners of war, showing their total number per camp and occupations, as well as languages spoken and religious affiliation. At the same time, commandants were told to report any instances in which western Allied prisoners of war were shot.[34] The keeping of lists was declared to be important by the OKW, who sought thereby to obtain similarly good information on the condition of their own prisoners of war in Allied captivity.[35]

A year later, at the start of July 1941, the OKW forwarded a list of British soldiers and sailors who were missing in action to the camp commandants, to be checked in case some of the men were prisoners of war. This was done, according to the OKW, with the aim of obtaining similar treatment for German soldiers who were missing in action.[36] And in the event that two camps became amalgamated quickly, and prisoners of war of more than one nationality were being kept together, the monthly reports to the ICRC and Protecting Power were to continue as normal, reflecting this fact. Missed notifications were to be caught up on, and then regular reports sent as per previous regulations.[37]

3.2 Early days: issues surrounding capture and early captivity

The Geneva Convention required belligerents to evacuate prisoners of war to "depots sufficiently removed from the fighting zone for them to be out of danger" as soon as possible after capture. The only exception was allowed for wounded prisoners, whom moving would prove a greater risk to life than leaving at the front. Belligerents were to also ensure that the prisoners not be "unnecessarily exposed to danger" while being transported, and that they normally not be forced to march more than 20 kilometers per day, unless necessary for the sake of obtaining food and water.[38]

The initial experience captured British and American soldiers could expect remained, in terms of structure, generally consistent during the course of the war years. They would be sent by either route-march or lorry back from the front lines to a prisoner-of-war collecting center which reported directly to the headquarters of each division. From there, they were again transported to a collecting station, which reported to each Army command. Finally, usually by rail, the prisoners of war were sent to a Dulag (final transit camp), and then to either a Stalag or Oflag. Captured Allied airmen were turned over to the nearest Luftwaffe office, which would transport them to Dulag Luft, the transit camp for the Luftwaffe where the prisoners of war were processed and underwent an interrogation. Naval staff, after being rescued, would be taken to Marlag Nord by the shortest or most efficient route.[39] The procedure was consistent for army and naval personnel; airforce personnel, in the later stages of the war, had to hope that they did not fall into the hands of a hostile crowd before being taken into military custody,[40] while Allied commandos operating out of a major combat area were often executed, as a result of the infamous "Kommandobefehl" issued by Hitler.[41]

In terms of early captivity, the OKW, in its 1939 manuals, stated that though the main purpose of the Dulag was to collect and sort prisoners of war according to officers, men, and civilians, the wounded among them had to be examined, treated, and, if necessary, sent directly to a hospital for further attention.[42] Upon entry into any camp, prisoners of war were to be searched for weapons and military documents, and subjected to a medical examination/disinfection.[43] The main indicators of a prisoner of war's status, his insignia and his paybook, were not to be taken away from him. The official notifications of captivity to the WASt came from the Stalags and Oflags; the Dulags' job was merely to sort the prisoners of war so they could be sent to the appropriate permanent camps as quickly as possible; the only lists necessary in Dulags were official transport lists. The Dulags had to report to WASt deaths in the Dulag, successful escapes, the transferral of prisoners of war directly to Arbeitskommandos outside the Dulag, and the retention of individual prisoners of war whose talents were required as staff at the Dulag. Problems arising from transport were to be reported to WASt by the destination camps.[44] Once in the Dulags, the prisoners of war were to be organized into companies of no more than 250. The right of the prisoners of war to appoint a "Man of Confidence," as per article 43 of the Convention, was considered "essential" by the OKW.[45]

A Dulag was normally to comprise of 6,000 prisoners of war, while Stalags and Oflags could house as many as 10,000 prisoners of war, with approximately one German guard/staff for every 7 to 10 prisoners of war.[46] Housing regulations had to be posted in the language of the prisoner of war, and they were to be fed according to the rations for the Reserve Army, as per regulations.[47] In the event that conditions changed, rationing or other alterations in the portions could be ordered.[48] Formal lists of all the prisoners of war in Oflags or Stalags were to be sent every 10 days to WASt.[49]

The prisoners' tents in the Dulags were to be furnished with the bare necessities; if possible, officers were to receive beds rather than palliasses. Private money found on the prisoners was to be taken, with the corresponding amount inscribed on an "account" card. As noncommissioned officers and other-ranks received no pay under the Geneva Convention unless they worked, the Dulag did not have to worry about the issue of pay. Officers did receive pay, but were to be told that their first pay would be given to them upon arrival in their Oflag.[50]

Early movements

Prior to transport, one prisoner of war from the group about to be moved was to be recognized as the "transport leader"; he was to be warned explicitly that any attempts at escape, mutiny, or insubordination would be put down by force of arms. Anyone who left the train without authority would be shot.[51] Transport arrangements to the relevant Oflag or Stalag were the responsibility of the relevant Wehrkreiskommando. The prisoners of war were to be sent by rail whenever possible, in a third-class compartment together. Unless otherwise ordered, responsibility for providing food for the journey rested with the Dulag.[52]

At the end of December 1941, German soldiers were warned to pay special attention while searching captured British airmen; apparently, they possessed escape kits including a small steel saw, maps, chocolates, and nutrition tablets.[53] In December 1942, orders were issued stating that the same precautions aimed at British airmen were also to apply to captured American airmen.[54] Further, it was noted that newly arriving prisoners of war had occasionally been shot at, and in some instances seriously wounded or even killed, because they were contravening camp regulations they were unaware of. This was partly because regulations varied somewhat from camp to camp. Clearly displayed notices or regulations concerning order and discipline on blackboards near the entrances were not sufficient; henceforth, noncommissioned officers or the camp Man of Confidence were to be made available to go over the rules with new arrivals.[55]

The capture of "especially important" prisoners of war (*Prominente*) by units outside the regular OKW prisoner-of-war structure, had to be reported to the OKW as soon as possible.[56] Likewise, the OKW had to be notified of the escape of any senior officer (colonel and higher) prisoner.[57]

In the interest of conducting more effective interrogations of captured American and British airmen, all valuables taken from them were to be transported with them as quickly as possible to the interrogation center at Dulag Luft Oberursel. And given the risks of escape, the captives were not to be sent on civilian but only on military trains.[58]

In mid-January 1944, the OKW clarified the status of British and American paratroopers, glider troops, and anti-aircraft troops. They were members of their respective armies, not airforces; consequently, they were not to be interned in the Luftwaffe prisoner-of-war camps, but rather in the OKW's Stalags or Oflags. However, as these branches fell within the airforce in the German military structure, Luftwaffe interrogators were best suited to carry out the interrogations, and were therefore to be brought in to question these prisoners of war.[59]

And when the going got tough

With the fighting in Normandy continuing in earnest during the summer of 1944, Germany's Fifteenth Army, located east of the Seine, was held in reserve by Hitler, who feared a second invasion front, until August, when they were finally placed into combat against the British and American armies. In preparation for the impending combat, the divisions of the Fifteenth Army were issued a circular in mid-July entitled "Instructions for the Treatment and Interrogation of Prisoners of War in the Army-area," to be passed along to their soldiers. Though not necessarily indicative of the policy of the entire German Army, its focus on American and British prisoners of war, the date at which it was issued, and the high office of its provenance provide a good indication of the actual attitudes toward prisoners of war held by the army most likely to capture prisoners at that stage of the war. As well as treating obvious administrative issues, the instructions called on the soldiers to: separate officers, noncommissioned officers, and other-ranks; not let them talk with one another; not let German soldiers talk to them; not get friendly with them, as it would only be taken advantage of by them in escape attempts; not let the prisoners of war have any contact with civilians; and watch carefully what they got their hands on, as they could try bribing either guards or civilians to help in escaping. Interrogations were to occur at the division level, which was why it was important not to ruin the interrogation by letting the prisoners of war talk with anyone. Officers and special soldiers could be carrying escape aids, such as compasses, which had to be removed; however, a search of the prisoner could only be conducted with a German officer present. In the meantime, they were not to be allowed to destroy papers of military value. The prisoners could hold on to personal papers. Finally, the German soldiers were warned that American, Canadian, and British soldiers were especially likely to try to escape soon after capture. Immediately following this letter was a list, from OKW headquarters in Berlin, of 10 guidelines to be posted in sight of German soldiers, concerning the handling of prisoners of war. In addition to some of the same points mentioned above, others included: excessive severity toward prisoners of war was as uncalled for as excessive friendliness; the interrogation of the prisoners of war was to be left to the professional interrogators; paybooks, personal letters, identification cards and insignia, and other personal belongings of the prisoners of war were not to be removed; to help with the later interrogation, any paper that had military value was to be sent up the chain of command, with a short notice describing the time and place at which the prisoner was captured. The last item on the list was an exhortation to the soldiers to maintain their reserve toward the prisoner of war, and thus be true to the dignity of German soldiers; the enemy remained the enemy.[60]

In an update of a similar order dated December 1941, the OKW in July 1944 reiterated the need to remove valuables from captured enemy airmen. Apparently, money and valuables were standard parts of the escape kits with which enemy pilots were issued before each mission. Upon capture, these were to be removed. A receipt for the total amount of the money and valuables had to be given to the prisoner. As only personal money could be credited to the prisoner's account, the military district administration would be responsible for separating escape money from the prisoner's personal money.[61]

Dismissed prisoners of war who had again been captured and were in German captivity were to be treated as any other first-time prisoner of war, in accordance with the Geneva Convention.[62]

And again in the interests of reciprocity, transfers of British and American prisoners of war to new camps were to be reported every 10 days, by use of new forms, as of the beginning of September 1944. To prevent the enemy from possibly mounting raids to liberate British and American pilots, under no circumstances were these forms to bear the location of the new camp, or any camp stamps.[63]

Keeping things neat

In late November 1939, the OKW reminded the military districts that all its guidelines and instructions were in strict accordance with the Geneva Convention of 1929 (ratified in 1934).[64] That copies of the

Geneva Convention were in fact available in the languages of the prisoners of war was apparent from an information bulletin sent out by the OKW, letting camp commandants and work-detachment leaders know from where they could be ordered.[65]

The OKW received reports that some of its orders meant for subunits within the prisoner-of-war organization had been sent in fragments, after a delay, or not at all. As of the beginning of June 1944, the previously common practice of passing along complete orders was made mandatory: all future orders for the OKW were to be passed along in full and in good time to the various camps, prisoner-of-war hospitals, work detachments, guard units, assistant guard units, etc., so they could be acted upon fully.[66]

3.3 General camp infrastructure

A place to call home

According to article 9 of the Geneva Convention, prisoners of war could be "interned in any town, fortress or other place with fixed limits," such as fenced camps. Prisoners of war "captured in districts which were unhealthy or whose climate was deleterious to persons coming from temperate climates [were to be] removed as soon as possible to a more favorable climate." As far as possible, the belligerents were to avoid mixing together in the same camp prisoners of different "nationalities or races." Most important, no prisoner could at any time be sent to an area "where he would be exposed to the fire of the fighting zone, or be employed to render by his presence certain points or areas immune from bombardment." Beyond these prescriptions, nothing else was stated concerning the location and design of prisoner-of-war camps: much flexibility was granted to the belligerents.

Given the relatively few specific guidelines in the Geneva Convention, therefore, it is not surprising that the German military district (Wehrkreis) administrations, which retained responsibility for planning and building the camps,[67] often used pre-existing structures and compounds, such as castles, forts, and even former schools, to house the prisoners of war. Most of the specific details satisfying the specific needs of each camp were to come from the military district administrations. Camps were generally located relatively close to a rail stop, as the railway was the preferred method for transporting prisoners of war within Germany; beyond that, the types of sites chosen for the location of camps ranged considerably, from the isolated Stalag

Lufts in the eastern military districts, to Oflag IV C, located in the main Schloss (castle) in Colditz.

In his 1942 update of Germany's general military policies toward prisoners of war, Dr. Waltzog spent little time discussing issues surrounding the prisoner-of-war camps themselves. With regard to article 9, which allowed for the separation of prisoners of war based on nationality and race, Waltzog treaded carefully: soldiers who shared barracks in their own armies were to share barracks as prisoners of war. For political reasons, ethnic Germans (*Volksdeutsche*) such as Alsatians could be separated into a different section of the camps, however.[68] But as Jews formed a specific race, he argued, it was legally permissible to place them into separate camps, or use them in a segregated work detachment.[69] With regard to the placement of the prisoner-of-war camps, Waltzog wrote (seemingly in contradiction with article 9) that areas prone to enemy air-raids, but not actual zones of fighting by enemy armies, were legitimate sites. The presence of anti-aircraft guns altered nothing. The enemy, according to Waltzog, had frequently placed German prisoners of war in direct danger, thus violating the provision of this article: the French used German prisoners of war as human shields in militarily important areas, while the British practice of sending Germans to Canada by boat, through war zones on the seas in which they were liable to be torpedoed, was also viewed by him as a violation of international law.[70] Waltzog made no other significant references to issues surrounding the prisoner-of-war camps themselves.

The prisoner-of-war camps, and all units associated with them (administrative, guards, work detachments, and branch camps), could only be dissolved with the permission of OKW headquarters in Berlin.[71] Later, at the start of May 1944, this was expanded to include any substantial aspect of prisoner-of-war affairs within the military districts, even the creation or dissolution of small units such as transit camps. In all cases, the authority for such changes existed only with the Chief of Prisoner-of-war Affairs of the OKW; military districts had to seek approval for changes, rather than act on their own initiative.[72] The ultimate authority in matters concerning the existence of the individual camps, as well as their location, rested with the OKW in Berlin.

Design matters

The 1939 manuals expected prisoner-of-war camps to hold a maximum of 10,000 prisoners; no minimum number was given. The commandants were warned that camps would occasionally not yet be ready before the sudden arrival of prisoners, and so the first priority was to construct the enclosed barbed-wire fence. When completed, the camps would ideally be surrounded by two rings of barbed wire, with obstacles placed in the space between them to make walking or crawling difficult for escaping prisoners. Realizing the potentially unique security requirements of each different camp, the OKW allowed the commandants discretion over the location and sighting of the machine-gun manned guard towers, and the barbed-wire fences. The general guidelines they expected the commandants to follow, however, were that the rings of wire were to be illuminated, and the machine-gun posts in the guard towers were to be situated in such a way that they afforded a clear range of fire both into the camp and along the perimeter wires.[73] In late May 1940, the previous practice of allowing guard dogs to run freely between perimeter fences was prohibited; from then on, all guard dogs had to be kept on a leash.[74] The OKW was also concerned, in October 1942, about the growth of weeds around the fences surrounding the prisoner-of-war camps. Where clearing the weeds was not practical or feasible, the camp commandants were to string a "warning wire" at least two meters within the fence, as another level of perimeter warning. As a result of some recent escapes, all camps were also to check their fences and wires carefully for rust and breaks, as many of them were now three years old.[75] By June 1944, the previous measures were viewed as inadequate and updated; henceforth, a perimeter of two meters within the barbed-wire enclosures was to be cleared in all camps.[76]

After fences, the priority in construction was to go to the barracks for the guards; the prisoners of war could, if necessary, be housed in tents or makeshift huts until their permanent barracks were ready.[77] The number of prisoners of war held in each barrack room could be as much as 20. When double- or triple-tier bunks were not yet created or available, fresh straw was to be provided for them to sleep on the floor. Where the materials for huts arrived without furnishings, such as wardrobes or closets, these were to be constructed locally. With the aim of ensuring the good health of the prisoners and to prevent the outbreak of any epidemics, frequent inspections of the barracks were to be conducted in conjunction with the German camp medical staff.[78] As part of their basic allotment, each prisoner-of-war was to be given two blankets, a towel, eating utensils, and a food-bowl.[79] A room of 20 prisoners of war was expected to require a 100-watt bulb.[80] Cleaning supplies were to be provided for the prisoners' to use, though rules for their use could not be left to the prisoners to decide.

Local camp housing regulations were to be posted in the prisoners' own language, indicating instructions for cleaning the common areas and rooms, the times at which the windows had to be open (even in the winter) to ensure healthy ventilation, heating and illumination times and rules, instructions regarding black-outs and lights-out, reveille, as well as the need to salute upon the entrance of a superior officer into a room. Fire-alarm regulations also had to be posted, as well as instruction for air-raid actions. The regulations in place for work detachments located outside the main camps were to mirror the camps' rules.[81] Generally speaking, thrift and savings by the commandant were encouraged only insofar as the health of the prisoners was not thus compromised.[82]

Taking cover

An important responsibility of the Detaining Power was the provision of shelters for use during air-raids. In October 1942, the OKW ordered the military district headquarters to check all prisoner-of-war air-raid shelters and make sure they were sufficient; where not adequate, they were to be improved immediately.[83] In early April 1943, the OKW issued general instructions concerning air-raid protection measures for prisoners of war: they had to always be available to prisoners of war, and whenever possible were to match those offered to German civilians. Work detachments which consistently showed good behavior during air-raids could be rewarded by being switched with another work detachment further away from areas likely to be bombed, though why any prisoners were in areas known to be likely to be bombed in the first place went unexplained.

With the increasing duration of the war, the OKW wrote, it was ever important for both camps and work detachments to become better prepared to deal with air-raids. Where air-raid shelters underground were not available, prisoners of war were to be given access to zigzagging covered trenches. In work areas near rail installations, the air-raid shelters had to be placed away from the rail tracks. Whenever air-raid alarms provided advance warning, prisoners of war were to be allowed to carry, insofar as was possible, some of their belongings (especially clothes and shoes) with them, or place them in special storage areas. The doors and housings of prisoners of war had to be unlocked during air-raids. Sand and water had to be available in plentiful quantities so that fires could be controlled. Guards were to keep their steel helmets within reach at all times; prisoners of war were permitted to receive both steel helmets and gas-masks for this purpose from their home countries. When working at private businesses, prisoners of war and guards had to be made aware of the location of all fire hydrants in the vicinity.[84]

In September 1942, the OKW decided that, should prisoner-of-war barracks be destroyed in the course of an air-raid, the new barracks were not to be situated at the site of the old ones, especially if the prisoners of war were near a "war-important" armaments business or factory.[85] Previous orders concerning the safety arrangements of prisoners of war during air-raids were to be supplemented, as of June 1944, so that prisoners of war were able to seek protection in their barracks or workplaces in the exact same manner as was permissible for Germans.[86] On July 15, 1944, in response to a series of refusals by prisoners of war to construct air-raid trenches, the OKW ordered that, notwithstanding their desires, such refusal ran contrary to the Geneva Convention. Therefore, whether they wanted to or not, prisoners of war were to construct adequate air-raid shelters as soon as possible.[87]

Flowers and flags

The camp commandants had the flexibility, after security concerns were met, to deal with local issues surrounding the housing of prisoners of war; the OKW steered clear of offering advice on issues concerning the physical makeup of the camp, with very few minor exceptions. Recognizing the obvious benefit of having the prisoners grow some of their own vegetables, and the relative harmlessness of permitting the activity, the OKW gave permission, in late May 1940, for them to grow their own gardens, provided the cost of materials used to create and maintain them were deducted from camp expenses.[88] In early July 1941, prisoners of war were permitted to plant flowers and to improve the outlook of their barracks.[89] But by November of that same year the shortage of raw materials in Germany was proving cause of enough concern that requests from prisoners of war for materials to beautify their camps, that were not absolutely necessary, were to henceforth be rejected; this went especially for products made of iron.[90]

In the early stages of the war, the OKW had permitted British prisoners of war who so requested the right to fly their own flag within the camp. This changed in late October 1942, when British flags were no longer permitted to be flown in prisoner-of-war camps. This was in reprisal for a British measure forbidding German prisoners of war from flying the German flag in British camps. If British prisoners of war complained about the measure, they were to have the reasons for it explained to them.[91] Also at this time, the OKW ordered that propaganda posters designed for use inside Germany [i.e. for Germans] be "inconspicuously" removed from the walls of prisoner-of-war camps and hospitals.[92]

Interior accommodations

Whereas article 9 of the Geneva Convention provided the basic prescriptions concerning physical siting of the prisoner-of-war camps, article 10 addressed the interior accommodations within the camps: the prisoners were to be "lodged in buildings or huts which afforded all possible safeguards as regards hygiene and salubrity. The premises [had to be] entirely free from damp, and adequately heated and lighted. All precautions [had to be] taken against the danger of fire." As regards the dormitories themselves, their total area, minimum cubic air space, fittings, and bedding material, the conditions had to be the same as for the depot troops of the Detaining Power. As can be seen from the relative few direct orders concerning prisoner-of-war accommodations, the OKW seemed to view the implementation of this issue as within the prerogative of the commandant's personal discretion.[93]

Conservation

An obvious source of concern for the OKW was the amount of electricity consumed by the camps. Their orders on the use of electricity in the camps reflected a desire for balance between rights of the prisoners of war and the need for conservation measures. In mid-May 1942, the OKW ordered that British prisoner-of-war officers be permitted to have electric light until 22:30 hours every evening, for reasons of "reciprocity."[94] Also in the interests of conserving electricity, the OKW ordered the camps on January 11, 1943, to physically check the wiring for every light source, and remove any wiring not necessary for this purpose. In rooms housing four officer prisoners of war, one 40-watt bulb was permitted; in rooms with 5 to 8 officers, a 75-watt bulb was allowed. They were allowed 10 additional watts of power for each officer in the room above 8. Electrical appliances for cooking private food supplies could only be used with the written permission of the commandant;[95] but before commandants gave their approval to appliances used by prisoners of war that consumed electricity, they had to inform the military district administration.[96] With regard to night illumination in the camps, the OKW ordered, in late September 1942, that lights be now turned out in the Oflags at 21:00 hours, instead of at 22:30 hours as decided in May; however, the camp staff had to make certain that doctors and medical staff continued to have access to electricity, so they could provide service throughout the night.[97]

Another attempt at conservation was made with regard to heating fuel in the camps. As the fuel supply in Germany had become scarcer by January 1944, the OKW ordered camps, where possibly, to try heating the prisoner-of-war quarters with heating bricks made of a mixture of charcoal dust (comprising half to three-quarters of the total) and clay. The results of this experiment were to be reported back.[98]

Clutter

The OKW reminded the commandants, in June 1941, that for reasons of security, the amount of luggage allowed in the prisoners' personal quarters was to be strictly controlled, with surplus supplies being put into storage; increased luggage allowances were to be made for officer prisoners of war.[99] In March 1943, the OKW noted that the prisoners' barracks were becoming increasingly cluttered with boxes and suitcases, making security inspections difficult. From then on, the prisoner of war could only have as much luggage as he could carry. With the supervision of the Men of Confidence, the remainder of the prisoners of war's possessions were to be locked up in storage.[100] By September 1944, the issue had become more serious than one of security inspections; the housing situation for prisoners of war was becoming more and more serious, the OKW wrote at this time, and to free up housing for increased numbers of prisoners of war, all camps had to restrict storage spaces to as small an area as possible, so that as many huts as possible could be converted into barracks. Discomforts had to be expected and accepted. In all Stalags, prisoner-of-war officers and nonworking noncommissioned officers were to be restricted to huts on the perimeters of the camps, in order to free up room in the main sections for more prisoners. The monthly notification of free spaces was to be carried out with very careful diligence on the part of the camp commandant. It was the responsibility of the commandants to inform the OKW of any unforeseen shortages in occupancy levels since their last report.[101]

Finally, while straw filled palliasses were considered acceptable sleeping material for prisoner-of-war soldiers, the right of prisoner officers to receive bedlinen was reaffirmed by the OKW in April 1940.[102] Two final measures concerning prisoner-of-war accommodations were unremarkable. In May 1943, the OKW ordered that pictures of French leaders who had turned to the other side (de Gaulle, Giraud, Darlan) be removed from prisoner-of-war barracks.[103] And at the start of April 1944, OKW ordered that female prisoners of war be housed separate from male prisoners; this was to be done, however, in such a way that escaping was impossible.[104]

Food

In keeping with the official military policy of adherence to the Geneva Convention, the initial German prescriptions regarding food mirrored those outlined in article 11: the rations had to be equivalent to what the Detaining Power would provide for its own depot soldiers; the prisoners of war had to be given means to prepare for themselves any additional food they might receive in parcels; and sufficient drinking water supplies had to be provided. To assure the prisoners of war that they were in fact receiving their full allotment, it was standard practice to publish a complete menu indicating the calories and rations, thus allowing the Men of Confidence and the Protecting Power delegates to compare the prisoners' menu to the official German rations. And in keeping with article 11, the prisoners of war themselves were to be employed in the preparation of the food, under the direct supervision of a German noncommissioned officer. Most importantly as regards discipline, all collective disciplinary measures affecting food were prohibited by the Geneva Convention.

In December 1941, perhaps the most important official change in German policy regarding the size of the rations was implemented. Henceforth, the OKW ordered, portions of food given to prisoners of war by the German authorities were to be reduced where possible by a third, with the reduction in food being compensated by the food reserves sent from abroad in collective parcels (such as from the ICRC). In certain cases, the order was reported to be untenable, because of the refusal of the Man of Confidence to cooperate. The OKW did not view this as a valid reason, and reminded the commandants that the implementation of the order was not dependent on the Man of Confidence's acquiescence.[105] At the same time, the OKW ordered reaffirmed that any food sent to prisoners of war undergoing disciplinary punishment had to be forwarded to either the camp infirmary or the prisoner-of-war hospital.[106]

Baking their daily bread

The OKW acknowledged that many complaints of prisoners of war concerning their right to have some say over the preparations of their food had been validated by foreign inspections; this led, in March 1942, to a reminder sent to all camps that previous orders allowed for prisoner-of-war input. Although these orders did not restrict the responsibilities of the German kitchen noncommissioned officers, they had to be followed.[107]

The OKW also noted at this time that proper cooking habits were important not only to prevent waste of food, but also to make sure that prisoners of war were healthy, and thus able to work. They therefore advised the camps to: avoid too much waste when cleaning vegetables and especially potatoes; not let food soak in water for days at a time; learn the difference between foods that took long to cook, and those that could be cooked quickly; cook potatoes in the peel, as it could save water; use small pieces of onion to provide vitamin supplements and improve the taste and nutrition of food; take care that the food was palatable to the prisoners of war, and to learn their preferences, for example, for spices.[108]

On August 10, 1942, the OKH sent a memo to the camp commandants setting the daily bread rations for prisoners of war at 800 grams per day.[109] In mid-October of that year, the OKW passed along the newest regulations concerning food allotments for non-Soviet prisoners of war, in various types of work. First, sick prisoners of war in either prisoner-of-war hospitals or the camp infirmaries were entitled to receive 225 grams of sugar per week. Prisoners of war working regular shifts in the armaments industry[110] were to receive the same food as German civilians similarly employed. However, prisoners of war deemed working either long hours or night shifts were entitled to two-thirds of the rations issued to civilians likewise employed. The same two-thirds ratio applied to those prisoners of war employed in "hard" and "very hard" labor. In all circumstances, the prisoners of war could be rewarded with a full 2 kilo and 850 gram bread ration per week if they met the standard German worker performance objectives. Prisoners of war working in farms were to receive the same, reduced, portions as their civilian counterparts, because the farms were considered to be self-feeding up to a certain point, and better able to deal with any shortages of rations by tapping into local sources of food. Notices concerning the OKW's policy toward horse meat were to be posted as necessary.[111]

At the end of January 1942, the OKW further stipulated the monthly rations for British, French, and Serbian prisoners of war for beer, wine, and fruit juice: 3 to 4 liters of beer, and no wine or fruit juice.[112] By June 1944 this was amended to allow for the delivery of up to 5 liters of beer to all prisoners of war (except Soviet and Polish) per month. The camp commandant would decide, based on local considerations, how close to this ceiling each prisoner of war in his camp would be allowed.[113] But one month later, in August 1944, British prisoners of war were no longer allowed to receive wine or fruit juice, in either individual or collective parcels. Wine or fruit juice which had arrived before that time was to be handed over to the communal camp kitchen. The prohibition was apparently instituted in response to a similar one imposed on German prisoners of war in British captivity.[114]

In mid-October 1942, it came to the attention of the OKW that in some camps, canned goods were being opened for inspection, and then the opened cans were being turned over to the prisoners of war; in other cases, during transport, the prisoners of war were given unopened cans of food. The OKW reminded the commandants that it was forbidden to give prisoners of war cans, for security reasons (they could be used to assist escapes). The contents of the cans were to be emptied into other containers before being turned over to the prisoners of war. Only in exceptional circumstances could the prisoners of war retain the cans, and even then only if security permitted.[115] The general prohibition against giving prisoners of war empty cans from collective parcels was reiterated in August 1943; for this reason, up to two plates were now to be issued to a prisoner of war.[116]

Reflecting both the need for security and the fact that there had been some inconsistency in the application of previous orders concerning the issuing of canned foods directly to the prisoners, the OKW ordered, in July 1944, that cans from either collective or private parcels be handled by prisoners of war only under conditions of strict supervision. The reasons for this were: (a) to prevent the covert accumulation of food supplies by prisoners of war; (b) to prevent empty cans from being used for escape attempts (as shovels for tunnel digging or in the making of pass-keys for locks); and (c) to prevent news and other information from being smuggled in to the prisoners of war. An individual prisoner could have up to six cans available to him at one time. Before a can was given to the prisoners of war it had to be opened and its contents checked; cans which arrived in standard packages from the American or British Red Cross needed to be subject only to occasional spot checks. Before a new can was distributed, an old one had to be returned empty. The camp commandants had to ensure that these regulations were followed in even the smallest work detachments.[117]

On January 11, 1943, the OKW formally ordered that prisoners of war be allowed to cook supplementary food for their meals. This was to be accomplished where possible by the creation of additional cooking facilities; nonetheless, commandants were to pay close attention to ensure that fuel supplies were used carefully and with thrift.[118]

By May 1944, reflecting the general shortages being felt throughout Germany, the OKW authorized the utilization of substandard, but treated, meat (*Freibankfleisch*) in cooking in prisoner-of-war camps.[119] Also at this time, the OKW noted that individual prisoners of war were reportedly hoarding supplies from individual and collective parcels, and storing them in closets or, especially, using warehouse space at the work detachments. The maximum supplies allowed to be held in storage for each prisoner of war were: 10 tins of meat, 5 of chocolate, and one half pound of coffee, which would exceed four weeks' reserves.[120] Further clarification of this order was given by the OKW one month later. Individual prisoners of war could only retain in their possession one day's food; the four weeks' reserve mentioned above was to be kept in a storage area where the two-key system, according to which a responsible German official would carry one of the two keys needed to unlock the room, and the Man of Confidence would carry the second key.[121]

In the last order specifically referring to food, issued in mid-October 1944, the OKW clarified that previous orders (dating back to December 1941) concerning the reduction of food portions for prisoners of war were to apply only if there was a large surplus of food from collective parcels, or in situations where the prisoners of war wasted too much German-issued food.[122]

Clothing

The specifics of clothing policy regarding prisoners of war could not be drawn from the Geneva Convention. Article 12, which ostensibly dealt with the issue, only stated that clothing, underwear, and footwear had to be supplied to prisoners of war by the Detaining Power, with regular replacement and repair of those articles being assured; workers were to receive work clothes wherever the nature of the work required it. As stated in the more specific German manuals given to commandants at the start of the war, the prisoners' basic clothing allotment was: one battle-dress (shirt and pants), one pair of boots, one pair of shoes or slippers, two pairs of socks, two pairs of undergarments, two shirts, two collars, one coat and a pair of gloves (in winter only) and, if necessary, work clothes; in addition, each Stalag or Oflag had to maintain a reserve of clothing for 500 men.[123]

The first additional order concerning clothing came in late August 1940. After acknowledging that many reports from various military districts in Germany indicated poor overall clothing situations, the OKW conceded to all military district headquarters that shortages for the prisoners of war would be inevitable, due to shortages for even the German military. As much as possible, then, measures were to be taken to make clothing last longer (hanging washed clothing on barbed-wire to dry, for instance, was banned). As well, permission to secure any available cobbling equipment was given. The tendency of British officers to give their "hand-me-downs" to Polish prisoners of war housed nearby was noted, and not forbidden; clothing of prisoners of war with uniforms of a different nationality was deemed undesirable, but hardly stoppable in the circumstances. Heavier items of clothing, such as coats, were to be placed in storage until absolutely necessary, in order to prevent wear and tear. A thorough review of the clothing situation was ordered, with a detailed list of needs to be forwarded back to Berlin.[124] It was with shortages in mind that the OKW next authorized, in March 1942, the prisoners of war to be furnished with civilian underwear, with the understanding that no other pieces of civilian clothing be given to prisoners of war, for security reasons.[125]

In early February 1943, the OKW sought to settle a recurring source of confusion concerning private clothing from individual parcels.[126] Clothing which arrived in individual (that is, private) parcels was the private property of the prisoner of war, and was not to be counted toward the main clothing stocks. However, if a prisoner had more clothing than he needed, clothing from the collective parcels which were nominally earmarked for him could instead be put in the collective stocks. Private clothing placed in storage had to be signed for, and was to be under the supervision of the Man of Confidence.[127] This practice was extended to include private blankets, that autumn: in September 1943, prisoners of war who had their own private blankets were prohibited from receiving blankets from the collective parcels beyond the regulated number; if prisoners were entitled to two blankets, and a prisoner already had one of his own, he would only be issued one more from the collective stocks.[128] The OKW also reaffirmed that clothing from the collective parcels was obliged to be treated with respect; prisoners were to be charged for wantonly damaging clothing from the collective stocks.[129]

As of July 1943, any prisoner-of-war clothing damaged during an air-raid was to be replaced immediately by the camps or the employer at the work detachment. A list of damaged goods had to be forwarded to the OKH in Berlin.[130] Later that month, the OKW decided that winter clothing was to be taken away from the prisoners of war and placed in secure storage, to guard against fire or potential air-raid damage. It was up to the local commander to determine when coats were to be issued, and the use of coats as blankets was prohibited.[131]

It had also come to the attention of the OKW at that time that some prisoners of war, especially French and British naval officers and pilots, were having their second uniforms confiscated and altered by local German staff, either by cutting or dyeing. Though this procedure was apparently being done for security reasons, in order to prevent the clothes from looking like civilian clothing, it was illegal: every prisoner-of-war had the legal right to his proper uniform. The practice was to be stopped immediately, even if doing so required closer guarding and supervision of the prisoners of war in question.[132]

January 1944 saw officer prisoners of war being generally prohibited from receiving and possessing any civilian clothing. An exception could be made for sports shorts, provided they were worn with other clothing, which clearly indicated prisoner-of-war status.[133] And to prevent contact between prisoners of war and the civilian population, prisoners were no longer allowed to give their laundry to a German for washing without the presence of a guard. Preferably, large groups of prisoners would collect their laundry together, and the guard would supervise its handing over to a laundry company.[134] As of June of that year, prisoner-of-war officers and protected personnel who sent their laundry out for washing could be charged RM1.50 (*reichsmarks*) per month for the service.[135]

In no circumstances, the OKW decided in March 1944, were prisoners of war to be issued with German goods, which were in short supply, beyond their proper entitlements. This order, however, did not affect any such supplies, which arrived in collective parcels, provided they had been vetted under security considerations.[136] As of July 1944, civilian clothing sent to prisoners of war was not only to be not delivered, but formally to be confiscated as well. As all prisoners of war had been warned that they were unable to receive such items for security reasons, any such confiscated clothing was to be handled as "refugee" supplies.[137]

Later that month, in the last significant general order concerning clothing issued by the OKW during the war, prisoners of war were again reminded that they could not have any civilian clothing in their possession, and that any such clothing arriving in parcels would be confiscated. Sports apparel (especially shorts) would only be permitted to be retained if it could be made to obviously look like prisoner-of-war clothing; the markings required were left to the discretion of the individual camps. Prisoner-of-war accommodations were to be searched again for any civilian clothing.[138]

Health issues/protected personnel

Issues of general hygiene and health were obviously of great significance for the prisoners of war, and the overall rules concerning them were laid out in articles 13, 14, and 15 of the Geneva Convention. The first of these required belligerents to take all necessary measures to ensure good hygiene: day and night access to clean toilets, use as far as possible of showers, and enough water for personal cleanliness. As well, the prisoners of war had to be given opportunity and facilities for physical exercises and the benefits of being outdoors.

Article 14 dealt with the establishment of camp infirmaries, where the captives could receive any kind of attention needed, including isolation areas for those suffering from infectious and contagious diseases; all costs were to be borne by the Detaining Power, and, if necessary, prisoners of war requiring more advanced treatment or surgery had to be transferred to the nearest appropriate military or civilian medical facility. At the prisoner's request, an official statement outlining the nature of his illness and duration of treatment had to be issued. In the camps, the Detaining Power could retain, by means of special agreement among the belligerents, captured enemy medical personnel to minister to the needs of the prisoners of war.

The last of these articles, article 15, stated that the prisoners had to be medically inspected at least once a month, the object being the supervision of the general state of health and cleanliness, and the detection of infectious and contagious diseases, particularly tuberculosis and venereal complaints.

The German military manuals at the start of the war simply stated that medical affairs within the prisoner-of-war camps were to be governed by articles 13–15 of the Geneva Convention.[139] The camp doctor had final authority in matters pertaining to health and hygiene in the camps, and there had to be at least one doctor per thousand prisoners.[140] Incoming prisoners had to be kept initially in a quarantine area, for the safety of the camp.[141]

The first additional order concerning issues of health or hygiene came in early October 1941, when the OKW ordered that security vetting of medical supplies sent to prisoners of war in packages be conducted at the military district (Wehrkreis) level. If cleared, they were to be distributed to the prisoners of war by the camp doctor.[142] Prisoners of war who, as a result of medical conditions, were not able to resume work at full capacity, had to be issued a certificate to this effect by the German camp doctor.[143]

At the end of December 1941, the OKW formally stated its position on prisoners of war who had suffered serious medical problems in the First World War, such as amputation, but who had been drafted into enemy armed forces nonetheless and were subsequently captured: they could only be sent home for medical reasons if they suffered another serious medical problem in this war.[144]

By March 1942, for reasons of both hygiene and security, prisoners of war were prohibited from wearing beards. This reiteration of a previous order further specified that razors were to be given to Soviet prisoners of war only if shaving machines were unavailable.[145] It was not clear whether the order would apply to British Indian prisoners of war, as well, but two months later, the OKW revised the order to allow prisoners of war to wear beards for religious purposes, or if they were medical personnel or clergy.[146]

As of May 1942, any collective parcels or medical parcels sent by the British Red Cross to hospitals with prisoners of war had to be signed for by the Man of Confidence and the Senior Medical Officer. If the consignments included a drug that was not well known, it was to be kept aside until its authenticity could be verified by the military district's medical personnel.[147]

In one of the few instances in which Nazi ideology was implemented to the apparent direct detriment of the German medical war effort, the OKW in August 1942 prohibited, for reasons of "racial hygiene," prisoners of war from donating blood to be used by Germans; it was deemed impossible to eliminate the risk of contamination by "Jewish hybrid" blood.[148] No follow-up to this directive was issued in subsequent orders during the remainder of the war.

By late September 1942, with the aim of improving its lists, the OKW ordered the individual camps to inform it of every occasion when a prisoner-of-war officer was sick for more than three days.[149] A few days later, the OKW ordered that prisoners of war who were convalescing from illness or injuries suffered in a work detachment be sent back to the main camp after they were well, and not back to the work detachment; from the main camp, they would be assigned to a different work detachment.[150] Infirmaries located in work detachments were still having trouble receiving medical supplies as of mid-November 1942; the OKW reminded commandants that these infirmaries were to receive medical supplies from the main camp's stocks.[151]

It had been noticed by the OKW, in August 1943, that many prisoners of war were faking illness to get out of work. One of the more common ruses, especially among the French prisoners of war, was to swallow a piece of silver foil, and then claim an ulcer. In the x-rays, the silver paper in the stomach looked very much like an ulcer. Doctors were to be on guard for such ruses.[152] French prisoners of war were also apparently becoming adept at faking eye inflammations by rubbing into their eyes a fine powder that gave the appearance of conjunctivitis. Camp doctors were to be aware of this in examining prisoners of war of all nationalities.[153]

The OKW reminded the camps, in January 1944, that prisoners of war who were insane, but who did not need to be locked up, could be kept in military hospitals provided special measures were taken to ensure no accidents occurred, such as possibly wandering over to the barbed-wire fence, where a guard might shoot them.[154] Further, all cases of British prisoners of war in hospitals or infirmaries who, due to memory losses, were not able to be identified, were to be reported to OKW Berlin as soon as possible.[155]

With the aim of avoiding repetitive questions concerning the state of health of ill British prisoners of war, each British prisoner in a hospital was to be given one postcard per week for the purpose of updating the condition of his health, as of August 1944. These would be transmitted to the ICRC.[156]

On November 10, 1944, a lengthier circular was sent by the OKW concerning the reporting of illnesses of prisoners of war, faking of illnesses, segregation of ill prisoners of war from others, and security measures in prisoner-of-war hospitals and infirmaries. Given the sacrifices being made by German workers, prisoners of war were not to be placed out of work for only marginal illnesses, the OKW wrote: doing so gave in to their plans for sabotaging the German war effort. The first line of defense against this, then, was the close supervision of prisoner-of-war doctors, who were generally too quick to certify their comrades as unfit to work. Large companies employing prisoners of war could make arrangements with the camps for civilian German doctors to be subcontracted to provide medical opinions. Newly arrived prisoners of war in military hospitals were to be separated from longer-term prisoner-of-war patients, because they could undo some of the propaganda benefits being won by introducing either news or rumors detrimental to Germany. Any suspicious actions were to be reported immediately to the security officer, who in turn had to contact the local security detachment if greater troubles arose.[157]

Healers in uniform

Captured enemy religious and medical personnel, including doctors, were not legally prisoners of war, according to article 9 of the Geneva

Convention for the Amelioration of the Condition of the Wounded and Sick in Armies in the Field, but "protected personnel." While the Geneva Convention on Prisoners of war stated that they could be held to care for their compatriots, they were nonetheless supposed to receive greater privileges than prisoners of war. Bearing in mind the need for security, the privileges granted usually came in the form of mail benefits – protected personnel were allowed to write double the letters and cards per month normally granted to prisoners of their same rank, and often were permitted parole walks as well. One of the more enduring difficulties faced by them during the war was the continuing struggle to receive their proper privileges, despite continuous OKW support in orders to the lower levels of command. A further problem was the official "recognition" that a person captured in uniform was in fact a member of his army's medical or religious corps, and thus entitled to special treatment.

In mid-July 1941, the OKW reminded camp officials that enemy doctors, medics, and clergy were not to be treated as other prisoners of war. Despite being in German captivity, they were to be treated according to more lenient rules.[158] There appeared to have been continuing problems in getting prisoner-of-war doctors, medics, and clergy the preferred treatment that was their right under the Geneva Convention, and at the start of September 1941, the OKW, noting problems in compliance with earlier directives, reaffirmed their rights to better treatment than other prisoners.[159] The rights of British medics, like doctors, to receive an unrestricted number of packages was confirmed at the same time.[160] That not all captured medical personnel and clergy were receiving the benefits due their status was confirmed by an OKW order bemoaning this fact, and reminding camp authorities that article 9 of the Geneva Convention (for the Amelioration of the Condition of the Wounded and Sick in Armies in the Field, of 1929) demanded they be treated differently from (that is, better than) other prisoners of war.[161]

The OKW recognized the American Field Service, within the British and American militaries, as a volunteer-help organization, in the sense of article 10 of the Geneva Convention.[162] In late September 1943, this recognition was also extended to members of the American Field Service who were captured while serving with the French armed forces.[163]

In May 1944, the OKW stated that unrecognized British medical personnel could be recognized officially upon the receipt of duplicate certificates of their status. Immediately upon their receipt, the prisoner of war was to be informed of the change in his status, and could not be placed to work: his privileges as "protected personnel" under the Geneva

Convention were guaranteed.[164] One month later, the last significant directive of the war concerning protected personnel was issued by the OKW. It began by stating that the treatment of enemy medical personnel was to be regulated by chapter 3 of the Geneva Convention of 1929. The previous practice of dividing enemy medical personnel into the categories "practicing" and "nonpracticing" was replaced by "recognized" and "nonrecognized." After a previously unrecognized medical prisoner of war received formal recognition, the first thing to happen was that his proper pay was to be instituted, and delivered, at the regulated intervals. Enemy medical staff who, for disciplinary or judicial reasons, had some of their privileges restricted (i.e. for assisting or attempting escapes) could temporarily be prohibited from practicing their medical trade. Further restrictions could include suspension of walking privileges and reduced monthly mail privileges. No disciplinary punishment, however, could affect the attributes of recognition as "protected personnel," such as pay, and possible repatriation.[165]

Religion

Prisoners of war, according to article 16 of the Geneva Convention, were to be permitted "complete freedom in the performance of their religious duties, including attendance at the services of their faith, on the sole condition that they comply with the routine and police regulations prescribed by the military authorities." Ministers of religion, who were prisoners of war, were allowed to minister to their coreligionists. No other comments concerning the practice of religion were made in the Geneva Convention.

As to the routine and police regulations prescribed by the military authorities, the only mention in the German military manuals of 1939 on the subject was that, inside the camp, the prisoners were permitted the free practice of their faiths.[166] Indeed, given the stress involved in captivity and the desire to maintain as good relations as possible (both for better general security and to have a happier laborforce), the commandants were specifically instructed to meet, wherever possible, the wishes of the prisoners in this area.[167] Throughout the war, the OKW's main concern with regard to the practice of religion concerned security. No formal mention or special provisions was made regarding Jewish prisoners of war.

Padres and prisoners

In July 1940, instructions for printing sermons were issued by the OKW. After security vetting, they could be produced at cost of a sliding scale, depending on total number ordered, with the cost to be borne by the prisoners of war.[168] In December 1941 the OKW allowed that, in church services attended only by British prisoners of war, the customary prayer for the King as well as the singing of the national anthem could be permitted.[169]

The OKW noted, in February 1943, that an increasing number of enemy clergy were abusing their privilege to conduct services by fomenting unrest among prisoners of war. The ministers were to be reminded that they were to only speak on religious themes in their sermons, and not on politics. Clergy who continued to use the pulpit for political purposes were to be immediately prohibited from conducting services, and to be reported to the military district headquarters. Camp commandants were also reminded that services could only be conducted if there was a German interpreter present, and that services conducted by a clergyman traveling to several work detachments could, in times of tension, be suspended. Further, it was the responsibility of the camp, and not the employer, to find a suitable space for the conduct of religious services for the prisoners of war in a work detachment.[170]

The OKW sent, in July 1943, a list of religious holidays for British Indian prisoners of war, on which they were to be exempted from work. These included holidays for Muslims, Hindus, Sikhs, and the Birthdays of Guru Nanak and Govind Singh. The dates were calculated based on the 1938 and 1939 calendars, but to be certain, the commandants were instructed to consult with the Indian prisoners themselves.[171] In subsequent years, the OKW continued with the practice of giving approval for (British) Indian prisoners of war to celebrate their Muslim, Hindu, and Sikh religious holidays. As much as possible, support was to be offered to them for these celebrations; to that effect, prisoners of other religions were to be put to work in their place in work detachments where possible, so that work was not interrupted.[172] As of June 1944, measures instituted for the slaughter of animals for the Muslim diet for German military units were to be extended to Muslim prisoners of war; this was to be done for propaganda reasons, so the prisoner could practice his religion, and to make Muslim prisoners more willing laborers.[173]

In an administrative order concerning the allocation of prisoner-of-war clergy among camps, the OKW stated, in December 1943, that they were not to be stationed at work detachments on a permanent basis for security reasons. Instead, the clergy stationed at the nearest camp were to make occasional trips to provide religious services for these prisoners of war.[174] In April 1944, the OKW decided that prisoners of war serving sentences in military prisons were not normally entitled to spiritual services;

only in cases of life-threatening illness or if a prisoner was condemned to the death penalty would the nearest civilian, military, or prisoner-of-war clergyman be made available to offer religious services.[175] At the same time, the OKW decided that requests from prisoner-of-war clergy concerning issues in prisoner-of-war camps were no longer to be dealt with individually, but on a quarterly basis instead.[176]

In September 1944, the OKW attempted to clarify the position of "unofficial" prisoner-of-war clergymen. Prisoners of war who could prove they were clergymen in civilian life, but who were captured as regular fighting soldiers and were now located in Stalags, could, should the need arise and should there be a surplus of them, be permitted to act as temporary medical-assistant personnel in prisoner-of-war hospitals. Officer prisoners of war who were clergy in civilian life could volunteer to provide religious services in Stalags, prisoner-of-war hospitals, and work detachments.[177]

In the last general order of the war concerning religious issues, the OKW announced, in December 1944, that it had teamed up with a German Protestant relief organization to publish officially approved sermons for use in Protestant services for British and American, as well as Dutch, French, and Polish, prisoners of war. These sermons could be ordered from OKW Berlin, and would be distributed through the camp administration. They would bear a censorship approval mark, and needed no further examination once this mark had been verified.[178]

Recreation

As part of the measures for the health of prisoners of war in article 14, the Geneva Convention stated that they were to be allowed facilities for exercise and outdoor activities. Further measures for recreation were given in article 17, which simply stated: "Belligerents shall encourage as much as possible the organization of intellectual and sporting pursuits by the prisoners of war."

The 1939 German military manuals stated that daily exercise was healthy and desirable, and to that end sporting activities and calisthenics were to be organized and encouraged. Requests regarding sports were to be granted as widely as was practical, with the prisoners themselves being responsible for the maintenance of such facilities and fields as were required.[179]

Health and happiness

In May 1940, the German military authorities, claiming to be under pressure from German public opinion, curtailed supervised walks of

French and British officer prisoners of war outside of their camps. In compensation, the camps were ordered to expand their playing fields as much as possible, to permit football, handball, and, where equipment was available, tennis and gymnastics. Only with consultation with the local civilian authorities were prisoners of war allowed to use sports fields outside of their camps, in cases where there was no room in the camps to expand these facilities. Drawing from the experience of the First World War, special care in guarding prisoners of war during sporting events was cautioned, as many of their escapes in that war started from such activities. With this in mind, each officer would be required to offer his personal guarantee that he would not attempt to escape, before he was permitted to participate. After the first escape attempt, the privilege was to be withdrawn. Prisoners of war were permitted, by the same order, to receive minor sports equipment in packages from home.[180] By late August, worried that the portion of the order concerning the withdrawal of recreational privileges would make Germany appear as though it were breaking the terms of the Geneva Convention, a follow-up order was issued, stating that prisoners of war had to be permitted walks and sports in the camps.[181]

In early May 1940, permission was granted for prisoners of war to receive musical instruments and records from home, subject, of course, to a security check. Sheet music, radios, and loudspeakers remained prohibited.[182] By the start of February 1942, the OKW instructed the camps to stop passing along the prisoners' requests for oil paints; they were not to be issued with oil paints.[183] Prisoners of war who wanted to hold exhibits of their artwork were permitted to do so, within either a main prisoner-of-war camp or work-detachment barracks. However, no civilians and no members of the Wehrmacht not directly related to prisoners of war were permitted to visit such exhibitions.[184]

It had been brought to the OKW's attention, in January 1943, that some prisoners of war were being kept back from outside work detachments because they were members of the prisoner-of-war theater company or orchestra. This was not considered a valid reason for keeping an able-bodied prisoner in the camp. Such prisoners of war were to be put to work in their proper detachments; they could practice with the theater group or orchestra on their time off and Sundays.[185]

Because brawls between prisoners of war of different nationalities were becoming more and more common during sports matches, the OKW prohibited organizing matches along national lines in November 1942.[186] But with the aim of improving morale among prisoners of war, the OKW permitted the YMCA to issue special sport insignias to be worn by prisoners of war who performed exceptionally well in sporting events or competitions. A prisoner of war could be issued this only once, and the awards were to be rotated. The responsibility for choosing the prisoners of war so honored would fall to the Men of Confidence.[187]

By June 1944, the material shortages in Germany had reached a low enough point that the OKW curtailed many of the supplies for prisoner-of-war recreation activities. In pursuit of the total war effort, the OKW wrote, prisoner-of-war work stations (not including cobblers and tailors) must no longer provide material for artistic or theatrical leisure endeavors. The most important tasks of prisoner-of-war work detachments were to be war related. However, during leisure time, prisoners of war could make use of material which had no other strategic use for their own purposes.[188]

Canteens

The existence of canteens for prisoners of war was considered significant enough to be included in the Geneva Convention. Thus, within article 12, the belligerents were instructed to install canteens in all camps, so the prisoners could obtain, at local market prices, "food commodities and ordinary articles"; profits from these canteens were to be utilized for the benefit of the prisoners.

Likewise, in the German manuals of 1939, commandants were instructed to establish canteens selling minor items for personal use; prices were to be set by the commandant or his designate, with, as per the Convention, profits being used for the benefit of the prisoners of war and their amelioration.[189] On the whole, the OKW avoided micromanaging the camps on this issue, and issued only a handful of general orders.

In February 1942, the OKW noted that some camps, in which the prisoner-of-war canteen was poorly stocked, were allowing staff to purchase products for the prisoners of war from Wehrmacht canteens. At a time when the German population was suffering hardships, it was considered unacceptable that the few material benefits available to German soldiers were being used up by enemy prisoners of war. The practice was henceforth forbidden.[190]

According to a decision taken by the Reich Finance Ministry, sales from prisoner-of-war canteens were considered as all other domestic business sales within Germany, and were thus subject to sales tax. This measure was made effective for sales made after December 1,

1943, and was to be collected by the OKW.[191] To ensure no fraud was being practiced in the canteens, the OKW ordered random inspections of the financial books of the canteens to be conducted in each military district.[192]

In October 1944, the OKW noted that prisoners of war had also been using colored pens and ink-sticks to color their clothing and to mark their outgoing mail, lately. All such material was to be confiscated, and all canteens were to be forbidden from carrying them.[193]

Transportation and transfers

Aside from evacuation after initial capture, dealt with above and in article 7, the Geneva Convention's rules surrounding the transportation and transfer of prisoners of war were set out in articles 25 and 26. The first of these dealt with the possibly deleterious effect of transportation on a sick or wounded prisoner of war, stating that unless the course of military operations demanded it, such prisoners were not to be transferred if their recovery might be prejudiced by the journey. Article 26 dealt with more common issues for healthy prisoners of war: in the event of transfer, prisoners had to be informed in advance of their new destination, and they were authorized to take with them their personal effects, their correspondence, and parcels which had arrived for them. The Detaining Power had to make all necessary arrangements so that correspondence and parcels addressed to the prisoners of war would be forwarded to them at their new camp without delay. Just as important for the prisoners, the financial sums credited to their accounts in the old camp had to be transmitted to the competent authority of the new place of residence. Lastly, expenses incurred by the transfers were to be borne by the Detaining Power.

The German military manuals of 1939 laid downsome further instructions for the commandants. Prior to any transport, a prisoner of war from the group to be moved was to be recognized as the "transport-leader" among them; he was to be warned explicitly that any attempts at escape, mutiny, or insubordination would be put down by force of arms; anyone who left the train without authority would be shot.[194] Transport arrangements among the relevant Oflags or Stalags were the responsibility of the relevant Wehrkreiskommando. Prisoners of war were to be sent by rail whenever possible, in a third-class compartment without civilians. Unless otherwise ordered, responsibility for providing food for the journey rested with the camp of origin; also, the prisoners of war were to be dressed **warmly** (in bold in the original) during transport.[195] In late November 1939, the OKW informed the military districts that only it had the authority to transfer prisoners of war from one camp to another, and its permission had to be sought before any future transfers.[196]

Moving complications

In November 1941, the OKW noted that prisoners of war being transferred to new camps often had delays in getting their pay-credits transferred over as well. To prevent future confusion, the camp to which the prisoner was sent was given the primary responsibility for making sure that all the proper documents made it from the old camp to the prisoner's new camp.[197] Likewise, the OKW ordered that mail sent to them at their old camp be forwarded to them, and not returned to the sender marked "undeliverable"; to that end, the camps were to keep lists of where their former prisoners of war had been sent.[198]

In December 1941, the OKW reported upon an incident in which, to make room for British officers being transported by rail, German citizens were asked to clear out of second-class compartments. This led to many Germans, including women and children, being forced to stand in the aisle for the duration of their trip. This unacceptable situation could have been avoided if four days' notice had been given to the transportation authorities, so that they could better plan to accommodate the prisoners of war. Furthermore, prisoner-of-war officers, with the exception of generals, were henceforth to ride only in third-class compartments.[199] Individual military districts were permitted to make independent arrangements for the transport of up to 30 prisoners of war in a group. However, the prisoners of war could not mix with the German population in the train compartments, nor should they be placed in "pack" cars. To ensure proper accommodations, the military districts had to inform the railways at least 24 hours in advance of a prisoner of war transfer, so enough compartments could be reserved for them. The railways had the authority to refuse transport to groups of prisoners of war, if they did not receive proper advance warning.[200] Similarly, the OKW noted that providing sleeping accommodations for large numbers of prisoners of war traveling through Berlin was no longer possible. Therefore, the military districts had to arrange the prisoner transport in such a way that an overnight stay in Berlin was not required. In general, the transport of groups of prisoners of war through Berlin was generally not desired; where possible, prisoners of war were to be routed around Berlin.[201]

As a result of trouble caused by Soviet prisoners during transport, the OKW in January 1943 ordered that, henceforth, all prisoners of war (regardless of nationality) who were recaptured escapees or otherwise "troublesome" were not to be transported at night. If night transport was inevitable, such prisoners of war were to have at least two guards watching them.[202] As of March 1943, prisoner-of-war camps from which western prisoners of war were being sent to new camps in the General Gouvernement area, were not permitted to send collective parcels to the transferring prisoners of war, as they would already have these provided for them in their new camps. Individually addressed parcels were to be forwarded. Each shipment of parcels to the General Gouvernement area were to be shown to the Commander of Prisoners of War in that area, so he could best judge where to send them, to avoid deprivations.[203]

With an eye to greater security and escape prevention, the OKW decided, in March 1943, that both for transfers to new camps and in the event of escapes, photographs and negatives of prisoners of war (especially "Prominente" [prominent personalities], higher ranking officers, and British and American pilots) were to be forwarded both to the new camp and the local criminal police station. This was to occur at the same time that the prisoners of war's personnel cards were sent.[204]

In late July 1943, the OKW lamented the delays of some transit and permanent camps in sending reports of prisoner-of-war transfers to Berlin; all camps were reminded of the need to send prompt reports so Berlin remained informed of the current location of the prisoners of war.[205] Prisoners who were to be transferred to a new camp were to be informed as late as practically possible, and were not to be told of the destination, so as to prevent potential escape preparations.[206] In mid-October 1943, the OKW required that greater care be taken in examining the identities of prisoners of war prior to transfers. The responsibility for keeping track of the identities lay with the camp from which they were sent.[207] Further, only the OKW could issue authority for prisoners of war to be transferred from one military district to another.[208]

Guards were reminded, in the early summer of 1944, that groups of prisoners of war being led through parts of a city could not take up the sidewalks, but should instead be marched in formation along the side lane of the road. Only prisoner-of-war groups granted special exemptions, as well as prisoners who were permitted to go to work without a guard, were permitted to use sidewalks, if there was no space on roads.[209] Also at this time, previous orders concerning the mandatory fixing of bayonets on rifles by guards were expanded to include the guards of prisoners of war being transported; it was noted that French bayonets, which were longer than the German ones, could in fact be fitted onto German rifles.[210]

In August 1944, the OKW issued instructions for actions to be taken by German guards during an air-raid on a train containing prisoners of war. If the prisoners of war were being transported in a general train (i.e. one containing German civilians), the Guard and prisoners of war were to take the same evasive action as the rest of the train, ensuring all the while that the prisoner was never out of the guards' sight. In special trains, bearing the designations "Igel" or "666," in which many prisoners of war were transported (the order did not specify of which nationality), they were in most cases to remain locked in their compartments. The prisoners of war could be released by guards to take cover only if there was no possibility of escape in doing so. The German transport leader would generally take actions after considering the specifics of his particular situation. In general, good plans had to be made for the possibility of air attacks before each journey was undertaken, and both guards and transport officials had to be made aware of them.[211]

Requests for enemy medical personnel to be transferred to specific camps could be made by the camp commandants, but would ultimately be decided upon by the military district headquarters, in consultation with the military district senior medical staff.[212] Two months later, the OKW decided that, given the present transportation situation, enemy prisoner-of-war officers or pilots could no longer be allowed to travel in civilian trains, even if under guard.[213] And generally, only the Commander of Prisoner-of-war Affairs in the military district needed to be informed of prisoner-of-war transports, including the number of prisoners involved and the trains they were taking. Only in exceptional circumstances was OKW Berlin to be notified of such details.[214]

On February 14, 1945, in response to an inquiry concerning British and American prisoners of war who were too ill to march with others being evacuated from the camps at Sagan and Lamsdorf, Hitler personally decided, contrary to both the Geneva Convention and previous official German policy, that they were not to be left behind. They were to be brought back with the first available train returning after delivering supplies to the Front.[215]

The last OKW comment on prisoner-of-war transportation or transfer during the war years, a very small pamphlet concerning their possible evacuation, also came in mid-February 1945. It stated that only whole prisoner-of-war units could be marched out together, with all work detachments being kept together as well. Daily marches were to be between 20 and 25 kilometers, with allowances to be made for unforeseen difficulties such as bad weather or poor routes; housing possibilities were to be explored by advance parties. Because of the possibilities of air-raids, no group was to contain more than 200 men. Rest time was 5 minutes after the first hour, and 15 minutes for each subsequent two-hour period. Any alcoholic consumption was strictly prohibited.[216]

4
Crimes and Punishment of Prisoners of War

4.1 Basic issues

"Prisoners of war shall be subject to the laws, regulations and orders in force in the armed forces of the Detaining Power. Any act of insubordination shall render them liable to the measures prescribed by such laws, regulations, and orders, except as otherwise provided in this Chapter."[1] Thus began the section of the Geneva Convention which fundamentally defined reality for prisoners of war: they were captives under the legal authority of the Detaining Power. While the Geneva Convention cemented the authority of the Detaining Power, it also served notice, with the second part of the article, that the Detaining Power's control over the prisoners of war was not absolute, and would be subject to some restrictions. But before the Convention distinguished in detail between two forms of rules to which the prisoners of war were subject, disciplinary and judicial, it laid out some main points regarding the general application of justice toward prisoners of war.

A basic precept of the Geneva Convention was equality of treatment between prisoners of war, on the one hand, and soldiers of the same rank belonging to the Detaining Power, on the other, for punishment of similar offenses; the prisoners could not be subject to more severe punishment than that given to the home army's soldiers for the same crimes or infractions. But regardless of the rules in place for the Detaining Power's soldiers, however, certain practices were prohibited: corporal punishment; collective punishment for individual acts; confinement in a cell not lit by daylight; and "all forms of cruelty whatsoever."[2]

The procedure to be followed in cases of disciplinary or judicial infractions was also laid out in general, and sometimes vague, terms by the Convention. A statement of fact had to be drawn up, and any time served in detention was to be deducted from any eventual punishment; the time spent in custody awaiting a final decision was to be kept to "a strict minimum." Judicial proceedings were to be conducted "as quickly as circumstances allow" by the Detaining Power.[3] Upon the completion of a disciplinary or judicial punishment, the prisoner of war was not to be treated differently from other prisoners of war.[4] The Detaining Power did not have the authority to demote the rank of a prisoner of war, and the prisoners were to maintain whatever privileges their rank accorded; officers could not be placed in cells along with noncommissioned ranks.[5] If a prisoner of war was eligible for repatriation he could not be held back by the Detaining Power for a disciplinary punishment; if he was undergoing a judicial punishment, repatriation would have to wait until the prisoner served out his full sentence.[6] These general comments in the Convention served to set up the remaining discussion of disciplinary rules, which were local regulations for the maintenance of order and discipline, and judicial rules and punishments, which dealt with contravention of German law leading to courts-martial, possible prison sentences, and, in the case of capital crimes, the death penalty.

4.2 Matters of discipline

Disciplinary rules were those applied by the Detaining Power to maintain (as the name implied) discipline and order. Given the wide possible range of measures that could be deemed necessary to maintain discipline in a future war, it was not surprising that the Geneva Convention provided only six articles, containing general guidelines and prohibitions, dealing with the issue of disciplinary punishments.

The most severe disciplinary punishment which could be inflicted on a prisoner of war was 30 days' imprisonment; in cases when the prisoner had to answer for more than one offense requiring 10 days' imprisonment or more, he had to be given a rest-break of 3 days before serving the subsequent punishment. Any food restrictions (such as a bread and water diet) in place for soldiers of the Detaining Power could also be implemented against the prisoners of war, provided that they did not contravene the last paragraph of article 11 ("All collective disciplinary measures affecting food are prohibited"), and only if the prisoner's health permitted such measures.[7] In no cases could a prisoner of war be transferred to penitentiary establishments (prisons, penitentiaries, or other convict establishments) in order to serve disciplinary sentence there; the establishments in which disciplinary sentences were served (arrest cells in camps) had to be hygienic, and facilities for the prisoner to keep himself in a state of personal cleanliness had to be provided. Further, the prisoner had to have the opportunity of taking exercise, or remaining outdoors, for at least two hours each day.[8] Though prisoners of war undergoing disciplinary punishments could not be restricted in terms of their ability to receive or send letters, they could be prevented from receiving parcels and remittances of money until after the sentence was served; if the undelivered parcels contained perishable foodstuffs, these would be given to the camp infirmary or kitchen.[9]

And if they should wander

Given that escape was a likely ambition for many prisoners of war, the Geneva Convention offered provisions for dealing with this disciplinary issue.[10] The only exception to article 48's requirement that prisoners be treated as all other prisoners of war upon completion of their punishment was for escapists: they could be subject to a regime of heightened surveillance by the Detaining Power after the punishment was served, but could not thereby be deprived of basic rights given to all prisoners of war. Recaptured escapees could only be subject to disciplinary punishment for their escape (which, along with assisting an escape, was defined as a disciplinary, rather than a judicial, offense). Further, attempted escape could not be considered as an aggravating factor for any crimes against persons or property committed by a prisoner of war during the course of his escape. Belligerents were to exercise "the greatest leniency" in deciding whether an act was to be considered a disciplinary or judicial infraction, especially in dealing with cases of escape; in any event, a prisoner of war could not be punished more than once for any given offense.

Prisoners undergoing disciplinary punishment had the right to present themselves, upon their own request, for daily medical inspection; they had to be given any medical treatment as was deemed necessary by the camp medical officers and, if required, be evacuated to the camp infirmary or to a hospital.[11] Lastly, and "[w]ithout prejudice to the competency of the courts and the superior military authorities," disciplinary sentences could only be given by an officer vested with disciplinary powers in his capacity as commander of the camp or detachment, or by a responsible officer acting as his substitute.[12]

In accordance with article 50, the OKW stated at the start of the war that a prisoner of war who successfully escaped and rejoined his own armed forces could not, if later retaken into captivity, face punishment for his escape; an unsuccessful escape attempt, or assisting an escape attempt, could only be treated as a disciplinary offense.[13] In March 1942, Waltzog's handbook on international law commented further on the issue.

Though Waltzog accepted article 50's prohibition against punishing escaped prisoners of war who, after rejoining their armies, were recaptured, he held that they were only spared punishment for the escape itself. Actions committed in the preparation of the escape (such as damage to goods), conspiracy to escape, and any other crimes (such as assault or murder) committed in the process of the escape were still offenses for which the recaptured prisoner could, and should, be held legally liable. And from the moment a prisoner of war successfully escaped his captors, Waltzog wrote, the legal state of captivity ended. Thus, if he conducted acts of violence, sabotage, or espionage as an individual (i.e. before having rejoined his army), he could, if recaptured, be treated as a partisan, saboteur, or spy.[14] Article 51 was deemed to deal only with actions surrounding the fact of the prisoner of war's escape at the beginning, then, and not all subsequent actions the prisoner could commit.[15] "Escape" was initially defined by the OKW, in October 1942, as the unauthorized removal by a prisoner of war of himself from either his workplace or housing;[16] in May 1943, it was redefined as the removal of a prisoner of war with the intent of remaining outside the custody of the Wehrmacht.[17]

Given the serious threat to security caused by escapes and the drain on German manpower involved in tracking down escapees, it was unsurprising that the OKW sought to tighten the rules of punishment surrounding escape as much as possible. In late August 1943, the OKW, seeking additional ways to punish prisoners of war caught while attempting escape, heightened the penalties for damage to property, in accordance with Waltzog's 1942 analysis. The OKW began the order for this reassessment by examining its interpretation of articles 50 and 52 of the Geneva Convention. The first of these, as the OKW faithfully reproduced, stated that prisoners of war could only be subject to disciplinary punishments for escape attempts. The second article, also accurately restated, urged the belligerents to exercise the greatest leniency in deciding whether or not a prisoner of war should be punished by disciplinary or judicial measures, especially in cases surrounding escapes. According to previous OKW orders, prisoners of war had earlier been subject only to disciplinary punishments when there was no great damage as a result of their escape, or if no Germans were threatened or harmed during the escape. Due to the current war situation, in which shortages in the war economy resulted in all Germans exercising great thrift, the actions of prisoners of war consequent to their escape could no longer be ignored, especially if their escape was made possible by the theft of tools and raw materials, or destruction of furnishings, buildings, or any other object which would require considerable manpower to replace or repair. The prisoners of war, in this instance, were to be treated as German soldiers would be who were caught doing the same things, as per article 46 of the Geneva Convention. In the future, then, any attempted or actual escape that was conducted by harming a man or damaging or destroying war-related materials was to result in judicial proceedings.

War-related materials were defined as: (a) building- or barrack-parts (such "destruction" would be breakage through walls and floors); (b) furnishings (bed boards for tunnel construction, lighting systems); (c) uniforms which did not *personally belong* to the prisoners of war (emphasis in original) and which were altered; (d) tools, raw materials, unwarranted consumption of electric current during the tunnel construction. All of these sorts of infractions, the OKW instructed, could be punished as judicial rather than disciplinary offenses.[18] Therefore, the "greatest leniency" in deciding whether to punish an offense as disciplinary rather than judicial required by article 52, especially with regard to events surrounding escapes, had effectively been declared superseded by the exigencies of war, and Waltzog's prescriptions on the issue of escape were formally adopted by the OKW.

The OKW concurred with the Geneva Convention, naturally enough, that prisoners of war undergoing punishment for an escape attempt could be subject to closer guarding than normal, either by being placed in a specially guarded company or camp.[19] But Oflag IV C Colditz was quickly being turned into a dumping ground for frequently offending officer prisoners of war; as of June 1941, escaped and recaptured officer prisoners were to be sent to Colditz after serving their disciplinary sentences in their original Oflags.[20] The general policy using Oflag IV C Colditz as a camp for officer prisoners of war with disciplinary problems was, in October 1941, still leading to overcrowding there. Upon investigation by the OKW, it was discovered that some officer prisoners of war were sent there as a result of problems with a single German officer, or violation of disciplinary rules. Henceforth, and in accordance with the previous policy, only officer prisoners of war with serious disciplinary problems, such as repeat escape attempts and notorious anti-German comments, were to be posted to Colditz.[21]

By January 1945, it had become habit among the German guards to refer to "special companies," in which previously punished noncommissioned prisoners of war had been placed for greater security, as "criminal squads." As this gave the impression that the prisoners of war were being punished twice for the same offense, and had led to complaints from Protecting Power delegates (regarding article 53 of the Geneva Convention), all guards were to refrain from using this term: the special companies were merely considered work detachments with greater levels of security in place.[22]

Who was boss

German military policy in place at the beginning of the war in this area mirrored the prescriptions of the Geneva Convention, with the OKW instructing the commandants to look to individual articles of the Convention to find out certain rules. At first, the German military manuals designated the camp commandant, or work-detachment leader (provided he was an officer), as the authority responsible for dealing with disciplinary issues over the prisoners of war under his care.[23] But in February 1942, the OKW noted that disciplinary infractions in work detachments had been difficult to deal with at times, because of the distance between the appropriate disciplinary authority and the prisoners of war. In several instances, too much time passed for the punishment to have been of any effective use. In situations where several work detachments existed under the authority of a single officer, then, the squad leaders (i.e. noncommissioned officers) could henceforth have this authority delegated to them.[24]

Ostensibly an attempt to provide a pragmatic solution to the problem, this contravention of the Convention was quickly contested by the prisoners of war themselves, and the Protecting Power, with the result that only one month later, the OKW reversed itself: in March 1942, the OKW decreed that German noncommissioned officers no longer had the authority to issue disciplinary punishments against prisoners of war, ordering that such punishment was again permitted only by the camp commandant or a commissioned officer so delegated by him.[25] In June 1942, the OKW attempted to cement the practice of having only officers exercise command and disciplinary authority over the work detachments: in normal circumstances, the OKW instructed, a lieutenant would command a work detachment, a major would command a battalion or very large work detachment, and a lieutenant-colonel would be the camp commandant.[26] Assistant-guards (*Hilfswachmannschaft*) carried the authority of guards in dealings with prisoners of war. However, in situations in which a prisoner of war was charged with failure to obey an assistant-guard, the guiding principle as to whether or not the prisoner would be punished had to be whether or not he was aware the assistant-guard was in fact an assistant-guard at the time the offense was committed. This was why assistant-guards were generally to wear armbands indicating their status.[27]

Unruly doctors

The issue of authority over prisoner-of-war medical ("protected") personnel was ultimately clarified in September 1944. Prisoner medical staff who committed disciplinary infractions in prisoner-of-war hospitals and infirmaries fell under the authority of the senior German medical officer, and had to be dealt with by him. Sick prisoners who committed disciplinary infractions while in a hospital or infirmary, however, were only temporarily under the authority of the doctors, and only for medical purposes; for disciplinary problems, the prisoner remained under the authority of his original camp's commandant, who would formally dispense any punishment for infractions of discipline committed in the hospitals (though, as before, he could delegate his authority to another officer closer to the scene).[28]

Information management

From the beginning of the war, the camp commandants had been ultimately responsible for announcing regulations and orders to all the prisoners of war within the camp; in December 1944, the OKW made some provision for them to draw upon the assistance of the Man of Confidence (or senior officer) in the task of promulgating orders. In situations where the Man of Confidence or senior officers did not pass along orders, the OKW decided that they could be subject to disciplinary or, in extreme situations, judicial punishments.[29]

Information concerning the reason and extent of a disciplinary or judicial punishment against a prisoner of war could only be given without their approval to senior departments, courts, police authorities, and the Protecting Power. Such information would only be given to anyone else, such as the Man of Confidence, relatives, or any other private person, with the approval of the condemned prisoner of war. Any other distribution of the information without the prisoner's permission was strictly prohibited.[30]

Every case in which a British, American, French, or Belgian civilian or military prisoner of war was shot or seriously injured was to be investigated by either a court-martial or an authorized officer. The comrades of the prisoner had to be interviewed in the course of the investigation. The results of the investigation were to be forwarded directly to OKW headquarters, Berlin, along with a recommendation as to whether or not further judicial or disciplinary action was warranted.[31]

Equality of punishment

In accordance with the Geneva Convention, German policy at the start of the war stated that prisoners of war were liable to disciplinary and judicial punishments in the same manner as a German soldier of equal rank, and greatest leniency, as per article 52, was to be used in deciding whether to treat an infraction as disciplinary or judicial.[32] The principle of equality of treatment was reaffirmed in February 1943, at which point the OKW also reminded commandants that a prisoner of war could not be charged with a judicial offense if he had already been given a disciplinary punishment for the same offense; the commandants were referred back to articles 46 and 52 of the Geneva Convention.[33]

Another example of equality of treatment concerned a complaint from the Protecting Power for the British prisoners of war concerning the OKW practice of placing sick prisoners of war accused of committing a crime or disciplinary infraction into "arrest cells" within the prisoner-of-war hospitals. The OKW instructed camp commandants, in late September 1942, to reply to any such complaints by reminding the Protecting Power delegates that the British prisoners of war were merely being subjected to the same disciplinary procedures which existed for German prisoners of war in similar circumstances.[34] One month later, the OKW further stated that, in accordance with the rules in place for German soldiers, if circumstances prevented the immediate execution of a disciplinary punishment, the prisoner was to be kept under guard, severe if necessary, until he could be removed to a suitable location.[35]

The principle delineated in the Geneva Convention that only one punishment could be imposed for a single offense (and if an incident had already be punished as a disciplinary offense, a judicial punishment for the same event was prohibited), was confirmed by the OKW at the start of the war.[36] It was for this reason that, in January 1943, commandants were instructed not to apply disciplinary punishments too hastily when dealing with prisoners of war who formed romantic relationships with German women. Judicial proceedings were deemed more appropriate to the severity of the problem, but often could not be instituted because disciplinary punishments had already been meted out by camp commandants seeking an "easy solution" to the problem. The commandants, when faced with a decision whether or not to proceed with disciplinary or judicial punishments, had to take a tougher stand on the issue, so that such problems were more sharply avoided in the future.[37] Likewise, in May 1943, the commandants were reminded that prisoners operating radios could face judicial punishments for violating federal broadcasting laws, rather than mere disciplinary punishments.[38]

Both collective punishment for an individual's actions and reductions in rank were prohibited by the Geneva Convention and German military policy, at the start of the war.[39] When a camp commandant was reported to have interrupted delivery of prisoner-of-war post as a form of mass punishment, the OKW took the opportunity, in June 1941, to forbid such future punishments, reminding commandants that article 36 of the Geneva Convention prohibited such collective measures.[40]

Clearing the air

For the execution of disciplinary punishments, the prewar directives of the OKW instructed the commandants to refer directly to the requirements set out in article 54 of the Convention.[41] In October 1942, the OKW further specified that when a prisoner of war entered into prison or a disciplinary cell, he was only allowed to carry with him the items needed for his immediate personal care; all other possessions were to be placed in storage, with a receipt given, until the prisoner was released, at which time his things would be returned.[42]

In August 1944, the OKW attempted to dispel some apparent confusion which had arisen as a result of differences between the German varieties of penal arrest and the rules of the Geneva Convention: disciplinary penalties could not be enforced against prisoners of war already in prison because they were already being deprived of their freedom, as per article 56 of the Geneva Convention; "close arrest" was forbidden by article 46 of the Geneva Convention; multiple disciplinary sentences of more than 10 days had to be interrupted by a period of 3 days between each; and though a prisoner of war could be required to work, he could not do any labor directly related to the war effort, and no dangerous work or work to which the prisoner was not suited could be demanded of him. Thus, where the Geneva Convention specifically prohibited something, it carried greater legal authority than standard German disciplinary/judicial practice.[43]

The OKW ordered at the start of the war that commandants follow article 56 of the Geneva Convention, with regard to rules for the serving of disciplinary punishments. Reading, writing, and mail privileges were to follow the conditions outlined in article 57; any incoming mail or packages for any prisoner of war had to be examined for security purposes, but only in the presence of the recipient or his designate.[44] In June 1941, the OKW further instructed that, in accordance with article 57 of the Geneva Convention, packages and valuables could only be withheld from a prisoner of war who was serving a disciplinary punishment for the duration of the punishment, and not afterwards.[45]

The German military agreed with the Convention at the start of the war that disciplinary punishments could not be served in a prison, and that in cases of repatriation, a prisoner of war could not be held back for a disciplinary infraction.[46] But by January 1944, the OKW declared an exception to the first part of this policy: in serious cases (such as for experienced escape specialists) prisoners of war could be sent to Wehrmacht prisons to serve out disciplinary punishment.[47]

The remaining general guidelines of the Geneva Convention dealing with disciplinary punishments, which were confirmed by the OKW in its 1939 manuals, received no alteration during the course of the war years – just the occasional reminder that they were still in force. Specifically: the maximum length of time for a disciplinary punishment was outlined in article 54 of the Convention (that is, 30 days);[48] two hours minimum per day of outside exercise was guaranteed by article 56; and medical needs for prisoners of war undergoing disciplinary punishment were to be conducted as indicated in article 58.[49]

Common local rules

For the prisoner of war arriving in a camp, the first thing which occurred after delousing and other medical issues had been dealt with, was his acquaintance with the camp's orders and regulations. As noted above, it was the commandant's formal responsibility to ensure that this happened, though the task was usually delegated to the security officer, drawing on the assistance of the Man of Confidence. The specific rules, after taking into account the requirements of the Geneva Convention and the OKW's general instructions, could vary with each camp, depending on the necessity of local circumstances. But in addition to the main directives of 1939 and the alterations noted above, the OKW occasionally added its own specific rules to be added to the every camp's standing orders. Usually in the form of prohibitions, the list over the course of the war years was long and varied, and contravention of these regulations constituted disciplinary infractions for which all British and, later, American prisoners of war were held liable, regardless of their location.

Twigging about disrespect and sarcasm, the OKW in mid-December 1939 forbade prisoners of war from using the German greeting "Heil Hitler" in the camps.[50] A few days later, a further addition of prisoner-of-war camp regulations was ordered, to the effect that normal military courtesies (saluting) were to be required between officer prisoners of war and men, on the one hand, and German officers and military staff, on the other.[51] In September 1942, the prohibition on unauthorized military courtesies was extended: prisoners were not allowed to salute or greet each other in manners not used in their own military forces.[52] According to article 18 of the Geneva Convention, prisoners of war were required to salute all officers of the Detaining Power. Included in this group, according to the OKW, were members of officer rank of the Waffen-SS, the police, and the Gendarmerie.[53] The standard German military orders concerning daily flag parade was determined to be also applicable to prisoner-of-war Stalags and Oflags.[54]

At the start of September 1941, all British officer prisoners of war were refused permission to go for walks outside the camp compound; this was because, despite repeated warnings, there were many escape attempts.[55] In a display of understatement and without any elaboration of the matter, the OKW, in late June 1942, formally prohibited prisoner-of-war visits to brothels.[56]

As a result of complaints from agricultural businesses, prisoners of war were no longer permitted to smoke in areas deemed to be "dangerous," especially farms. To enforce this, guards were to post no-smoking signs in the language of the prisoners of war, as well as watch for violations. Prisoners who smoked despite having been warned not to would be subject to disciplinary punishment.[57] In a further attempt to prevent forest fires, as well as poaching, prisoners of war were also prohibited from crossing forests unsupervised.[58] Prisoners were also prohibited from picking up or examining leaflets dropped by enemy planes either in the camps or their workplaces.[59] They were further expected to turn over to the German guards any other forbidden objects, such as arms or ammunition, which were dropped to them during the course of an enemy airraid. The prisoners of war were to be informed that failure to comply with this order would lead to penalties against them.[60]

Orders prohibiting prisoners of war from poaching had gone largely ignored, especially by French prisoners of war. Therefore, in order to prevent poaching, all prisoners of war were henceforth prohibited from leaving public areas during their leisure time. At the same time, they were to be warned in writing that future poaching violations would be punished severely.[61]

In many instances, prisoners of war were constructing uniforms to look like German uniforms, for the purpose of escape, from parts of two or more other uniforms. As a result, the OKW authorized the camps to conduct searches of prisoners' personal effects (including officers), and to seize and confiscate any pieces of clothing which looked to be used for this purpose.[62] It had also been noticed, by April 1943, that prisoners of war were often either altering their prisoner-of-war "identification markings" or switching them with those of other prisoners, to facilitate escape attempts. In addition to being careful of this, the camps were instructed by the OKW to issue disciplinary punishments to prisoners of war caught doing this.[63]

The Swiss Legation, in October 1943, sent out a newsletter in English, followed with a German translation, to British Men of Confidence, stating that British prisoners of war could offer a written guarantee that they would not escape in return for greater privileges (parole for walks). These guarantees could be signed for a group by the senior ranking officers or noncommissioned officers, and were applicable to officers, warrant officers, and noncommissioned officers. These guarantees were to apply for specific time frames and purposes. The OKW approved of this arrangement.[64] The group-signing practice was later prohibited by the British government. However, individual British officers could still sign paroles in order to be allowed to go on supervised walks in the countryside. Otherwise, the previous OKW rules regarding close guarding of British prisoners of war applied to those who were permitted to go on supervised walks or use sports fields outside the Stalags.[65]

As the war progressed, the OKW noted, in January 1944, the temptations for profiteering through black-market activities between prisoners of war, using supplies from their parcels, and civilians, were proving stronger. For both political and security reasons all such dealings had to be stopped, and the guilty parties disciplined.[66]

A perimeter of two meters within the barbed-wire enclosures was to be cleared in all camps, in June 1944. The OKW ordered that all prisoners of war be told, in their own language, that any prisoner who touched or crossed the wire would be shot. Each new arrival to the camp was to be likewise informed.[67]

At the start of February 1943, the OKW warned camp commandants that some of the railway posters being put up by British prisoners of war as decorations were in fact subversive, and had to pass through the censors before being put up. Inappropriate posters were to be sent to OKW headquarters.[68] For security reasons, they were also prohibited from making glider models.[69] In December 1944, prisoners were forbidden to sing while outside of their living areas. Within their barracks, singing was only permitted if it did not disturb the surrounding neighborhood. Guards and interpreters were to pay close attention to the singing.[70]

At the same time, the OKW banned lotteries that had a financial pay-off. These were deemed to be a security threat, as they could lead to relations between foreign or German civilians and the military prisoners of war.[71]

Prisoners of war serving prison sentences were entitled to continue receiving their mail. However, due to the absence of interpreters at the military prisons, mail being sent to prisoners of war in jail had to first be examined by the postal censor in the main prisoner-of-war camp. From there, bearing a mark showing it had been censored, it was to be forwarded to the prisoner in prison. Likewise for parcels, though any food was to be removed and turned over to the camp kitchen for use by other prisoners of war. Portions of collective parcels being sent to imprisoned prisoners of war were also to bear a mark certifying that they had been inspected at the main camp.[72]

In June 1942, the commandants and work-detachment leaders were told, by the OKW, that announcing the sentencing of prisoners of war who had been found guilty of judiciary offenses, either on the announcement board or verbally during roll-call, could have a desirable impact on the other prisoners of war, as it might deter them from committing similar acts.[73]

And in June 1944, it was decided that prisoners of war who were about to begin marches in the course of fulfilling a disciplinary punishment had to have clothing which would not require repairs in the near future.[74]

4.3 Justice matters

Given that prisoners of war were subject to the judicial laws of the Detaining Power, the Geneva Convention offered only few, general guidelines concerning the application of judicial proceedings, most of which were designed to ensure that the prisoner went through the process fully aware of his rights, and that his home army remained fully informed of the results. To this end, the Protecting Power delegates played a key role;[75] they informed the home army of the nature of charges against the prisoner, ensured that he had proper legal representation, and kept the home army abreast of any final judgments against the prisoners, especially the death penalty.[76] The Convention guaranteed the prisoner the right to defend himself with legal counsel, the right of appeal, the right to be judged by the same tribunal which would conduct the trial for a soldier of the Detaining Power, and the right to address any complaints to his Protecting Power.[77]

The German military manuals in place at the start of the war confirmed these rights, stating as well that any judicial offense committed by a prisoner of war (against the Militärstrafgesetzbuch, Reichstrafgesetzbuch, or any future judicial laws) had to be tried by the appropriate German military legal authority. Prisoners of war had the right to address any complaints to the commandant or their Protecting Power delegate, by communication with the Man of Confidence.[78]

Dr. Waltzog, in his 1942 analysis of the Geneva Convention, made an effort to establish the right, in most circumstances, of the Detaining Power to hold prisoners of war legally responsible for actions they committed before entering into captivity. As he noted, no articles of international conventions prohibited this, with two exceptions: article 50 of the Convention prohibited the punishment for escape of an escaped prisoner who, after rejoining his own army, was recaptured; and article 31 of the Hague Convention stated that a spy who succeeded in returning to his own army, but was later captured, could not be punished for his previous espionage. With the exception of the two points, then, prisoners of war were to be held liable for any crimes they committed before becoming prisoners.[79] As mentioned earlier on the issue of escape, Waltzog also defined the steps involved in an escape as judicial offenses (destruction of property, theft, etc.), with the net effect of making every action necessary for an escape to be punishable by court-martial, rather than disciplinary punishment.[80] Aside from this issue, Waltzog adhered to the principle of equality of treatment: prisoners of war would be subject to the military laws and consequences in place for German soldiers.

The only policy directives issued by the OKW over the course of the war years concerning judicial issues dealt with few minor clarifications, or were announcements of what types of offenses would henceforth be dealt with as judicial, rather than disciplinary, offenses.

Trials and tribulations

In June 1941, the OKW provided guidelines concerning who could represent prisoners of war during judicial proceedings. The judicial and disciplinary jurisdiction of Germany over captured prisoners of war was first explained in terms of German laws and the Geneva Convention, and after discussing several purely administrative minor issues, the pamphlet stated that prisoners of war were to be represented by a fluent German speaker who was neither a Jew nor a Communist, and that the prisoner did not have the right to know the name of the judge presiding over his case. Not only the verdict, but also the main reasons for the verdict had to be translated for the prisoner, and he had to sign a written acknowledgment of understanding at the end of proceedings. Also, "colored" prisoners of war were to be considered for more lenient sentences than "white" prisoners of war, due to their inherent racial weakness and inferiority.[81]

In September 1943, the OKW clarified its interpretation of article 47 of the Geneva Convention. The third paragraph stated that time spent in "preventive imprisonment" (in the English version of the Convention, "under arrest [awaiting punishment or trial]") should be deducted from the length of the sentence, provided this was permitted for the soldiers of the captor state. However, the first paragraph spoke of "preventive arrest" (in the English version of the Convention, "detained in custody"); therefore a distinction was made between the two forms of restriction of freedom. The time served in "preventive arrest" was not, according to the Convention, to be credited against the final sentence. However, as German law allowed for crediting time already spent in "preventive imprisonment" against the final sentence, this rule applied as well to the prisoners of war.[82]

Minor points on the nature of arrest were also discussed in an order from the OKW in January 1945. In reiterating regulations concerning close arrest of prisoners of war (including officers) during investigations, the OKW stated that the conveyance of food from any parcel source (including the ICRC) was strictly and unequivocally prohibited. If prisoners of war were well behaved, they could be permitted to purchase minor items of comfort; in each case, it was up to the camp commandant to decide. In border areas, smoking was only permitted with the possession of a smoking-card, and if there were no fire hazards nearby. If the prisoner was being held pending an investigation, these potential privileges could only be granted with the permission of the investigating officer.[83]

With regard to the cost of prisoner-of-war legal representation during judicial proceedings, the OKW clarified its interpretation of article 62 of the Geneva Convention in July 1941. The cost of defending the prisoner would fall on the Protecting Power; however, if the prisoner chose his own counsel, then he would pay for the lawyer himself.[84] The OKW also reaffirmed the right of prisoners of war who were facing criminal procedures to contact their defense counsel in writing at any time, without the letters being credited to the prisoner of war's monthly mail allotments. The prisoner and his counsel were also permitted to meet in person at least once, at least one day before the proceedings were to begin, to discuss their case.[85]

In January 1944, the OKW, referring without elaboration to a "recent special case," reminded camp commandants that prisoners of war were not to be subject to more judicial measures than were allowed for by the Geneva Convention. Prisoners of war were exclusively under the judicial authority of the Detaining Power, especially with regard to interrogations and investigative authority, and concerning investigations into shootings. Senior prisoners of war and Men of Confidence were prohibited from conducting so-called "additional judicial" activity, under threat of being charged with fraudulent use of authority and insubordination.[86]

Prisoner-of-war officers who were under investigation or temporary arrest pending charges had to be given two-thirds of their salaries on "free" days, the OKW decided in November 1944. Prisoner officers who were serving sentences in prison did not get any pay until they were released again.[87] The first part of this order, concerning the payment of only two-thirds or the prisoner-of-war's salary, was rescinded on January 1, 1945, and orders were instead given that they receive their full pay.[88]

Those prisoners of war serving sentences in military prisons were permitted to receive letters from their relatives, and parcels including food and clothing. The maximum monthly contingent was to be decided by the commandant of the military prison. Further issues concerning prisoner-of-war correspondence could be settled directly between the camp and the prison authorities.[89] The regulations which allowed for prisoners of war serving sentences of longer than 6 weeks in a military prison to be transferred for part of their sentence to a Stalag applied only to those prisoners who were required to perform labor as part of their sentence. This did not apply to prisoners of war who were not obliged to work: prisoner-of-war officers and work-refusing noncommissioned officers. They were simply to be returned to their original camp upon completion of their sentence in the military prison.[90] Before any prisoner-of-war serving a lengthy prison sentence was sent to a military prison, all his valuables and money were to be taken away from him, and credited to his Personnel Card.[91]

As early as January 1942, the OKW decided that all "untrustworthy" or lazy prisoners of war were to be formed into "special companies" within each camp. Membership in such a company could influence the sentence a prisoner would receive for committing a judicial infraction: time spent in these companies had to be reported to the judicial authorities, who would later consider a prisoner of war's sentence. Though such prisoners of war could be subject to greater restraints on their freedom than other prisoners of war, such as being locked up after dusk or attending more roll-calls than the others, they could not have Red Cross parcels held back, nor could their post be restricted. Such detainment should not be considered a form of punishment; the company was to be described only as a "special" one.[92] On August 1, 1944, reacting to reports that treatment of prisoners of war suspected of having committed offenses varied greatly from area to area, the OKW ordered that this order be followed more literally in the future.[93]

Tightening definitions

In addition to these few general points of clarification concerning the application of justice to prisoners of war, the only other directives from the OKW on the issue consisted of new prohibitions, or the redesignation of some actions as "judicial" offenses rather than disciplinary offenses.

In an attempt to deter escape attempts, the OKW ordered, in January 1944, that prisoners of war in a camp in which an escape occurred be informed of judiciary penalties imposed against the recaptured prisoners of war for offenses committed during their escape, as well as instances in which German guards had shot escaping prisoners.[94] As prisoners had been caught using both German uniforms and civilian clothing in escape attempts, the camps were to search prisoners of war returning to camps from the outside for any such clothing. The prisoners were also to be warned that the possession of such could be considered to be the judicial offense of "espionage," and thus could be punished by death.[95]

Prisoners of war who had been recaptured after an escape had often been giving false names and identification numbers at their new Stalags. Occasionally, these were of other prisoners of war of the same nationality in their old camp. Henceforth, such prisoners of war were to face judicial, rather than disciplinary, charges. The security officers of camps into which recaptured prisoners of war were brought had to be very alert to the possibility of misinformation.[96] Prisoners were also to be reminded that they could be subject to the death penalty for "looting" if they left the confines of their housing or shelters during an air-raid.[97]

The OKW noted, in October 1943, that according to articles 27 and 45 of the Geneva Conventions, all prisoners of war except officers and unwilling noncommissioned officers were required to do work. Refusing to do work was disobeying a lawful military order, and could be punished accordingly, by judicial court-martial. These facts were to be translated in the prisoners' languages, and posted.[98] On November 7, 1944, the OKW issued instructions to deal with prisoners of war who faked illness to get out of working. It was, they wrote, understandable that prisoners would avoid work as much as possible, but faking illness was having a serious negative impact on overall labor efficiency. Therefore, no sick-leave was to be granted until the prisoner's illness had been certified by a doctor. When possible, during recuperation, prisoners of war were to be given light tasks (though not on Sundays or holidays). If a prisoner of war was suspected by a doctor of faking illness, he was to be warned that he was breaking German military law, and told that any future faking would result in military charges being laid against him.[99]

Friends and poachers

Fraternization between prisoners of war and German women was, from the number of directives issued by the OKW on the particular subject, significant enough a concern as to warrant judicial remedies. Toward the middle of October 1940, a one-page notice was sent from the OKW to be posted within sight of prisoners of war. It warned prisoners of war that any unauthorized contact between prisoners of war and German women was strictly prohibited, and that violations would be considered as breaches of German law carrying a sentence of up to 10 years in prison, or, in especially severe circumstances, life-imprisonment or death. Possible claims by prisoners of war that they were unaware of this order would be ignored.[100] Further, it was the duty of each guard, immediately upon becoming aware of any "relations" between a prisoner of war and a German woman, to intervene immediately and report the matter to his superiors. Under no circumstances were such prisoners of war to be permitted to continue coming into contact with German civilians, especially with German women; any guard who failed to prohibit this would face serious disciplinary consequences.[101]

Camp commandants were reminded that members of the enemy's medical staff were not, according to article 9 of the Geneva Convention of 1929, to be treated as regular prisoners of war. Therefore, the prisoner-of-war punishments for entering into relations with German women did not apply. However, the enemy medical personnel were prohibited nonetheless by an order from mid-September 1940, and they were to be held accountable to the terms of this order, and not the other, if they became involved with German women.[102] In accordance with article 12, para. 3 of the Geneva Convention of 1929,[103] the OKW ordered, on November 11, 1941, that medical personnel who attempted to escape would have their privileges either partly or entirely taken away.[104]

Early in June 1941, a military pamphlet concerning judicial punishments against prisoners of war was sent out by the OKW, dealing exclusively with the issue of relations between German women and prisoners of war. It reiterated previous prohibitions, elaborating that they were needed to protect the purity of German blood. Not only could the women who were seduced be expected to bear harsh punishments, but the prisoners of war could expect a court-martial, with a minimum sentence of 3 years' imprisonment; the maximum sentence would be death or life imprisonment. The harshness of these sentences was explained in terms of German civil and military laws.[105] Toward the end of January 1942, the OKW took steps to ensure that prisoners of war who were under investigation for criminal activities would not be repatriated before the investigation could be completed. Specifically, prisoners of war under suspicion of either having committed a crime or of having an affair with a German woman, whether before or after their entrance into captivity, would not be released from captivity, and would not join a work detachment.[106] For prisoners of war in work detachments who were accused of breaking the rules regarding relations with German women, the OKW ordered, in August 1942, that: should the working area be completely separated from the German population, the prisoner was to remain there until further disciplinary procedures progressed; in all other cases the prisoner was to be separated from the other prisoners in the work detachment, and returned as soon as possible to the main camp; in no circumstances was a prisoner of war to remain in a work detachment which mixed with German workers.[107] To further dissuade prisoners from breaking the fraternization rules, the OKW ordered, in November 1944, that all prisoners of war be informed of the case of a Serbian prisoner, named Pantalija Kabanica, who was charged with having relations with a German woman, and sentenced to death and executed.[108]

Another frequent occurrence which led the OKW to reevaluate its status was poaching. As early as March 1942, camp authorities were told by the OKW that illegal poaching by prisoners of war was becoming a problem, and that poachers must be punished strictly.[109] In September 1943, camp commandants were reminded by the OKW that prisoners of war caught poaching were not to be subject to disciplinary punishments. Instead, in each case that occurred, an action report was to be sent up the chain of command, so that judicial proceedings could be launched against the prisoners instead.[110] Lastly, German fire marshals complained to the OKW that prisoners of war were smoking in forests, hence increasing the risks of forest fires. The OKW, in turn, reiterated that smoking by prisoners of war in forests was strictly prohibited, and would be punished with the full force of German law.[111]

4.4 Related security issues

Over the course of the war, the OKW issued numerous instructions to its staff concerning security issues and prisoners of war. Though not policy decisions which involved an interpretation of the Geneva Convention or alterations to the 1939 German manuals, they nonetheless had an impact on the nature of captivity experienced by all British or American prisoners of war, and thus ought to be examined in order to provide a fuller picture of overall German policy toward these prisoners. The orders were directed to the commandants of the individual camps; to ensure that the security of the state was maintained, it was unsurprising that as the war years progressed and new lessons were learned, the OKW increasingly gave specific directions to the guards of prisoners of war, including on the permissible use of firearms against the prisoners. In addition, prisoner-of-war escapes and sabotage were also deemed significant enough security concerns by the OKW to warrant at least some specific instructions to the level of the camps.

How to guard

At the end of September 1939, in an order signed by Keitel, the OKW approved the possibility of deputizing German civilians to serve as assistant-guards for the guarding of prisoners of war. The only point made by the OKW at this point was that assistant-guards would be subject to the same rules and regulations concerning use of firearms as regular soldiers.[112] Should a prisoner of war suffer mistreatment at the hand of an assistant-guard, the guard could be punished judicially under German military law. If the issue was minor in nature, the assistant-guard's superior officer could dispense disciplinary punishment instead, and remove the assistant-guard from further dealings with prisoners of war.[113] In late November 1939, the OKW reminded the military districts that suitable measures during possible mutiny, insubordination, and refusals to work by prisoners of war included maintaining close contact between the guard detail and the local Gendarmerie, so that the latter could be brought in to help intervene should the situation require it.[114]

At the end of July 1942, the OKW issued additional special measures for guarding prisoners of war. These were deemed necessary because of the increased tensions among prisoners of war of all nationalities, but especially the French, Belgians, and British, following increased enemy parachute activity in the west. In the main camps, guards were told to direct their efforts against increased escape attempts, mutiny, and attempts at liberation from outside the camp. They were exhorted to act promptly with strength, energetically wrapping up tense situations, quietly and without nervousness, in order to best guarantee peace and order. Though each military district could have slightly different needs, in general a highly mobile reserve battalion, under the direct control of the district commander for prisoners of war, was to be within easy rail transport from the prisoners of war. All German staff were to have their training brought up to date in order to handle such situations. When necessary, reserve army units were to be made available to help out the local guards of prisoners of war. Arrangements were also to be made with the local police departments, and air-defense forces, to provide backup if necessary. The same went for the Reichskriegerbund and with individual components of the party (SA, SS, NSKK).[115]

On September 22, 1942, the OKW ordered harsher but simpler guarding methods. In the camps, the prisoners of war had to be kept together when on the sportsground or during walks. By written and vocal commands, prisoners of war were to be warned that whoever touched or crossed the perimeter wire during the day would be shot from the guard towers if they did not stop after three warning shouts had been given by the guards; at night, they would be shot without warning if caught on the wires. Where possible, prisoners of war would remain in their barracks at night; patrolling units were to shoot without warning if prisoners of war were found wandering outside of designated areas at night. Spotlights on the towers were henceforth to be operated at irregular intervals. The principal methods that the camp security officer could use to prevent escape attempts included frequent, unannounced searches of prisoners of war and their barracks, to be conducted at random times during the day and night. Every German soldier regardless of rank was authorized to conduct searches, even against prisoner-of-war officers. There would also be at least two, if not three, roll-calls in the Oflags, the last of which would be conducted before dusk. All tools were to be returned quickly at the end of each work period. And lastly, well-illuminated rings of wire were to surround the camp when possible, to reduce the risk of sabotage and infiltration.[116]

From the November 8, 1942, due to the Allied landings in north Africa, the OKW had ordered French and British prisoners of war to be more closely guarded. At the start of February 1943, this measure was rescinded; the OKW decided that it was up to the individual commandants and work-detachment leaders to determine what level of guarding was necessary for the British and French prisoners of war under their command.[117]

In early January 1943, responding to inquiries concerning legitimate uses of force against prisoners of war, the OKW sent out a copy of an earlier order, outlining its position. According to article 46 of the Geneva Convention, prisoners of war could not be punished with any forcible measures that were not also applicable to German soldiers. Self-defense was a permissible reason to use force to subdue prisoners of war, not only in reaction to a specific attack, but also to prevent an attack against a third party. While this was the case, corporal punishment against prisoners of war was specifically forbidden; guards could use only enough force as was needed to bring prisoners of war under control. Also, only guards and their assistants could intervene directly against prisoners of war. If a prisoner of war refused to obey a direct order from one of them, then the guard had "the *right, if trapped in a situation of extreme danger and having exhausted all other options, to force compliance with arms*" (emphasis in the original). The guards were entrusted with looking over the prisoners of war, and the rules were deemed clear as to what could and could not be done to them; the guards should not, however, shy away from being firm and ensuring that work which was rightfully demanded be completed.[118]

In mid-January 1943, the OKW issued to guards yet another pamphlet summarizing their duties. Before it got down to specifics, the German guards were reminded of several general facts. The prisoners of war were described as the enemy's soldiers, the most valuable part of the enemy state's manpower. Under the terms of the Geneva Convention, Germany had the legal right to use prisoners of war as workers; prisoners of war were the manpower of Germany, and had to be exploited for the German economy. So that prisoner-of-war labor really did benefit the German people, the guards had to ensure that the prisoners of war were given proper accommodations, sufficient food, financial compensation, and, from their guards, correct treatment. The guards had to make sure the prisoners worked as long and hard as German workers in the same task. However, the prisoners were not entitled to the same benefits of citizenship as German workers; it was always to be remembered that prisoners of war were members of the enemy's military. The three major duties of the German guard were: (1) guarding the prisoners of war; (2) keeping them working; and (3) protecting the German people from possible sabotage. Regardless of the prisoner's rank, the guard was his superior, in terms of command. Prisoners of war had to be dealt with strongly but legally. If necessary, obedience was to be enforced with arms. The work-detachment leaders and guards had to sharply prevent any attempts by prisoners of war to withdraw from working. Escape, mingling with German workers, or sabotage were all things the guard had to watch against.

The German guard was neither to abuse prisoners of war nor allow others to abuse them. Again, the OKW reiterated that even though the prisoner of war could come into limited contact with German workers during the course of work, he was always a member of the enemy's military, and not part of German society. Civilian German workers who cultivated any personal relationships with prisoners of war, or adopted an easygoing manner with them, could be punished with prison sentences for threatening the health of the German society: grave dangers lay in contacts between prisoners of war and German civilians. They were only to speak together as much as was required for work. German women especially had to recognize the dangers posed by relations with prisoners of war; sexual contacts were undesirable, because they promoted the political intentions of the enemy. Relations between prisoners of war and foreign civilian workers also had to be hindered as much as possible, because they were prone to lead to plans for propaganda, sabotage, or espionage. The German peasantry, Nazi Party, Wehrmacht, guards, and national economy had the common goal of winning the war. Thus, the Wehrmacht could count on the support of the local Party and civilian leadership. Any misunderstanding between these groups and the guards was to be immediately reported, so it could be sorted out, and close cooperation could resume.[119]

On April 5, 1943, guards were instructed by the OKW to pay especially careful attention to their duties when guarding British prisoners of war. According to the OKW, the measures outlined in the pamphlets on guarding prisoners of war needed to be followed especially in the case of British prisoners of war, because they were extremely likely to constantly attempt to test the authority of the guards, and consort with the civilian population for propaganda purposes. Such instances were to be dealt with sharply and immediately. In supervising prisoner-of-war private soldiers, the only British noncommissioned officers to be used were those who could be sure of getting a favorably subordinate response from them. British noncommissioned officer prisoners who were unable or unwilling to subordinate their prisoners of war were to be immediately replaced, and sent to Stalag 383 Hohenfels.[120]

One month later, on May 8, 1943, the OKW announced that it had made arrangements with the Head of the SS and German Police (Himmler) for greater support in guarding prisoners of war in work detachments. Due to the number of prisoners of war in work detachments, the number of guards and assistant-guards was proving insufficient; in order to maintain both discipline and work efficiency, a certain level of supervision was necessary, which OKW guards were no longer able to offer alone. Consequently, the camp commanders now had the authority to request members of the Gendarmerie to assist in guarding duties for prisoner-of-war work detachments. The disciplinary authority of the Wehrmacht guards over the prisoners of war would not be affected by this arrangement. In the absence of Wehrmacht guards, however, the members of the Gendarmerie would have temporary command authority over the prisoners of war. The Gendarmerie was responsible for carrying out the orders of the camp commandant with regard to the prisoners of war, and had to be properly instructed by the camp staff on the rules and regulations pertaining to the guarding and supervision of prisoners of war in work detachments.[121]

Guards of prisoners of war of all nationalities were ordered by the OKW, on May 17, 1943, to make sure that they had enough room in which to employ their firearms if necessary, without being easily overwhelmed by rioting prisoners of war. This order was deemed necessary as, in several recent instances, Soviet prisoners of war had attacked and temporarily overpowered their guards because the guards did not allow for enough distance between them and the prisoners. The lessons of the events with the Soviet prisoners of war were to be learned by the guards of all other prisoners of war.[122]

By October 1943, the OKW instructed all guards of prisoners of war to have their bayonets fixed onto their rifles while they were on duty. This measure was taken to decrease the likelihood that prisoners of war would cause trouble, and only in situations where the guards' field of fire was hampered by the bayonet was he not to have it fixed on the end of his rifle.[123] Later, it was noted by the OKW that guards who were transporting prisoners of war at night had been attacked and killed. Prisoners of war were only to be moved at night if absolutely necessary, and then only with special security arrangements in place.[124]

In January 1944, the OKW clarified that firing a warning shot was not always necessary before shooting at prisoners of war. So long as the preconditions for the proper use of firearms (three warning yells or shouts, for the western prisoners of war) by guards against prisoners of war had been made, there was no need for further warnings.[125]

In May 1944, the OKW issued more orders on the use of firearms by guards. It was acknowledged that in some circumstances prisoners of war did have cause to leave their barracks at night (such as to use outdoor latrines); the commandant had to take all measures necessary to remove such needs, including the issuing of pails and buckets with sand, for latrine use within the barracks at night, and also providing some sort of alarm so that prisoners of war could get the attention of the guards without having to leave the barracks. The behavior of prisoners of war during night air-raids was to be thoroughly regulated. The prisoners of war were to be given both written and verbal instructions concerning their movements at night. At least once a month, the guards were to have the night rules reexplained to them as well, so that they knew of their authority to shoot at prisoners of war outside their huts without warning. Camp orders weakening the authority of guards to shoot without warning at night were prohibited; such measures would only undermine the authority of the German command. It was very important that the measures adopted to keep prisoners of war in their barracks at night, and the regulations given to guards, were clear, so that mistakes did not occur, and shooting errors were avoided.[126] One month later, the OKW ordered that all prisoners of war be told, in their own language, that any prisoner who touched or crossed the perimeter wire would be shot; each new arrival to the camp was to be likewise informed.[127]

In mid-July 1944, the OKW issued further supplementary orders concerning the use of firearms by guards against prisoners of war. These began by reiterating the right of guards to shoot without a warning shout at prisoners of war who were outside their barracks before morning reveille without permission; the same went for prisoners of war who touched or attempted to cross the perimeter barbed-wire fence. Again, these measures were to be announced, verbally and in writing, to the prisoners of war in their own language. This was to be done for each individual new arrival to the camp, and also to all prisoners of war within one month following any shooting incident. As a result of complaints from the Protecting Powers, all staff were to be reminded that these rules had to be followed in the strictest obedience, and that to further avoid misunderstandings, signs were to be placed warning of the danger in front of the fence.[128]

Based on (unspecified) disturbances in August 1944, the OKW warned the camp commandants that illegal organizations among prisoners of war had been increasingly active. In the interests of security, the camps had to diligently investigate any suspicious activity, no matter how small it appeared, and coordinate their efforts with the local state police detachment, as per previous agreements.[129]

At the start of October 1944, the OKW reaffirmed that in general, security searches of prisoner-of-war accommodations should only take place in the presence of either the prisoner or his representative (i.e. the barrack senior or the Man of Confidence). However, in "wholly exceptional circumstances" in which the prisoner's presence could not be allowed, the camp commandant could oversee the search instead.[130]

On January 1, 1945, the OKW noted that in the course of visits to work detachments it had been proven possible for visitors to enter past the guards without being challenged for their identifications. Guards of all work detachments were to be reminded that they had to demand to see proper identification from any person seeking to enter.[131] Guards were also to be reminded that prisoners of war often tried to escape through the lavatories during transport. Guards were therefore to accompany the prisoner to the lavatory, and keep an eye on him at all times. Should the prisoner slam the door shut on the guard in an attempt to escape, the Guard could shoot the prisoner through the door without issuing a warning.[132]

In mid-January 1945, a series of orders for camp security officers was issued by the OKW. The first stated that newsletters from the American Red Cross were now being vetted centrally before being sent to the individual camps, and so they did not need to be reexamined for censorship, but could be immediately be distributed. Greater thrift in distributing paper to the prisoners of war was urged, due to the increasingly difficult problems of supply. In addition to providing factual details of escapes in their Escape Reports, the security officers must henceforth also include information as to any material factors which might have inspired the escape. Although a reciprocal agreement was reached with the American government regarding the returning of mail of already repatriated prisoners of war, the camps had to ensure that the returned items did not bear any German administrative stamps or markings. It had also come to the attention of the OKW that the Allies set up a small school in Belgium to train and organize a German-speaking police corps. Security officers were to find out what they could about this unit through interrogations, and report their findings to the OKW.[133]

The costs of escapes

The threat to national security by escaped prisoners of war was the reason for the increasingly stringent guarding regulations described above. However, on several occasions, the OKW issued comments and instructions to the guards dealing with the problems of escape more directly.

In addition to guarding the prisoners of war, the OKW decided, on June 5, 1942, that instituting a system of monetary rewards for helping capture escaped prisoners would both minimize the length of time it took to capture escaped prisoners and ultimately decrease the total security threat. Financial rewards could be given for the capture of escaped prisoners of war: only to people who were not members of the military, the police, or the customs department; to a maximum of RM30, though the standard would be RM10; in exceptional circumstances, and with the permission of the OKW, even RM100. Rewards could be also be given to prisoners of war who saved a life, offered exceptional help during unexpected crises, such as fire or natural disasters, or who helped out during either an attempted or actual escape by a prisoner of war or civilian laborer. The rewards could be in the form of either military citation, money (to be determined at the time), special privileges (increased postal rights, new outfitting from stores), or even release from captivity (either the result of one exceptional act, or on the third act for which a reward could be given).[134]

In October 1942, to supplement previous orders concerning the issuing of rewards for capturing escaped prisoners of war, the OKW decreed that rewards could also be given to people (not members of either the military or the police) who prevented an escape attempt. These cases were to be judged individually by the camp commandant.[135] In May 1944, Reichsführer-SS Himmler ordered that civilians who captured escaped prisoners of war or other sought-after persons were eligible to receive rewards of up to RM100. Should several people have been involved in the recapture, the award was to be split up between them equally. The prisoner-of-war camps were no longer to disburse money for such rewards; they would be given out directly, and all previous orders concerning rewards for recapturing prisoners of war were to be considered superseded by this one.[136]

A specific problem, which led to successful escapes, was forged identity cards. To deal with it guards were reminded, in May 1940, to keep close watch over photography equipment; pictures of prisoners of war were only to be taken for their camp identity cards.[137] Those prisoners of war who had not yet been photographed were ordered by the OKW to have their pictures taken, and any prisoners of war who had changed their appearance (with a beard, for instance) were to have a new picture taken, and were to bear the expense themselves.[138] Also that month, the OKW noted that police, when called in to help with searches following escapes, had also brought in their own assistant policemen to help. The camp staff was instructed to make use of this additional resource in the future, not only for searches following escapes, but also for major inspections of the camps when large escape plans were suspected of the prisoners of war.[139] And any instance in which an escaped prisoner was caught wearing civilian clothing was to be immediately reported to the OKH in Berlin.[140] Because of the increasing use by prisoners of war of civilian clothing in their escape attempts, greater care was to be taken during searches looking for hiding places for such clothes.[141] As another cause of successful escapes was the lax storage of keys, the OKW reminded all camps that they should have a secure procedure for storing camp keys.[142]

In September 1942, the OKW issued a general comment on prisoner-of-war escapes, and followed it with new rules to be passed down the chain of command. Thus far that year, 1,175 Officers (of who 678 were Russians) and 77,628 noncommissioned officers and men (of whom 35,208 were Russians) had escaped their captivity. Dealing with this problem cost 620,000 lost work hours for the German economy, in addition to the increased threat to the internal security of Germany. Therefore, the primary responsibility of the guards had to be the prevention of escapes; in cases where the escape was made either possible or easier because of negligence, the guard would face court-martial. Should "prominent" prisoners of war escape, the criminal police and the RSHA were to be notified immediately. More careful censorship of mail was required, and the issuing of unopened tins of food was henceforth strictly prohibited. Responsibility for apprehending escaped prisoners of war outside the camp was firstly the task of the police and the Gendarmerie. The military district headquarters had to notify all relevant authorities (rail police, etc.) of the details of the escape as soon as possible. The search for prisoners of war in the immediate vicinity of the camp was the responsibility of the camp commandant; police assistance might be called in to help, if needed. If the escape occurred during rail transport, and there was no military authority at hand, the Transport Leader had to notify the nearest rail administration office. Lastly, all fleeing non-Soviet prisoners of war were to be given three warning shouts before being shot at; no warning shouts were to be given to Soviet prisoners of war.[143] Before transport to a new camp, prisoners of war were to have all letters and writing equipment removed from them; these supplies were to be sent later by separate transport, and reinspected for security reasons at the new camp.[144]

The OKW also, on January 11, 1943, ordered the camps to reassess their security measures with the aim of preventing prisoner-of-war escapes. Specifically, they were to make sure obstacle wire placed between the inner and outer perimeter fences actually did prevent an individual from either crawling or running easily. All shrubbery was to be removed from these areas, so guards could have a clear line of fire. Lastly, guard towers were to be sighted in such a way that they gave not only a view into the camp, but also a clear line of fire along the fences; the precise sighting would be left to the discretion of the commandant. These measures, by heightening the difficulty of escaping, were expected to act also as a deterrent.[145]

To warn German guards about the consequences of accepting bribes to look the other way during escape attempts, the OKW informed all guards of an occasion in which a German guard of prisoners of war had been bribed with chocolates and cigarettes to look the other way during an escape attempt. He was condemned to death for willful neglect of duty. The OKW ordered that all guards be informed of this, and reminded of it every three months.[146] In April of that year, the OKW also reported that a German guard was found guilty of providing a Polish officer prisoner with maps and tools for the purpose of escape. The guard was sentenced to death and executed, and, again, all members of the guard teams were to be informed of the event.[147] Additionally, the OKW sought to improve the quality of guarding: during a recent transport of 529 Russian prisoners of war, 61 of them escaped. As a result of the investigation, it was determined that they had in their possession pocket knives, scissors, and razors, to use as escape tools. As a result of the improper conduct of the search of the prisoners of war before transport, the Security Officer of their Stalag was charged and sentenced for negligence leading to an escape.[148] And in addition to simple negligence, the OKW also decided to punish guards who, in hesitating to use their weapons, indirectly contributed to a prisoners' escape. Such infractions were to lead to courts-martial in the future. Due to hesitancy on the part of guards, many prisoner-of-war escape attempts which could have been thwarted were instead successful.[149]

The OKW conceded, in March 1943, that the previous procedure of checking the identifications only of persons unfamiliar to the guards at the camp gates was not proving particularly effective as a security measure. Henceforth, all personnel leaving or entering the camps were to have their identification checked by the guards at the gates.[150] From March 19, 1943 onward, the entrances to Oflags were to have double gates; when one gate was opened, the other would remain locked until the first one was again locked. This was to prevent escape attempts while the guards had the gates unlocked while letting someone else in or out.[151] In July 1944, the OKW decided that all previous orders concerning the showing of identification upon entrance and exit from prisoner-of-war camps were to apply to all members of the Wehrmacht, regardless of rank.[152]

It was clear to the OKW, in June 1944, that prisoners of war were somehow manufacturing German military administrative stamps in the camps, and using them to forge false papers for escape purposes. To hinder this, all receipts bearing official stamps were to be confiscated from the prisoners' personal possession and locked up in storage.[153] Likewise, camp money henceforth could not carry any administrative marks or seals. Any such camp money in circulation was to be withdrawn and destroyed.[154] In mid-August 1944, orders were issued to tighten up control of any papers issued to prisoners of war which bore German administrative stamps of any kind. As such stamps could be used by prisoners of war, especially in the Oflags, for forged documents, the commandants were instructed to keep them locked up, and give receipts to the prisoners of war for them.[155]

Cooperation with the SS

On August 19, 1943, a detailed order was issued which set out the parameters of cooperation between the Wehrmacht and the SS, for the prevention of prisoner-of-war escapes. Mass escapes in the previous months made it clear that a closer cooperation between the two was necessary. Accordingly, at Hitler's behest, the Wehrmacht entered into an agreement with Himmler to employ the Security Police in closer cooperation with the security branch of the military. Henceforth, if a mass escape occurred, the security police were to be informed immediately by the commander of prisoners of war of the relevant military district, and a man-hunt would be coordinated between the two. Members of the security police would assist the commander of prisoners of war in each military district in implementing measures designed to decrease the likelihood of escapes. The commander, for his part, had to maintain a close liaison with the security police representatives in his military district, discuss with them all questions relevant to the escape of prisoners of war and the experiences learned from past escapes, and request the security police to assist in searches of prisoners of war, their barracks and work detachments, and any related investigations arising from the searches. Further, the commander would inform the security police of any decisions he took concerning prisoner-of-war security arrangements, and would respond to the security police's recommendations concerning prisoner searches. While individual camp commandants retained their overall authority on prisoner security, they were now obligated to support the measures of the local security police units designed to prevent prisoner escapes, including searches of the prisoners of war and their barracks. The security police measures would extend to cover all work detachments away from the prisoner-of-war camps and investigations into the causes of escapes, including interrogations. Prisoners of war, however, remained in the custody of the Wehrmacht, and so any security police questions had to be delivered in conjunction with the local camp officials. The security police would create search units in the vicinity of camps, to participate at the side of the Wehrmacht during searches of Oflags and Stalags with an officer of the Abwehr, of the military district administration, the camp commandant, and the security officer of the relevant camp. In work detachments, searches could only be conducted by the security police with the cooperation of an officer from the main camp, the Abwehr officer or his delegate, and the control officer. Upon conclusion of searches involving the security police, a written report was to be made by the camp commandant and forwarded up the chain of command.[156]

Visions of Normandy and mass escapes

In May 1944, a "mass escape" of prisoners of war was defined by the OKW as any escape of 7 or more prisoners of war, regardless of their rank or nationality. At the same time, the OKW ordered that any escape by an officer prisoner, regardless of rank or nationality, was to be immediately reported to OKW headquarters by telex.[157]

Anticipation of future problems in the prisoner-of-war camps after enemy landings in Europe prompted the OKW, on May 25, 1944, to issue new warnings and instructions for the guarding of prisoners of war. Repercussions following an enemy landing in the west could include revolts in the camps, with or without external military support. To prepare for this possibility, camp commandants had to ensure that: all guards were fully trained and competent with their weapons; enough ammunition existed and was distributed among the guards to be able to put down such a revolt; a clear and simple alarm system was put in place, assigning every guard to a specific place and task; alarm practices be held, to improve the efficiency of the guards; the game plan was kept secret if possible from prisoner-of-war observation.[158]

That the issue of the expected Allied landings in France was paramount in the minds of the soldiers guarding prisoners of war was made further clear by the staff of the OKW. On June 1, 1944, they issued a four-page summary of previous rules for guarding prisoners of war, with special emphasis on preventing revolts and attempts at mass escapes among both prisoner-of-war officers and soldiers, following the possible Allied landings. No new instructions or orders were issued, however; the camps were just told to be ready for the worst-case scenario, and reminded of their duties and obligations to prevent escapes.[159] This was further made clear when the same office suspended all leaves of absence until further notice for all members of the prisoner-of-war administration, right down to guards, on June 6, 1944; all guns were to be inspected for readiness, and adequate ammunition was to be distributed.[160]

In an intimidation attempt designed to inhibit escape attempts, the OKW issued, on June 14, 1944, a security "warning" to prisoners of war concerning the possible treatment they might receive at the hands of the German civilian population. Prisoners of war, and especially British and American pilots, were to be told that as British and American airforces had been attacking civilian areas in addition to military targets (a "scorning of all principles of humanity"), a "dark emotional current," whose specific outlets the OKW did not define, had been noticed in the German population, which had been given expression in the behavior of civilians against prisoners of war.[161]

Mass escapes and individual escapes of officers of the rank of colonel and above, as well as of prominent military personalities, carried such a high level of security danger for Germany that disciplinary hearings would henceforth be conducted into the activities of the guards, to determine whether or not negligence played a role. Full details, therefore, had to be given in the Escape Report filed after such events.[162] For reasons of national security, previous orders calling for investigations against camp commandants in the event of a mass escape, or an escape of prisoner-of-war officers ranked colonel or higher, or of prominent prisoners of war, had to be maintained. The investigation against the commandant was to be conducted as quickly and thoroughly as possible; if necessary, it would be conducted by the local criminal police unit. It was especially important in the cases of mass escapes to determine if the conditions of the work assignment were a factor. If fault appeared to lay with the commandant, the OKH was to be notified immediately.[163]

And lastly, in late March 1945, the continuing problem of escapes had so vexed the OKW that Jodl sent a telegram to the commander of prisoner-of-war affairs in military district XIII stating that the commandant of a prisoner-of-war camp "in which even one prisoner-of-war escapes, will pay for it with his head." [164]

Sabotage

Given the relatively few specific policy directives issued by the OKW on sabotage during the course of the war years, it appears that the issue was dealt with as an offshoot of good general inspection of incoming parcels, and the proper guarding of the prisoners of war. Exhortations to increased vigilance seemed the main way in which the OKW sought to deal with the problem. The German manuals in place at the start of the war reminded the commandants that, from the experiences of the Great War, it was evident that the enemy's personnel, even if unarmed, could be expected to carry on, whenever possible, their fight through espionage and sabotage,[165] and that the danger was especially great in the employment of prisoners of war in labor.[166]

It was in early December 1941 that the OKW first responded directly to growing problems of sabotage being reported by the camps. Specifically, the OKW ordered that: prisoners of war be given new razors only if they turned in their old ones; special receptacles for used razors and broken glass be placed far from the garbage used for leftover food.[167]

With regard to the reception of sabotage materials through the mail, the OKW specifically ordered, in March 1942, that the retention by prisoners of war of heat-pads with chemical filling was strictly prohibited; any heat-pads sent to prisoners of war in parcels, either collective or individual, were not to be delivered.[168] The pieces of the game of darts, likewise, were to be confiscated from the prisoners and from any incoming parcels, as their parts could be used for sabotage.[169]

In the work detachments, the danger of sabotage was considered especially great. As a countermeasure, guards were to consider locking up prisoners of war in their barracks immediately upon return from work, supervising the workplaces in cooperation with the civilian and local military authorities, and reinforcing secure transport for prisoners of war from endangered or difficult work detachments back to the main camp.[170] British noncommissioned officer prisoners of war who had signed up to work, but whom were no longer prepared to work, were to be returned to their camps. They were not to be considered "unwilling" laborers; given the frequency with which such prisoners attempted acts of sabotage, their return to their camps was more of a benefit than the disadvantage of lost labor.[171]

A critical time to watch out for sabotage, wrote the OKW in early April 1943, was in the immediate aftermath of an air-raid. For that reason, it was imperative that guards watch prisoners of war especially closely during these times.[172] The same point was made again by the OKW in March 1943, when guards were instructed to be especially vigilant against acts of sabotage upon the sounding of the "all clear" signal after an air-raid.[173]

The possibility of sabotage being planned in hospitals by prisoners of war who were recuperating or not seriously ill was mentioned by the OKW on November 10, 1944; the only point made was that the German staff had to be especially vigilant.[174]

And in a final and ominous note on sabotage, the OKW ordered, at the start of January 1945, that British or American prisoners of war who were found with a small glass bulb, approximately 10 centimeters in diameter and filled with a yellow liquid,[175] in their luggage were, upon notification from the Befehlshaber des Ersatzheeres, to be sent immediately to the special representative of the Reichsführer-SS in Auschwitz for reasons of sabotage.[176]

5
Economics and External Relations of Prisoners of War

5.1 Labor and finance

After the average prisoner of war had been captured, processed, and sent to a permanent camp, the next major evolution in his captivity which he could expect was the beginning of a work regime. It was, according to all of the countries which had signed the Geneva Convention, entirely reasonable to expect that at least some of the costs for maintaining the prisoners would be defrayed by putting them to work, and the Convention dedicated a separate section, comprised of articles 27 to 34, to this issue. The basic rule was that, with the exception of officers, the Detaining Power had the right to require labor of any prisoner who was physically fit. Noncommissioned officers could only be compelled to work in a supervisory capacity. Officers could, upon their request and if work "suitable" to their rank existed, be employed for pay; noncommissioned officers could likewise be employed for pay as general laborers (and not supervisors), if they so requested. Accident benefits and compensation for prisoners of war were to be the same as those which existed for normal workmen in the country.[1]

The Detaining Power was responsible for the conditions of labor, payment of wages, living arrangements, and treatment of the prisoners of war in the workplace. No prisoner could be forced to work in a position to which he was "physically unsuited," the duration of the workday was to equal that of civilian workers likewise employed, and one 24-hour rest period per week, preferably on a Sunday, was to be allowed to each prisoner.[2]

It was forbidden to employ prisoners of war in any work which had a "direct connection" with the war operations; specifically, using them in the manufacture or transport of arms or munitions, and the transport of any material destined for combatant units, was expressly forbidden. In the event that prisoners of war believed they were employed in war-related work, they had the right to present their complaints, through their MOC, to their Protecting Power delegates.[3] Unhealthy or dangerous work was also forbidden, and the conditions of employment could not be made more difficult by the introduction of disciplinary measures.[4] Labor detachments were to have the same conditions and rights, as regards accommodations, hygiene, post, food, and healthcare, as the main prisoner-of-war camps; each work detachment was to be a subunit of a specific camp, and the representative of the workers was allowed contact with the Man of Confidence of the main camp.[5]

The last article on prisoner-of-war work in the Convention stated that no pay was to be given to the prisoners of war for work done for the administration and internal maintenance of the camps; any other mandatory work resulted in an entitlement to a wage, to be determined by the belligerents. As well, the Detaining Power had the right to determine how much money could be held in the immediate possession of the prisoners of war, and how much would be placed in an account. Generally, the arrangements for pay were: (a) the same pay for prisoners of war as for soldiers of the home army employed on similarly tasks, or on the work being done by civilian workers; if prisoners of war were used for labor by private companies, the wages were to be agreed to in advance by the Detaining Power and the prospective employer; pay was the personal property of the prisoner, and had to be credited to him – in the event of death, the remainder of a prisoner's savings was to be forwarded to his next-of-kin through diplomatic channels.[6]

The German regulations in place at the start of the war followed the terms of the Geneva Convention closely; as with other subjects concerning the treatment of prisoners, the commandants were often instructed to refer directly to the Convention, in this case articles 27–34. Prisoner-of-war regular soldiers, and volunteer noncommissioned officers, could be employed for the upkeep of the camp without remuneration. Prisoner-of-war labor could be a boon and a danger for Germany – a boon if the prisoners of war were properly supervised, but a danger because of the risk of espionage and sabotage. And as stated in articles 27–34, the prisoners could be compelled to work. Special attention had to be given to the prohibitions listed in article 31. As for possibly dangerous work mentioned in article 32, prisoners of war could only be employed in work that German workers also performed, provided they met the physical requirements, as per article 29.[7] Private money found on the prisoners of war was to be taken, with the corresponding amount inscribed on an "account" card. Noncommissioned officers and other-ranks received no pay under the Geneva Convention unless they worked; working prisoners of war and officers (who received pay regardless of whether they worked) were to be given their first pay upon arrival in their permanent camps.[8] Any future amounts of money sent to a prisoner of war were to be noted in a credit account, and removed from his possession. The total was to be converted into *Lagergeld* (camp money), which the prisoner could then withdraw and use for purchases at the camp canteen. No one outside the camps was allowed to use camp money; it was for internal circulation only, as a security measure. Pay received by prisoners of war who worked was to be arranged between the camp administration and the employer, and no money was to be given directly to the prisoner.[9]

Dr. Waltzog's 1942 update to German policy on prisoners of war did not depart from most of the previously held policy of the OKW. It preserved the privileges of the noncommissioned officers to be obliged to work only in a supervisory capacity, unless they specifically requested regular work. He further elaborated from the text of the Convention in that once such a request had been made, the noncommissioned officer was required to work as a normal prisoner-of-war until the end of his captivity; he could not request work for a specific duration, or later ask to have his privileges reinstated.[10] According to Waltzog, Germany was under no legal obligation under international law to provide a written explanation of this policy in advance; the OKW later overruled Waltzog on this point.[11] While prisoners of war received the full protections and privileges granted to German workers regarding accidents, illness, or work-related disabilities, these benefits, by act of German law, existed only for the duration of formal captivity; at death, for instance, when captivity legally ended, so too did the prisoners' privileges, and Waltzog argued that the Detaining Power had no further financial obligations to the prisoner's next-of-kin.[12]

Waltzog also agreed that prisoners of war could not be employed in work that was directly related to the war effort. But indirect contributions, he continued, which led to the amelioration of the general economy and society (road and rail repair, for instance) could not be included in the definition: the same train tracks which might carry troops also carried basic goods. He extended this analogy to argue that the same principle allowed the employment of prisoners of war in repairing airfields that were used by civilian planes, regardless of whether they were also used by the Luftwaffe; conceivably under this interpretation, all the Luftwaffe had to do was allow for an occasional "civilian" plane to land at an airfield to justify using prisoners of war to repair damages after air-raids.[13]

Gentleman volunteers

Both the Geneva Convention and the German regulations stated that officer prisoners of war could not be compelled to work; in the absence of a prohibition against volunteer labor, however, the German authorities made the effort, as per article 27, to find supervisory work suitable to their rank for officers who requested it. Toward the end of November 1941, the commander of military district IV, with the approval of the OKW, decided to use postal incentives to get more officer and noncommissioned officer prisoners of war to volunteer to perform regular labor. Prisoner-of-war officers were entitled to 3 letters and 4 postcards per month, while noncommissioned officers who refused to work were allowed 2 letters and 2 postcards per month. Officer and noncommissioned officer prisoners of war who volunteered to work would be entitled to two or three more letters a month, depending on their rank. These measures would have no effect on the amount of mail a prisoner of war could receive, however.[14] On April 20, 1942, the OKW replaced its previous instructions concerning prisoner-of-war officers who were willing to work with a new one: from that point to the end of the war, British and American officer prisoners of war officer were not permitted to work, regardless of whether or not they so desired.[15]

The issue for noncommissioned officers was more complicated. Even though the Convention obliged them to do supervisory work, many British and American noncommissioned officer prisoners of war simply refused. German policy over the course of the war evolved between the need to employ all legitimate sources of labor on the one hand, and the need to minimize trouble and the extra guarding necessary for recalcitrant prisoners on the other. The issue was further complicated by the fact that many noncommissioned officers requested to be placed in general work in order to be paid more (as per article 27), but later tried to rescind their "volunteer" status, and return to either supervisory work or none at all. In mid-November 1940, the OKW sent out an order listing the conditions under which noncommissioned officers would be permitted to work: (1) they had to pass a health exam from the camp doctor, to be entered on their personnel card; (2) they had to receive security clearance from the camp commandant; (3) the work to be done had to be cleared by the local work-bureau and, when possible, be related to any specialty the prisoner might have; (4) the noncommissioned officers would work at the rates set by the OKW, with no distinction made between them and other-ranks in this regard; (5) the noncommissioned officer would get paid in the camp, according to established regulations.[16]

In early March 1941, the OKW further clarified its position concerning the use of noncommissioned officers in labor. Apparently, some noncommissioned officers were under the impression that they had the right to revoke their written request to work, and hence leave employment at their discretion. The OKW disagreed. Its position was that, in signing a written request to work, the noncommissioned officers waived the privileges granted them under article 27, para. 3 of the Geneva Convention, for the duration of their captivity. In order to make things perfectly clear in the future, when noncommissioned officers made a written request to work, it had to be made clear that they were undertaking a formal obligation to work for a definite length of time, not to exceed the duration of their normal captivity.[17] However, British noncommissioned officer prisoners of war who had signed up for regular labor, but who no longer wanted to work, were to be returned to their camps. They were not to be considered "unwilling" laborers; given the increase in sabotage attempts by them, their return to their camps was more of a benefit to the German war effort than a disadvantage.[18]

While prisoners of war were permitted to make donations to their poorer comrades also in captivity, the recipients of such goodwill aid could not be noncommissioned officers who refused to work. They were able to make money at any time by accepting work.[19]

Forbidden labor

With regard to prohibited labor, both early OKW policy and Dr. Waltzog's 1942 update of that policy remained consistent with the requirements of the Geneva Convention, noted above. During the course of the war, however, non-British and non-American prisoners of war were often used in the German munitions industry. Though most orders from the OKW on the use of prisoners of war in prohibited industries specifically mentioned the nationalities of the prisoners involved (and these rarely included, as a matter of policy, British or American prisoners), a few directives did not, and for the sake of completeness are also described below.

In late November 1940, a secret order was issued by the OKW concerning the use of English (i.e. British) prisoners of war in air-raid shelter construction projects. The use of English prisoners of war in such capacities was, apparently, causing German prisoners of war in English captivity to be put to similar use in England. Given the greater likelihood of bombings in London and other southern English cities, German prisoners of war were thus being put at greater risk than their English counterparts in Germany. With this in mind, the further use of English prisoners of war in air-raid defense construction projects was prohibited. Instead, prisoners of war of different nationalities, or civilian internees, were to replace the English prisoners of war.[20]

In March 1941, the OKW noted that a large munitions company had noted, in a report, that gaps in its company were being filled occasionally with prisoner-of-war labor. The OKW ordered that even though such assignments did occur and were compatible with the Geneva Convention (though this compatibility was not explained), they should not appear on future reports.[21] A few months later, in May 1941, regulations were sent by the OKW concerning the mixing of prisoners of war and foreign civilian workers in firms of the armaments industry. Previous mixing of them was leading to efficiency problems; therefore, both groups were to be kept strictly segregated from one another, both at work, and in accommodations. When unavoidable, their interaction was to be kept to a minimum, for security reasons.[22] After seeing to it that the labor demands in their areas had been met, the Commanders of Prisoners of war in the military districts had to immediately put any surplus prisoners of war, especially trades specialists, at the disposal of the armaments industry.[23]

Carrots and sticks

Regardless of the specific use to which American or British prisoners of war were put, it remained a constant interest of Germany that they work as hard as possible, and not slack off. To that end, a constant stream of orders was issued by the OKW on how to obtain the most labor from prisoners of war.

In late March 1941, the OKW noted that prisoner-of-war labor performance could stand to be improved. The problem, as they saw it, was that guards were solely concerned with preventing escapes, and not supervising the work being done. The OKW order therefore reminded guards that though security was their primary responsibility, they also had to pay closer attention to the work being done by the prisoners, to prevent them from slacking off. It was, the OKW continued, unacceptable that the German population worked hard, while the prisoners of war received the same food allowances for less work. Therefore, the guards were ordered to supervise prisoner-of-war labor more closely, and, where necessary, withhold some portions of their food allowance if prisoners were deemed not to be working hard enough.[24]

Included as an appendix to the first fortnightly collection of orders (eventually called *Befehlsammlungen*) issued to the camps in June 1941 was a report from the Reich minister for labor to the various Wehrkreis labor offices concerning the use of prisoners of war. In it, district work offices were berated for wasting prisoner-of-war labor in sectors which did not directly help the German war effort. It further stated that requests for prisoner-of-war labor by businesses not involved in work crucial to the war effort were to be refused.[25]

The less-than-stellar work habits of prisoners of war was again noted by the OKW in June 1942. This was apparently especially prevalent in work areas where there were no German workers to set a good example. An occasional cause of this had also been lack of proper diligence on the part of the guards. The guards were once again to be reminded that, in addition to guarding the prisoners of war, they also had the responsibility of ensuring that they worked hard. To this end, guards were expected to: make sure each prisoner of war was fully engaged in his work to the best of his ability; inform the prisoners of the guards' rights under German law to punish them for not trying hard; ensure that the hours being asked of by the employer were being given in full by the prisoners; adopt measures which could lead to the greater cooperation of the prisoners; strongly punish any prisoners of war who continued not to give their full effort. The guards had a vital duty to the state to ensure that prisoners of war were working hard; with this in mind, all unofficial visits by guards to either private houses or restaurants during work hours were prohibited. The leaders of the work detachments were to make this order known to the prisoners.[26] On August 19, 1942, reacting to newer reports that prisoners of war were not in many cases being pushed hard enough at work by their guards, the OKW ordered the military districts to permit the Nazi Party functionaries in each district to personally oversee the fulfillment of the previous orders concerning prisoner-of-war productivity. In any cases where they reported that the guards had been negligent in allowing prisoners to slack off, the situation was to be sharply corrected.[27]

Complaints had been received that it was taking too long for prisoners who had recuperated from illnesses or minor injuries to be returned to their old workplace. Apparently, they were being kept in hospitals or infirmaries longer than necessary. Camp commandants were therefore ordered to take more care to ensure that convalesced prisoners of war be returned to their old work detachments as quickly as possible upon recovery.[28] Although the OKW believed, in June 1944, that more measures had to be instituted to increase the efficiency of prisoners engaged in the mining industry, accidents to prisoners were considered to be an even greater drain on the war effort. Therefore, guards and work detachment leaders had to take whatever reasonable measures were necessary to reduce the incidence of accidents.[29]

To ensure maximum efficiency from prisoner-of-war labor, the work-detachment officers were instructed by the OKW, in July 1944, to work even more closely with the senior Nazi Party labor official of the area.[30] Also, Concentration Camp workers were no longer to work with prisoners of war in the same German business, as they had been proven to have unfavorable influences on the prisoners. They could only be employed by the same company if their workplaces were entirely separate from each other.[31]

On August 17, 1944, the OKW again gave directives aimed at improving the productivity of prisoner-of-war laborers. These were issued due to complaints from the Nazi Party offices as well as local business leaders that the implementation of previous measures had not led to the desired levels of efficiency. As a first step to rectifying this situation, there was to be closer cooperation between the Wehrmacht and the Nazi Party. To this end, a liaison officer from the Party was to be attached to each military district commander to work more closely with him on all issues relating to prisoner-of-war issues. The goals of this greater cooperation were to increase the efficiency of prisoner labor, to overcome local obstacles as soon as they appeared, and to ensure that the disposition of prisoner labor fit the military needs of the German economy for that particular area. Concerning the treatment of prisoners of war, security measures were instituted only so that they improved the efficiency of the prisoners. Close supervision was important so as to ensure that they received the housing and food required for their jobs. Situations in which the prisoners of war were allowed to become physically weak were to be strongly prevented. Further, guards were to be reminded that prisoners of war were soldiers, and thus subject to military obedience, which could be enforced by arms if necessary. Prisoners of war who slacked off were to be subject to immediate disciplinary punishments, and these punishments were to be made known to the other prisoners of war as well. Prisoners who underperformed could also be given less food as a result; this was especially applicable in the case of prisoners of war doing "very-hard-labor" tasks who instead did not work hard enough to justify their rations. The new cooperation between Nazi Party and Wehrmacht was also needed to ensure that the orders of the local area commanders were carried out fully. Through greater supervision, suggestions for disciplinary punishments for slackers could be heard from more sources, and the Wehrmacht could thus crack down harder on those prisoners of war avoiding their duty. The Party leaders would also work to ensure smooth cooperation between the business leaders and the guards, who had the task of supervising work efficiency in addition to maintaining basic security. The adequate supervision of prisoners of war was as much a political task as it was a military task. Therefore, guards could be assigned based on any political consideration which might arise, in cooperation with the Party staff. They could also, then, receive political commendations for a job well done. "Marginal violations of the treatment of prisoners of war by guards, so long as they act to improve efficiency, are not to be pursued [for disciplinary punishment of the guards]."[32]

On October 5, 1944, the OKW issued instructions dealing with leisure time, designed to increase the efficiency of prisoner-of-war labor. Total war, the directive began, demanded the highest levels of efficiency from all labor. With regard to prisoners of war, increasing their efficiency was of vital importance, second only to concerns for national security. At a time when the German public had to do without such distractions as theater, it was inconceivable that prisoners of war enjoyed privileges not available to the public. In consultation with the Party Chancellery, the Propaganda Ministry, and the representatives of labor it was therefore ordered that the pursuance by prisoners of war of leisure activities and the execution of any previous orders pertaining to their free time be modified to take into account the following measures. First, walking to the place of employment was still permitted, whereas movement in the prisoner-of-war camps, work detachments, and prisoner-of-war hospitals was to be constricted so as to conserve energy for work. The cooperation and agreement of the local Party and police detachments was to be sought on a case-by-case basis, if needed. Prisoners of war were to be marched to work in orderly columns, with no fraternization with the guards, and under armed guard at all times. Second, though films could still be seen within the camps and the larger work detachments, public houses could not be used for this purpose. In cases where there was no film apparatus available, arrangements could be made to see a film in a foyer or hall only with the cooperation and agreement of the local Party and Police detachments. Third, participation in public arrangements for entertainment was not permitted. If a factory owner wished to organize a film showing for his foreign-labor employees, the prisoners of war who worked there could also attend, provided proper security measures were in place. Fourth, no working time could be lost due to leisure activities. And fifth, leisure-time measures were to be enjoyed for workers offering a normal level of efficiency; if the prisoners' efficiency was reduced, their leisure-time privileges would be reduced.[33]

On December 3, 1944, the OKW yet again sent out a short memo to all military districts and offices, which dealt with prisoners of war, exhorting the improvement of prisoner-of-war labor efficiency. It started by noting that demands on the German workers at this stage of the war were very great, and although they were doing a wonderful job, Germany had to take greater advantage of every source of available labor, including prisoners of war. Broadly put, there were two simple ways in which prisoner-of-war efficiency could be improved. First, within the realm of common sense, they had to be treated correctly and firmly, and be given good professional guidance and purposeful work tasks. Second, they had to be given suitable, if spartan or stern, supplies and accommodations, and also be made aware of the futility of escape attempts. Good, clear guarding and watchfulness were very important in this regard. German guards should not be surprised that prisoners of war were not especially concerned with working hard or efficiently. That was why proper supervision combined with propaganda was necessary – to make them feel like they wanted to, and should, work harder. Guards had to always be firm, because prisoners of war would take advantage of whatever perceived weaknesses they saw, but not abusive. If everyone, at all levels of command, tightened up their professionalism and treated the prisoners firmly but correctly, they would become more efficient workers.[34]

On December 10, 1944, the OKW ordered that the various mixed nationalities in work detachments be separated and reorganized into individual units; the mixing of nationalities and races in work detachments, up to 8 in some instances, had led to poor work performances. The situation originally began as a result of shortages in the armaments industry and harvests, and spread from there to other types of work detachments. The reasons given for the segregation of the prisoners of war now were that it allowed for: easier treatment of individual large groups of like prisoners of war; better possibilities for propaganda; easier implementation of orders; savings on the number of interpreters and security personnel needed; better exploitation of housing needs in the camps; security measures (material and other) to be more easily implemented; better volunteer and motivation attitudes, especially as regards the eastern areas. The reasons that mixing had proven a big problem were that it led directly to labor disturbances, and that due to the present transportation situation, the displacement of larger groups had become almost impossible. For these reasons, a general order to segregate all prisoner-of-war units was impracticable; however, the military districts were urged and instructed to investigate ways of segregating prisoners of war by nationality as much as was possible.[35]

A day of rest

With regard to the right of prisoners of war to have one 24-hour rest period per week, the OKW, in June 1941, provided a brief summary of permitted work times for prisoners of war, as per the Geneva Convention. It reiterated the main points of the Geneva Convention, and went by the general rule that prisoners of war were expected to perform as well as German workers doing the same task, and for the same amount of time.[36] The time it took prisoners of war to march to and from work was not to be considered working time; this, stated the OKW, corresponded with regulations in effect for German workers. However, as long marches to work impaired the effective usage of prisoner-of-war labor, employers were encouraged to set up housing for the prisoners of war near the worksite. If this was not possible, the work detachment could be replaced.[37]

In reply to specific enquiries from military districts, the Head of the Reserve Forces of the OKW reaffirmed that not allowing prisoners of war a 24-hour rest period per week constituted a violation of the Geneva Convention.[38] One month later, however, the OKW further clarified its position on the issue of rest periods for prisoner-of-war labor: a prisoner was obliged to put in the same hours of labor as a German worker doing a similar task. Every three weeks at the latest, however, the prisoners of war had to be given 24 consecutive hours of rest. If the company for which the prisoners of war worked closed on Sundays, then the prisoners of war's request for Sundays off could be accommodated. However, the rest day did not have to fall on a Sunday. These measures, however, did not apply during times of emergency, such as a late harvest, when sacrifices were being demanded of German workers.[39] In October 1941, the OKW noted that prisoners of war had been complaining that they were made to work more Sundays than German workers doing the same task. This was to be prevented from occurring in the future; not only was this creating diplomatic problems with the Protecting

Powers, but thefts in the relatively deserted workplaces were also increasing.[40]

Boots, pants, and security

With regard to security, a recurring problem for the OKW (with somewhat odd consequences) was what to do to minimize the risk of escape by prisoners of war from work detachments. The most simple solution seemed to be to remove their boots and pants from their possession in the evenings. However, with the prospects of air-raids, this policy caused problems for the safety of the prisoners. After initial opinions to the contrary, the OKW decided, in October 1942, to allow prisoners of war in large work detachments located in areas prone to air-raids to retain their pants and boots at night.[41] By July 1943, the OKW changed its mind again: when possible, prisoners of war being housed in a new work detachment were to have their boots and pants taken away at night, so as to prevent escape attempts.[42] In September 1943, the initiative for deciding what to do was delegated downwards: due to the increase in damage caused by enemy air-raids, the leaders of work detachments were to decide on their own judgment whether or not prisoners of war should retain their pants and boots with them, at night.[43] This appeared to lead to unwanted results, so that, by June 1944, the OKW again decided that, to hinder escape attempts, the pants and boots of prisoners of war in work detachments were not only to be removed at night, but they were to be kept in a place normally inaccessible to the prisoners.[44] Not surprisingly, the OKW noted in September 1944, the previous orders concerning the taking away of pants and boots at night from prisoners of war in work detachments had led to a variety of security measures by different units. The head of the work detachment could henceforth decide that such arrangements were not necessary or undesirable, for instance in cases in which the area was prone to enemy air-raids, or if the prisoners of war in the detachment consisted of volunteer noncommissioned officers.[45]

Other security issues included the OKW's reminder to the camps that private employers of prisoners of war did not have the authority to use force with prisoners. If there was a problem getting prisoners to work, they had to turn the issue over the leader of the work detachment, or the nearest camp control officer. In no cases (except absolute emergencies) were either the employers or their assistants permitted to use force against prisoners of war; such action would be considered bodily assault, and treated accordingly.[46]

Allowing prisoners of war to occasionally leave the workplace had led to abuses of the privilege and escape attempts. Bearing in mind the diverse range of work detachments, prisoners of war in general were only to be allowed to leave the workplace if they were ill and if it was brought to the attention of the Stalags; they, in turn could coordinate proper measures between the work-detachment leaders and the businesses in which the prisoners of war were employed.[47] In certain circumstances in which a trustworthy prisoner-of-war was accommodated far from his workplace, the employer could, with the permission of the camp commandant, issue the prisoner with a bicycle for the trip to and from work. Strict control was to be exercised so that prisoners of war so privileged did not use the bicycles for escape purposes. They had to wear clothing which clearly indicated they were prisoners of war, and carry a pass issued by the camp authorities. The local police were to be informed of the arrangement. At the first instance of abuse, this privilege was to be revoked, and the prisoner would be subject to disciplinary punishment.[48]

By early July 1942, the OKW noted that, in many instances, prisoners of war were threatening either strikes or work stoppages unless ultimatums were accepted. The most common complaints, the OKW wrote, concerned wages and food. The OKW reiterated that under the terms of the Geneva Convention, prisoners of war were obliged to work; the order to work carried the force of a regular and legal military command. Refusal, therefore, constituted disobedience and mutiny. When faced with such situations, the leader of the work detachment had to warn the prisoners that they were refusing a direct and lawful military command, and that they would be court-martialed if they persisted. If the prisoners of war still refused to work, the guards were to force them to work at gunpoint. Should the prisoners of war resist and take up any arms, the guards in extreme circumstances could resort to using their weapons against the prisoners. Recognized or suspected organizers of such strife were to be captured, and an action report was to be sent up the chain of command. All leaders of work detachments, and their guards were to be instructed to take this course of action in such an event.[49] The previous practice of posting prisoners of war to work away from work detachments was, due to a lack of guards, no longer permitted; exceptions could be made only in special circumstances.[50]

A medley of plans

Throughout the course of the war, the OKW issued many specific directives applicable to working British and American prisoners of war. The orders are wide-ranging in topic, and often there are no subsequent orders on the same topic. The cataloging of these orders is the lengthy, if occasionally tedious, necessary final step to providing comprehensive coverage of German military policy on the issue.

The right of the prisoners of war to appoint a Man of Confidence, as per article 43 of the Convention, was considered "essential" by the OKW.[51] In late April 1944, the commander of Wehrkreis XII gave an outline concerning Men of Confidence and prisoners of war. If an MOC represented more than 100 prisoners of war, he was to be given no other work. If he represented between 50 and 100 prisoners of war, he was to be given a half day free per week to fulfill his duties as Man of Confidence. If he represented less than 50 prisoners of war, he was to complete his duties as Man of Confidence on his own leisure time.[52]

Early in May 1942, a single-page handout was issued by the OKW concerning behavior toward working prisoners of war, for use by all who would come into contact with them. It stated that the war-economy necessitated the full employment of all available persons, and therefore the prisoners of war were to be used in a full range of jobs in the service of the economy. Prisoners of war were to be treated in such a way that their full capability was used, in both industry and the agricultural economy. Sufficient nutrition was a precondition for this, but this had to be reciprocal with a willingness to work. Each work-hour lost to illness or malnutrition, was declared a loss for the German economy. The general treatment was to be severe but correct; the Wehrmacht would punish a lack of willingness to work. Lest fraternization seem tempting, Germans were reminded that prisoners of war did not belong to the communities in which they worked; they were not part of the "German family." They fought as soldiers of their land against Germany, and were therefore enemies. Whoever treated them better than German workers became a traitor to the *Volksgemeinschaft*. German women who had relations with prisoners of war placed themselves outside the *Volksgemeinschaft*, and would receive the correspondingly just punishment; even the appearance of a relationship was to be avoided. Whoever became too friendly with prisoners was assisting enemy espionage and sabotage, directed against the German people. The participation of prisoners of war in civil celebrations and events (as well as church functions) attended by Germans, was not permitted. When prisoners of war celebrated an event, it would be by themselves. Individual prisoners of war, who were deemed deserving due to special performances, could be allowed unguarded free movement on parole from their responsible camps. Prisoners of war had to receive all the basic necessities. The appropriate work clothing for specific jobs, e.g.

for mining, chemical or different special tasks, was provided not by the Wehrmacht, but by the businesses in which they were employed. Prisoners of war were not to receive money and valuables, and least of all alcohol, beyond what was necessary for the completion of their regular duties. Their working time depended upon how closely the business was related to the war effort. The prisoners of war had the right to a rest period as well as certain leisure time for the upkeep of clothing and housing. It was necessary for all Germans to heed these basic principles in all their dealings with all prisoners of war; any violation of these guidelines would be considered sabotage against the war effort, and be strictly punished.[53]

One week later, a 12-page pamphlet was issued by the staff of Wehrkreis XVII outlining the OKW's policy on the general duties of employers who received prisoners of war for labor. Though much of this was administrative in nature, concerning the details of issues between the camp staff and the employer, several points concerning the prisoners of war were made. First, the prisoner-of-war was not in an individual labor relationship with the employer; the camp and the employer had a relationship which required the camp to provide a set number of prisoner-of-war laborers. The camp staff could make deductions from the employer if the prisoners of war had to march too great a distance to and from the worksite. The employer could not transfer a prisoner of war to a different employer; each employer had to have an individual contract with the camp; this prohibition could be relaxed in certain cases where rural agricultural work was being undertaken. The total working time of the prisoners of war, including the march to and from work, was not to exceed that of German workers performing a similar task. Likewise, if a German worker had to work Sundays, so too could the prisoners of war. Their 24-hour rest time per week, which was to be granted when possible on a Sunday, was authorized only insofar as a German worker in the same period had the same amount of time off. The employer had to obtain the prisoner's signature acknowledging receipt of pay, which was to be given at the end of each week. Small amounts of reichsmarks (as opposed to camp money) could be issued to the prisoners of war in certain cases, for the procurement of small items (such as cigarettes or razors). The employer did not have to pay prisoners of war for work days lost to bad weather, rest days, sick days, and days in which the prisoners of war had to be deloused or have their clothing or shoes repaired. The employer was responsible for providing the same food as that given to German workers performing the same task, including extra portions for hard labor. Likewise, the employer had to provide food for sick prisoners of war and during bad weather days. The prisoners of war would be sent to the employer with good clothing, and the expense for either replacing clothes worn out at work, or special work clothes, had to be carried by the employer. Lastly, the German employer was obliged to provide the same accident benefits for injured prisoners of war as were available for German workers.[54]

On July 1, 1943, another one-page handout on the handling of prisoners of war, first issued in 1942, was updated. The new version unequivocally ordered that prisoners of war be sufficiently fed, stated that their firm handling was essential to achieving benefits for Germany, and replaced "each encounter with insufficient distance being maintained" with simply "each encounter" between Germans and prisoners of war to be counted as espionage or sabotage against the German people. It also gave further emphasis to the view that prisoners of war were to be considered valuable manpower, and any business which misused or neglected the possible manpower worked directly against the German war effort. The labor of a prisoner of war was of greater consequence than the individual interests of the businesses which employed them.[55]

The OKW made provisions for the allocation of prisoners of war who were either asked for individually or who had expertise in a given field. In late May 1941, prisoners of war who were asked for by name by a firm, were allowed to be transferred to the appropriate work detachment, provided they passed the necessary security clearances.[56] In early July 1941, the OKW began to ask camps to inform the Wehrkreise and OKW of prisoners of war possessing specialized skills, so it could be decided how best to employ them.[57] Some prisoners of war, according to the OKW, were being entrusted with scientific research, such as with German research institutes. So that no misunderstandings occurred, the names of these prisoners of war were to be announced (to their coworkers). However, hints as to the details of their captivity or ancestry were not to be permitted.[58] Where possible, guards were to allow prisoners of war to work in fields in which they had some experience as civilians. Though there would be transportation difficulties, these would be more than offset by the increase in productivity that came from using previously well-trained personnel.[59] Businessmen requesting prisoner-of-war laborers had to make their application to the local civilian labor boards, and not the prisoner-of-war camp commandant. Prisoners could only be sent to work for a business if the approval came through the regular channels from the military district headquarters.[60]

British prisoners of war could, the OKW decided in July 1943, be used as tractor drivers in agricultural businesses, provided that proper security conditions were met.[61] Prisoners who tended to the prisoner-of-war graveyards should preferably be of the same nationality as the dead prisoners of war. They were to fulfill their chore during leisure time, and tend to the crosses, paths, and weeding of the graves.[62]

On the general issue of air-raids, the OKW ordered, in September 1943, that leaders of work detachments ensure that they designate a backup meeting place for prisoners of war to assemble at, should their barracks be destroyed during an air-raid. This meeting place was to be clearly indicated and made known to all prisoners in the detachment.[63] On June 8, 1944, the OKW stated that working prisoners of war had the same obligations toward making up lost time due to air-raids as German and foreign civilian workers. Injuries sustained as a result of an air-raid at the workplace were to be considered as work-related.[64] Further measures for action to be taken by prisoners of war upon enemy air-raids were laid out by the OKW in July 1944. At the workplace, the employer was responsible for posting clear notices describing air-raid procedures for his workers. The guards and assistant-guards, however, retained the responsibility for security. If prisoners of war were surprised by an air-raid in the midst of a march, there was to be no question as to whether or not they were permitted to seek shelter in the nearest private or public shelter; the only condition was that German civilians had priority, and that the prisoners of war were to be kept in one large group, preferably away from the civilians. Under no circumstances were prisoners of war to intermingle with German civilians. Only if enough guards were present could the prisoners of war be broken down into smaller units, and seek protection in different shelters.[65]

With regard to food, the OKW, on April 8, 1942, responded to complaints from prisoners of war in work detachments, who said they weren't receiving even one hot meal a day, by ordering the commandants and employers to make sure that the midday meal was a hot meal.[66] For security reasons, unused portions of collective parcels, such as tins of food, were to be kept under locked storage away from prisoners in work detachments. Only the leader of the work detachment, or his designated guard, could have a key; the Man of Confidence was to have regular access to the stores. Prisoners of war in any event had to sign to acknowledge receipt of these and individual parcels.[67] In May 1942, the OKW prohibited prisoners of war from bringing to work, items from their collective parcels which were scarce in the German civilian population, such as coffee or chocolate. The prisoners of war had to consume these items in their barracks.[68] In December 1942, the OKW ordered the camp commandants to personally oversee the application of a previous order forbidding the prisoners of war from consuming chocolate or coffee while at work. The previous order prohibited it to maintain the morale of German workers, who, because of war shortages, were having to do without such luxuries.[69]

On the issue of clothing, the camps were reminded by the OKW, in August 1942, that the provision and maintenance of work clothing to prisoners of war in work detachments were the responsibility of the employers. The prisoners of war were not to be charged for these items.[70] The private employers of prisoner-of-war workers were also responsible for making sure their undergarments were in good condition. Therefore, they recommended sending prisoner-of-war clothing out to be privately laundered. They could charge a maximum of RM1.5 per month for laundry costs.[71] Regulations concerning the responsibility of the employer of prisoners of war to provide protective work clothing were amended, in December 1942, by the addition of the following: "The employer is obliged to provide work and protection clothing for prisoners of war in the same scope as required by the responsible Economic-offices for German manpower, and to obtain them at his own expense."[72]

At the end of October 1939, camp commandants were reminded that prisoners of war in work detachments were only to be sent to a German civilian doctor in case of emergency; in all other cases, the prisoner was to be seen by a German military doctor in the camp infirmary.[73]

In early November 1941, the OKW issued emergency orders to help with the potato harvest. Due to a shortage of workers, according to the order, everyone who was able had to take part in helping bring in the harvest. This included every unassigned prisoner of war from all the camps, both Oflags and Stalag. All the officers' orderlies had to report for duty for the duration of this measure. This special bulletin was regretted, but considered justifiable, as everyone, including prisoners of war, would be eating potatoes the upcoming winter. The order was to last for three weeks.[74] A few weeks later, the same terms were ordered for the sugarbeet harvest.[75] Toward the end of August 1942, the OKW decided that prisoners of war would once again be pressed into working for the upcoming harvest season.[76]

Regarding the canteens in the work detachments, the OKW, in January 1943, prohibited the sale of any prisoner-of-war crafts or works of art, either with or without the help of German guards. Such works were only to be placed in the canteen's storage if they were no longer needed out.[77] On March 9, 1943, the OKW reaffirmed permission for prisoners of war to raise Angora rabbits and sell their pelts through the military district agricultural administrator. The proceeds from such sales were to go to the prisoners' canteen.[78]

A notice from the OKW demanding that all German staff have one gas-attack drill day per month included the statement that, as members of Germany's economic manpower, prisoners of war were also to be in a position to function at work during a gas attack. Therefore, the camps had to make at least nominal provisions for prisoners of war in this regard.[79]

Wages

In July 1943, the OKW reiterated that private employers of prisoners of war could only pay them in camp money, and not in Reichsmarks. The prisoners of war could be permitted to exchange camp money for RM for the purpose of purchasing supplies from merchants, but these exchanges were only to be conducted through the camp's administration.[80] To prevent too much camp money from getting around, and to reduce the strain on the camp money's printers, the OKW ordered the camps and the employers of prisoners of war to credit surplus balances of pay to the prisoners' accounts in the main camps, instead of paying out cash.[81]

Prisoner-of-war officers sent to Stalags in the performance of their duties were to be paid by the Stalags, and not their original Oflags. However, prisoner officers who were in hospital or infirmary at the end of each month (pay day) received their base salary from their Oflag, and supplemental sick pay from the hospital's funds.[82]

Fewer wages

A common practice among all the major belligerents purportedly adhering to the Geneva Convention regulations concerning prisoner-of-war labor, was the deduction of money from the prisoners' wages for room and board. On May 10, 1940, an update to the initial deduction rates were issued for working prisoners of war in Germany. Earlier, the daily deductions from pay for accommodation were set at RM0.20 for summer months and RM0.40 winter months. Food deductions were set at RM1.20 per day. It turned out, however, that these rates were in fact too high. Therefore, the new rates were: for food, RM0.80 per day (0.90 for hard work and 1.00 for extremely hard work, with no deductions for the days the prisoners of war didn't work); for accommodations, RM0.40 per day for winter months was too high, so it was henceforth RM0.20 per day all year round.[83]

At the end of June 1940, new rates were set by the OKW for deductions from the pay of western prisoners of war for clothing and camp materials. The previous rates for clothing were RM0.15 per day. The new rate was set at RM0.09 per day. Camp material costs were deducted from prisoners of war at a rate of RM0.50 per month. Now, for Western prisoners of war, the rate was to be set at RM0.01 per day. The new rates were to apply only to the Western prisoners of war.[84] Employers of prisoners of war could deduct from their wages expenses for food and housing for only the first three days of an illness. No more deductions than that were permitted, and employers were to be warned against making unjustified deductions.[85]

Prisoners of war had been subjected to financial deductions of their accounts in some areas, for the purpose of "administration expenses contribution." Camps, which had limited administrative supplies were passing along part of the costs to the prisoners of war. This was not justifiable. In the future, deductions of prisoner-of-war money made without the permission of the OKW were expressly forbidden.[86]

It had been noticed by some Stalag administrators that German employers of prisoners of war were placing the general tax (*Pauschalsteuer*) on prisoners' wages after the deductions for food and accommodations; the tax was to be placed before the deductions were made.[87] The federal ministry of finance decided, in January 1944, that prisoner-of-war wages were not to be subject to income tax. In instances where tax was being deducted, the practice was to be stopped, though without recompense.[88]

Working overtime

Overtime pay for prisoners of war, the OKW decided in June 1941, was not permitted; prisoners of war who were occasionally required to work more than the scheduled hours would be paid the regular rate. Prisoners of war could only receive increases in pay if they were engaged in piecemeal work. As prisoners of war were provided to businesses at a flat rate, interruptions of labor due to air-raids were not the responsibility of the OKW; the burdens of such lost time were to be borne by the businessman himself.[89]

In March 1942, the OKW slightly changed its stance on the issue of overtime pay for prisoners of war. After defining overtime as hours put in beyond a regular work day (defined as what was required of German workers), three main points were made: the employer set the preconditions for which overtime pay could be given; the employer set the maximum amount to be paid to the prisoner; and overtime pay could be disbursed at a rate of RM0.20 for the first hour and RM0.30 for each additional hour. These rates and conditions applied to Sundays and holidays as well. However, the same regulations did not apply to prisoners of war engaged in agricultural or forest labor; employers in these fields could give increases in pay to recognize willing and especially hard-working prisoners of war.[90] In May 1942, the OKW decided that prisoners of war who worked especially hard could be paid a performance bonus, to be no more than 20 percent of a German worker's bonus for similar work.[91]

Pay, rank, and status

The OKW also issued policy directives on two fundamental factors which could determine the pay given to a prisoner of war: his rank, and his status (medical personnel or clergy, versus regular prisoners of war). The OKW noted that delays often occurred before a prisoner of war's claim to medical personnel status; when the status was finally clarified, the difference in pay was to be retroactively applied to the period of delay.[92] For the payment of medical personnel, it was crucial, the OKW deemed in late October 1942, that their recognition as such be confirmed from the home army. Until that point, they had to be considered as normal prisoners of war performing volunteer medical tasks.[93] Prisoner-of-war clergy and medical personnel waiting to be repatriated were to be paid their salaries up to the day they were to be handed over, out of German custody. Remaining financial credits were then to be transferred to them by the same procedure as other repatriated prisoners of war.[94] British Warrant-Officers who were medical personnel were, as per the Geneva Convention on the Sick and Wounded of 1929, to be paid the same as personnel of the same rank and position of the Detaining Power.[95]

The OKW noted that exact translations of ranks between the British and German militaries was impossible, and issued this clarification to be acted upon immediately. Henceforth, all Midshipmen, Warrant-Officers, and Acting Pilots were to be regarded as officers, and be transferred, if they were not already there, to Oflags. Monthly pay for them was, respectively, RM60, RM60, and RM72. Corporals and Bombardiers were to be treated as noncommissioned officers; Lance-Corporals and Lance-Bombardiers were the equivalent of the German Gefreite.[96] After the OKW decided, in May 1943, that United States Army, Navy, Marine

Corps, and Coast Guard Warrant-Officers and Chief Warrant-Officers were to be treated as officers, it concluded that Warrant-Officers were to be paid RM60 per month, while Chief Warrant-Officers were to be receive RM72 per month.[97]

Ranks of the Indian Army were clarified for the purposes of pay by the OKW in September 1943. There were two major categories: (a) British officers with the King's commission, Indian officers with the King's commission, and Indian officers with commission; and (b) officers with the Vice-Regal's commission, consisting of Risaldar Major and Subadar Major (equivalent to the German rank of Major), Risaldar and Subadar (the equivalent of First Lieutenant), and Jemadar (the equivalent of Lieutenant). The first group held ranks equivalent to regular British officers, and were to be paid accordingly. The second group were to be treated as British officers, but to be paid RM45 per month, regardless of which rank they hold.[98]

As American authorities paid German noncommissioned officers and men up to a maximum of $3.00 a month regardless of whether or not they worked, American noncommissioned officers and other-ranks in German captivity were to be paid up to RM7.5 per month. The American prisoners of war were to be informed of this through their Men of Confidence.[99] At the start of June 1944, the OKW moved to give back-pay to British Army Warrant-Officers who had not received their correct pay while in captivity before June 1943, when their precise status and entitled pay was settled.[100]

On January 2, 1945, the German government noted the differences between payment of German officers and American officers. The American monthly pay rates were: Leutnant and Oberleutnant – $20 (RM50); Hauptmann – $30 (RM75); Major and higher ranks – $40 (RM100). The German monthly pay rates were: Leutnant – RM72; Oberleutnant – RM81; Hauptmann – RM96; Major – RM108; Obersleutnant – RM120; Oberst – RM150. The German government asked that both countries use the German payscale, but the American government refused, and was paying German prisoner-of-war officers according to their scale. Accordingly, the German government decided to make up the difference in pay for the German officers in American captivity, and would reduce the pay they gave to American prisoner-of-war officers in turn, by the following, every month: RM25, 37.5, and 50 respectively, commencing March 1, 1945. American prisoner-of-war officers were to be informed of these measures accordingly; the American Government was being told through the Protecting Power.[101]

General finance

In addition to labor conditions and pay, the OKW also regulated the process by which money and foreign currencies could be held by prisoners of war. These regulations and orders to the camps usually concerned the rights of prisoners concerning foreign currencies, financial transfers, and other such general issues dealing with money. In no section of the German military manuals in place at the start of the war, were these issues dealt with – the OKW determined policy in this field as it went along.

Foreign currencies and transfers

In early July 1940, the OKW sent out two orders clarifying the procedure to be followed for taking care of foreign currencies held by prisoners of war in hospitals, and in the main camps. In the hospitals, for security reasons, all currencies were to be confiscated, with a receipt given. The currencies would be sent to Berlin, while a credit for the amount taken would be added to the prisoners of war account back at his main camp. Prisoners of war in the main camps who wished to send money home to their families had to do so through the Deutsche Bank in Berlin, with the exchange rates set by the German authorities.[102] On April 19, 1943, the OKW further clarified that, in the main camps, it was up to the prisoners of war themselves to either hold onto their foreign currencies in storage, or to sell them for German currency. Should they wish to sell, it was to be done by the camp administrative staff through the nearest major German bank branch. If they sold, though, the prisoners of war ran the risk of not being able to take the money with them if they were released from captivity.[103] British prisoners of war were not permitted to send home British currencies. They could only send home money transferred first into Reichsmarks. However, no transaction could take place without the prisoner's agreement as to the exchange rate. These conditions did not apply, however, for the remaining valuables of deceased prisoners of war.[104] Currencies removed from American prisoners could, with their approval, be sent to the Deutsche Bank in Berlin for either conversion into Reichsmarks or to be sent to a specified recipient in the United States. The individual prisoners of war had to be given a receipt for the transaction. The remittance of the Reichsmarks to the prisoners of war in their camps would be regulated later.[105]

In July 1941, the OKW responded to requests from prisoners of war that receipts be given for currency transfers, so that, in the event of later confusion, proof could be offered that the transaction had taken place. The OKW was of the opinion that issuing formal receipts for every such transaction would be too much of an administrative burden. The notable exception, however, was when prisoners of war paid for a currency transaction in cash [camp money] to the German head of a work detachment; anytime money was given to the administration in this fashion, an acknowledging receipt was to be given to the prisoner. Further, the Men of Confidence were to be given a receipt for collective remittances; their own lists of the individual contributors could be used should a later problem arise.[106]

As of November 1, 1943, British prisoners of war were allowed to arrange for money from their credit amount on their personnel cards to be sent home. On the tenth day of each month, the camps could submit a relevant list to the OKW for this purpose. Requests were to be signed in duplicate by the prisoners of war, and receipts were to be issued by the camp authorities. On the list, the prisoners of war were to write the name and address of the recipients. The moneys would eventually be disbursed by the British Government.[107]

Foreign currency and money found on captured British and American airmen were to be treated as any other valuables found on any other prisoner of war: the value and description of the objects taken were to be recorded on the prisoners' personnel card. Only in the case of uncommonly large amounts of money was the issue to be referred to higher authorities.[108]

Loose change

Prisoners of war were prohibited from opening accounts at German financial institutions. The Men of Confidence, so as not to be held completely accountable for the prisoners of war's collective money, could open a special account with the camp administration, from which deductions for prisoner canteen purchases could be made daily. These accounts would be subject to periodic audits.[109] Those being transferred to camps in the General Gouvernement area were to have their camp money taken away from them before transfer, with the amounts taken inscribed on their personnel cards.[110] In mid-December 1942 the OKW noted that prisoners of war seemed to be hoarding their money. This was to be halted; from now on, prisoners of war could keep a maximum of RM30 on their person. The rest of their money was to be kept in their "bank" credit accounts in the camp.[111]

In February 1942, the OKW laid out its policy concerning prisoner-of-war private property damaged due to air-raids: they were not to be reimbursed for damage claims from Reich funds, because the orders concerning damaged goods due to air-raids did not apply to prisoners of war.[112]

In early April 1942, the OKW determined that any purchases made for the direct benefit of the prisoners of war should come from profits of the camp canteens if there were any; only if there weren't any should the camp funds pay.[113]

The valuables and money of prisoners of war who had escaped but not been recaptured could be turned over to the camp funds, the OKW stated in May 1942.[114] At the end of October 1942, the OKW ordered that any costs from repairing material damages to the camps from either sabotage or escape attempts be incurred by the prisoners of war, if necessary through their canteen funds, as was apparently the practice in England and Canada.[115] On April 19, 1943, the phrase "canteen funds" was ordered cancelled by the OKW.[116]

In a final minor addendum to financial issues concerning prisoners of war, the OKW decided in March 1944 that dental costs were to be borne by the camps if the dental work was of medical necessity. Wreaths for burials of prisoners of war were also to be paid for by Germany, but any other decorations were to be paid for by the other prisoners of war. Working prisoners of war were not to be charged for laundry costs. Replacement of lost or misdelivered tobacco was to be paid for by Germany. Other minor costs, such as those pertaining to the running of the prisoner-of-war canteens, were to be carried by the prisoners of war themselves.[117]

5.2 External relations of prisoners of war

Legal angels

Under the terms of the Geneva Convention, the Protecting Power was a neutral state which represented the legal concerns of the prisoner-of-war's home country. The United States, until its entry into the war in 1941, served as the Protecting Power for the British Commonwealth prisoners of war; thereafter, Switzerland served in that capacity for both the United States and the British Commonwealth countries.[118] The main description of the duties and rights of the Protecting Power and its delegates came in article 86, which allowed for the appointment of delegates, subject to the approval of the Detaining Power, who would be "authorized to proceed to any place, without exception, where prisoners of war are interned. They shall have access to all premises occupied by prisoners and may hold conversation with prisoners, as a general rule without witnesses, either personally or through the intermediary of interpreters." The belligerents undertook to facilitate the task of the Protecting Power delegates in any way they could. Elsewhere in the Geneva Convention, the Protecting Power was mentioned only sporadically, in relation to prisoners' rights.

The prisoners of war had the legal right to correspond, via their MOC, unhindered with the Protecting Power delegates, and to address any requests, complaints about their treatment, or possible violations of the Convention to them. Specifically, the opportunity for the involvement of the Protecting Power was envisioned in: article 31, for labor; article 39, for receiving books; articles 42, for the general conditions of captivity; articles 43–4, for the rights of MOCs to be in contact with the Protecting Power; articles 60, 62, 65, and 66, for assistance and notifications during judicial proceedings; article 77, for communications between the belligerents regarding information bureaus and relief organizations; and article 87, as the diplomatic intermediary between the belligerents, to help settle, with the ICRC, any disputes between the warring countries.

The specific area in which the role of the Protecting Power was most explicitly described – as opposed to more general mentions in passing – by the Convention concerned the issue of judicial proceedings against prisoners of war. At the start of any judicial hearing against a prisoner of war, the Protecting Power had to be notified as quickly as possible, and at least three weeks, before the opening date of a judicial hearing against a prisoner of war. The following information had to be included in the official notification to the Protecting Power: the status and rank of the prisoner, the place of residence or detention, a statement of the charge or charges, and a statement of the legal provisions applicable.[119] The right to choose legal counsel went first to the prisoner. However, failing a choice by him, the Protecting Power could appoint an attorney to represent the prisoner; upon the Protecting Power's request, the Detaining Power was obliged to provide a list of qualified counsels. The Protecting Power representatives also had the right to attend the hearing, except in cases where national security demanded secrecy; in such cases, the Protecting Power had to be notified of the situation in advance.[120] Sentences against the prisoners had to be communicated immediately to the Protecting Power.[121] In cases where a sentence of death was passed, a detailed communication describing the nature and circumstances of the offense had to be given to the Protecting Power, who would in turn pass it along to the prisoner's home army; the sentence was not to be carried out until at least three months after the communication was given to the Protecting Power.[122]

The German manuals in place at the start of the war did not comment very much on the role of Protecting Power delegates, except to reaffirm the rights of the prisoners of war to be in contact with them during judicial proceedings, and to confirm the rights of the prisoners to complain to them.[123] In 1942, as well, Dr. Waltzog wrote that the legal position of the Protecting Power was merely as the intermediary between the home state of the prisoner and the Detaining Power for legal purposes. Most of his short commentary on this matter was devoted to the issue of states, which no longer existed, a situation not relevant to the British or American prisoners.[124] Overall, then, and as will be seen from the relatively few additional comments made regarding the Protecting Power by the OKW over the war years, their position and function was regarded as being an uncontroversial intermediary between the belligerents, concerning prisoner-of-war affairs.

In November 1941, the OKW responded to complaints from American Protecting Power delegates that British prisoners of war were not given enough advance warning of the delegates' visits to camps. It was in Germany's interest, the OKW reasoned, that the prisoners of war be prepared for the visits, so that there were fewer delays while the delegate waited for prisoners' representatives (MOCs or senior officers) to get organized, and the visits were accomplished more quickly. Therefore, the prisoners of war were henceforth to be given more advance notice of the visits, so that they could better prepare themselves.[125] This was still the case by January 1943, when the OKW noted that on many occasions during visits by foreign delegates to prisoner-of-war camps, the prisoners' requests to the delegate took up an inordinate amount of time. Henceforth, any requests the prisoners had for the visiting delegate were to be made in writing, and passed along from the Man of Confidence to the camp commandant, who would then present them.[126] Complaints by prisoners of war which could not be immediately addressed to their satisfaction by the camp commandant, had to be expedited as quickly as possible to either the Protecting Power or the ICRC, with a German translation containing the opinion of the commandant.[127]

The OKW reminded camp commandants, in July 1943, that all complaints and requests from the prisoners of war to their Protecting Power had to be expedited as quickly as possible, without delays. Further, if the complaint turned out to have been groundless, no punishment could be given to the prisoners of war (article 42 of the Geneva Convention). Requests and complaints directed to the camp commandant or other military departments could, on the other hand, be rejected by the appropriate departments if necessary.[128] Regarding the general issue of complaints coming from prisoners of war, the OKW decided that although greater haste had to be attempted in dealing with them, this should not come at the expense of refusing a potentially time-consuming investigation; the repeat of a single complaint provided sufficient grounds for this to occur.[129]

Reacting to rumors that "Western" prisoners of war had been told by their superiors that, if captured by the Germans, they would be shot, the OKW ordered, in mid-June 1942, that camp commandants were to try to get statements from individual prisoners of war who were told this, so that a formal complaint could be lodged with the Protecting Power and the ICRC.[130]

The rules regarding the right of the prisoners' representatives to contact their Protecting Power were slightly modified by the OKW in June 1942. Though British prisoners of war were permitted to write directly to their Protecting Power, the Swiss Legation in Berlin, they could not, decided the OKW, address an individual inspector, but rather the Prisoner-of-war Department of the legation.[131] At the same time, the OKW decided that, for reasons of reciprocity, the Protecting Power could receive monthly statements concerning the receipt of collective parcels from the British Men of Confidence.[132] In any instance in which a British prisoner-of-war was shot or wounded, a military investigation had to be launched, led by an officer appointed by a military court. The prisoner-of-war's comrades were to be kept together so that the officer could have the chance to interview them. The resulting report would be sent to the Protecting Power and the OKW.[133]

In Oflags containing prisoners of war of different nationalities, each nationality was to have its own senior officer. The senior officer represented the interests of the officers of his own nationality, and not those of others. He was the liaison to the ICRC, the Protecting Power, and the camp commandant. He was not responsible for the interests of other prisoners of war.[134] The right of the Men of Confidence or Senior Medical Officers (for prisoner-of-war hospitals) to present the visiting foreign delegates with a list of complaints or needs was also reaffirmed by the OKW. When possible, the list was to be forwarded in advance, so the discussion between the delegate and the Man of Confidence or Senior Medical Officer could be conducted as quickly as possible.[135]

In the final significant directive concerning the Protecting Power for the British and American prisoners of war, the OKW noted that some American prisoners of war had received notice of their promotion from the visiting Swiss protection power delegate; the OKW ordered the camps not to recognize the promotions until they could be officially confirmed by the US Government.[136]

Medical angels

The International Committee of the Red Cross (ICRC), based in Geneva, was expressly designated as a relief agency with significant responsibilities, under the Geneva Convention. While the Protecting Power acted as legal guardian for the prisoners of war, the ICRC acted as their general physician, responsible for inspecting the camps to ensure satisfactory levels of health and hygiene existed, and attempting to ensure that adequate levels of food were provided.[137] In addition to its inspections, the ICRC also acted as a humanitarian intermediary between the belligerents: "collective consignments" (the Convention's phrase for the collective food and clothing parcels) sent from the various British and American national Red Cross societies were delivered to the prisoners of war through the efforts of the ICRC in Geneva,[138] which also coordinated efforts with the prisoners' representatives to deal with the needs of individual camps.[139] Also, the "capture cards" sent by the prisoners of war immediately upon capture went to their home countries' Information Bureaus[140] via the ICRC, who ran the Central Agency for information about prisoners of war.[141] In the event that a conference was required to work out further agreements between the belligerents via their Protecting Powers, the ICRC could appoint delegates to facilitate the task.[142] No diplomatic chores accepted by the ICRC, however, were to act as an obstacle to the humanitarian work it performed, which was its primary task.[143]

The tasks of the ICRC received no mention in the 1939 German manuals for the commandants of prisoner-of-war camps; likewise, Dr. Waltzog's 1942 reassessment of the Geneva Convention provided no commentary alongside the reprint of the articles, which dealt with the ICRC's responsibilities. Presumably, then, the OKW felt the Convention's general description of the duties of the ICRC was self-explanatory; the directives issued during the course of the war had more to do with the mechanics of the keeping of updated lists of prisoners of war for transmission to the ICRC, and collective parcel deliveries, than anything else.

That there was concern as to the speed with which the German military was releasing the names of captured prisoners of war was apparent in a letter sent by ICRC official Carl J. Burckhardt on June 22, 1940, to the OKW's Prisoner-of-war Department. In it, he forwarded complaints from the British government that, after the sinking of the *Glorious*, the

Ardent, and the *Castra*, they had a list of more than 100 sailors thought to be prisoners of war who had not yet had their names forwarded by Germany. The letter urged to OKW to move with greater haste in such circumstances.[144]

Two days later, an administrative order was sent out requiring, among other things, that: Oflags and Stalags send in updated lists of prisoners of war every 10 days to WASt, starting September 25; a personnel card be filled out for each prisoner and a copy sent up the chain of command, as required by the Geneva Convention; hospitals send in prisoner-of-war lists every 7 days to WASt; lists of prisoners of war be forwarded to the Protecting Power representatives and the ICRC, as required by articles 77 and 79.[145] In early February 1941, more and more wounded prisoners of war in France were being treated in local, private clinics, rather than being sent to military hospitals and infirmaries. The OKW ordered that a list of all such enemy soldiers be sent to OKW for transmission to the ICRC in Geneva, so that their families could be informed of their situations.[146] Brief summaries of the medical condition of ill prisoners of war had to be sent to the ICRC in Geneva, via the OKW, as of October 1941. In addition to a brief description of the medical illness, it was to be noted if the prisoner was a candidate for repatriation, and if so, when it was proposed to occur.[147]

With the entrance of the United States into the war, parcels and letters which had previously been sent through American aid agencies, no longer could be. The ICRC in Geneva had agreed to act as an intermediary in the future for donor organizations. Therefore, packets would be sent through Geneva, including a stamp indicating the nationality of the prisoners of war involved.[148]

On June 20, 1942, the OKW published a small booklet on the visits of foreigners to prisoner-of-war camps, which reiterated and repeated many of the previous guidelines. It reaffirmed that the ICRC was a "recognized aid agency" (article 78); the representatives of the ICRC had as primary concerns the material conditions of the prisoners of war, such as food, clothing, and medicine. To this end, visiting delegates had the legal right as well to speak with the prisoners of war, without supervision from German officials. Private conversations between other foreigners and the prisoners of war were prohibited, unless prior approval had been granted by the OKW. Greeting of foreign visitors was the responsibility of the camp commandant, or, if he was indisposed, his representative. The language of the visit was German; translators had to be made available if necessary. The course of the visit was to be discussed in advance with the camp leadership; the Security Officer was in charge of these preparations. Inspections of hygienic facilities by the delegates of the MMC or the ICRC were to have the German camp doctor present. It was important, the OKW stressed, that the visits be hosted with correct courtesy and politeness; a good relationship with the delegates helped to ensure that their visits to German prisoners abroad would be conducted properly. In general, the delegates could only pose questions to the leading officers of the camp; officers were not allowed to answer any questions concerning other camps. All political conversations with the delegates were prohibited. Offering or accepting any special favors was prohibited; however, the delegates could, if they wished, join the visit leaders for meals. Photographic equipment was not to be forcibly removed from the delegates; they were to be informed, however, that taking pictures was strictly prohibited. In exceptional circumstances, the visitor who was allowed to take pictures would show proper authorization from the OKW. In general, delegates were allowed to visit work detachments attached to the camps; special permission was not required. However, the delegates could only visit the prisoners' housing at the work detachments, and also speak with the prisoners of war; they were not permitted to visit the workplace. It was to be explained that, for reasons of military security, such visits were not allowed. Visits by foreign delegates to work detachments were to be led by an officer. The OKW liaison officer was responsible for coordinating the visits; in conjunction with him, therefore, was the duration of the visit to be decided. The reports of the delegates went not only to the OKW and the Foreign Office, but also to the ICRC, and from there, to all the countries of the world. It was therefore important that the delegates received as favorable an impression as possible; the reports would likely affect the treatment of German prisoners of war held by the enemies.[149]

In addition to lists of the total number of British prisoners of war being sent in reports to the ICRC, the number from each Dominion was also to be included (Australia, New Zealand, South Africa, Canada, Ireland, India).[150] And for the upcoming Christmas of 1942, the OKW decided to permit the distribution of 200,000 Christmas brochures from the YMCA, the British king's book gifts for Canadian and Australian prisoners of war, as well as a Christmas Greeting from their prime ministers.[151] Newsletters from the ICRC were only to be passed along to the Men of Confidence if it was clear that the OKW had approved them. Doubtful cases were to be referred to the OKW for clarification.[152]

British prisoners of war could, according to the OKW, make donations to the British Red Cross. The donation was to be collected in bulk, sent to the OKW, and from there would be transferred to the British Red Cross through the ICRC.[153]

A collective necessity

The collective parcels (or "consignments") of food and clothing were vital to the health of the prisoners of war; as noted above, the German military calculated on generous shipments to the prisoners of war when it decided to cut its own food rations to them by a third. Generally speaking, and after taking note of the low initial German rations issued to the prisoners of war, the problems of the prisoner food rations which occurred in the final stages of the war came about as a result of the increased difficulty of sending collective parcels either by road or rail in an increasingly chaotic Germany, to the prisoner-of-war camps.

On August 21, 1940, before the American entrance into the war, the OKW ordered that, in the interests of ensuring that German prisoners of war in British captivity receive American Red Cross parcels, the British prisoners of war in German captivity should be given the same number of parcels, of equal value, from the German Red Cross without delay.[154]

Guards were reminded, in June 1940, to open prisoner-of-war packages only in the presence of either the prisoner or his agent; missing tobacco led some prisoners of war to complaints and accusations of theft against the guards.[155] In September 1941, due to complaints from the Protecting Power inspectors and many Men of Confidence, the OKW reaffirmed its previous instructions, that collective parcels be opened and stored only with the participation of the camp Man of Confidence, and never without them or his delegate.[156] Further, in response to complaints of delays in delivering packages to sick prisoners of war, the camps were ordered to make any necessary improvements to their storage facilities so this would not be a problem in the future.[157]

On February 1, 1942, the OKW reminded camp commandants of the need to receive written receipts from the Men of Confidence acknowledging delivery of the collective parcels. Men of Confidence who wished to send clothing to another camp had to do so through the offices of the commandant; direct contact was prohibited.[158] Two months later, the OKW again felt it necessary to precisely delineate who was responsible for what, concerning collective parcels. Responsibility for administering the release of collective parcels to the prisoners of war was given to the

Administration branch of the camp, and not the camp security officer. The security officer was only permitted to go through the parcels with the aim of ensuring no illegal items slipped by into the camp.[159] The delivery of collective parcels of the ICRC to BABs was the direct responsibility of the military district headquarters, who were expected to use the distribution network of the nearest Stalag as much as possible.[160]

From the collective parcels, the ICRC, according to the OKW, wanted to create a one-month reserve supply of both food and clothing for the prisoners in each camp. As it would be administratively difficult for the OKW to collate a list of needed material, the camp commandants were authorized to cooperate directly on this matter with the Men of Confidence, who would then contact the ICRC to obtain the necessary supplies.[161]

To ensure the proper delivery of adequate ICRC parcels, the Man of Confidence was to countersign the list sent from the camp to Geneva, verifying the total number of prisoners of war in the camp.[162] Standard British Red Cross parcels could henceforth be examined by spot checks, rather than individually. Collective parcels sent by companies licensed by the British Red Cross (usually containing books, sports equipment, and tobacco), would still be individually examined by the censors.[163] Also, parcel request slips could now also be mailed to charitable organizations in the United States.[164] To avoid undesirable repercussions for German prisoners of war and civilian internees, the OKW permitted the British and American Red Cross to send parcels to prisoners of war of other nationalities, with the exception of those from the Soviet Union.[165]

British and American prisoners of war were permitted to receive parcels of up to 10 kilos in weight, provided the contents were indivisible.[166] With the aim of reducing the amount of luggage prisoners of war had in the camps, British prisoners were permitted to send superfluous pieces to the ICRC in Geneva for safe storage.[167] In general, camps were to only store parcel reserves relative to the storage space available for this purpose. Clothing parcels, including blankets, were to be continued to be accepted, but with regard to parcel foods, delivery of them was to be stopped only if the Men of Confidence requested it, and through the camp commandant, with immediate notification being made to the ICRC. The supplies of the individual nationalities were to be kept separate.[168]

As of October 1943, all packages and collective parcels which could not immediately be delivered due to security or other reasons would be placed in storage using the two-key system.[169] On June 15, 1944, this order was repeated, with the addition that this system was to apply to all areas within the camps and work detachments in which collective parcels were stored.[170] According to the OKW, German law stated that Germany only had to replace damaged clothing or goods from collective parcels if it could be shown that the damage was the result of an individual's malice. Prisoners of war were not, therefore, entitled to replacements of goods damaged in the normal course of transportation. An exception to this was only valid for prisoners of war from Canada and Great Britain, based on an earlier arrangement with the governments of those countries. In the event that goods arrived damaged, the prisoners were to declare it immediately, so these could be withdrawn by the Men of Confidence. Camp canteen profits could no longer be used for covering these damages.[171]

In collective parcels from the American Red Cross, tobacco had occasionally arrived in packages bearing propaganda, usually the word "Freedom." It had been determined by the OKW that these packages were not sent with malicious intent, but had initially been intended for propaganda uses domestically within the United States. And as there was no malicious intent on the part of the senders, confiscation of the tobacco packages was not necessary, provided they did not contain specifically anti-German sentiments; the tobacco was to be passed along without the packaging. The American Red Cross had been informed of the problem and promised not to send anymore such packages, but asked that those already en route be accepted.[172] Likewise, personal letters and parcels arriving for American prisoners of war were held back on occasion because of objectionable ink-stamp slogans used by the American post office on the stamps. The American government assured Germany that these were the same ink-stamps as were used domestically, and promised that future mail destined for Germany would not bear ink-stamps with any references to the current war. Therefore, all letters and parcels currently being held back were to be delivered, provided the ink-stamp slogans were not distinctly anti-German and did not imply a malicious intent.[173]

In June 1944, the OKW made arrangements for the establishment of local-area Men of Confidence. These were needed to coordinate parcel deliveries and other matters between Men of Confidence who were each looking after hundreds of prisoners of war in individual camps. There were to be several local-area Men of Confidence in each military district, working with the military district administration. The borders of their respective areas of concern were to be established by the military district commanders.[174]

Confiscated items from prisoner-of-war collective parcels were only to be used for the prisoners. Thus, confiscated food was to be sent to the camp kitchens for use in collective meals; confiscated items such as coffee, tea, or cocoa were likewise to be sent to the kitchens for use by all prisoners of war for breakfast; confiscated soaps were to be sent to laundries where prisoners washed their clothes, or to prisoner-of-war hospitals for use by them; confiscated tobacco was to be used as rewards for prisoners of war of all nationalities. Receipts were to be given acknowledging the confiscation. Special attention was to be given, however, to ensuring that no member of the Wehrmacht or German civilian shared in the confiscated items; any use of such items by anyone other than prisoners of war could lead to grave repercussions with both the ICRC and the Protecting Powers.[175]

For British and American prisoners of war, parcels which for some reason could not be delivered were to have the name of the addressee sent to WASt, to see if they could track down his location. If WASt could not find the prisoner, then the parcel was to be opened in the presence of the Man of Confidence, the general contents distributed for collective use by the prisoners of war, and the personal items found within sent back to the sender.[176]

Requests by the Men of Confidence to the ICRC for collective parcels were to be sent by mail and spaced in such a way that a steady supply of parcels arrived. Only in very exceptional cases of shortages could the Men of Confidence be allowed to send their request, through the military districts, by telegram. In such circumstances, the messages were to be kept as brief as possible. Follow-up telegrams to the ICRC concerning a previous request were not permitted.[177]

Finally, several of the directives from the OKW concerning collective parcels dealt with the prohibition or general requests for specialized items. Ethnic Arab prisoners of war had been receiving smoking substances called "Kif," "Takrouri," and "Souffi" in tobacco packages in the collective parcels. As these substances were even banned by the French colonial forces for health reasons, they were to be confiscated from the prisoners of war, as were any future shipments of them.[178] On a different issue, prisoners of war skilled at repairing clocks were permitted by the OKW to ask the ICRC for spare parts.[179] Cigarette paper and tops, as well as empty notebooks, in Red Cross parcels were to be allowed to be delivered to prisoners of war.[180] The sale of ink and cellophane envelopes to prisoners of war was forbidden by the OKW at this time, at these materials were commonly used in escape preparations.[181]

Mail call

The Geneva Convention required some measure of coordination between the belligerents in order to provide equal mailing privileges to the prisoners of war held by each country. The Detaining Power undertook to provide a set number of letters and postcards for prisoners per month, and to deliver them by post by "the shortest route." Post could not be detained for disciplinary reasons, and no later than one week after arriving in a camp, each prisoner of war had the right to send a post-card (later known as the "capture card") to his family, informing them of his capture and the general state of his health. Prisoners had the right, "as a general rule," to write home in their native languages, though final approval was up to the belligerents.[182] With regard to transfers, it was the responsibility of the Detaining Power to ensure that mail and parcels arriving at the prisoner's old camp be forwarded to him at the new camp.[183]

Prisoners of war were also permitted by the Convention to receive personally addressed parcels containing food and clothing, subject to a security check.[184] Parcels and letters sent through designated information bureaus (the ICRC) were exempt from postal duties and charges; in cases of urgency, prisoners could be permitted to send telegrams home, at their own expense.[185] Consignment of books could be received, subject to censorship, from both the recognized Protecting Power and relief organizations (YMCA and ICRC); it was forbidden to delay delivery of such items due to the pretext of difficulties of censorship.[186]

While exhorting the belligerents to accomplish censorship of post and parcels as quickly as possible in the presence of either the recipient or a designated representative (MOC), the Convention also recognized that the exigencies of war would occasionally lead to the prohibition of any correspondence, for political or military reasons; the Convention required, in these instances, that the delay be only temporary, and for as brief a time as possible.[187] The belligerents were also required to make available notary functions – such as authentication of signatures, power-of-attorney, and wills – for the prisoners of war.[188] Lastly with regard to correspondence (and located in the Convention on the section dealing with disciplinary and judicial punishments and measures), the right of prisoners of war undergoing disciplinary punishment to read, write, as well as send and receive letters, was guaranteed; delivery of parcels and money could be delayed until the expiration of the sentence, with any perishable foodstuffs going to the camp or infirmary kitchens for communal use.[189]

The sections of the German manuals dealing with prisoner-of-war postal privileges essentially reprinted or paraphrased the articles of the Geneva Convention.[190] The only addition made was that despite the Convention's exhortations for quick delivery of mail, security should never be compromised by hasty censorship. At the start of the war, then, the official German policy was, as in many other areas, to implement the terms of the Geneva Convention quite literally. Dr. Waltzog, likewise, interpreted these articles of the Convention in the same fashion as the 1939 manuals. His only addition was to point out, without any further comment, that while stopping mail for disciplinary reasons remained prohibited, the Convention foresaw that it might be necessary to temporarily halt post for political or military reasons.[191]

A month into the war, in October 1939, clarification orders were issued concerning prisoner-of-war correspondence. The postal provisions for transferred prisoners of war, listed in article 26 of the Geneva Convention, were to apply not only to prisoners of war who were sent on to other camps, but to any prisoners of war detached from the main camp, such as those in work-details, hospitals, or prisons. This meant that all mail and packages were to be delivered directly to the prisoner personally, and not just to his main camp. Regarding the general handling of post, as delineated in article 36, the term "shortest way" was taken to apply between the postal censors and the foreign countries. Not delaying post for disciplinary reasons was taken to mean only as a criminal punishment; the ability to withhold mail for "special [unstated] reasons," for a specific time, was reserved by the German authorities. Although the prisoner was already allowed, in the Dulag, to send a postcard announcing the fact of his capture and the state of his health, another similar postcard, not counted toward his monthly quota, was also to be allowed sent upon arrival at the main prisoner-of-war camp; priority in delivering these postcards was to go to the sick and wounded.[192]

Languages permitted for correspondence were to be defined at a later time by the OKW; in any event, a convincing reason would be required for the use of a language that was not the prisoner-of-war's native language. Commenting on article 37, the OKW stated that excessive transmission of food to the prisoners of war in mail parcels was, in fact, in Germany's interest, because it provided relief of the domestic food situation. For security reasons (such as possible use during an escape), civilian clothing sent to prisoners of war was not to be delivered to them, but held in properly identified storage until the end of their captivity. The right of prisoners of war to pay for and send telegrams in urgent situations, listed in article 38, was reaffirmed; they were to be restricted to the most extreme circumstances, and allowed only if they were fairly brief, and in clear, comprehensible text.[193]

As per article 39, all books sent to prisoners of war had to be thoroughly checked before being released. Regarding that same article's admonition that books not be delayed on the pretext of censorship, as much time as was necessary was to be taken before a book was released to the camp library. Regarding general censorship of prisoner-of-war mail, the "shortest time" mentioned in article 40 was to be taken to mean the time needed for an appropriately thorough examination. In order to avoid possible later complaints, packages were to be opened and distributed only in the presence of the addressee or his designated agent, with signatures of receipt to be verified against their identity cards. A written request was required before a prisoner of war could act as such an agent on another prisoner's behalf.[194]

Regarding the Man of Confidence's correspondence with the Protecting Power, the commandant could add information to the MOC's letters with the aim of clarifying aberrant or inapplicable statements, but he could not alter the MOC's letter itself. He was, therefore, allowed to offer his opinion on the points being made by the Man of Confidence. While article 57 guaranteed prisoners of war serving disciplinary sentences the right to receive and send letters, it also allowed for packages and parcels addressed to the prisoner to be held in storage until the sentence was served. Such parcels were to be opened in the presence of the Man of Confidence, and any perishable items, which could spoil before the sentence was served, were to be given to either the camp infirmary or the kitchen. These measures were clearly permitted, but the prisoner being disciplined had to be informed of them.[195]

Just a few days after these instructions, a shorter set of orders concerning prisoner-of-war post was sent out by the OKW. In addition to basic security and administrative issues, it specified that: prisoners of war were allowed two letters and four postcards per month, or, for officers, three letters and four postcards; the prisoners could send letters written only on standardized, approved forms, to be obtained from the camp canteens; all letters and postcards had "Prisoner-of-war Mail" clearly written on the front; incoming letters and packages be no heavier than 250 grams and 5 kilos, respectively; the address of the prisoner be listed in the follow manner – last name, first name, captive number, Stalag (or Oflag/Dulag), Germany (Allemagne); delivery of foreign newspapers not be permitted; delivery of money and valuables, as well as minor printings, business-paper, and merchandise not be permitted; and that all letters and incoming packages for the prisoners of war be conveyed toll free and duty free.[196] These instructions were reconfirmed by the Reichspostministeriums in mid-December 1939.[197] At the end of that month, however, the Reichspostministeriums ordered that letters from abroad bearing only the prisoner's name be forwarded to the WASt in Berlin.[198]

By late February 1940, the OKW was concerned that the rules concerning prisoner-of-war post, set out a few months previously, were not being followed stringently enough. Therefore, they sent an eight-point reminder down the chain of command, stating: registered mail sent to the prisoner of war was not permitted; registered mail sent by the prisoner was permitted only with the permission of the camp commandant; the camouflaging of the destination or origin of postage was not permitted by prisoners of war – they had to use the accepted camp name, as specified by the commandant in his regulations; post could not be sent directly from, or received at, the prisoner's work detachment – all post had to go through the camp post-office; no letters or correspondence were permitted between prisoners of war in any circumstances (even between fathers, sons, or brothers), nor was any allowed between a prisoner of war and any individual in Germany, especially members of the Wehrmacht; post for the prisoner sent from within Germany was not permitted, and had to be returned to the sender stamped "not permitted"; prisoners of war could only write in German, in the official language of their state, or in their native language – international languages (Esperanto, Volapük) and codes of any sort were strictly forbidden, and any material so sent was to be returned to the prisoner; not complying with postal regulations was a grave offense, equal in some instances to espionage – it was in the best interests of the state that they be followed.[199]

In order to facilitate communication between transferred prisoners of war and their relatives, the right of the prisoners to send a postcard home notifying their relatives of their new address, upon arrival at a new camp, was reaffirmed; this postcard was not to be counted toward their total monthly allowance. If whole camps were to be moved or dissolved, similar provisions were to be made for the prisoners of war.[200]

Camp commandants were reminded in early autumn 1941 that the cost of notepaper for writing letters was to be borne from the camp canteen's funds.[201] This order was followed a short while later by another, listing complaints by British prisoners of war that their mail was often returned home as "undeliverable" without any serious attempts by the German authorities to deliver them. In order that German prisoners of war in British captivity continue to receive their mail, the OKW ordered the postal staff to make greater efforts to ensure the British prisoners of war received their mail.[202]

The OKW relented slightly on the issue of allowing prisoners of war who were closely related (father, son, brother) but captive in different camps, to correspond with one another, in October 1941. These letters and postcards were to be subject to careful scrutiny, but were not to be allowed in addition to the prisoners' normal monthly allotment, so as not to overstrain the censors.[203]

Prisoners of war had occasionally needed to take care of important personal family affairs by post. In reply to requests of the Men of Confidence for permission to write directly to the concerned parties in the home state, the OKW responded by restating that it was prohibited for any prisoner to have any direct contact with the home state. To deal with exceptional circumstances, the offices of the Man of Confidence could be used to contact the Protecting Power. However, no correspondence was to be permitted unless it went through the Protecting Power. This was to be explained to the prisoners of war as being in everyone's best interests, so that there would be no future misunderstandings, and possible resulting delays in correspondence.[204] The ICRC planned, in May 1942, to send a newsletter to all British Men of Confidence concerning ways to speed up mail contact between prisoners of war and their families in Australia and New Zealand. The OKW agreed to the distribution of this newsletter by the commandants.[205]

Registered mail for prisoners of war was not permitted; up to this point, these types of letters had been delivered anyway, once a month. Starting July 1, 1942, they would no longer be accepted, and would instead be returned to the sender. The Men of Confidence were to be informed of this measure.[206] Regarding prisoners of war who had been transferred to different camps, the OKW again ordered that mail sent to their old camp be forwarded to them, and not returned to the sender marked "undeliverable"; to that end, the camps were to keep lists of where their former prisoners of war had been sent.[207]

On July 20, 1942, the OKW issued another pamphlet concerning prisoner-of-war post. Among many administrative issues, it indicated that British and American prisoners of war were to receive identical privileges to one another. They were allowed to receive parcels from both aid societies and private persons, from hostile and neutral states (as per article 37 of the Geneva Convention). They were permitted to write to and receive letters from private individuals in both hostile and neutral countries, including areas under German administration (General Gouvernement and the Protectorates); within Germany proper, they could only write to or receive letters from immediate family members (parents, children, siblings, grandparents). They could also write to their Protecting Power, which for both was Switzerland. Outgoing monthly mail permitted for British and American prisoners of war was: three letters and four postcards for officers; two letters and four postcards for other-ranks. All were allowed to receive an unrestricted number of letters. All medical personnel were permitted double the outgoing letters and postcards of the other prisoners of war of their rank. The prisoners of war were allowed to write to their Protecting Power concerning material and mental needs, but could not write about statistical data or collective troubles. Letters from the prisoners of war to the ICRC were permitted to be about their collective parcels and investigations of missing personnel. British and American prisoners of war were also permitted to send letters via air-mail, provided they paid the appropriate dues. All correspondence between prisoners of war and private persons within Germany, members of the German military (with the exception of camp commandants), departments of hostile governments, and all legations, embassies, and consulates both inside Germany and abroad, was strictly prohibited.[208]

The right of francophone Canadian prisoners of war to correspond in French was reaffirmed by the OKW in October 1942; if a French-speaking censor was not available in their camp, their mail was to be forwarded for examination to the next nearest camp which had one.[209] Letters in uncommon languages used by prisoners of war in correspondence with their relatives, not known to the German translators at the camps (especially Hindi, Urdu, Farsi, Arabic, Kurdish, Georgian, Armenian, Afrikaans, and Swahili) were to be sent to Berlin for censorship. The prisoners of war were to be informed that this measure would lead to delays in their outgoing and incoming mail.[210]

In July 1943, the OKW stated that any stoppage of prisoners of war's mail coming to or from the camps, without authorized supervision, was strictly illegal. There were to be no delays of prisoner-of-war mail before it reached the camp.[211]

With the aim of reciprocity, the German military attempted in August 1943 to outline, once and for all, rules concerning postal correspondence of British and American prisoners of war. With regard to letter mail, the number allowable per month depended on rank:

Generals could send five letters and five postcards per month; other officers could send three letters and four postcards per month; non-commissioned officers and other-ranks could send two letters and four postcards per month. Recognized medical personnel and clergy were allowed double the regular amount given to other prisoners of war of the same rank. Letter mail could only be written on the paper and postcards provided through the camps. Special mail was permitted under article 42 of the Geneva Convention; this had to be forwarded through the Men of Confidence to the ICRC. Direct correspondence between prisoners of war and enemy states was prohibited. The Men of Confidence were allowed unrestricted correspondence with the ICRC to discuss issues such as collective parcels, missing soldier inquiries, and issues concerning the sending of mail by prisoners. Men of Confidence were permitted by article 78 of the Geneva Convention to correspond with representatives of the national Red Cross societies as well as recognized prisoner-of-war help organizations. Correspondence with the YMCA was restricted to issues concerning leisure time and mental and spiritual health. Air-mail letters were to be counted as part of the monthly quota of outgoing mail.[212]

Not credited against the monthly mail quotas were: short telegraphic messages of no more than 25 words; letters from the Men of Confidence to prisoner-of-war help organizations or the Protecting Power; the notification-of-capture postcard sent to the prisoner's relatives and the ICRC; receipts confirming the arrival of a parcel; one letter or postcard per month to a relative who was also a prisoner of war in German captivity. The full additional cost of airmail letters was to be paid by the prisoners of war. Registered mail was prohibited, either to receive or to send. The language of the letters sent and received by prisoners of war had to be in either the prisoner's first language, or in German or English. To assure faster censoring, German or English were recommended. Within Germany, correspondence with a prisoner of war was only permitted to his immediate family, meaning parents, children, siblings, and spouse. The noting of the current date was permitted, but numbering the letters or postcards was not. Personalized postcards were not permitted. With the exception of authorized group photos, photographs could not be sent by the prisoners of war. Messages concerning the welfare of people other than family were permitted. No charge would be made for sending regular letters and postcards.[213]

Censored portions of letters or postcards were to be blotted out with ink, so they could not be read. In the interests of expediting the processing of mail and censorship, prisoners of war were encouraged not to write too often or too long letters, if possible. Each prisoner who had not heard from a relative for over three months could send a special rush-inquiry message through the ICRC, to be no more than 25 words long; this would be sent by the ICRC as quickly as possible, and the prisoner-of-war might have to pay airmail charges if applicable. Such a special rush-inquiry message was not to be credited against the prisoner's regular monthly quota. Prisoners of war were permitted to receive parcels from private individuals and help organizations from both neutral and enemy countries. From within German-controlled territory, the prisoner could only receive a parcel if it was from his next-of-kin. Parcels were permitted under the terms of article 38 of the Geneva Convention. The standard weight for each parcel was up to 5 kilos. If the contents were indivisible, the parcel could weigh up to 10 kilos. The cost of mailing the parcels was charged only at the source of the mailing, and not the reception. The following objects could not be sent to prisoners of war: any type or currency of money; civilian clothing (exceptions could be made for special outer clothes needed for work); medical-personnel armbands, for those who were not medical personnel; weapons or objects which could be used as weapons, such as large pocket-knives or scissors; ammunition or explosives, tools which could be used for either sabotage or escape; reproduction machines, charcoal or tracing-paper; compasses, backpacks, maps, cameras, binoculars, and lenses; electric lights, lighters, fuses, and candles (with the exception of Christmas candles sent in Red Cross Christmas parcels); spirits and alcoholic beverages, excluding wine; hard spirits, or other inflammable objects; any heaters; any radio reception or sending devices, including blueprints for making them; drugs and salves like Vaseline (help organizations and the ICRC could send such objects for medical reasons to the camp); chemicals or plant leaves; books and prints containing unsavory content; foreign newspapers and books with news inserts; cigarette holders and paper, blank paper, memo pads, notebooks, and other mail or postcards; potatoes. If a parcel contained such things, they would be removed, and the remainder of the parcel would be forwarded to the prisoner.[214]

Book parcels were allowed, but could not contain any other objects. Help organizations were allowed to include books within larger parcels. In general a list of authorized book titles could be obtained from Berlin. To prevent theft and damage, all parcels were to be covered with solid wraps and tied with rope. Censorship of the parcels would occur at the camps or work detachments. The parcels or packages would only be opened in the presence of either the addressee or an agent authorized by the prisoner. The examination of collective parcels from help organizations would generally be conducted by spot checks. The examinations were also conducted so that the prisoner knew no food or objects designated for the prisoner's enjoyment were damaged.[215]

Any postcards or letters sent to prisoners of war which bore either advertisements or propaganda slogans (e.g. "For Victory," from the USA) were not to be delivered. They would be returned to sender, and the recipients were to be informed of the reason.[216]

As of April 1944, non-Soviet prisoners of war were to be provided with postal letter-forms free of charge. The cost of these forms were to be deducted from the profits of the prisoner-of-war canteen, or, if these were exhausted, from the OKW.[217] For the promotion of better mail service for prisoners of war, they were to be encouraged by the camps to write the addressees' names and addresses more legibly in the future. This was especially to be stressed for British prisoners of war, for whom poor penmanship had led to many letters returning undelivered.[218]

Recently, prisoners of war had been seeking approval to send manuscripts and other writing home to relatives, in the hopes that they could be published. As no facility for censorship beyond existing postal requirements existed, the manuscripts were to be returned to the prisoners of war.[219] In the interests of reciprocity, American prisoners of war were allowed to send a group picture home to their relatives, the size of a postcard, and with their signature on the back. No messages could be written, and the picture-card was not to be counted toward their monthly mail quotas. For security reasons, no prisoners of war (American or otherwise) were allowed to take pictures which could conceivably be altered to look like a military pass.[220] A few months later, the OKW ordered that, in addition to group photographs, British and American prisoners of war could also be permitted to have photographs taken of sporting, theater, and other special events, to send home to their relatives.[221] The OKW also noted that recent pamphlets sent from the Australian Red Cross contained peace messages and propaganda; they were not to be delivered to the prisoners of war, but destroyed instead.[222]

At this time, the OKW gave a list of European languages, as well as Arabic, which prisoners of war were allowed to use in correspondence with their relatives. Where there was an Indian interpreter in a camp, the prisoners of war of that camp could also write in that language. Letters written in any other language by prisoners of war were to be sent back to them, and they were to rewrite them in a more common language. Letters written in an nonapproved language which arrived for prisoners of war were not to be delivered, but sent back instead. Commandants and commanders could direct enquiries concerning exceptional situations to the OKW.[223]

In the interests of reciprocity with the United States government, the OKW instructed the camps at this time to lend support to any inquiries from the German Red Cross concerning postal deliveries to specific prisoners of war.[224]

Lastly, in response to the previous orders concerning undeliverable mail sent to prisoners of war, the WASt received requests for information from camps for 120 packages for American prisoners of war. Of these, 100 were in fact properly addressed, and could have been easily delivered to the prisoners of war. To save the department from doing unnecessary work, camp commandants were instructed to make sure that the addresses were more carefully examined by camp staff before they were sent off to WASt.[225]

Ends of captivity

Unable to fight anymore

There was, the signatories to the Geneva Convention agreed, no point in detaining enemy soldiers who were too sick or wounded to be able to recover and continue in the fight; further, their maintenance could only be a burden on the Detaining Power, as these prisoners could hardly be expected to work either. Thus, mechanisms for the repatriation of seriously wounded or sick prisoners of war, after an examination by a Mixed Medical Commission (or MMC), were discussed in articles 68–74 of the Convention.

The first of these articles stated that belligerents were required to send back to their own countries those prisoners of war who were seriously ill or wounded, directing the Detaining Power to take what steps were necessary for transportation; until a formal agreement on repatriation was signed, the signatories to the Convention were directed to use as a guide a model draft agreement which had been included as an appendix to the Convention. Next, article 69 described the creation of MMCs, consisting of two neutral doctors and one doctor of the Detaining Power, who had the responsibility for examining the seriously ill or wounded prisoners and assessing their rights to repatriation; a neutral doctor would serve as chair of the commission, and their decisions would be reached by way of a simple majority. The list of those with a right to be examined by the MMC was given in article

70. Included in addition to those prisoners who had been recommended by the Detaining Power camp's medical officer, were: (a) prisoners who made a direct request to that effect to the medical officer of the camp; (b) prisoners presented by the prisoners' representatives (MOC or senior officer), the latter acting on their own initiative or on the request of the prisoners themselves; and (c) prisoners nominated by the Power in whose armed forces they served or by a relief society duly recognized and authorized by that Power.

The source of the illness or wounds to be considered for repatriation were not confined to those received in battle; article 71 extended the same rights to those who met with accidents at work, unless the injury was self-inflicted. The belligerents could also, upon further negotiations, arrange for the repatriation of prisoners who had been in captivity for a long time.[226] Articles 73 and 74 gave final instructions regarding repatriation: the Detaining Power was responsible for the cost of transport up to its frontiers, after which the home power was responsible; and no repatriated person could be employed on active military service.

The German manuals of 1939 stated that seriously injured or ill prisoners of war would generally be repatriated as soon as their medical condition permitted transport. The mechanism by which they were to be judged and examined was laid out, the OKW wrote, in articles 68 and 69 of the Convention. The only additional point made was that the German doctor on the MMC would report directly to the WASt the details of those prisoners approved for repatriation, and the OKW would then organize their transport and trip home. The details of the final journey home of the prisoners would be dealt with by specific orders at the time.[227] With regard to these articles of the Convention, Waltzog did little more than reprint them, with no differing commentary from the earlier position of the OKW.[228] The majority of orders and directives issued by the OKW on this subject dealt with the mechanics of MMC visits to camps, or the administrative issues surrounding a prisoner of war's repatriation.

In July 1941, the OKW noted that many repatriated prisoners of war, upon their return home, lodged claims with both the ICRC and their Protecting Power concerning the loss of objects of value left behind in the camps. The OKW felt that most of these claims were baseless, and the occasionally legitimate one only affected objects of little or no value. However, due to the enormous administrative work that needed to be done to clarify each claim, the camp commandants were to obtain, henceforth, a written statement from the soon-to-be-repatriated prisoners of war that they were leaving with all their valuables with them. If for whatever reason they were unable (due to rushed transport, for instance) to take what they had arrived with, such as foreign currency, then the statement was to list the value of the objects missing. This statement had to be written in both German and the prisoner's language, and any refusal by the prisoner to sign the statement was to be explained. This way, future claims could be checked against the prisoner's own words.[229]

Prisoners of war being sent home also complained, as reported in September 1941, that they were not getting enough notice to set all of their affairs, especially financial, in order; for instance, a prisoner of war was informed one evening that he would be leaving the following morning, even though the camp administration had known about his release for days. This was, according to the OKW, unacceptable, and should cease to occur.[230] Prisoners designated for repatriation had often, after being gathered into departure centers, faced delays due to transportation before going home. As they left their main camps, though, they had to turn in all their camp money. Thus, waiting for transport, the prisoners of war had no money with which to purchase minor things, and they thus eventually left with a very poor impression of Germany. To prevent this, the prisoners of war were to be allowed to take some money with them to these assembly camps, with the provision that they did not take it with them when they finally departed.[231] By March 1942, the OKW again noted that repatriated prisoners of war were continuing to complain that they were not allowed to leave with all of their personal property; apparently, objects were being temporarily confiscated during transport, receipts were issued to the prisoners of war, but the objects were not returned in time for the prisoners' departure. The OKW drew the attention of the camp commandants once again to existing orders on this issue.[232]

On June 20, 1942, the OKW published a small booklet on the visits of foreigners to prisoner-of-war camps. With regard to repatriation, the OKW noted that an MMC, as per article 69 of the Convention, consisted of three doctors, two of whom would be neutrals and one a German. The MMC worked in accordance with article 70 of the Geneva Convention, especially as concerned prisoner-of-war-hospitals, and decided which seriously wounded prisoners of war could be repatriated. Private conversations with the prisoners of war were prohibited; the MMC fulfilled a fundamentally medical function and no other. Inspections of hygienic facilities by the delegates of the MMC or the ICRC were to have the camp doctor present.[233]

Upon dismissal from captivity, a prisoner of war was to be relieved of all his camp money; the amount taken was to be credited to his personnel card.[234] Those prisoners placed in separate quarters pending repatriation were not to receive individually addressed packages. They were to be compensated for foods from the collective supplies of the camps.[235] Sick or wounded prisoners of war who were to be repatriated following hospitalization had to be given an opportunity to turn in their camp money, so it could be credited to their personnel cards. Likewise, their home addresses were to be double checked, so that valuables and their money would be correctly sent.[236] The OKW reminded military districts and camps of this again in July 1944: camp money could only be used in Germany, and was not allowed to leave the country. Prisoners of war who were being repatriated were to receive a credit on their personnel card for the camp money they left behind.[237]

The German staff of prisoner-of-war camps were reminded by the OKW, in August 1943, that foreign members of the MMCs traveling through Germany underwent many discomforts in the course of executing their duties under the Geneva Convention. They were guests of the German state, and were to be treated as officers by members of the German military forces, and welcomed accordingly. All German non-commissioned officers and other-ranks were to show them the same military compliments as German officers.[238] During the visits of the MMC to a camp, the only persons who needed to appear before it were the camp commandant, the security officer, and any relevant medical staff, according to the OKW in an order of March 1944. If the MMC had previously recognized a prisoner of war as worthy of repatriation, the prisoner did not have to reappear before them; even if the prisoner had become better, his status for repatriation did not change. In the lists submitted to the MMC only medical issues were to be stated; no security-related comments could be submitted. If an ill prisoner was in a different hospital from the one normally responsible for prisoners of war from his home camp, the prisoner-of-war doctor treating him was to make a submission to the MMC.[239]

British and American prisoners of war and surplus medical personnel awaiting repatriation should not be told in speeches by the camp commandant or German doctors about how well they had been treated, the OKW decided, in August 1944. Good treatment and accommodation were of outstanding propaganda value in and of themselves, without the prisoners of war having to be told about it.[240]

If there were security misgivings about the genuineness of a prisoner of war's illness or wounds, the OKW noted in January 1944, these were to be passed along to the OKW before the prisoner was scheduled to appear before the MMC for possible repatriation.[241] On November 10, 1944, a lengthier circular was sent by the OKW concerning the reporting of illnesses of prisoners of war, the faking of illnesses, segregation of ill prisoners of war from others, and security measures in prisoner-of-war hospitals and infirmaries. With regard to those prisoners proposed for appearance before the MMC, it had also been noticed by the OKW that prisoner-of-war doctors were often actively assisting prisoners of war in faking illnesses so they could be repatriated. Special supervision was put in place for British and American airmen; they were to be placed out of the reach of prisoner-of-war doctors, for observation only by German medical personnel in military hospitals.[242]

On February 23, 1945, the OKW issued new orders concerning the appearance of British and American prisoners of war before the MMC. Priority for appearance before the MMC was to be given to British and American prisoners of war;[243] the rule for determining the nationality of a prisoner of war was the uniform in which he was captured. In accordance with earlier orders, prisoners of war who had already been deemed repatriable by German doctors did not need to reappear before the MMC. Given the current transportation difficulties, priority in transport was to be given to prisoners of war who were asked to appear by the MMC in October and November 1944. The British and American Men of Confidence were to be informed that there would be more sittings of the MMC in April and May, so that, in accordance with article 70 of the Geneva Convention, timely notice could be given to have prisoners of war examined first by German doctors. Camps requesting to send prisoners of war for examination by the MMC on March 15, 1945, were to notify the military district headquarters by telegram of the numbers (broken into British and American), location, and potential housing possibilities for the MMC.[244]

Letters which arrived for American prisoners of war who had already been repatriated were to be forwarded to the Swiss Legation in Berlin. Parcels which arrived were to be opened by the Man of Confidence, and any objects not of personal value could be used by the remaining American prisoners of war. Personal objects were to be returned to the sender.[245]

A few days later, more instructions were issued pertaining to the MMC. Changes in German medical staff soon before a visit by the MMC were to be avoided, as the new doctors would not have enough time to familiarize themselves with the prisoners' cases. Special care was to be given to claims of asthma or epilepsy, as, due to insufficient time for observation by the MMC, their judgment was heavily based on reports of enemy doctors, in the absence of reports from German doctors. Given that proof of deafness offered by specialists was often just the whispering of a prisoner of war, unofficial observations to the contrary could be brought against it to defeat it according to the regulations of the Geneva Convention. For claims of kidney problems concrete lab test results were to be sought as corroboration. For the determination of heart troubles, an important consideration for the MMC was proof of decreased work ability; therefore, strain tests were important to conduct. For judgments of psychiatric illness, it was imperative that the treating doctor be a German specialist. For examination of lung problems (such as tuberculosis), it was important that adequate charts of changes in weight were kept. For the creation of lists of prisoners of war for examination, the following had to be observed: separate lists were required for American and British prisoners of war (but not for the individual British Dominions); only the diagnosis of the German doctor was to appear on the list; repeated complaints were to be brought to the MMC at the first available instance; officers and men were to be presented and introduced one after the other; the Protecting Power delegate or Man of Confidence was to be presented and introduced lastly; at the presentation of a wounded prisoner the time of his wounds was to be told to the MMC.[246]

Dying in captivity

The Geneva Convention's provisions for the deaths of prisoners of war were straightforward. The same rules which applied to the soldiers of the Detaining Power regarding the opportunity to draw wills and certification of death had to be extended to the prisoners of war under their care; further, the Detaining Power had to ensure an honorable burial, with the necessary grave markings noted for transmission to the home state, and respectful maintenance of the graveyards.[247]

The OKW's 1939 manuals vested the camp commandant with the legal authority to verify signatures and wills,[248] and required that prisoner-of-war deaths be reported according to regular military protocol by the camp doctor and the commandant to the WASt. Funerals had to be conducted with proper military honors and escort, with a maximum of 30 prisoners of war in attendance. Grave markings and indications were to be noted and sent to WASt.[249]

Dr. Waltzog's update of German policy left the issue untouched, except to note that, in the case of accident benefits offered to surviving relatives of German workers, the same did not apply to the relatives of prisoners of war killed at work: their benefits and rights under German law existed only for the duration of captivity, and as death ended captivity, so too did Germany have no further financial obligations to the prisoner-of-war's next-of-kin.[250]

In March 1940, the OKW decided to tighten up the administrative requirements following the death of a prisoner of war. Henceforth, prisoner-of-war death reports had to contain their camp personnel cards, a death certificate signed by the camp doctor, a description of the grave, and a communiqué to the OKW stating the nationality of the dead prisoner. One month later, a letter was sent from the OKW to the Foreign Ministry informing them that lists of prisoners of war who died while in German captivity would be forwarded through the ICRC in Geneva for transmission to the states concerned. In November 1940, the policy was spelled out to the ICRC directly, in a letter sent to Geneva from the OKW in Berlin.[251]

The administrative process to be followed in case of a prisoner-of-war death was reiterated by the OKW in July 1941. The camp was to notify the WASt immediately, as well as send a death-report to the German Red Cross, so that the next of kin could be notified. The report could contain comments from the deceased's friends, as well as clergy, written in the prisoner-of-war's native language. The main questionnaire, however, had to be completed in German. The last will of the prisoner could be included, as well as a detailed and precise description of the burial plot (row, grave number, cemetery) in order to avoid unnecessary specific enquiries from the next-of-kin. Legibility was stressed as important, so that the relatives of the deceased had as precise an understanding of what had occurred as was possible.[252] In November 1941, the camps were reminded that the responsibility for providing lists of deceased British prisoners of war lay not with the camps, but with the WASt and the ICRC, to whom the Protecting Power delegates ought to be referred.[253] When the photograph of each deceased prisoner-of-war grave was taken, the national flag of the prisoner was to be placed on the coffin, with a sign stating name and other details in the background.[254]

For reasons of reciprocity, the OKW ordered, in February 1942, that the graves of deceased British prisoners of war were to be photographed, including a sign that showed the prisoner's name, birthplace, nationality, identification number, and country. The costs of the picture were to be borne by the prisoners' canteen. Further, there had to be a formally dressed honor guard of German soldiers (fewer than would be present for a German burial) and a wreath with a red bow and ribbon with the words "Die Deutsche Wehrmacht" on it, in the picture. The coffin was to be draped, where possible, with the flag of the prisoner's country.[255] Also for reasons of reciprocity, these measures were extended to include American prisoners of war, as of September 1944.[256] Further in the interest of reciprocity, the OKW ordered new measures to be taken in the event a British prisoner died while in German custody (i.e. jail). In addition to the death reports to be sent to WASt and then the German Red Cross, the OKW's Prisoner-of-War Office should be notified as well, so that a telegram could be sent to the ICRC, to be forwarded to the British authorities. The format of the telegram was to be, for example, "British prisoner-of-war William Smith, prisoner-of-war Number 270448, born 11/11/1910 in Cambridge, deceased 18/3/42 in Stalag VIII B. Cause of death: Illness (accident, shooting, etc.). Next of Kin: Mary Smith, Cambridge, 17 Bedford Road."[257] Also in the interest of reciprocity, this order was extended to include American prisoners of war, in mid-August 1943.[258]

In response to an inquiry as to whether or not prisoners of war who were killed during escape attempts should be buried with military honors, the OKW decided that they should. Escape alone was not considered an action which rendered a soldier dishonorable. However, if in the course of the escape attempt, the prisoner conducted dishonorable actions, then he was not to be buried with military honors.[259]

Displaying a sense of tact, the OKW ordered in May 1942 that mail arriving for prisoners of war who were deceased be returned to the ICRC in Geneva, after being stamped, "Undeliverable – Return to Sender."[260] Should the return address of mail sent to deceased prisoners of war lie in enemy control, the OKW later decided, the mail was to be forwarded to the ICRC in Geneva instead.[261]

In the general event that a prisoner of war died in captivity, the OKW ordered in March 1943 that a death report be completed and sent to the WASt. This report had to contain the details surrounding the death, including the immediate circumstances, the location, the name of the prisoner's work detachment or camp, as well as the full personal details of the deceased prisoner. The detailed completion of this form was deemed necessary to avoid later complications should follow-up questions arrive. The death report would form the basis of the death notice sent to the German Red Cross, which would be used by the ICRC to inform the prisoner-of-war society in the deceased prisoner's country, who would then inform his next of kin. Disclosure of the details surrounding the death were not to be made by the commandant to either the Man of Confidence or the Protecting Power delegates.[262]

The deceased prisoner's estate (all valuables, and currencies) were to be forwarded to the WASt, and not to either the Red Cross or to the Protecting Power; only the WASt was authorized to make the administrative arrangements necessary to send the deceased prisoner's estate to the next of kin. The only items not to be sent to the WASt were: RM credits, which, by previous OKW order, remained at the camp; and currencies, which were to be sent to a finance section of the OKW, with a copy of the amount forwarded to the WASt.[263] The German Foreign Office, working through the offices of the Protecting Power, came to agreement with the British Government for the handling of money and valuables of deceased prisoners of war, in September 1943. Henceforth, following the death of a prisoner of war, the financial credit amounts were to be transmitted to OKW headquarters Berlin, from where they would be transferred, eventually, to the British government. The British, upon receipt of the amount to be sent, would immediately disburse the total to the deceased's descendants. The format for reporting this information to OKW was: rank, family name, given name, prisoner-of-war number, British unit, Dominion if applicable, date of birth, date of death, name and address of next of kin, and the credit balance in the camp (in RM).[264]

ICRC questionnaires concerning the death of a prisoner of war were to be filled out immediately after a prisoner of war died, and forwarded to the President of the German Red Cross. Camp commandants and the doctor of prisoner-of-war hospital or infirmary were responsible for ensuring this was completed.[265] The OKW sent out a reminder to the camps that the death questionnaire had to be filled out after a prisoner of war died, including those killed during air-raids, and sent to the German Red Cross. As these would be read abroad, caution and precision were recommended in choosing the words.[266] In mid-September 1944, the OKW ordered that they be notified by telex of prisoners of war killed during an air-raid only if there were more than seven killed. The other normal monthly procedures for reporting prisoner-of-war casualties remained unaffected by this order.[267] In mid-November 1944, the OKW reconfirmed that, in the event of death or serious injury of a prisoner of war, notification was to be sent using regular channels of communication, including the camp, prisoner's name, identification number, and home address. If further investigation was deemed necessary, the results were to be sent along as soon as possible, including the cause of the death or serious injury. In the event a British or American prisoner was killed as a result of an enemy air-raid, the particulars were to be forwarded to the OKW immediately, as per previous orders.[268]

Liberation

Aside from repatriation and death, the only formal way for captivity to end was liberation at the end of the conflict. To that end, the Convention added one general article stating that the belligerents, in any possible armistice convention, were obliged to make arrangements for the repatriation of prisoners of war. Prisoners of war who were subject to criminal proceedings could be detained until the end of the proceedings or the final sentence. The belligerents were also, upon cessation of hostilities, to create commissions to assist in searching for scattered and missing prisoners.[269]

The German manuals of 1939 only stated that, upon cessation of hostilities, the repatriation of prisoners of war would be dealt with by special regulations.[270] Regarding the earlier military practice of releasing prisoners of war back to their home countries on parole, Waltzog only noted that releasing prisoners of war on parole, a previous practice, was not foreseen by the current Convention; Germany had released prisoners of various nationalities out of captivity, but only by special arrangements.[271] Waltzog added little else to the general subject except to note that, should a prisoner successfully evade his captors and rejoin his army, the state of captivity legally ended, and an entirely new one would begin should the same individual find himself captured in the future.[272] However, as the war years progressed, some additional ways in which prisoners of war could be "released" or "dismissed" from captivity, not foreseen by the Convention, were decided upon by the OKW.

Despite the fact that the Geneva Convention only recognized three means by which prisoners of war could end their captivity (medical repatriation, death, and liberation upon cessation of hostilities), the OKW provided for other methods as well. The first such method indicated in an order during the war was as a reward for a heroic act. The ability of prisoners of war to receive cash rewards, or even their freedom, for risking their lives to save the life of a German was confirmed by the OKW in early October 1941. Generally speaking, cash rewards were to be given, unless a prisoner of war seized the initiative and put himself in grave danger to commit the selfless act.[273] This was reconfirmed one month later, when, in response to enquiries from camp commandants, the OKW stated that though personal emergencies were not sufficient grounds for repatriation under the terms of the Geneva Convention, saving a German life could result in freedom being awarded.[274]

On February 10, 1943, the OKW issued administrative orders for the possible release of prisoners of war from captivity for service in combat on the eastern front. These orders simply stated the procedure to be followed for prisoners of war who either volunteered or were recommended by their commandants. The order was valid for prisoners of war of all nationalities.[275] In November 1944, the OKW noted that prisoners of war who expressed a desire to join the Waffen-SS often had their lives threatened by other prisoners of war, because of their friendliness to Germany. Prisoners who wished to join special units of the Waffen-SS were to be collected as soon as possible by the camp commandants, to be transferred to an SS recruitment office. If they were found to be unfit to serve, their original camp was to be so notified, so that they could be transferred to a new camp.[276]

In July 1944, the OKW issued an order, without reference to specific Western nationalities, which allowed prisoners of war to be dismissed from captivity and turned over to the Gestapo "if ordered or necessary." A prisoner who was dismissed out of captivity and handed over to the Gestapo could not remain in the prisoner-of-war camp, but had to be handed over to the responsible Gestapo department immediately. At the time of the actual surrender of the prisoner to the Gestapo, the prisoner was considered dismissed from captivity. If Soviet prisoners of war so dismissed had either tuberculosis or other contagious diseases, the Gestapo was to be informed. The execution of a prisoner of war in a camp was not permitted, unless in individual cases expressly ordered by the OKW, for special reasons. The photographing of all executions was generally prohibited. In the special event that a photograph was needed for administrative reasons, permission had to be obtained from an officer holding at least the rank of division-commander; the negatives were to be sent marked "Secret," undeveloped, to OKW headquarters. In carrying out the order for an execution, the employed military units were obliged to take all precautions necessary to keep away all spectators. Any pictures or negatives taken of earlier executions were to be sent, insofar as possible, to OKW Berlin. The order was signed by General Westhoff, and made no other references to the nationalities of the prisoners of war for whom this order applied.[277]

The last note from the OKW on the case of ending the prisoners of war's captivity by means other than repatriation or death came on April 20, 1945. A one-page notice issued by Berlin to the military districts stated that the Legal Department of the Foreign Office had determined that prisoners of war could be released as the fighting front approached their camp, provided the advancing enemy armies gave assurances that these prisoners of war would not be used in combat. The Swiss government had been asked to forward this proposition to the Western powers for consideration. The British government responded on behalf of itself and the British Commonwealth governments that their prisoners of war who were released to their advancing armies on the western front in Germany would not be used in combat against Germany, provided the German government gave assurances that the rest of their prisoners of war behind the western front would not be relocated further to the rear. The British government expected that prisoners of war left in their camps in this way would be left with adequate food and medical supplies. The government of the United States chose to reserve its opinion on the matter.[278]

6
Final Assessments

6.1 What the inspectors saw

The reports of visits by delegates of the Protecting Power and International Committee of the Red Cross (ICRC)[1] together form the most impartial, contemporary, and comprehensive assessment of the general conditions experienced by the British Commonwealth and American prisoners of war during the Second World War.[2] Inspectors generally tried to visit each camp every three or four months, they were generally given unfettered access in inspecting the camps,[3] were allowed to conduct interviews with the leading prisoners of war of each camp in privacy, to guarantee that all grievances were in fact being aired without undue influence from Wehrmacht officials, and copies of their reports were sent to both the home governments of the prisoners of war as well as the Detaining Power.[4]

As described in the introduction to this study, the Protecting Power and ICRC delegates reported on their visits in a fixed format. In many instances, however, whole sections (i.e. Food, Clothing, etc.) were either left blank or contained only phrases such as "nothing to report," or "nothing new." In general, the section which were consistently and diligently filled out by the inspectors was the general assessment, written at the end of the reports. Here, the inspectors offered their overall opinion on whether the material conditions in the camps could be considered "excellent," "good," "fairly satisfactory," "seriously deficient," or "wholly inadequate" (or words or phrases similar in meaning).[5] Quite separate from the evaluation of material conditions was the reporting of any instances of harassment or serious violations of the Geneva Convention. In assessing the reports of visits to the camps in which British or American prisoners of war were detained, then, two categories can be consistently examined: the overall material conditions of the camps (meaning the location and structures of the camps, interior accommodations, food, clothing, health issues, protected personnel,[6] religion, recreation, transportation and transfers, general disciplinary and judicial issues, labor and finance, mail, external relations, complaints, collective parcels, and repatriation), and the instances of harassment (which could be categorized as "none/minor issues," "significant harassment," or "serious violations of the Convention").

The first part of this chapter, therefore, will consist of providing an overview of the findings of the ICRC and Protecting Power inspectors on these two main issues.[7] Given the limitations of what is an essentially statistical survey, the next portion of this chapter will seek to flesh out the various categories with specific examples of "excellent," "good," "satisfactory," "deficient," and "wholly inadequate" camps to demonstrate what the standards actually meant. Likewise, examples of the instances of minor, significant, and serious harassment or violations of the Convention will also be provided. The final portion of this chapter will consist of marrying the findings of the inspectors' reports to the German policy decisions described earlier in this study, as well as the findings of other academic literature, in order to attempt to provide conclusions on the overall nature of captivity experienced by the American and British prisoners of war.

The first thing to be noted from the examination of the reports made by Protecting Power and ICRC delegates is that their numbers increased steadily from the spring of 1940, reaching a peak in late 1943 and early to mid 1944. In the spring of 1945, as Allied armies rapidly converged on the Berlin, the number or reports dropped to its lowest point since the first spring of the war. (See Figure 3.)

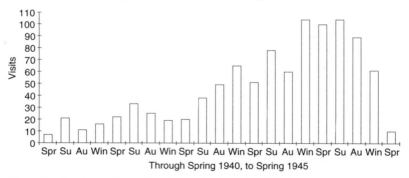

Figure 3 Total number of reports of visits, by ICRC or Protecting Power, per season

Material world

From Figures 4 and 5 (indicating the material conditions indicated in the reports, and as a percentage of the total reports made each season), it is clear that, save the troubles which were encountered in developing satisfactory accommodations up to the spring in 1940, the general material conditions remained either "fairly satisfactory" or better throughout most of the seasons of the war years, until the winter of 1944/5. In fact, except the winter of 1943 when the proportion slipped to 65 percent, most seasons yielded reports of satisfactory or better conditions in over 70 percent of the cases. The significant decline came as the fronts around Germany were collapsing. During the winter of 1944/5, 52 percent of the reports made to the camps indicated significant material problems for the prisoners of war. In the spring, given the state of collapse in Germany as a whole, it is unsurprising that the indications of dangerously inadequate conditions comprised over one-third of the cases, poor conditions comprised another third, and the satisfactory conditions were reported in just under one-third of the reports.

A slice of "excellence," for officers

Indicative of the reports showing supposedly excellent conditions was the visit by an ICRC representative to Oflag IX A Spangenberg, which housed 200 British officers and 50 British noncommissioned officers, on August 6, 1940. The physical attributes were almost picturesque: an old castle, with courtyard, made up the British section. It had most recently been used as a forestry school, which accounted for its modern furnishings, including electric lighting and central heating. It

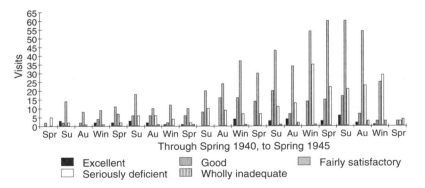

Figure 4 Material conditions in the camps

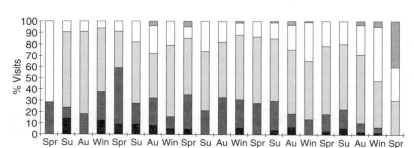

Figure 5 Material conditions in the camps (as a percentage of total reports of visits)

was situated on raised ground with a view of the land surrounding it. The interior arrangements consisted of variably sized rooms, with the occupants numbering 3 to 61 per room; they were billeted according to rank and branch of the service. The rooms were well ventilated and furnished with iron beds; in some of the larger rooms, the inspector felt the beds were placed a little too close together. The prisoners of war had common rooms and a good library at their disposal for use during the day. They were allowed one hot shower per man per week, and cold showers at other times; a very poor supply of soap resulted in a request to the Red Cross to send more as soon as possible. The kitchens for the prisoners of war were well equipped and sufficient for their number. The prisoners were issued standard German depot rations, which could be checked against a posted menu, as required by the Geneva Convention; the men complained, however, about both the quantity and quality of the potatoes. A recent reduction in the number of parcels received from England meant there was less than usual available to supplement their German rations, as had been the previous practice. The prisoners were well clothed, and as clothing parcels arrived from England, there was no foreseeable shortage in supplies; clothes were cleaned regularly at a laundry. The canteen was also considered by the inspector to be relatively well stocked, though there was no food at all available for purchase; beer, lemonade, and objects for personal hygiene could be purchased. The British prisoners complained about the poor quality and supply of Polish cigarettes they were able to buy. Religious services were available as well; a German minister who used to live in the United States came every week, and his visits were apparently greatly appreciated by the prisoners. There was plenty of opportunity for exercise, though most prisoners didn't seem to want to, blaming their lack of enthusiasm on the food. Gardening was possible, and an equipped gymnasium was at their disposal as well. Two-hour walks into the surrounding countryside, under armed guard, were organized twice a week. The prisoners also participated in their own orchestra. Outgoing mail was in order, but a recent decrease in incoming mail worried the prisoners greatly; mail had been arriving with some regularity up to July, before the current lack. The British officers received only a portion of their pay up front in cash, as was the practice elsewhere in Germany (the remainder of their salary was credited to their accounts). The prisoners of war enjoyed "perfect courtesy" from the German officers. Despite the complaints concerning the mail, potatoes, soap, and tobacco, the overall impression on the inspector was that it was an excellent camp. The discipline among the British was fine, and their only other request was that some extra medical personnel among the officers who were there be transferred to other camps where their skills could be put to better use.[8]

Examples of excellent camps for working soldier prisoners of war were the two autonomous work battalions containing British prisoners of war, BAB 20 and 21, which were visited by the ICRC on October 31, 1943. The inspectors stated that the almost 1,200 prisoners of war in each BAB lived in model circumstances; they had been there for the past year and a half. In BAB 20, straw for their palliasses was changed every three weeks, and each prisoner had one pillow and two blankets. They had stoves for the preparation of their Red Cross food in their rooms, one hot shower per day, no vermin, and adequate coal for heating. The hygienic installations were also good. The prisoners of war were employed as "heavy" laborers, and received the corresponding German rations for such. Though the prisoners of war did not like the taste of the German-issued food, the commandant felt this was because they received so much from the Red Cross that they did not appreciate or eat all that the Germans gave them. The linen for prisoner-of-war patients in the infirmary were regularly washed. The doctors, however, did not have a good supply of drugs, and requested more from the Red Cross. The prisoners of war had, in general, two full uniforms each, of which one was in good condition; their footwear was also in good shape. Only half of them also had received working clothes, but there was some debate as to whether or not the other half had a uniform which they chose not to wear for that purpose. The prisoners of war were mostly employed in building work, usually six and a half hours per day, with Saturday afternoons and Sundays free. There was a canteen, and though there was limited choice in the items for sale, the prisoners of war did get beer. There was a camp library, sports equipment, theater, three orchestras, a dramatic society and a debating club. Regular religious services were conducted by a Presbyterian minister. Letters from home arrived quickly, and all prisoners of war were able to write 2 letters and 4 postcards per month; the protected personnel here wrote 6 letters and 8 postcards per month. The disappearance of 10 cases of cigarettes from September's collective parcels was being investigated. Overall, the camp was excellent, and the discipline was good. BAB 21 was virtually identical in organization and in terms of the benefits of the prisoners of war. The only difference was that some prisoners had a harder time getting work clothes, and that American parcels seemed to be arriving damaged, of late. Overall, though, there were no problems of treatment here either, and it was considered excellent as well. In both camps, the Men of Confidence asked if any arrangements could be made to have superfluous medical orderlies repatriated; the ICRC delegate promised to investigate the matter.[9]

Enough to be "good"

Indicative of a report indicating "good" material conditions was that made by the Swiss representative who visited the 450 prisoners in the major work detachments attached to Stalag IV A Hohenstein on April 5, 1943. At Grube Brigitta, especially, the Man of Confidence and the Kommandoführer worked exceptionally well together, with the result that the camp gave a good impression in every way. More Red Cross parcels were needed, and prisoners of war were issued with a second uniform rather than work clothes, but there were no new complaints. At Grube Erika, the main complaint of the prisoners concerned the food. It was prepared by civilians, for prisoners of war of all nationalities; the rations were considered adequate, but the soups were thought to be far too watered down and thin. Long working hours were required of the prisoners of war here, though there were no major complaints about this. Some items of clothing were in almost desperate demand (especially trousers and boots), and the Red Cross had been informed to send more. A complaint that medical orderlies were working in the mines would be investigated by the Protecting Power. Despite these points, the representative thought the general conditions here were good. At Grube Ostfeld, where just under 100 prisoners of war were employed, conditions were satisfactory in every way, and there were no complaints or requests made. As elsewhere, the prisoners here received only one Sunday free each month, and worked 9 hours daily. Grube Heye III, where 50 or so prisoners of war worked, had a few more problems than the other detachments. Lighting was still very poor, and one barrack ceiling leaked. Working uniforms were in very bad condition, as even overalls were not provided. The Kommandoführer threatened to punish all prisoners of war by forbidding football, because of one prisoner's misbehavior; the prohibition of collective measures was pointed out to him. The recognized member of the medical corps who was previously not allowed on paroled walks, now was. The impression of the Swiss representative here was that conditions could be improved if the Man of Confidence showed a little more initiative. On average, however, the prisoners of war attached to Stalag IV A Hohenstein generally lived and worked in what the representative considered to be good conditions, and serious disciplinary problems were rare.[10]

"Satisfactory," in the end

In the opinion of the Swiss representative who visited Oflag XIII B Hammelburg on March 25, 1945, despite the generally deteriorating situation in Germany, the German authorities there managed to provide somewhat satisfactory conditions for the almost 1,500 prisoner-of-war officers and their orderlies. All the barracks in the compound had now been placed at the disposal of the officers, and the rooms, which were previously in a primitive state, had been improved. Though the camp was at its full capacity, each prisoner still had a bed, palliasse, and two German blankets. Stronger light bulbs had been promised to improve the lighting in the barracks. Due to coal shortages, wood-gathering parties were allowed out. There had been little improvement in the washing facilities, though; only 8 of 13 taps worked. Prisoners were still able to have one hot shower per month. There had been improvement in the toilet facilities, though there was still a shortage of toilet paper. There were no complaints regarding any of the facilities by the prisoners. The kitchen was well equipped, but there was not enough coal for much hot water; despite promises of more cleaning supplies, it was also difficult to keep clean. German rations were small, and the commandant promised to get whatever vegetables he could; Red Cross parcel supplies were also low, and more were needed. More medical orderlies were requested to deal with the increased number of prisoners of war. The infirmary was clean, lighted, and airy; serious cases went to the hospital in the attached Oflag for Serbs. This hospital, according to the American Medical Officer, was "absolutely first class." A list of needed supplies and drugs had already been sent to ICRC. There were many clothing shortages; heavy socks and shoe-repair material were needed most of all. There was little supply of materials for indoor or outdoor recreations. Especially requested were books, cards, and art supplies. Requests for theater supplies had been sent to the YMCA. Outgoing mail was in order, though there was so far no incoming mail. There were no complaints at all regarding treatment. All things considered, even with the deficiencies noted, the Swiss representative considered this camp satisfactory for the prisoners, especially when compared to conditions elsewhere in Germany.[11]

Not up to par

Stalag VIII B Lamsdorf, visited by the Swiss on September 14, 1944, was materially unsatisfactory in most regards. There was some mixing of nationalities in the compound, which led to some friction between them. Further, the camp was infested with bugs and fleas – there was no way to get rid of them. A thousand of the 13,000 prisoners of war were at the main camp, and the rest were in the work detachments; the base camp was overcrowded by approximately 250 prisoners. The most recently arrived prisoners slept on sacks filled with wood-wool on the theater floor, and cleaning utensils were almost non-existent. Some prisoners of war wanted heavy-labor rations for their work in building new barracks, but were denied. Though medical facilities had been improved, problems still existed – one wall of the infirmary was actually the back of a urinal, and had some leakage and smell. Only the German Medical Officers had the authority to grade prisoners of war for different levels of labor, and the British Medical Officer was not allowed to visit the Stalag Lazarett for security reasons. The drug supply was satisfactory. The British Medical Officer complained that he was often ignored regarding the selection of orderlies. Though the clothing situation was generally satisfactory, the stocks were almost exhausted, and shortages were imminent. Despite earlier ICRC protests, only half the parcels were being given to the men. This showed up especially in soap shortages affecting the mining work detachments. Pay was correct, but it was very difficult to purchase even small items, such as razors and matches. Religious services were held, but the ministers were only allowed to go to a detachment if return transport existed for that same day; consequently, some detachments had not received a visit from a clergyman in quite some time. The commandant promised that a minister would soon be stationed closer to the affected detachments, so this problem would be alleviated. Theater was forbidden by the Military District headquarters, because the German civilian population no longer had access to the theatre. Hockey-sticks and bats were recently confiscated, as they could possibly be used as weapons. Outgoing mail was regular, and incoming letters also arrived fairly regularly, though no parcels had arrived for several weeks. The main complaints of the Men of Confidence were: the storage of Red Cross parcels; the confiscation and loss of personal effects, both on arrival and later; the fact that only working prisoners of war were now allowed to purchase cigarettes from canteen, apparently according to a OKW order;[12] and the view that air-raid trenches were unsatisfactorily constructed. Thirty-eight British prisoners of war were accidentally killed by Allied bombardment when they refused to go into their air-raid trenches so they could "watch the Show"; they worked at IG Farben, Auschwitz, and their deaths were considered their own fault. Conditions in some of the labor detachments had improved a little (less Sunday work and fewer hours), but in general, material conditions had become worse since last visit, especially as regarded the vermin. The camp authorities could not cope and the commandant seemed too weak to effect change; his orders were often curtailed by his security officer, who really ran the Stalag. There were no reports of problems regarding either discipline, or the general treatment of the prisoners of war by the Germans.[13]

"Completely unsatisfactory"

The ICRC inspector visiting Stalag XVIII D Marburg, on October 23, 1941, found it to be completely unsatisfactory. Previously established for Polish prisoners of war, it had been taken over for use by British prisoners during the summer months. The terrible condition of the barracks had not been improved in any way. For example:

> The earth of the courtyard is covered with clinging mud; the three houses which constitute the Stalag are dilapidated and dirty, and there are piles of bricks and scaffolding everywhere. The outside air, which is already very cold, penetrates everywhere and the greater number of the rooms are not heatable. In the courtyard, in pouring rain mixed with snow, a long line of prisoners waits for the distribution of soup which is made in the open air. In brief, the general impression is miserable.

Closer inspection of the camp confirmed his initial bad impression. Three of the five large rooms designated for the 3,500 prisoners of war were unheatable. Ventilation and lighting, further, were inadequate, and only some of the prisoners of war had two blankets. One of the rooms, in which almost 230 prisoners slept, could only be reached by way of a small and narrow staircase; the inspector worried about their safety should a fire occur. Though several British prisoners of war prepared their food under the supervision of German noncommissioned officers, they found their diet very poor in meat and vitamins. Not having been captured long beforehand, the British generally had good-quality outer uniforms. However, 90 percent of those in work detachments had no socks and 80 percent had no woollen underclothes; boots were in a bad state both in the work detachments and the main camp. Further, the Man of Confidence had absolutely no control over the Red Cross clothing supplies sent to him; one full wagon-load of clothing was moved directly into German clothing stores without his supervision or inspection. No hot water was available for laundry. The only washing stations in the camp were outdoors in the courtyard; though covered by boards, they were subject to inclement weather, and especially the cold. British prisoners of war were allowed one hot shower per week, but the Man of Confidence claimed the German soap supply was halted with the arrival of the first Red Cross parcels. The latrines were both unhygienic and insufficient in number. An infirmary existed, but had no provisions for separating infectious cases from the other patients; serious cases were sent to a nearby hospital. The beds in the infirmary had a palliasse and two or three blankets, but no mattresses or sheets; the night before the inspector's visit, two patients had to sleep on the floor for lack of space. Some recreational diversions (books, games, and musical instruments) recently arrived from the YMCA. The detention cells were completely inadequate. Prisoners of war of all nationalities were mixed in small cells, and were only allowed out three times a day, for five minutes each time, during which they had to go and fetch their food. Most prisoners of war in detention had no palliasse or bed, and only one blanket; the cells remained unheated, even though the outside temperature dropped occasionally to freezing. Two cases were reported by the Man of Confidence of British medical personnel having been beaten by German medical staff; as the cases also involved a disagreement of some sort between the British Doctor and his staff, the matter was under investigation. Overall, the inspector wrote: "We can conclude that Stalag XVIII D [Marburg/Drau] is absolutely inadequate for its purpose. Everything is in disorder and very badly organised. The sanitary conditions were deplorable. The camp is a real danger to the health of the prisoners, and it is to be hoped that very serious measures will be taken before the winter to improve the present conditions in this Stalag."[14]

So bleak as to be dangerous

Instances of abuse or harassment were almost non-existent at Stalag X B Sandbostel, visited near the war's end, on March 13, 1945, by an ICRC delegate and one month later by a Swiss delegate; however, the material conditions of the camp were so terrible that "the prisoners' lives are in danger." Though the principal cause appeared to be the almost physical breakdown of Germany, the poor conditions there were nonetheless indicative of what could be found in the rare other circumstances, earlier in the war, in which inspectors found a camp's material conditions to be wholly inadequate. Physically, the camp was still situated far from any apparent war targets, near the northern town of Sandbostel. Of the 2,143 American and British prisoners of war, 1,700 were American, almost 400 were British, and the remainder were a mix of the two who had just arrived. Many of them had recently been transferred here from other camps out east, in the face of the Soviet advance. The interior accommodations were terrible: they were extremely shoddy in their construction, had no beds, and were overcrowded; many of the Americans slept on the floor without even straw. Even in the infirmary there were no beds, and the patients slept on the floor. In response to the complaints of the Men of Confidence, the commandant usually replied that the German civilian population suffered as well, and that there were limits to what improvements he was able to effect. Though most rooms had a stove of some sort, many were entirely without; the prisoners were trying to make some on their own, with bricks. There had been almost no normal heating all winter, as the little coal which existed had been used for the camp kitchen. Wood-gathering parties had been allowed out, but as two prisoners of war recently escaped during one such excursion, the practice had been stopped; at the request of the Swiss delegate and the accompanying OKW officer, the commandant promised to reconsider, using a parole-scheme worked out with the MOC which seemed to work in camps elsewhere. There was a shortage of blankets (both German and Red Cross). The food allotments were so low as to make malnourishment a serious problem, especially given the paucity of Red Cross parcels arriving. Though the British were rather well-clothed, many of the Americans recently arrived with almost no possessions, and lacked almost everything.

The American Man of Confidence, who served in the same capacity for the British prisoners of war as well, also asked the delegate for the immediate shipment of over 100 ICRC food parcels. The medical condition of the prisoners of war was also poor: all suffered from some amount of malnourishment, and serious cases of malnutrition were likely to develop within one month. The recent bombings of Bremen (from where the camp used to receive its bread supplies) meant that there was no more bread available, and the prisoners were given more potatoes instead; the commandant assured the delegate that bread would soon be arriving from Hamburg. Noise, smoke, and parasites all led to conditions in the infirmary being described as "deplorable." Medical supplies were also running very low. Perhaps the only thing which worked properly in the camp was mail; British and American prisoners of war all received mail regularly, and were allowed to send out the normal quantities of letters and postcards per month. Though Belgian and French prisoners of war in other compounds of the same the camp were detailed to do work directly related to the German war effort (fortifications and antitank defenses), the Americans and Britons were not. Recreational activities still existed in the camp, including theater, orchestra, sports, courses, lectures; their continuation was threatened, though, by the shortages of food, and the increase in prisoner-of-war numbers in the camp. Religious services were held regularly. Despite the material conditions of the camp, relations between the Anglo-American prisoners of war and the Germans were not bad; all serious disciplinary problems in the camp involved prisoners of war of other nationalities. The ICRC delegate's final assessment, however, left no doubt as to the wholly unsatisfactory conditions: "This is a bad Stalag, whose Authorities are doing nothing to improve the lot of the prisoners."[15] The Swiss delegate noted that, during the transfer of some prisoners of war from Stalag II B Hammerstein to this camp, a local SS officer demanded they turn over the 6,000 American Red Cross parcels located at the old camp. The Stalag's second-in-command, a German army lieutenant-colonel, refused, but was unable to prevent the SS men from physically carrying the supplies away anyway; the same thing apparently happened at various work detachments attached to Stalag II B before their evacuation to Stalag X B. Given that the fighting front was relatively close, the Swiss inspector believed the German staff had thought he would not visit the camp, and so "the Camp Commander and his staff did not bother to ameliorate conditions more than could possibly be helped."[16]

By service

It is also interesting to contrast the relative levels of material comfort enjoyed by prisoners of war based on the type of camp in question: Luftwaffe-run camps (Dulag Luft and the Stalag Lufts), the Kriegsmarine's Marlag, and the camps run by the German army for the officers (Oflags) and other ranks (Stalags and BABs). As can be seen from Figures 6 and 7 (indicating the percentage of reports made to each type of camp, and the material conditions found in the reports to the different types of camps), British and American prisoners of war held by the Kriegsmarine were most likely to endure better average conditions than those held by the Luftwaffe, or the Heer. The Stalags and BABs (Army – Other Ranks) suffered the highest proportion of "deficient" and "wholly inadequate" conditions, while the prisoners in the Dulag/Stalags Luft were most likely to have "excellent" or "good" conditions.

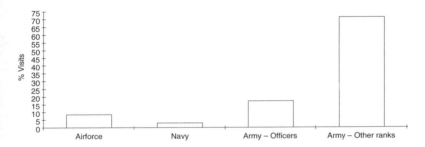

Figure 6 Visits made to each type of camp (as a percentage of total visits)

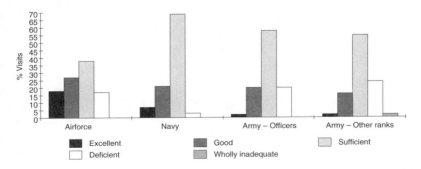

Figure 7 Material conditions (as a percentage of all visits to each type of camp)

Mistreatment by the captors

Of considerable concern for both the prisoners of war and their home governments were the instances in which the prisoners suffered from mistreatment at the hands of their German captors. No caveat is needed in assessing these criteria; what was protested as harassment or a serious violation of a prisoner's rights did not change in the course of the war years. Figures 8 and 9 provide a look, by season again, at the types of reported violations as a percentage of total reports made each season. As can be seen, for the duration of the war, reported significant violations never passed the 20 percent mark. Instances of serious violations were reported in the summer of 1941, and then in three of the four seasons of 1944.

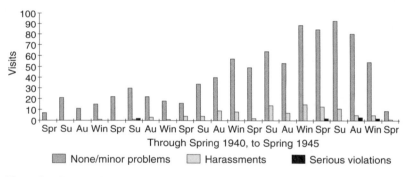

Figure 8 Geneva Convention violations

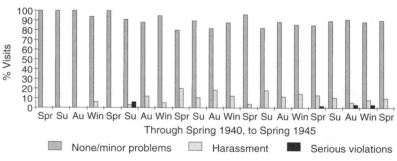

Figure 9 Geneva Convention violations (as a percentage of total reports of visits)

Harassment

The ICRC and Swiss inspectors visiting the camps containing British or American prisoners of war, reported significant harassment in 107 of their reports. The range of offenses classified in this way (as opposed to "minor problems," which could be solved on the spot by consultation between the inspectors and the German staff, and the "serious" or "grave" violations, described below) varied greatly, but can be summarized nonetheless.[17]

The most reported harassment concerned the shackling incident, in which Canadian and other British prisoners were handcuffed as a reprisal measure for the discovery of German soldiers who had been killed with their hands bound together after the Dieppe Raid,[18] in late 1942.[19] As the reports themselves indicate, the diligence with which the OKW order was carried out depended not only on the camp, but also on the date of the inspection. For instance, the ICRC inspector sent to Oflag VII B Eichstädt on November 10, 1942, to investigate conditions for the manacled (since October 8) British prisoners of war, found that the number of manacled prisoners of war was fixed at 381, of whom 321 were officers and the remainder orderlies. They were drawn first from the ranks of British captured at Dieppe (93 Canadians of the 97 captured there), and then randomly from British prisoners of war of all parts of the Commonwealth. They wore flexible manacles with either chain or bars links measuring 10 centimeters across. They were housed separately from the other prisoners, and wore the manacles from 08:00 in the morning to 21:00 at night, removing them for one hour at midday, and whenever they needed to go to the latrines. Unlike the remaining prisoners of war of the camp, who had their German rations reduced by a third, the manacled prisoners of war continued to receive the full German ration, and were apparently shown every kindness possible given the circumstances by both their peers and the German authorities. No injured or ill prisoner was manacled, and if a manacled prisoner fell ill, he was unshackled during his treatment and convalescence, and another prisoner took his place, so that the total number of shackled prisoners of war remained constant; the replacements were drawn from a large pool of willing volunteers. The manacled prisoners were also allowed one extra hour beyond lights-out, to enjoy as best they could without the manacles, which were removed when the rest of the camp had lights-out (21:00). The commandant was also hopeful of receiving more comfortable chain manacles soon.[20] The same camp was visited almost one year later by a Swiss inspector, November 5, 1943: the implementation of the "shackling" order by the German staff was by then so lax that it was almost considered to be a breach of the Geneva Convention in principle only. The guards entered the barracks of the designated prisoners at 08:00 in the morning, placed the handcuffs on their wrists, but left without either locking the manacles or checking to see that the chains which linked them were in fact connected. The prisoners kept up the charade by placing their handcuffs on just before each of the two daily roll-calls, and were left to their own devices for the remainder of the days. "Local authorities appear to disapprove of the order, which is carried out with tolerance and consideration ... [T]he German guards turn the blind eye to the fact that [the handcuffs] are removed before and after the parades." The otherwise satisfactory conditions of this camp led to the assertion that it was an inconvenience as it was applied, rather than a serious problem.[21]

Other reprisal measures instituted by the OKW and noted by the camp inspectors included those taken in retaliation for Camp 306 in Egypt (in which Germans had apparently been mistreated by Jewish guards of the Palestine League),[22] Camp F in Canada (poor conditions for German prisoners of war),[23] and mail delays to German prisoners in Australia (for which Australians in Stalag VII A Moosburg had their mail withheld until diplomatic efforts apparently were undertaken to defuse the situation).[24] In all of these instances, the reprisal measures were ended much more quickly than for the shackling incident. Other instances of collective reprisals were for local causes, as prisoner-of-war escapes often resulted in a general curtailment of privileges for all the prisoners of the camp in question, despite the prohibition of such mass measures by the Geneva Convention.[25]

The other activities which the inspectors considered to be forms of significant harassment included: questionable or unsuitable physical location of the camp or work detachment;[26] local shooting policies for German guards;[27] physical and verbal abuse, by German guards and work-detachment leaders as well as the occasional civilian employer of prisoners;[28] irregular disciplinary procedures (especially the use of solitary confinement); "special" companies of prisoners awaiting punishment;[29] harassment of Allied NCOs who refused to work as general laborers;[30] difficulties in obtaining medical attention in distant work detachments due to the German guards;[31] the search of prisoners' quarters without an MOC present, and resulting loss of property;[32] and problems faced by the MOCs in communicating directly with the Protecting Power or in controlling their ICRC parcels;[33] and illegal, war-related work.[34]

With the exception of the shackling incident (mentioned in 20 reports), the reprisal camps (7 reports), and the relocation of Dulag Luft to central Frankfurt, all of the above-mentioned reports of harassment revolved around low-level misuses of authority, rather than concerted efforts by the OKW. In many instances, it was the actions of a single guard or individual which resulted in the problems,[35] while in other cases, such as for the shooting policies, the German commandant's policies were the problem. Most of the problems noted by the inspectors were rectified to some degree or another either by negotiation on the spot, or after the Protecting Power intervened at the Wehrkreis level or with the OKW itself.

Serious problems

Eight reports over the course of the war years indicated very serious violations of the Geneva Convention (forming less than 1 percent of the total reports of visits made during the war); an overview of them is worth indulging in to highlight the nature of serious violations in general, and their causes. Aside from two reports concerning a single camp in 1941, the remainder occurred in the spring and autumn of 1944, and the winter of 1944/5.

The two reports in the summer of 1941 both concerned Stalag XX B Marienburg, where guards had been shooting into prisoners' barracks, and severely beating others for reasons related to work.[36] After protests lodged by the Swiss, no other instances of this nature occurred at this camp for the remainder of the war.

The shooting of the 47 recaptured prisoners of the "Great Escape" from Stalag Luft III Sagan constituted perhaps the single greatest crime against British or American prisoners of war during the war. The report noting the occurrence, of April 17, 1944,[37] further pointed out that the commandant of the camp, who was well-regarded by the prisoners, was replaced for health reasons, as he had suffered a heart-attack because of the incident. As was made clear at the Nuremberg Trials,[38] the actual murders of the prisoners were not carried out by Wehrmacht troops, but by the SS, and were conducted further at the personal behest of Hitler.

The serious violations of the Convention noted in a May 1944 visit to Stalag V C Offenburg occurred in one of the few instances where material conditions were so willfully terrible that their continuance could only be taken by the inspectors to be a form of cruelty.[39] The problem concerned the lodging of British Indian prisoners of war next to a machine room, leading to sleep deprivation and complete nervous breakdowns, and was rectified after the Swiss strongly urged the work detachment be dissolved and sent elsewhere.

The transfer of American and British airmen from Stalag Luft VI Heydekrug to Stalag Luft IV Groß Tychow formed the basis of the serious violation of the Convention noted in both the Swiss and ICRC reports of early October 1944.[40] This seems to have been the fault of the commandant and the military-district commander personally, rather than the result of any orders from the OKW at this time. No other transfers were noted to have occurred under such brutal conditions and with such blatant disregard for the Geneva Convention, but it should be noted that no further serious incidents concerning these prisoners occurred again.

The situation of the British prisoners in the Sonderbarracke of Stalag 317 Markt Pongau, noted during a Swiss visit in October 1944,[41] was blamed mostly on the threats and intimidation coming from the German noncommissioned officer who was in charge of the detachment; no such serious problems were noted in the next visit to that camp, or in any of the previous visits to the camp under its previous name (Stalag XVIII C).

The terrible conditions suffered by the British and especially the American prisoners of war at Stalag IV A Hohenstein, noted in the visit of late February 1945, were, in the opinion of the ICRC delegate, the result of the commandant's prejudice against prisoners of those two nationalities.[42] Americans were singled out for harsh treatment and occasional beatings by the guards, and the American and British Red Cross parcels were distributed to other nationalities but not to them (leading to general malnourishment and, as a consequence of the general weakening of the prisoners' constitutions, leading to a spate of deaths from pneumonia). The commandant countered every request for improvement by effectively stating that the bombing of Dresden was the cause of the problems (i.e. that he refused to attempt to improve conditions in retaliation for the raid), despite the fact that the living conditions of the prisoners of other nationalities at the camp (French, Belgian, Dutch, Yugoslav, and Polish) were bearable.

Examining the issue of harassment and serious violations of the Geneva Convention in terms of the types of prisoner-of-war camp in question leads, as Figure 10 indicates, to interesting conclusions. Visits to prisoners of war held by the Kriegsmarine and those in the OKH's Oflags indicated no serious violations of the Geneva Convention, whereas 4 percent of the visits to the Luftwaffe's camps and 1 percent of the visits to the Stalags and BABs showed that grave violations had occurred. On the other hand, the prisoners of war held by the Kriegsmarine and those held in the Oflags were more likely to suffer from varying forms of harassment. But when the proportions are viewed alongside the total numbers of visits (Figure 6), it is clear that more Other Ranks in the Stalags and BABs suffered from both harassment and serious violations of the Geneva Convention than either the officers in the Oflags or the prisoners held by the Luftwaffe and Kriegsmarine.

6.2 Policy versus evidence

Comparing the evolution of specific policies of the OKW toward American and British prisoners of war alongside the findings of the ICRC and Protecting Power reports over the course of the war years allows one to see if or how any specific instructions correlated with the changes in conditions noted in the camp reports.

There was nothing in the orders from the OKW from the outbreak of war through the spring of 1940 which would seem to account for the unsatisfactory conditions noted in five of the seven reports made during this time. Once the camps had been running for some months, the general conditions reported by the inspectors remained constant over the next year. Aside from one report indicating some harassment (retaliation, the Germans claimed, for alleged poor conditions suffered by German prisoners of war at one camp in Canada), there were no problems in any of the camps until the summer of 1941, with over 90 percent of the reports also indicating "satisfactory" living conditions.

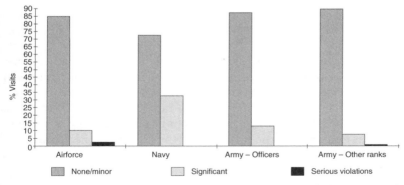

Figure 10 Geneva Convention violations (as a percentage of all visits to each type of camp)

From the OKW's orders, there appears no one reason why the instances of serious violations of the Geneva Convention and harassment increased as much as they did, in the summer and autumn of 1941. In one camp, the issue was clearly an overstepping of authority by the commandant. In two others, though, instances of guards beating prisoners to force them to work, could be taken as a direct result of the OKW's orders making the guards responsible for the prisoners' labor efficiency, as well as guarding them in the workplace. During the autumn of 1941, the major problem, with relation to treatment, was the continuing use by commandants of collective punishments for infractions committed by individual prisoners. These clear violations of the Convention did not result from any explicit order from the OKW.

Following a decrease in reported instances of harassment during the winter of 1941/2, inspectors noted a significant increase in the spring of 1942. Most of the problems noted by the inspectors to the camps revolved around increased shooting occurrences, and occasional mistreatment at the workplace. The mistreatment at the workplace might be considered to have been foreseeable, given that the OKW in the winter of 1941/2 allowed for disciplinary authority over prisoners of war in work detachments to be delegated to noncommissioned officers if no officers were present. Though less than one month later the OKW reversed its position by stating that only officers had formal disciplinary authority after all, the ambiguity the order created seemed to already have had an effect. No specific orders were issued at this time which could be said to have led to the increase in shootings, though the inspectors' reports made clear that escape attempts occurred with increasing regularity.

More problematic was the increase in reports indicating poor material conditions, which began in the summer of 1941 and remained (proportional to the total visits made each season) somewhat stable through to the summer of 1943. The first significant increase in reports indicating poor material conditions, in the summer and autumn of 1941, coincided with the formal implementation of the food-reduction orders which had been hinted at as early as the spring of 1940. Naturally, some adjustment in the volume and frequency of supplies from the Red Cross to the prisoners of war can be assumed to account for part of the sudden rise. However, an examination of the camp reports also demonstrates that a significant problem was general material shortages: there were not enough barracks, bunks, blankets, cleaning stations, and latrines for the increasing number of prisoners of war.

Though the sudden influx of British prisoners after Dunkirk seemed to have been absorbed without difficulty, it appears that the increase in prisoners from the Balkan campaign, as well as general war shortages, may have contributed to this state of affairs. Certainly, once the Red Cross supply lines were organized, the prisoners of war had enough food from their collective parcels. The remaining material problems in the camps at this time did not seem to be the result of OKW orders intending to lead to the material deprivation of the prisoners. Materially, then, this level of unsatisfactory conditions (hovering between ten to twenty percent of the reports) stayed constant through the autumn of 1943.

In the summer of 1942, the OKW, recognizing that previous efforts to induce greater productivity from working prisoners of war were not successful, allowed for Nazi Party officials to assist in overseeing their efforts. Given the combination of the legitimate authority vested in guards to compel prisoners to work hard and the advice the guards were obliged to consider from Nazi officials, it is not surprising that, with some fluctuations, instances of harassment were reported in approximately 15 percent of the visits over the remaining war years. The largest single act of harassment visited upon British or American prisoners of war was the shackling of thousands of preferably Canadian, and otherwise other British, prisoners starting in October of 1942. It did not increase the average number of instances of harassment reported during the period of its implementation, meaning that other forms of harassment seemed to have decreased during this time. Other reasons for the level of harassment included instances in which commandants instituted forms of collective punishment for the ever-increasing number of escape attempts by the Anglo-Americans.

6.3 Conclusions

Having examined the evolution of the OKW's policies toward British and American prisoners of war, as well as the reports of the ICRC and Protecting Power reports of visits to camps containing the prisoners of these nationalities, some general conclusions can now be made with reference to the major fields covered in this study.

Prisoner-of-war administration

Changes during the war years in German policy on the general command and control of British and American prisoners of war gave some concern for the safety of the prisoners. In most countries, including Germany at the time of the signing of the Geneva Convention in 1929, there was little question as to who would exercise command over the prisoners of war: the armed forces of the Detaining Power. But with the rise of a parallel military structure (the SS) within Nazi Germany, the issue became more complicated.

Hitler's desire, after the July 20, 1944, assassination attempt on his life, to place the Ersatzheer more firmly under loyal command resulted in the appointment of Heinrich Himmler to Commander-in-Chief of the Reserve Army in September 1944. As the Reserve Army was responsible for running the prisoner-of-war administration in Germany, the potential SS influence did not bode well. Until the later phases of the war, however (as indicated in the reports of visits by the ICRC and the Protecting Power), the SS and Gestapo influence in the camp was held at arm's length in most circumstances, and the umbrella of military command over the prisoners of war was maintained.[43] The use of the Gestapo in conducting searches and in rounding up escaped prisoners of war, and the OKW orders requiring closer coordination between the commandant and military district staff and the various Nazi party organizations, were not illegal in principle: these activities were conducted under the nominal command of the OKW. And as noted earlier, the changes to the prisoner-of-war administration, resulting finally in the appointment of SS-General Gottlob Berger as Chef Kriegsgefangenenwesen, occurred at a high enough level above the camps as to have little direct consequence in most instances, with the exception of the requirements to more closely coordinate escape countermeasures and searches with the local police or Gestapo offices.

Identification and status of prisoners of war

Though the Geneva Convention identified persons who could expect to be treated as prisoners of war, changes in the definition of a prisoner of war by Germany excluded from this category many who had previously enjoyed the protection of the Convention, especially commandos and downed airmen. In the case of the former, Hitler ordered that small groups of Allied commandos be killed by all the forces under his command, both SS and regular military; in the case of the airmen who had been shot, civilians were encouraged to kill them in lynch-mobs before the prisoners were formally inducted into the prisoner-of-war administrative process, with guarantees given that the lynch-mob would not face prosecution for the criminal acts.

The Commando Order of October 18, 1942, was issued by Hitler in conjunction with the shackling order for Canadian and other British prisoners of war. After the raid at Dieppe, by mostly Canadian soldiers and British commandos, had been repulsed, members of both the German armed forces and the Todt organization had been found with their arms bound in such a way that they would eventually, and did, strangle themselves. Further, a British close-quarters combat manual was purportedly found which instructed commandos to keep prisoners alive only insofar as it was expedient. The one effect of these discoveries was the order to shackle many Canadian, and then British, prisoners of war, while the second effect of the discoveries made after the raid was that it stimulated (or gave an excuse for) Hitler to declare that the commandos had, by their actions, placed themselves outside the common rules of warfare. Henceforth, regardless of whether they fought in uniform or as spies or *franc-tireurs*, Allied commandos caught fighting outside major military beach-heads or war zones were to be killed rather than taken prisoner.[44] The defendants at Nuremberg did not try to deny the existence of the order (copies of which were entered as evidence), and even admitted at the time that killing commandos rather than making them prisoners of war represented "something new in international law, since the soldiers were in uniform,"[45] in Raeder's words. In the debates leading to the final decision to implement the Commando Order, Admiral Canaris of the Abwehr voiced his disapproval of the plan, arguing that "[m]embers of sabotage units who wear uniforms, are soldiers and are entitled to being treated as prisoners of war; if they wear civilian clothes or German uniforms they have no such rights (franc-tireurs)."[46]

The Commando Order was applied in all the theaters of the European war, from Italy to Norway, and was carried out by all branches of the armed forces,[47] in addition to the Party military branches. Given the explicit directives of both the Geneva Convention and the previous Hague Conventions, as well as the German military manuals and Dr. Waltzog's 1942 update of them, as to who warranted treatment as a prisoner of war, the Commando Order's implementation, affecting conditions of capture for specialized units of the enemy's armed forces, represented an obvious breach of international law committed by the OKW (not just the Nazi military structures), and was easily proven to be a war crime at Nuremberg.[48] As there was never any doubt that captured Allied airmen were prisoners of war, the decision made to encourage and allow civilian mobs to kill them before the airmen could be taken to a Dulag Luft was perhaps an even more egregious violation of the Geneva Convention affecting the identification and early captivity of prisoners of war.

The killing of American and British airmen who had been forced to bail out over Germany marked an attempt by the dictatorship to include all levels of German society, which was now being directly attacked by the Allies from the air, in the war. As noted in the evidence and testimony at Nuremberg, the primary architect of this policy was Martin Bormann.[49] As early as August 10, 1943, Himmler had instructed the police not to interfere in instances where the German public lynched downed airmen, writing that "[i]t is not the police concern to intervene into dealings of the German population with the shot down English and American airmen who practice terror."[50] Additionally, in a note of May 21, 1944, Hitler ordered that downed enemy flyers "be shot without summary trial in all the following cases: (1) When they fired at (German) airmen parachuting to safety; (2) When they attacked with deck-arms German aircraft and their crews on emergency landings; (3) When they attacked trains and railway lines; (4) When they attacked individual civilians with deck arms-fire."[51] One week later, in the *Völkischer Beobachter* of May 28–9, 1944, Goebbels published an article, "A Word on Enemy Terrorism in the Air," in which he stated that, in carrying out raids over cities, Allied pilots placed themselves

> outside every internationally accepted norm of the Laws of War... . Under such circumstances only armed intervention of the military or police could save the lives of shot-down airmen, but who has the right to exact that these airmen are treated humanely, that German troops and police are called to act against the German people when they treat the murderers of children as they deserve being treated[?] ... We can find ways and means to defend ourselves against these criminals.[52]

Two days later Bormann's circular to the local party organizations explained how they should behave in the event that "spontaneous" lynchings take place: "No police or penal measures [are to be] taken against citizens involved in incidents of this kind."[53] According to Göring's testimony at Nuremberg, he protested against the action to Hitler, citing possible similar reprisals on the part of the Western Allies. Hitler's simple alleged reply was that German pilots fighting on the Eastern Front already ran the risk of being lynched after bailing out – why should their comrades fighting in the West be placed in a preferential state?[54]

Despite Göring's apparent attempts at dissuading Hitler from pursuing the policy, members of his staff drew up a process for separating airmen who were suspected of carrying out "terror-crimes" from other captured airmen at Dulag Luft, and handing them over to the SD; a list of crimes justifying these measures was created by Warlimont and Colonel Brauchitsch of Göring's staff.[55] The German Foreign Office disagreed, saying such actions would amount to a renunciation of the 1929 Convention on POWs; Hitler's decision on July 4, 1944, was: "Every enemy airman who had taken part in this sort of attack and was shot down cannot expect to be treated as a prisoner of war – instead he should be killed immediately after being held by German hands (he should be treated as a murderer)."[56] An OKW order, referring to Goebbels' article, instructed soldiers not to intervene if airmen were being mobbed or lynched.[57] The end result of this order, which, like the Commando Order, was carried out by the regular German military as well as Nazi Party or police units, was the killing of many American and British airmen before they could be taken into formal captivity.[58] In one example of the impact of these measures, a German military captain named Heyer ordered, in late 1944, guards escorting three captured British airmen to the Luftwaffe Interrogation Center in Essen to not interfere if civilians were to mistreat them along the way; his gave this order in a loud enough voice that a nearby crowd could hear every word, and along the march they set upon the airmen, and threw them to their deaths over a bridge.[59] At Nuremberg, it was demonstrated that airmen were killed not only by civilians in lynchings, but also by the SS: 47 American, British, and Dutch airmen were beaten and eventually shot at Mauthausen in early September 1944 rather than being taken into captivity and turned over to the Luftwaffe.[60]

"Minorities" among Anglo-American prisoners of war

Given the genocidal nature of the Nazi regime, another obvious source of concern for both the American and British Commonwealth governments was the fate of Jewish members of their armed forces who might be captured in combat. For the British, this issue was especially important given the fact that 1,500 volunteers from Palestine (mostly Jewish, but also some Arab) fell into German hands with the surrender of British forces at Kalamata, Greece, in April 1941, and then in the following months in Crete. Initial fears that these Jews would be mistreated proved unfounded, as the German soldiers who arrived to take the British into captivity showed little interest in the subunits among them.[61] The difficult conditions suffered by these prisoners during their initial internment at Corinth was common to all the British prisoners; Jews among them were not set apart for different treatment.[62] The

6,000 British prisoners taken at Sphakia, Crete, were also separated into nationalities, and of the total British forces taken captive in Greece and Crete, the Palestinian prisoners of war were among the first to be sent to Germany.[63] Fears that the Jewish prisoners would be forced to wear the Jewish star after their arrival in Marburg in early July 1941 proved unfounded, though they were not allowed out of the camp in work detachments like the other prisoners at first.[64] By the end of July 1941, these prisoners were finally transported to Lamsdorf, where they were formally registered with the Red Cross for the first time, and were placed in the main British compound. At Lamsdorf, the German commandant initially refused to allow the Jewish prisoners to receive Red Cross parcels, and considered forcing them to wear a distinctive badge identifying themselves as Jews; the British Man of Confidence informed the commandant that all British prisoners would refuse their Red Cross parcels in sympathy, and that a formal protest would be launched with both the ICRC and the Protecting Powers unless the Jewish prisoners henceforth received the same treatment as the remainder of the British. The German commandant, reluctant to create a diplomatic incident, issued the Red Cross parcels and made sure the same measures were in place for all the British prisoners.[65]

Though few American accounts deal mainly with the issue of Jewish American prisoners in German captivity, those which have been written corroborate the experiences of the British Jewish prisoners, as well as the Red Cross and Protecting Power reports, in indicating that although there may have been individual antipathy and some insults or minor abuse, there was no concerted policy aimed against Jewish personnel caught in American uniform. In one memoir, a Jewish American officer recalled that a German noncommissioned officer guard slapped him for not confirming his religion aloud; the noncommissioned officer was ordered by his officers to apologize, but did not. The same American officer's guard on the train to Dulag Luft informed a fellow passenger, a German soldier, that the American was Jewish; the German soldier said nothing, and instead offered him a cigarette.[66]

Other soldiers who could potentially fear problems during capture for racial reasons were black soldiers of the American and British militaries, and on several different occasions from May 1944 onwards, small groups of black soldiers were killed upon capture by the SS rather than being taken into captivity. In one instance, after combat near Raids, France, in late June 1944, the commander of the 1st Battalion, 17th SS Infantry Division, specifically ordered that "no Negro prisoners were to be taken alive."[67] The most noticeable thing about the cases involving black Allied soldiers is that the alleged atrocities were carried out by members of the Waffen-SS, and not regular German military units; thus, with regard to OKW complicity on this matter, the evidence indicated that atrocities were committed by units of the SS.[68]

Generally speaking, when a prisoner of war had been accepted as such, and the process of registration was begun, acts of violence or public humiliation were rare. One notable example occurred in Italy in January 1944, when Field Marshal Kesselring ordered Lieutenant-General Kurt Maelzer to parade several hundred British and American prisoners of war through the streets of Rome, in an effort to boost morale. Maelzer was charged by the US Military Commission in Florence in September 1946 with violating article 2 of the Geneva Convention[69] and was sentenced to 10 years' imprisonment. "During the parade, onlookers threw sticks and stones at them. Numerous photographs were taken and published in the Italian press under the caption 'Anglo-Americans enter Rome after all ... flanked by German bayonets.'"[70] Events such as this, however, represented the exception rather than the rule with regard to both German military policy and practice.

In some cases, delays in the recognition of captured British and American soldiers contributed to almost desperate conditions and illegal uses of the prisoners. In mid-August 1944, in the face of the Allied advance in France, 168 American and other Allied prisoners were evacuated from the prison in which they were held in Fresnes, to Buchenwald, by the SS.[71] They had been evacuated before the process of registration had begun, with the consequence that no one from the German military knew they were there. Though not treated as cruelly as the main inmates at Buchenwald, some of the prisoners of war were beaten or placed in solitary confinement, and all suffered from the poor rations of food given to them. It was only through the cooperation of two British spies also being detained there, who were in contact with Russian prisoners of war employed at a nearby Luftwaffe airfield, that the Senior Allied Officer was able to smuggle a list of the names of the prisoners of war to Luftwaffe officers. Two days after the list was placed into the hands of a German airforce officer, two Luftwaffe officers arrived at Buchenwald itself and interviewed the prisoners; they were sent to Stalag Luft III Sagan soon thereafter. In total, these military prisoners of war spent two months in Buchenwald; given the confusion of the time, had the Senior Officer not shown the initiative necessary to get his charges noticed by the Luftwaffe, one may wonder how long they would have remained there. In smaller, less organized instances, delays also occasionally occurred in the accordance of recognition of prisoner-of-war status to captured American or British soldiers.[72]

There were several instances during the war in which American or British soldiers who would have been considered prisoners of war even by the changing German standards were killed for nontactical reasons, when holding them alive did not pose a threat to the capturing troops, rather than taken into captivity: 100 British officers and men of the 2nd Battalion, Royal Norfolk Regiment, taken prisoner near Le Paradis on May 26, 1940, by units of the SS-Totenkopf Division were killed; between June 7 and 21, 1944, the 12th Panzer Division, SS-Hitlerjugend, killed a total of 107 captured Allied soldiers (103 Canadians, 3 British, and 1 American) after fighting near the Normandy towns of Château d'Audrieu, St. Sulpice-sur-Rile, Les Saullets, Les Mesnit-Patry, Les Mains, Mouen, Authie, and Argentan; on July 25, 1944, the captured crew of a British Sherman tank were killed rather than taken into captivity by soldiers of the 11th SS Division; on July 28, 1944, 4 British soldiers were shot by members of the 752nd SS Infantry Regiment; and at Malmédy, on December 17, 1944, 129 captured and disarmed American soldiers were killed by members of the 150th SS Panzer Brigade.[73] But with the exception of the case of commandos and downed Allied airmen, the murder of regular American and British prisoners outside major combat zones, rather than their induction into captivity, was practiced by the SS, and not regular German military (that is, OKW); examples raised at Nuremberg of the murder of American and British soldiers who had already been taken into captivity also indicated that it was at the hands of forces of the SS, SD, or the Gestapo.[74]

In a final note regarding the limited implementation of the Geneva Convention toward American and British prisoners of war during the initial stages of capture or captivity, Hitler queried both Dönitz and Jodl on the possibility of simply repudiating the Geneva Convention in its entirety, on February 19, 1945.[75] Dönitz's reply was: "From the military point of view, as far as naval operations are concerned, there are no arguments in favor of this; on the contrary, more harm than good can be expected. Such a step would in fact in the opinion of the Commander in Chief of Naval Forces yield no benefits whatsoever. It would be better to make arrangements – considered necessary – without previous notice and to retain one's face outwardly for all eventualities."[76] Jodl suggested that the maintenance of outward acceptance of the Convention did not in fact have to mean its observance in practice; to deter "the terroristic air attacks of the enemy" it might be enough to put out more reports about the "unavoidable" cases of Allied pilots shot down over Germany, being lynched by the infuriated population, rather than simply repudiate the Geneva Convention.[77]

Early captivity

The trips back through the rear echelons to the Dulags often were arduous for the newly captured American or British prisoners.[78] Once there, the formal induction into the German prisoner-of-war system began, usually with an interrogation. In addition to seeking administrative information to register the prisoners (name, rank, serial number), the Dulags afforded an excellent opportunity to try to gain valuable military information through interrogations. This use of the transit camps, unforeseen by the Geneva Convention, was common to Germany, Britain, and the United States; indeed, some of the most valuable British and American military intelligence came from adding together the piecemeal information gathered at such interrogations.[79] The OKW generally did not interrogate captured army NCOs and other ranks; army officers usually spent from two to three weeks at the army interrogation center at Stalag III A Luckenwalde, some of it in solitary confinement. The most sophisticated and subtle interrogations within the OKW were carried out by the Luftwaffe at Dulag Luft.

Captured British and American airmen were subject to many ruses by the interrogators, including being given fake Red Cross forms to fill out which demanded far more information that the real ones did. The individual holding cells were sometimes heated to unbearable levels, and the food was monotonous, in a concerted effort to depress the prisoner and thus lower his resistance to friendly questions from genial interrogators who could make the discomforts end. The prisoners were often told that they would not be sent out to a permanent camp unless they answered all the questions asked of them, and in some cases were threatened with being turned over to the Gestapo if they didn't cooperate more fully. The threats were, however, empty, and the prisoners were, after up to three weeks in a Dulag, sent onward to a main prisoner-of-war camp.[80]

Attempts were made by both Germany and the western Allies, especially in the early stages of captivity, to use recently captured prisoners of war against either their own side or their allies. In addition to the OKW orders for the release of prisoners who volunteered to fight in battalions against the Soviets, Arab prisoners of the Palestinian League were sent to Stalag III D Berlin in July and August 1941 to undergo intensive propaganda from Arab collaborators, and were afterward given the opportunity to join the Arab Legion, to fight the British.[81]

Prisoner-of-war camps

With regard to the siting and physical location of the main prisoner-of-war camps and work detachments in which British or American prisoners of war were detained, Germany mostly abided by the terms of the Geneva Convention. The notable exception was the policy decision taken to move Dulag Luft to the center of Frankfurt am Main, in the hopes of dissuading the Allies from bombing the city center.[82] The Swiss inspector visiting the new camp on November 1, 1943, noted only that the "Senior British Officer strongly objected to its location. It is, if not right in the middle, at least in a large town which could perhaps be considered as a military objective";[83] the inspector did not add his own opinion on the matter. A less sanguine view was taken by the Red Cross delegate who visited the camp two weeks later, and wrote:

> [t]his transfer of the Camp is of great importance. It is the only point to which the report must pay extreme attention. While throughout Germany systematic evacuations of large urban conglomerations of population are proceeding, the German authorities are acting in altogether a different manner toward the British and American airmen, by transferring their camp which was previously situated in the countryside, to a town where the danger of aerial attack is very grave. This new step is contradictory to the provisions of Article 9 of the Geneva Convention. The old camp, which was excellent from every point of view, did not need any improvement.[84]

The complaints as to the location were reiterated by Swiss delegates visiting the camp again on January 24, 1944; the notation of the Canadian government to the report indicated that "[t]he only really unsatisfactory feature about this camp is the location and as two protests have already been lodged by the British to which we are awaiting replies no action is necessary at this time."[85] The situation was inadvertently resolved by the Allies themselves, as the report of the Swiss representative's visit to Dulag Luft, of May 22, 1944, indicated:

> Dulag Luft Wetzlar is in place of Dulag Luft Frankfurt a/M. which was destroyed in course of one of the latest air-raids on Francfort [sic].... On request of the German Camp Commander, speaking on behalf of higher quarters, the Delegate has to inform the US and British Government for information to their flying forces,[86] that should this camp ... be destroyed by bombs no other accommodation than tents will be provided for Air-Force personnel regardless of

weather conditions or season of the year... . There were no serious complaints. The men are quite satisfied with their present quarters and other arrangements ... "[87]

Thus, the German attempt to use the British and American airmen as human shields did not work, as the Allies bombed the city regardless of their presence.

The material conditions of the OKW's camps for American and British prisoners of war, as described in the Protecting Power and Red Cross reports, remained at a "satisfactory" level or above in the vast majority of reports of visits. However, "satisfactory" did not necessarily mean that the requirements of the Geneva Convention were being met. One of the most basic issues was overcrowding. The OKW tended to provide relatively acceptable levels of accommodation during the earlier war years; the general overcrowding in the camps became worse during the summer of 1944 and when the Soviets advanced closer.[88] And as noted above, the German decision to cut food rations by a third in early December 1941 effectively meant that prisoners relied on the supply of Red Cross food parcels for the maintenance of a basic diet; the rations actually issued to the American and British prisoners varied from camp to camp, and often depended on the local availability of produce, and the initiative of the commandant's staff.[89] As the war took a heavier toll on the German transportation infrastructure,[90] and food and clothing supplies at the camps dwindled, the quality of life fell accordingly; the food supply to most camps in 1945 was, in the words of an ICRC inspector visiting the camps, "very precarious";[91] in camps reporting seriously deficient or wholly unacceptable material conditions in 1945, prisoners usually suffered from significant malnutrition, and in some cases near-starvation.[92]

The many British and American complaints concerning the clothing (and especially blanket) situation for their prisoners in German captivity were met in the same way as for the food shortage: the Red Cross parcels proved a necessary part of keeping the prisoners well-clothed and fed. The general tone from the Protecting Power and Red Cross reports is the same. The heating fuel situation was again directly dependent on the availability of supplies to the local German staff. In reports of visits to camps made later in the war years, the existence of wood-gathering parties of prisoners, let out "on parole," is noted more frequently; from 1944 onward, the practice was so common in camps with coal shortages that the absence of wood-gathering parties in a given camp was considered grounds for complaint or further discussion between the Protecting Power and the OKW.[93] Though the prisoners depended as well on the Red Cross for medical supplies in addition to food and clothing, the Germans did prove able to provide medical materials in desperate situations.[94] German efforts in regard to other aspects of the material conditions (such as the quality of sanitation, heating fuel, structural integrity of the barracks and other camp buildings) often fell short of the requirements of the Convention.[95]

As was seen by the reports of the Red Cross and the Protecting Power, British and American prisoners of war were generally given the postal rights as outlined by the Geneva Convention. Frequent disruptions occurred, but these were usually the result of logistical problems, such as transportation deterioration or a shortage of translators and censors, rather than any concerted effort by the German military authorities to renege on their obligations.

It was clear to the German authorities that it was in their interest to keep idle officer or NCO prisoners of war occupied with other matters than escape; if Red Cross parcels arrived in enough quantities to allow for the food, clothing, and medical situation to become bearable, thoughts inevitable turned to both recreation and education, in an effort to make existence in the camps more viable. So long as much German material was not required and security was not threatened, the OKW generally encouraged such activities, and allowed for both YMCA delivery of recreational material and Red Cross supervision of reading and educational programs.[96] Among the British prisoners of war especially, education became a large part of their captivity.[97] By early 1942, a structure was in place to allow for university equivalency courses to be taught and examinations to be held, in conjunction with Scottish and English universities as well as many professional associations. By the end of the war, nearly 17,000 applications for examinations had been made; of the 10,000 candidates who sat their exams in the camps, almost 80 percent passed.[98] With regard to religious services and the increasingly limited (for working prisoners of war) recreation time, the German authorities tended to adhere to the requirements of the Geneva Convention in allowing the free practice of faith among the prisoners. Such activities were subordinate to the requirements of work, however, and when the prisoners had no time off, their leisure activities suffered accordingly. As was demonstrated by the OKW's orders, the camps exercised censorship over the sermons in an attempt to make sure they remained apolitical.[99]

Because of German refusal, the first exchange of prisoners for medical reasons took place only in October 1943. In May 1944, 698 Germans were exchanged for 990 American and British Commonwealth prisoners. In September 1944, an additional 50 British Palestinians were released, and a month later, a larger group of 200 British, most of whom were Palestinians, were also released. In January 1945, the last exchange was carried out.[100]

Once the American or British prisoners of war were liberated by the advancing Allied armies, their material privations ended; the armies of occupation took care of them and organized their eventual repatriation.[101]

Concerning the general modes of transportation, matters were generally acceptable until the final months of the war, with the withdrawal of thousands of prisoners of war from the advancing Allied armies. The worst reported case of transport of British and American prisoners of war, noted earlier, concerned the march of 10,000 Allied airmen from Sagan, as the Soviet army approached in February 1945; they marched for two weeks with no food, sleeping on bare earth or on the snow, and Hitler personally ordered that any attempting to escape be simply shot.[102]

Discipline

With regard to the maintenance of discipline within the camps, as could be seen from the many German exhortations to the guards to be "firm but correct" in dealing with the prisoners, German practice was usually correct in the early war years. The guards themselves were usually middle-aged or slightly infirm men not fit for duty elsewhere, who generally professed no enthusiasm for the war.[103] But with the increase in escape attempts, the subsequent threat to German internal security and the resulting drain on manpower, security restrictions were introduced which had the effect of limiting the remaining prisoners' quality of life: the collective parcels were distributed in small amounts, to prevent reserves being built up with a view to escape; officers were often no longer allowed to walk about the compound; and movements even within the camp were reduced. In accordance with the Geneva Convention, special camps were set up to provide "heightened security" to repeat escapees: Rawa-Ruska (Stalag 325), Colditz (Oflag IV C), and Lübeck (Oflag X C). Security generally became tighter across all prisoner-of-war camps following the mass escape at Sagan, and with the greater influence and participation of the Gestapo in "coordinating" security measures with the OKW's camp security officers.[104] Disciplinary problems involving Jewish prisoners of war were rare. While outbursts against them (verbal, usually) were not uncommon, they were the result of the personal initiative of the abuser, and not of orders from above.[105] Clashes occasionally occurred between British Arab prisoners and German guards, despite the general German efforts to entice them into volunteering for the Arab Legion.[106] And the OKW orders exhorting guards to improve the labor efficiency of the prisoners of war led, from early 1943 onward, to increased clashes between the two groups. Swiss delegates, investigating complaints from the British Palestinian prisoners at Stalag VIII B Lamsdorf work detachments, noted the increases of beatings and even shootings in the coal mines throughout the region at the time.[107]

Escape

When faced with the problem of escape, the OKW generally adhered to the terms of the Geneva Convention, with regard to the punishments offered against the recaptured British and American prisoners of war. The one significant exception to this, dealt with at Nuremberg after the war, was the shooting of the 47 recaptured British airmen after the mass escape from Stalag Luft III Sagan. Both the official British enquiry into the shooting of the prisoners and the Nuremberg trial records showed that the killings were carried out by the SS, and not the German army or airforce.[108] And despite the predictably self-serving nature of Göring and Keitel's postwar testimony regarding this massacre, the fact remained that some sort of attempt to prevent the murders was carried out by Göring, who cared greatly about possible repercussions on the fate of German airmen in Allied captivity, and that Hitler did not trust his military leaders to carry out the executions.[109]

Labor

The use of British and American prisoners of war in illegal war-related labor was generally the exception rather than the rule, and was usually remedied soon after complaints were made by the Protecting Power or ICRC. General directives concerning the necessity of using prisoners of war to assist the war effort, in direct and indirect ways, were produced at the Nuremberg Trial from before the war's beginning, on January 28, 1939.[110] And though the prosecutors, in discussing a August 17, 1944, directive concerning the use of prisoners of war in directly war-related efforts, referred in court to its impact on French and British prisoners of war,[111] the documentary evidence they entered referred only to French, and not British, prisoners;[112] both the OKW's policy and postwar Nuremberg trials indicate that the Anglo-Americans were exempted from such labor. Exceptions occasionally occurred at the lower levels of command, and were usually dealt with there: in February 1941, 3,600 British prisoners of war were thought to be working in one munitions factory; upon hearing that a Protecting Power delegate was on his way to investigate the matter, the head of the military district had them quickly replaced with French workers.[113] The overall impression left is that American and British prisoners of war were rarely employed directly in aid of the German war effort, but that French and Russian prisoners of war were, with ample evidence provided at the Trials to convict the German military and civilian leadership of the breach of the Convention with regard to these nationalities.[114]

The Wehrkreis commanders were responsible for making the prisoners of war available to local employers, through the auspices of the local labor boards. In this, the OKW competed directly against Sauckel's foreign-worker pool and the SS's provision of labor through the concentration camps. Each of these groups, in turn, also had conflicting interests with Speer's munitions ministry, which controlled its own workers. In general, the Wehrkreis commanders resisted the transferal of the valuable resource of prisoner-of-war labor even to other military districts.[115] By mid-1943, it was estimated that 20 percent of the workforce in the German coal industry consisted of prisoners of war; the demand was growing so great that Hitler decided to allow for the employment of even Soviet prisoners within Germany itself, and ordered partisans to be captured and put to work rather than being shot.[116] In July 1943, over two and a half million prisoners of war of all nationalities were at work in Germany.[117] In February 1944, there were almost 80,000 British prisoners at work in Germany.[118] Of the British, 23.5 percent worked in mines and metallurgy, 18 percent in other types of industry, 24 percent in construction, 10.5 percent in energy and transportation, 17.5 percent in agriculture and forestry, 3 percent in administrative work such as banking or commerce. The fairly even spread of the British in all branches of the Reich economy comes as a result of their not being placed directly to work in the war economy, as they were protected by the Convention.[119]

The changing economic conditions within the belligerent countries had a significant impact on the working conditions of the prisoners of war.[120] The general production needs and manpower shortages in Germany led the authorities, as was seen from the many directives on labor efficiency, to try to maximize their use of the prisoners. The working hours were usually longer for prisoners of war than for German workers. In industry, the length of the work day for prisoners ran from 10 to 14 hours, especially as the war progressed, while the number of free Sundays per month was reduced. In agriculture, prisoners of war could be employed for up to 17 hours per day at the height of the season, with free Sundays even rarer than in industry; the increase in hours was partially offset by much greater rations of food than was generally available in the main camps. The only effect the ICRC could hope to obtain was a promise that those prisoners working under the most difficult conditions and hours would be rotated from time to time. While the Red Cross and the Protecting Power intervened in cases in which American and British prisoners of war were employed in dangerous or unhealthy work, the Anglo-American prisoners were generally exempt from use in prohibited war-related concerns.

Reciprocity

The basic principles of reciprocity and reprisal required both sides of the conflict to be sensitive to the treatment of their soldiers in the other's captivity.[121] During the summer of 1942, German prisoners of war held by the British at Latrun, near Jerusalem, were maltreated by their guards, and protested to the Spanish Consul; in reprisal, in August 1942, 82 Palestinian NCOs and 68 other British prisoners of war were sent to Stalag 319 Chelm, a penal camp, where the treatment of the two groups was harsh.[122] In February 1943, a Red Cross inspector wrote, "Camp 319 is a camp which was built as a retaliation; it cannot be compared to any regular camp. It is more shoddily constructed than the others. In addition to this, relations between the prisoners and their guards are not the best." The Red Cross reported that the Germans were prepared to return the prisoners of war to their original camps if the British removed the Germans from Latrun. By the end of May 1943, the NCOs were returned to their original camps, as the British had apparently removed the German prisoners to other camps in Egypt.[123]

With regard to the Dieppe shackling incident,[124] the British did not dispute most of the facts of the German charges, but stated that rather than general battlefield policy, the actions at Dieppe had been justified under article 1, which stated that the Convention was "subject to such exceptions (derogations) as the conditions of such capture render inevitable." The Germans invoked the next sentence: "Nevertheless, these exceptions shall not infringe the fundamental principles of the present Convention," to which the British replied that, in any event, reprisals were specifically forbidden. An end was almost found on December 12, 1942, when the British and Canadians agreed to uncuff their German prisoners at the suggestion of Carl Burckhardt. The Germans agreed on the condition that the British officially prohibit, under penalty, the binding of prisoners and the use of handcuffs. The British agreed while at the same time stating that sometimes it might be inevitable (i.e. they didn't agree).

The decisive criteria for the application of reprisals by the German military were expediency and effectiveness.[125] The order to shackle Canadian and other British prisoners of war after Dieppe in 1942 was the direct result of a German investigation into the conduct of these troops during the raid.[126] The WUSt's investigations into war crimes committed by American and British forces, in some instances, appeared credible. But the extent to which these incidents influenced the resulting German military policy toward British and American prisoners of war appears negligible; only in the shackling order after Dieppe in 1942 can an Allied action be clearly linked to a German counteraction.

Overall treatment

In their postwar assessment of the plight of prisoners of war, the ICRC believed that an important factor affecting the quality of life and the material conditions for all prisoners of war was the economic situation of the Detaining Power and, to the extent that they could send supplies via the Red Cross, the home country.[127] But equally decisive in affecting the quality of life for the British and American prisoners of war were the personalities of the prisoners' representative (MOC or Senior Officer) and the German camp commandant. Aside from instances in which orders from above or material shortages limited action, the MOC's ability to maintain a firm but diplomatic presence with the commandant was almost as important as the commandant's professionalism. Further, in the larger camps, effective administrative ability was necessary from the MOC in keeping the Red Cross supplies properly rationed and organized. While the camp commandant was not able to change the instructions he received, or improve the quantity of rations when these were decided from above, he could often ensure that the remaining factors within his control kept circumstances as tolerable as possible; good governance from the commandant could lead to good relations with the prisoners and relatively bearable conditions despite material shortcomings, while ill-will from a commandant could make an already bad situation much worse.[128]

As regards the overall treatment of prisoners of war by Germany during the war, the evidence presented at Nuremberg mostly dealt with nationalities other than Americans or soldiers of the British Commonwealth. The OKW was responsible for several other violations, in addition to the already mentioned shackling order and the implementation of the Commando Order, including the decision to relocate prisoners of war (Dulag Luft, in the case of the Anglo-Americans) in German cities to "render by [their] presence certain points or areas immune from bombardment," in the words of article 9 of the Convention.[129] Another failure of the German military of its responsibility toward the prisoners of war concerned the woeful transport conditions, already noted in the Red Cross and Swiss reports above, which existed in the last few months of the war; the panic of the final months often led to atrocious conditions, in which shelter and food were often non-existent. Though many shortcomings in the OKW's treatment of British and American prisoners of war were noted at Nuremberg, they tended to be overshadowed by more serious violations against prisoners of other nationalities, leading the Soviet prosecutor to remark that he felt the OKW leaders were being handled too leniently by his Allied colleagues.[130]

Notes

Chapter 1: Introduction

1 See for instance Diether Cartellieri, "Erinnerungsveränderungen und Zeitabstand – Ein Beitrag zum Problem der Erinnerungsleistungen in Abhangigkeit vom Behaltensintervall," in Erich Maschke, ed., *Die deutschen Kriegsgefangenen des Zweiten Weltkriegs: Eine Zusammenfassung* (Munich: Verlag Ernst und Werner Gieseking, 1974). [Band XV of the multivolume series, ed. Erich Maschke, *Zur Geschichte der deutschen Kriegsgefangenen des Zweiten Weltkrieg* (Munich: Verlag Ernst und Werner Gieseking, 1962–74), hereafter referred to as the Maschke Series.]
2 The diaries and memoirs written soon after the close of the war are a useful source for fleshing out how the prisoners themselves saw the outcome of the policies of the OKW, as well as their perception of the effectiveness of the ICRC and Protecting Power reports. For instance, the assessment of Winston Churchill's nephew, Giles Romilly, a prisoner-of-war held at Oflag IV C (Colditz), that the inspectors were, simply, the prisoners' "angels": Giles Romilly and Michael Alexander, *The Privileged Nightmare* (London: Weidenfeld and Nicolson, 1954). Likewise for the ever-increasing number of articles and also monographs which continue to appear, touching on specialized aspects of the Wehrmacht's conduct during the Second World War. None of the recent work seen by the author since the completion of this book has affected the overall conclusions reached in this "top-down" evaluation of the policies and then general conduct of the OKW with relation to British and American POWs.
3 Yves Durand, *La Captivité, Histoire des Prisonniers de Guerre Français, 1939-1945* (Paris: Fédération Nationale des Combattants Prisonniers de Guerre et Combattants d'Algérie, Tunisie, Maroc, 1982).
4 Jean-Marie d'Hoop, "Lübeck, Oflag X C," *Revue d'histoire de la deuxième guerre mondiale* 10, pp. 15–29; *idem*, "Propagande et Attitudes Politiques dans les camps des prisonniers: le cas des Oflags," 31(122), pp. 3–26.
5 *Revue d'histoire de la deuxième guerre mondiale*, especially Janvier 1957.
6 More specifically, many articles on various aspects of prisoner-of-war history in some parts of occupied Europe have been written, such as: Stanislaw Senft on North Moravia, in *Slezský* [Poland] 1972, 70 (90), pp. 118–28; G. Hantecler, "L'origine et le nombre des prisonniers de Guerre Belges 1940–1945," *Revue internationale d'histoire militaire* [of Belgium] 29 (1970), pp. 949–61; Asbjorn Eide, "Humanitet I Vaepnet Kamp? Krigens Folkrett under Revisjon," *Internasjonal Politikk* [Norway] 2(2) (1973), pp. 341–58.
7 Gerhard Hirschfeld, ed., *The Policies of Genocide: Jews and Soviet Prisoners of War in Nazi Germany* (Boston: Allen and Unwin, 1986); Christian Streit, *Keine Kameraden: die Wehrmacht und die sowjetischen Kriegsgefangenen 1941-1945* (Bonn: Verlag J. H. W. Dietz Nachf., 1997); Alfred Streim, *Die*

Behandlung sowjetischer Kriegsgefangener im "Fall Barbarosa" (Heidelberg: Müller Verlag, 1981).
8 See the text of the 1929 Geneva Convention. Henceforth, all references to the "Convention" will be to this treaty.
9 Many articles have been written by Rüdiger Overmans and Otto Engelbert. See also volumes X/1, X/2, XI/1, and XI/2 of the Maschke Series (as above); K. D. Müller, K. Nikischkin, and G. Wagenlehner, eds., *Die Tragödie der Gefangenschaft in Deutschland und in der Sowjetunion 1941–1956* (Köln; Weimar: Böhlau, 1998), esp. the comprehensive bibliography pp. 439–62.
10 Siegfried Schönborn, *Kriegsgefangene und Fremdarbeiter in unserer Heimat 1939-1945* (Freigericht: Naumann, 1990); Erich Kosthorst, *Konzentrations- und Strafgefangenenlager im Dritten Reich: Beispiel Emslang: Zusatzteil, Kriegsgefangenenlager: Dokumentation und Analyse zum Verhältnis von NS-Regime und Justiz*, 3 vols. (Düsseldorf: Droste, 1983); Frank Eisermann, ed., *Main-Kinzig-Kreis: Dokumentation zum Schicksal der Zwangsarbeiter und Kriegsgefangenen, der Flüchtlinge und Vertriebenen im Main-Kinzig-Kreis* (Hanau: Main-Kinzig-Kreis, 1993).
11 David Rolf, *Prisoners of the Reich* (London: Cooper, 1988).
12 David Foy, *For You the War is Over: American Prisoners of War in Nazi Germany* (New York: Stein and Day, 1984).
13 Rolf, p. 205.
14 Rolf's bibliography refers only to four series of files as having been used at the the Bundesarchiv-Militärarchiv in Freiburg (BA-MA).
15 BA-MA MSg1/2011,2012 provides details of the postwar interrogations of General Westhoff as well as a series of affidavits and charts, tables, etc., on the workings and structure of the entire Kriegsgefangenenamt of the OKW.
16 Specifically, BA-MA RW 6/270 provides a very nearly complete collection of the Befehlsammlungen, or fortnightly orders and updates, issued during the course of the war years by the OKW's prisoner-of-war branch.
17 David Alden Foy, "'For You the War is Over': The Treatment and Life of United States Army and Army Air Corps Personnel Interned in Pow Camps in Germany" (Ph.D. dissertation, University of Arkansas, 1981).
18 For example, in a section describing the dangers of escape on p. 125, Foy, *For You the War is Over*, refers to German Regulation Nos. 29, para. 462, and 32, para. 504. These are the Befehlsammlungen found at BA-MA in RW6/270, but, as is clear from his footnote references on pp. 179–80, he drew them from secondary sources, and not from either the German archives themselves or the microfilms of captured German records held at the National Archives in Washington DC.
19 Andrew S. Hasselbring, "American Prisoners of War in the Third Reich" (Ph.D. Dissertation, Temple University, 1990).
20 Some of the more noticeable questionable and undersupported comments include Hasselbring's claim that Germany was influenced by both Jean-Jacques Rousseau and "the intangible reason of humanity" in its attitudes toward prisoners of war, without offering any citations or evidence for the generalizations (p. 2–3); his assertion that tobacco "deprivation" constituted a form of "physical abuse" during interrogations (p. 59); the repeated claim

that an exceptional spirit of chivalry existed between the Luftwaffe and captured pilots, while admitting that "no direct evidence" existed to support the claim (p. 7); his delineation of threats of abuse by German interrogators as violations of the Geneva Convention, before stating that "In the main, the techniques used by Germany were the same as those employed by Great Britain and the United States against Axis POWs" (p. 75), without either elaboration or citation of evidence; his ignoring of the existence of testimony from Allied former prisoners in describing what is known of SS General Gottlob Berger's tenure as Chef Kriegsgefangenenwesen in late 1944 (p. 107); and most egregious of all his misstatements, his claim that the executions after the mass escape at Sagan were caused in part by the disbelief among the escaping prisoners of war that damage committed during an escape could lead to a court-martial (p. 152), a view of the tragedy that doesn't even seem to take into account the widely available, published description of that atrocity in the International Military Tribunal records.

21 On page 70 he writes, "Recognizing every military's need for intelligence and the expediencies of war, the Geneva Convention excluded [military interrogation] and the other transit camps from inspection ... " There is no such exclusion in the Geneva Convention; moreover, para. 2 of article 86 of the Convention appears to guarantee the opposite: "The representatives of the Protecting Power or their recognized delegates shall be authorized to proceed to any place, without exception, where prisoners of war are interned. They shall have access to all premises occupied by prisoners and may hold conversation with prisoners, as a general rule without witnesses, either personally or through the intermediary of interpreters." The cumulation of this sort of problem in the work inspires suspicion of credibility whenever Hasselbring departs from the details of prisoner-of-war daily life for more general observations and conclusions.

22 Jonathan Vance, *Objects of Concern: Canadian Prisoners of War Through the Twentieth Century* (Vancouver: University of British Columbia Press, 1994).

23 The exception to this is Vance's discussion (see note 22 above) of the Canadian raid at Dieppe in 1942, and the subsequent shackling incident, which carefully examines the issue in detail from all sides.

24 Patsy Adam-Smith, *Prisoners of War, From Gallipoli to Korea* (Victoria, Australia: Viking Penguin Books, 1992), ch. 2, "World War II; Prisoners of the Germans," pp. 88–203.

25 Louis Althusser, *Journal de captivité: Stalag X A* (Paris: IMEC, 1992); D. Guy Adams, *Backwater: Oflag IX A/H Lower Camp* (New York, 1944); Jim Longson and Christine Taylor, *An Arnhem Odyssey: "Market Garden" to Stalag IV B* (Barnsley: Leo Cooper, 1991); Djamel Dib, *L'archipel du Stalag* (Algiers: Enteprises nationale du livre, 1989).

26 Walter Morrison, *Flak and Ferrets* (London: Sentinel, 1995); Jack Pringle, *Coldtiz Last Stop* (Sussex, UK: Temple House Books, 1995); and especially P. R. Reid, *Colditz: The Full Story* (London: Macmillan, 1984).

27 Werner Borgsen, *Stalag X B Sanbostel: zur Geschichte eines Kriegsgefangenen- und KZ-Auffanglagers in Norddeutschland, 1939–1945* (Bremen: Edition Temmen, 1991).

28 Arthur A. Durand, *Stalag Luft III: The Secret Story* (Baton Rouge, LA: Lousiana State University Press, 1988).

29 In his dissertation at least, Durand acknowledges the limitations of his scope, and the reasons for his choices: "most of the materials relating to the British, Dominion, and German roles are not available in [the United States] ... It would have been an ambitious project, indeed, that attempted an equally detailed study of all six compounds at one time, and also the German side of the story." Arthur Durand, "Stalag Luft III: An American Experience in a World War II German Prisoner of War Camp" (Ph.D. dissertation, Louisiana State University, 1976), pp. xiv–xv.
30 Durand, *Stalag Luft III: The Secret Story*, pp. 158–74.
31 Ibid., p. 161.
32 This aspect will be examined further with specific references below, in the section on food.
33 United States, Department of the Army, *United States Army in World War II* (Washington, DC: Government Printing Office, 1948–85).
34 W. Franklin Mellor, ed., *Official Medical History of the Second World War: Casualties and Medical Statistics* (London: HMSO, 1972), pp. 835–8.
35 C. P. Stacey, *The Canadian Army, 1939-1945* (Ottawa: E. Cloutier, King's Printer, 1948).
36 International Committee of the Red Cross, Report of the International Committee of the Red Cross on its Activities during the Second World War, Sept. 1, 1939 to June 30, 1945, vol. 2: "The Central Agency for Prisoners of War" (Geneva: 1948).
37 International Committee of the Red Cross, *Revue Internationale de la Croix-Rouge* (Geneva: published monthly, 1939–45 issues).
38 André Durand, *From Sarajevo to Hiroshima; History of the International Committee of the Red Cross* (Geneva: Henry Dunant Institute, 1984). The Institut Henri Dunant is the official research institute of the International Red Cross, whose archives are opened only to their own researchers, and not to the public.
39 Colonel George C. Lewis and Captain John Mewha, Department of the Army Pamphlet no. 20-213: *History of Prisoner of War Utilization by the United States Army 1776–1945* (Washington DC: Government Printing Office, 1955). Despite the sweeping range indicated in the title, this volume focuses mostly on the use of German prisoners of war in the United States during the Second World War.
40 BA-MA RW 6/184, 450, 451, 452, 453. These files provide monthly compilations of numbers of prisoners of war in German control, broken down by camp and nationality, from September 1940 to January 1945. They were the official tables sent by the OKW to the ICRC in Geneva. Copies of the same information can be found in Washington DC at the National Archives and Records Administration (NARA): Microcopy No. T-77, Serial/Roll 828 (First Frame 5564618) and Microcopy no. T-77, Serial/Roll 827 (First Frame: 556971).
41 John Ellis, *World War II: A Statistical Survey* (New York: Facts on File, 1993), pp. 253–6.
42 Article 43 of the Convention: "Such appointments [MOCs] shall be subject to the approval of the military authorities... . In camps of officers ... the senior officer prisoner of the highest rank shall be recognized as intermediary between the camp authorities and the officers." As will be

seen, tensions rose considerably on the rare occasions when the Commandant did not accept the prisoners' elected choice as MOC.
43 Vance, *Objects of Concern*.
44 National Archives of Canada (NAC): Record Group 24, and Reel C-5339.
45 NARA: Record Groups 59, 200, and especially 389.
46 Public Record Office of the United Kingdom (PRO): Record Groups FO 916, and WO 224.
47 The decision to rely on the reports of the Protecting Power and ICRC delegate visits to the camps was made because they were neutral citizens whose independent assessments came after visiting many camps (giving them a wide range of experience) and whose reports were complemented by those of colleagues visiting camps in other countries. Unlike individual prisoner-of-war memoirs or diaries, these reports provide a uniform and impartial standard assessment of the actual conditions found in the camps.

Chapter 2: Background Information

1 League of Nations Treaty Series 118, no. 2734 (343).
2 I Samuel XV 3. All biblical references are from the King James Version of the Bible (Owen Sound, Ontario: Gideons International in Canada, 1977).
3 Deuteronomy 20:16–18.
4 Deuteronomy 20:12–16.
5 Sun Tzu, *The Art of War*, tr. Samuel B. Griffith (Oxford: Oxford University Press, 1963), p. 77.
6 Frank Kierman and John Fairbank, eds., *Chinese Ways in Warfare* (Cambridge, MA: Harvard University Press, 1974), p. 27.
7 Frank Kierman, "Phases and Modes of Combat in Early China," in Kierman and Fairbank, pp. 31, 33, 34.
8 Ibid., pp. 45–6.
9 Ibid., p. 62.
10 Michael Loewe, "The Campaigns of Han Wu-ti," in Kierman and Fairbank, pp. 102–3.
11 Thucydides, *The Peloponnesian War*, tr. Rex Warner (Middlesex, England: Penguin Press, 1954), pp. 485–7.
12 Plato, *Republic*, Book V, sections 468–72, tr. G. M. A. Grube (Indianapolis: Hackett Publishing Company, 1974), pp. 128–32.
13 William Flory, *Prisoners of War; A Study in the Development of International Law* (Washington DC: American Council on Public Affairs, 1942), p. 12, with references to Coleman Phillipson and André Chotard.
14 Hugh Elton, *Warfare in Roman Europe, AD 350–425* (Oxford: Clarendon Press, 1996).
15 Ibid., pp. 53, 185.
16 Ibid., p. 56.
17 Ibid., p. 130.
18 Ibid., p. 133.
19 Ibid., p. 135.
20 Ibid., p. 248.

21 Robert Ward, *An Enquiry into the Foundation and History of the Law of Nations in Europe from the Time of the Greeks and Romans to the Age of Grotius*, 2 vols. (New York: Garland Publishing, 1973 (repr. of 1795 London ed.)), vol. 1, p. 216.
22 Philippe Contamine, *War in the Middle Ages*, tr. Michael Jones (Oxford: Blackwell, 1984), pp. 33–5.
23 For this and a full examination of the rules concerning ransom in this period, and recourses to courts should disagreements arise, see M. H. Keen, *The Laws of War in the Late Middle Ages* (Toronto: University of Toronto Press, 1965), ch. 10, "The Law of Ransom," pp. 156–89. The right-hand gauntlet signified the willful laying down of arms, or surrender, of a captive.
24 Ward.
25 Contamine, p. 42.
26 Ibid., p. 151.
27 Ibid., p. 152.
28 Flory, p. 13.
29 Quoted in Contamine, pp. 256–7.
30 Contamine, p. 257.
31 St. Thomas Aquinas, *Summa Theologica*, vol. 2, tr. Fathers of the English Dominican Province (Chicago: Encyclopedia Britannica Inc, 1953), pp. 577–81.
32 Aquinas, p. 578.
33 Mark C. Bartusis, *The Late Byzantine Army: Arms and Society, 1204–1453* (Philadelphia: University of Pennsylvania Press, 1992), p. 74.
34 Bartusis, p. 252.
35 Ibid., pp. 208–9.
36 Ibid., p. 134.
37 Cited in Flory, p. 11.
38 Ernst Gurlt, *Zur Geschichte der Internationalen und Freiwilligen Krankenpflege im Kriege* (Leipzig: Vogel, 1873). France signed 187, German Empire and Austria 102, Brandenburg and Prussia 80, Spain 49, England 46, Holland 37, Sweden 23, Bavaria and the Palatinate 11, Denmark 9, United States 9, Russia 8, Turkey 4.
39 Hugo Grotius, *The Law of War and Peace*, tr. Louise R. Loomis (Roslyn, NY: Walter J. Black Inc., 1949), p. 297.
40 Grotius, Book III, ch. IV, "Right of Killing Enemies in Lawful War and Other Bodily Violence," *passim*.
41 Montesquieu, *De l'ésprit des lois* (Paris: Librairies Barnier Frères, n.d.), pp 127–9.
42 David Hume, *An Enquiry Concerning the Principle of Morals 1751*, eds. L. A. Selby-Bigge and P. H. Nidditch (Oxford: Clarendon Press, 1975), pp. 183–92 (sec. III, pt. I, "Of Justice").
43 See esp. Hume's footnote concerning Montesquieu in sec. III, pt. II (p. 197).
44 Ibid., p. 187–8.
45 Ibid., p. 188.
46 Ibid., p. 188.
47 J. J. Rousseau, *The Social Contract*, Book I, ch. IV, tr. Christopher Betts (Oxford: Oxford University Press, 1994), pp. 49–53.

48 Ibid., p. 52.
49 Ibid.
50 American National Red Cross, *Historical Background of International Agreements Relating to Prisoners of War*, rev. Feb. 15, 1944. (Washington DC: ARC 313, 1944).
51 Ibid., p. 4.
52 Ibid.
53 Ibid.
54 Henry Wheaton, *History of the Law of Nations in Europe and America from the Earliest Times to the Treaty of Washington, 1842* (New York: Garland Publishing, 1973; repr. of 1845 ed.), p. 162.
55 Ibid., pp. 163–4.
56 American National Red Cross, p. 5.
57 Ibid., p. 4.
58 The following summary is extracted from David Wells, *The Laws of Land Warfare: A Guide to the U.S. Army Manuals* (Westport, CN: Greenport Press, 1992), pp. 133ff. Wells reprints the specific terms of the Lieber Code, in addition to providing commentary and analysis.
59 American National Red Cross, p. 6.
60 Ibid., p. 7.
61 Ibid.
62 Ibid.
63 American National Red Cross, p. 10.
64 Flory, pp. 21–3.
65 American National Red Cross, pp. 10–12.
66 Flory, p. 22.
67 Robert Jackson, *The Prisoners, 1914–18* (London: Routledge, 1989), p. 5–6. Though the summary which follows is drawn from Jackson's book, other works worth consulting further include: R. A. Reiss, *Le traitement des prisonniers et des blessés par les Austro-Germano-Bulgares* (Paris: Librairie Bernard Grasset, 1919); Ronald F. Roxburg, *The Prisoners of War Information Bureau in London* (London: Longmans, Green and Co., 1915); Daniel J. McCarthy, *The Prisoner of War in Germany* (New York: Moffat, Yard and Company, 1918). Desmond Morton, *Silent Battle: Canadian Prisoners of War in Germany 1914–1918* (Toronto: Lester Publishing, 1992), provides a current and thorough analysis of the experiences of Canadian prisoners during the First World War.
68 Jackson, pp. 137, 140–1.
69 Ibid., pp. 22, 66.
70 Ibid., p. 137, quoting the the US Ambassador to Berlin's secretary, Mr. John B. Jackson.
71 Ibid., pp. 24 ff.
72 Ibid., p. 77.
73 Ibid., p. 79.
74 Ibid., p. 80.
75 Ibid., p. 81.
76 Ibid., pp. 53–4, 106–8, 140–1.
77 Ibid., p. 113.
78 Please refer to the text of the 1929 Geneva Convention.

79 Germany did not treat Soviet prisoners of war according to the terms of the Convention despite article 82, which stated: "The provisions of the present Convention shall be respected by the High Contracting Parties in all circumstances. In time of war if one of the belligerents is not a party to the Convention, its provisions shall, nevertheless, remain binding as between the belligerents who are parties thereto."

80 The Convention's requirements and obligations for each given field will be presented in detail, along with official German policy at the start of the war, at the beginning of each of the relevant sections. What follows here is a general overview.

81 Canada, *Regulations Governing the Maintenance of Discipline Among and Treatment of Prisoners Of War* (Ottawa: King's Printer, 1939). Hereafter referred to as "Canadian Regulations."

82 Great Britain, War Office, *Regulations for Maintenance of Discipline among Prisoners of War* (London: HMSO, 1939). Hereafter referred to as "British Regulations." Given that the British and Canadian Regulations are virtually identical, the Canadian Regulations (which were obtained by the author first) will be cited as the source reference for the Commonwealth position, with the British Regulations being cited only if they differ.

83 Canadian Regulations, paras. 1–7.

84 Ibid., paras. 8–18.

85 Ibid., paras. 14, 19, 20, and 21.

86 Ibid., para. 23.

87 Ibid., paras. 25–39.

88 Ibid., paras. 42–9.

89 Ibid., paras. 53–63.

90 Ibid., paras. 64–105.

91 Ibid., Appendix A.

92 Ibid., paras. 4–5.

93 United States, War Dept., *Rules of Land Warfare: Basic Field Manual FM-27-10* (Washington, DC: Government Printing Office, 1940).

94 Wells provides an overview of how the rules concerning American policy toward prisoners of war changed, from the General Orders of 1863, to the Rules of Land Warfare of 1914, 1934, 1940, and 1956: Wells, pp. 133–66.

95 BA-MA RHD 4/38/2: Oberkommando der Wehrmacht, *Vorschrift für das Kriegsgefangenenwesen Teil 2: I Abkommen über die Behandlung der Kriegsgefangenen vom 27. Juli 1929, II Genfer Abkommen zur Verbesserung des Loses der Verwundeten und Kranken der Heere im Feld vom 27. Juli 1929*. Berlin: Reichsdruckerei, 1939. The also the English version of the 1929 Geneva Convention.

96 These are listed as sequential volumes of the BA-MA RHD 4/38 series. In March 1942, the OKW ordered (BA-MA RW 6/270, 11/3/42: OKW Az. 2 f 24. 20 a Kriegsgef. Allg [IVb] Nr. 2306/42. Zustellung des Buches "Recht der Landkriegsführung") all prisoner-of-war camps, BABs, and the Luftwaffe, Kriegsmarine, and Heer military district headquarters and administration branches to purchase a copy of book written by an official of the Kriegsgerichtsrat der Luftwaffe, Dr. Alfons Waltzog: *Recht der Landeskriegsfürung* (Berlin: Verlag Franz Vahlen, 1942). This book faithfully reproduced the French and German versions of the 1907 Hague

Convention, as well as the 1929 Geneva Conventions on Prisoners Of War and the Treatment of Sick and Wounded in the Field, with a interpretation provided by Dr. Waltzog on the meaning of each of the articles. Given the office of the author, the order to buy it, and the official endorsement by the OKW of this book that it was "superbly suitable" for use as a guide by German staff dealing with prisoners of war, it should be taken as an update statement of official German policy, and will thus be examined for any divergencies from initial German military policy in the individual sections which follos.

97 BA-MA RHD 4/38/4, 5, 6, [22/5/39, 16/2/39, 16/2/39]: Dienstanweisung für den Kommandanten eines "Kriegsgefangenen=Durchgangslager", "=Mannschafts=Stammlager", "=Offizierlager". Given the repetitive nature of much of these three handbooks, the relevant citation will come from the first one, unless otherwise noted.
98 BA-MA RHD 4/38/5, p. 7.
99 BA-MA RHD 4/38/4, p. 8.
100 BA-MA RHD 4/38/4, p. 9.
101 BA-MA RHD 4/38/5, p. 7.
102 BA-MA RHD 4/38/4, p. 8.
103 More detailed treatment of German military policy for specific fields (such as "Discipline" or "Clothing") will be introduced at the start of each of the relevant sections which follow, so the reader will be able to better appreciate how German policy evolved from the start of the war onwards.
104 See Great Britain, War Office, *Handbook of the German Army* (London : Imperial War Museum, Dept. of Printed Books, 1996), Appendix XXXIX, "Evacuation of Prisoners," pp. 210–11.
105 from G. Mattiello and W. Vogt, *Deutsche Kriegsgefangenen- und Internierteneinrichtungen 1939–1945*, Bd. 1: Stalag, Bd. 2: Oflag, Dulag (Koblenz, 1986 [Bd. 1], 1987 [Bd. 2]), vol. 1, p. 7.
106 The instigation of lynchings of Allied airmen, rather than capture in formal captivity, will be addressed in the section on German war crimes.
107 A notable exception to this process occurred later in the war as a result of the Commando Order, which led to the denial of prisoner-of-war protection to many captured British and American commandos, who were shot as saboteurs instead. This issue will be discussed in the section on German war crimes.
108 As Mattiello and Vogt write, "The Arabic designations were given without following any particular system; the camps were located in the most various [sic] Military Districts."
109 The information for the chart is from BA-MA MSg 1/2012.
110 The best single source for opening dates of the camps is the exhaustive, multivolume philatelist's guide to the prisoner-of-war camp postal system by Mattiello and Vogt, cited above. It provides the opening administrative dates, highest number of prisoners held during the war, and the nationalities present, for each of the camps. Comparing the information in their study with information from the Captured Records section of the National Archives in Washington DC (specifically, Microcopy T-77: Roll 828 [frames 5564853–5564907], and Roll 829 [frames 5565881–5566202]) gives one a thorough account of the opening dates of the camps and of the

212 *Notes*

numbers of prisoners of war held during the war years. Given the fact that Oflag II A was established on 28 Aug. 1939, and 30 more camps followed within approximately one month (see next note), the planning had to have begun well before the war's outbreak.

111 The following information is drawn from both volumes of Mattiello and Vogt.
112 Oflag II A, Stalags II A, B, C, D, E
113 Stalags VI A, B, C, D; Oflags XI A, B, Stalags XI A, B
114 Stalags VIII A, B, C
115 Stalags I A, B; Stalags III A, B; Stalags IV A, B; Oflag VII A, Stalag VII A; Stalags XVII A, B.
116 Stalag V A; Stalag IX A; Stalag XII A; Stalag XIII A
117 These numbers refer to the number of camps which existed as separate administrative entities at various points in the war, and which actually contained prisoners of war (some camps existed on paper only, and never saw a live prisoner). In some cases, a camp was formally closed, and reopened shortly thereafter with a new name to accommodate prisoners of war of a different nationality or rank. For example, Oflag III C was open from Aug. 1940 to June 1943; a few months after its closure, at the same location, it was reopened as Stalag 383, and ran from Dec. 1943 to Dec. 1944.
118 All of the following come from comparing Mattiello and Vogt to the reports of camps found in the Record Groups of the British, Canadian, and American archives described earlier. The place names in parentheses are for the nearest German town or city to the camp – if the camp moved, the first and last locations will be listed. A word of caution needs to be stated in regard to the opening and closing dates, also shown in parentheses. They are based on both Mattiello and Vogt and information from the reports of the ICRC and Protecting Power. As they were not found in any master list of the OKW, they should not be considered either "official" or completely accurate: they are better thought of as the best possible estimate based on the available sources.
119 As noted in an earlier footnote, these camps represented the OKW at its improvisational best: there was no pattern governing their location, and they are therefore presented together here. Many of these camps were located in General Gouvernment but moved locations during the course of the war; some of them began in the major Wehrkreise but migrated east later. The Stalags in this group which were located in France usually functioned as Dulags.
120 Determining the total number of prisoners of war held by Germany over the course of the war years entails piecing together information from two major sources. The OKW's official lists (containing the information sent to the ICRC in Geneva) on the numbers of prisoners of war in German captivity are located in the Bundesarchiv-Militärarchiv in Freiburg (RW 6, vols. 184, 450, 451, 452, 453) and run from Sept. 1940 to Jan. 1945. At the National Archives in Washington DC (NARA: Microcopy T-77, Rolls 827, 828, and 829), the monthly records compiled by a different branch of the Chef Kriegsgefangenenwesens organize much of the same material in a more accessible and convenient way, but only run from May 1941 through Nov. 1944.
121 BA-MA RW 6/184, p. 8.

122 BA-MA RW 6/184, p. 32, 41–2.
123 NARA, Microcopy T-77, Roll 829, frames 5565881ff.
124 NARA, Microcopy T-77, Roll 828, frames 5564853–5564907.
125 NARA, Microcopy T-77, Roll 829, frames 5565881ff.
126 NARA, Microcopy T-77, Roll 829, frames 5565881ff.
127 NARA, Microcopy T-77, Roll 828, frames 5564853–5564907.
128 BA-MA RW 6/450, p. 19.
129 NARA, Microcopy T-77, Roll 828, frames 5564853–5564907.
130 BA-MA RW 6/450, p. 103.
131 NARA, Microcopy T-77, Roll 829, frames 5565881ff. The general policy would henceforth be for the United States to house the majority of German prisoners of war captured by the Anglo-Americans.
132 NARA, Microcopy T-77, Roll 829, frames 5565881ff. Of these, 34,002 (including 1,758 officers) were held by the British, while 45,370 (of whom 3,281 were officers) were held by the United States.
133 NARA, Microcopy T-77, Roll 828, frames 5564853–5564907.
134 NARA, Microcopy T-77, Roll 828, frames 5564853–5564907: 149,721 were British (of whome 9,316 were officers), while 26,967 were American (including 7,348 officers).
135 BA-MA RW 6/453, p. 8. This date marks the last entry of the OKW's statistics in either of the two sources mentioned. Of that total, 164,406 were British (10,809 officers) and 61,590 were American (12,625 officers).

Chapter 3: General Issues on Policy and Prisoner-of-war Camps

1 BA-MA RHD 4/38/5, p. 9.
2 Ibid., p. 10.
3 Ibid., p. 11.
4 BA-MA RHD 4/38/4, p. 12.
5 BA-MA RHD 4/38/4, 5, 6, [22/5/39, 16/2/39, 16/2/39]: Dienstanweisung für den Kommandanten eines "Kriegsgefangenen=Durchgangslager", "=Mannschafts=Stammlager", "=Offizierlager". Given the repetitive nature of much of these three handbooks, the relevant citation will come from the first one, unless otherwise noted.
6 A. Waltzog, *Recht der Landeskriegsführung* (Berlin: Verlag Franz Vahlen, 1942), p. 114.
7 BA-MA RW 6/270, 16/6/41: OKW Az. 2 f 24. 12 a Kriegsgef. (I) Nr. 3712/41.
8 BA-MA RW 6/270, 16/5/42: OKW Az. 2 f 24. 73 e Kriegsgef. Allg. (Ia) Nr. 2944/42. Zugehörigkeit polnischer Soldaten zum französischen Heere.
9 BA-MA RW 6/270, 15/1/44: OKW Az. 2 f 24. 74 f Kriegsgef.Allg. (IIc) Nr. 9842/43. Kriegsgefangene US-amerikanischer Nationalität in brit. Uniform.
10 BA-MA RH 49/101, 1/8/44: OKW Az. 2 f 24. 12 c Chef Kriegsgef.Allg. (Ib) Nr. 3715/44. Britische Kriegsgefangene polnischer Abstammung.
11 BA-MA RH 53-17/191, 9/9/42: OKW Az. 2 f 24. 82 i Kriegsgef.Org. (IVc) Nr. 4363/42.

12 BA-MA RW 6/270, 26/10/42: OKW Az. 2 f 24. 77 s Kriegsgef. Allg. (I) Nr. 11756/42. Angehörige des brit. Royal Army Service Corps.
13 BA-MA RW 6/270, 26/6/42: OKW Az. 2 f 24. 10 a AWA/Kriegsgef. Ch Nr. 290/40, vom 30.1.40. Stellung kr.gef. Offz. gegenüber deutschem Personal.
14 BA-MA RH 49/66, 11/6/43: OKW Az. 2 f 24. Kriegsgef.Allg.(Ia)/Org (IV) Nr. 4733/43.
15 BA-MA RW 6/270, 15/1/44: OKW Az. 2 f 24. 77 z Kriegsgef.Allg. (IIc) Nr. 7920/43. Einstufung und Besoldung brit. Kr.Gef.
16 BA-MA RW 6/270, 15/8/44: OKW Az. 2 f 24. 77 u Kriegsgef.Allg. (IIc) Nr. 3641/44. Nachträgliche Anerkennung britischer Unteroffiziere.
17 BA-MA RW 6/270, 21/7/43: OKW Az. 2 f 24. 76 a Kriegsgef.Allg. (VIa) Nr. 6596/43. Kriegsgef.Geheimnisträger.
18 BA-MA RH 49/111, 22/12/44: OKW Az. 2 f 24. 73 AWA/Insp.Kriegsgef. (A Ia) Nr. 5505/44. Behandlung der Bandenangehörigen als Kr.Gef.
19 Gerald Davis argues that Hitler's decision to stop shooting captured partisans was made in order to make them available for work in coal mining, in which twenty per cent of the total workforce consisted of prisoners of war of all nationalities by mid-1943. Gerald H. Davis, "Prisoners of War in Twentieth-century War Economies," *Journal of Contemporary History* 12 (1977), p. 629.
20 "Kgf" for *Kriegsgefangenen*, or prisoner of war. The similar marking in the US and British Commonwealth was either "POW" or "PW."
21 BA-MA RW 6/270, 11/3/42: OKW Az. 2 f 24. 73 o Kriegsgef. Allg (Ia) Nr. 2140/42. Kennzeichnen der Juden.
22 BA-MA RH 49/28, 3/5/44: OKW Chef Kriegsgef. Org. IV 2068/44 geh.
23 BA-MA RW 6/270, 10/8/42: OKW Az. 2 f 24. 77 n Kriegsgef. Allg. (I) Nr. 6977/42. Tragen von Abzeichen.
24 BA-MA RW 6/270, 16/5/42: OKW Az. 2 f 24. 73 c Kriegsgef. Allg. (Ia) Nr. 3927/42. Abnahme von Ausweisen.
25 BA-MA RW 6/270, 15/1/44: OKW Az. 2 f 24. 84 k Kriegsgef.Org. (IV) Nr. 0391/43. Verlust von Erkennungsmarken.
26 BA-MA RW 6/270, 1/8/44: OKW Az. 2 f 24. 82 k Kriegsgef.Org. (IV) Nr. 3021/44. Verlust von Erkennungsmarken.
27 BA-MA RH 49/91, 11/7/44: OKW Az.: 31 t AWA/WVW (II W) Nr.: 1888/44.
28 BA-MA RW 48/13, 4/3/40: OKM AMA/M Wehr Ib B.Nr. 1626. Oberkommando der Kriegsmarine. Bekanntgabe der Namen von Kriegsgefangenen durch Rundfunk.
29 The capture postcards were the official, treaty-sanctioned method by which capture was announced. The point made here was that so long as the process of notification had been started (regardless of how long it would actually take for the cards to arrive in Geneva, and the various bureaucracies to then inform the next-of-kin of the capture), it would not be against any treaty provisions to make these broadcasts.
30 BA-MA RW 48/12, 19/4/40: OKW Az. 2 f 24. 30 b Kriegsgef. (III) Nr. 439/40g.
31 BA-MA RW 6/270, 15/1/44: OKW Az. 2 f 24. 63 e Kriegsgef.Allg. (V) Nr. 0277/44. Meldung der brit. und amerikan. Kr.Gef.
32 BA-MA RW 6/270, 15/1/44: OKW Az. 2 f 24. 74 f Kriegsgef.Allg. (IIa) Nr. 11837/43. Meldungen des Kr.Gef. und Zivilinternierten-Bestandes der Lager.

33 BA-MA RW 6/270, 1/5/44: OKW Az. 2 f 24. 63 b Kriegsgef.Allg. (V) Nr. 02211/44. Mitteilung des Kr.Gef.-Bestandes an das I.R.K.
34 BA-MA RH 53-17/185, 3/7/40: OKW Az. 2 f 24. 10 e (4) Kriegsgef. Ch 2 Nr. 2081/40. Inder in Kriegsgefangenenlagern.
35 The summaries of these lists were used for official correspondence between Germany and the ICRC, and are located at BA-MA, RW 6/184, 450, 451, 452, 453; they were retroactively compiled to run from Sept. 1939 to Jan. 1945.
36 BA-MA RW 48/12, 2/7/41: OKW Az. 2 f 24. 50a Kriegsgef. (V) Nr. 3817/41.
37 BA-MA RW 6/270, 1/10/44: OKW Az. 2 f 24. 74 f Kriegsgef.Allg. (IIa) Nr. 11837/44. Meldung an Schutzmächte, IRK usw.
38 Article 7.
39 *Handbook of the German Army*, 1940, p. 210.
40 Martin Bormann's attempts to incite the German population to lynch Allied "terror-fliers" met with some success; the details of this policy and its impact will be discussed the latter part of Chapter 5.
41 This issue will be discussed in detail in Chapter 6.
42 BA-MA RHD 4/38/4, p. 11.
43 BA-MA RHD 4/38/5, p. 11.
44 BA-MA RHD 4/38/4, p. 12.
45 BA-MA RHD 4/38/4, p. 13.
46 BA-MA RHD 4/38/4, p. 18.
47 BA-MA RHD 4/38/5, p. 16.
48 BA-MA RHD 4/38/5, p. 18.
49 BA-MA RHD 4/38/5, p. 13.
50 BA-MA RHD 4/38/4, p. 22.
51 BA-MA RHD 4/38/4, p. 16.
52 BA-MA RHD 4/38/4, pp. 14–15.
53 BA-MA RW 6/270, 31/12/41: OKW Az. 2 f 24. 82 h Kriegsgef. (I4) Nr. 8447/41. Englische Fliegerpackung.
54 BA-MA RW 6/270, 5/12/42: OKW Az. 2 f 24. 24 Kriegsgef. Allg. (IVa) Nr. 4670/42. Behandlung der den kriegsgef. brit. Fliegern abgenommenen Geldbeträge.
55 BA-MA RW 6/270, 31/12/41: OKW Az. 2 f 24. 82 l Kriegsgef. (I4) Nr. 8466/41. Unterrichtung neueintreffender Kr.Gef. über die Lagerbestimmungen.
56 BA-MA RW 6/270, 5/12/42: OKW Az. 2 f 24. 76 a Kriegsgef. Allg. (VIa) Nr. 12531/42. Meldung über besonders wichtige Kr.Gef. The prominent British and American prisoners of war were those who had significant family connections in their home countries. Kept in seclusion from the other prisoners of war in Oflag IV C, Colditz, they included Giles Romilly (Churchill's nephew), the Master of Elphinstone (son of the Viceroy of India), John Winant (son of the American ambassador to the UK), Michael Alexander (son of General Alexander), the Earl of Hopetoun, Max de Hamel (a cousin of Churchill), Viscount Lascelles, and Earl Haig. Himmler's final orders regarding them, that they should be shot, were disregarded by General (SS) Berger who, with the Swiss delegate Rudolph Denzler, saw them to eventual safety. See Giles Romilly and Michael Alexander, *The Privileged Nightmare* (London: Weidenfeld and Nicolson, 1954).

216 Notes

57 BA-MA RW 6/270, 5/12/42: OKW Az. 2 f 24. 82 u Kriegsgef. Org. (IVc) Nr. 5091/42. Meldung der Flucht höherer Offiziere.
58 BA-MA RH 49/116: 11/10/43: Der Oberbefehlshaber der Luftwaffe Führungsstab Ia Br.B.Nr. 26735/43 geheim (A). Abtransport von abgeschossenen englisch-amerikanischen Fliegern.
59 BA-MA RW 6/270, 15/1/44: OKW Az. 2 f 24. 11 a Kriegsgef.Org. (I) Nr. 5607/43. Britische und amerikanische Fallmschirmjäger, Luftlandetruppen und Flaksoldaten.
60 The copy found was that reissued by the 48th Infantry Division and was found among the captured collected papers of Stalags XII A, D, F, and G, within Wehrkreis XII, in the west of Germany. BA-MA RH 49/52, 14/7/44: 48 Infanterie Div/ Abt Ic Div.Gef.Std. Anweisung für die Behandlung und Vernehmung von Kriegsgefangenen im Armeebereich.
61 BA-MA RW 6/270, 15/7/44: OKW Az. 2 f 24. 24 e Kriegsgef.Allg. (IVa) Nr. 03805/44. Behandlung der den kriegsgefangenen Fliegern abgenommenen Geldbeträge.
62 BA-MA RW 6/270, 15/8/44: OKW Az. 2 f 24. 82 k Kriegsgef.Org. (IV) Tgb. Nr. 3673/44. Meldung bei der Rückführung in die Kriegsgefangenenschaft.
63 BA-MA RW 6/270, 1/9/44: OKW Az. 2 f 24. 882 k Kriegsgef.Org. (IV) Nr. 4133/44. Veränderungsmeldungen an die WASt.
64 BA-MA RH 53-17/185, 25/11/39: OKW Az. 2 f 24. 11 a Kriegsgef. Ic Nr. 2275/39. Breyer, OKW Berlin.
65 BA-MA RW 6/270, 11/3/42: OKW Az. 2 f 24. 50 c Kriegsgef. Org (IVa) Nr. 1044/42. Abdruck des Genfer Abkommens über die Behandlung der Kriegsgefangenen vom 27.7.1929.
66 BA-MA RW 6/270, 1/6/44: OKW Az. 2 f 24. Kriegsgef.Allg. (Ia) Nr. 1966/44. Weitergabe der Anordnungen des OKW an die unterstellten Dienststellen.
67 BA-MA RHD 4/38/5, p. 17. In these 1939 manuals, the reader is referred for more details to "Vorschrift für das Kriegsgefangenenwesen: Dienstanweisung über Raumbedarf usw," as well as two other publications – Wehrmachtverwaltungs-Vorschriften H.Dv. 320/2 and H.Dv. 320/3 Nr 109-111. These were not found at the Bundesarchiv-Militärarchiv (for instance in either RW 6, for records of the OKW/AWA, which included the Abteilung für Wehrmachtverwaltung; or RW 48, the WASt für Kriegsverluste und Kriegsgefangenen records) or among the Captured German Records at NARA, in Washington DC. The unfortunate result is that the following descriptions are weakened by the fact that they were culled from more general references in other sources, such as the commandants' manuals and the subsequent updates from the OKW.
68 Waltzog, p. 124.
69 Ibid., p. 125.
70 Ibid.
71 BA-MA RW 6/270, 15/1/44: OKW Az. 2 f 24. 12 c Kriegsgef.Org. (Ic) Nr. 0529/43. Auflösung von Einheiten des Kgf.-Wesens und von Kriegsgefangenenlagern. This order, though coming late in the war, was presented as a reminder of standard policy.
72 BA-MA RW 6/270, 1/5/44: OKW Az. 2 f 24. 12 c Kriegsgef.Org. (Ic) Nr. 0529/43 2. Angel. Einrichtung von Zweiglagern und Veränderung von bestehenden Einrichtungen des Kr.Gef.-Wesens.

73 BA-MA RH 49/112, 22/9/42: OKW Az. 2 f 24. 12c Chef Kriegsgef/Allg (VIa) Nr. 3252/42 g. Fluchterlaß; BA-MA RW 6/270, 11/1/43: OKW Az. 2 f 24. 82 k Kriegsgef. Org. (IVa) Nr. 5669/42. Sicherung der Kriegsgefangenenlager gegen Fluchtversuche. These orders, issued in late 1942/early 1943, were presented as reminders rather than new policy changes.
74 BA-MA RH 53-17/187, 20/5/40: OKW Az. 2 f 24. 11a Kriegsgef. Ic Tgb.Nr. 1721/40. Bewachung der Oflags und Stalags.
75 BA-MA RW 6/270, 26/10/42: OKW Az. 2 f 24. 82 u Kriegsgef. Allg. (VIa) Nr. 10617/42. Warndraht u. Nachprüfung der Drahtumzäunung in den Kriegsgefangenenlagern.
76 BA-MA RW 6/270, 15/6/44: OKW Az. 2 f 24. 76 a Kriegsgef.Allg. (Ib) Nr. 03846/44. Warndraht.
77 BA-MA RHD 4/38/5, pp. 16–17.
78 Ibid., p. 17.
79 Ibid., p. 18.
80 Ibid., p. 48.
81 Ibid., p. 18.
82 Ibid., p. 48.
83 BA-MA RW 6/270, 26/10/42: OKW Az. 2 f 24. 21 Kriegsgef. Allg. (IVa) Nr. 11485/42. Luftschutzmassnahmen für Kriegsgefangene.
84 BA-MA RW 6/270, 5/4/43: OKW Az. 2 f 24. 73o Kriegsgef.Allg. (Ia) Nr. 3019/43. Luftschutzmaßnahmen im Kriegsgefangenenwesen.
85 BA-MA RW 6/270, 18/9/43: OKW Az. 2 f 24. 82 k Kriegsgef.Org. (IVa) Nr. 4404/43. Wiederaufbau von Kriegsgefangenen-Unterkünften nach Fliegerschäden.
86 BA-MA RW 6/270, 15/6/44: OKW Az. 2 f 24. 82 u Kriegsgef.Org. (IV)/Allg.(I) Nr. 2704/44. Luftschutzmaßnahmen im Kr.Gef.-Wesen.
87 BA-MA RW 6/270, 15/7/44: OKW Az. 2 f 24. 21 f Kriegsgef.Allg. (IVc) Nr. 04517/44. Luftschutzdeckungsgräben.
88 BA-MA RH 53-17/187, 18/5/40: OKW Az. 2 f 24. 21 Kriegsgef. -(II) Nr. 1258/40. Pflanzungen in Kriegsgefangenenlagern.
89 BA-MA RW 6/270, 7/7/41: OKW Az. 2 f 24. 72 g Kgf. Ch 2 Nr. 4662/41.
90 BA-MA RW 6/270, 11/11/41: OKW Az. 2 f 24. 21f Kriegsgef. (II,1) Nr. 7150/41. Zuteilung von Rohstoffen für Kriegsgefangenen-Unterkünfte.
91 BA-MA RW 6/270, 26/10/42: OKW Az. 2 f 24. 12 a Kriegsgef. (Id) Nr. 1836/42, 2.Ang. Anbringung von Flaggen in den Unterkunftsräumen der Kr.-Gef.
92 BA-MA RW 6/270, 31/12/41: OKW Az. 2 f 24. 77 s Kriegsgef. (Z) Nr. 7224/41. Deutsche Propaganda-Plakate, die für innerdeutsche Propaganda bestimmt sind.
93 BA-MA RHD 4/38/4, p. 20-21.
94 BA-MA RW 6/270, 16/5/42: OKW Az. 2 f 24. 77 a Kriegsgef. Allg. (Ia) Nr. 2262/42. Beleuchtung in mit britischen Offizieren belegten Oflags.
95 BA-MA RW 6/270, 11/1/43: OKW Az. 2 f 24. 21 Kriegsgef.Org. (IV)/Allg.(IVa) Nr. 102/43. Verbrauch von elektr. Strom durch Kr.Gef.
96 BA-MA RW 6/270, 17/5/43: OKW Az. 2 f 24. 21 Kriegsgef.Allg (IVa) Nr. 3369/43. Verbrauch von elektr. Strom durch Kriegsgef.
97 BA-MA RW 6/270, 22/9/42: OKW Az. 2 f 24. 77 m Kriegsgef. Allg. (Ia) Nr. [sic – no number printed]. Besondere Massnahmen in Oflag.

218 Notes

98 BA-MA RW 6/270, 15/1/44: OKW Az. 2 f 24. 21 Kriegsgef.Allg. (IVa) Nr. 10330/43. Heizmaterial.
99 BA-MA RW 6/270, 16/6/41: OKW Az. 2 f 24. 12a Kriegsgef. (I) Nr. 3712/41.
100 BA-MA RW 6/270, 19/4/43: OKW Az. 2 f 24. 82 k Kriegsgef.Org. (IVa) Nr. 1431/43. Aufrechterhaltung der Ordnung in den Kr.Gef.-Unterkünften.
101 BA-MA RW 6/273, 5/9/44: OKW Az. 2 f 24. 12c Kriegsgef.Org.(Ic) Nr. 4418/44.
102 BA-MA RH 53-17/192: 20/4/40: OKW Az. 2 f 24. 21 Kr.Gef.-II. Nr. 1110/40.
103 BA-MA RW 6/270, 17/5/43: OKW Az. 2 f 24. 73 c Kriegsgef.Allg (Ia) Nr. 3570/43. Anbringung von Personenbildern in Unterkunftsräumen Kr.Gef.
104 BA-MA RW 6/270, 1/4/44: OKW Az. 2 f 24. 73 Kriegsgef.Allg. (Ia) Nr. 658/44. Benutzung von Fahrrädern durch Kr.Gef.
105 BA-MA RW 6/270, 8/12/41: OKW Az. 2 f 24. 22 a Kriegsgef. (II,2) Nr. 8110/41. Kürzung der Verpflegungsportionen.
106 BA-MA RW 6/270, 8/12/41: OKW Az. 2 f 24. 19 m Kriegsgef. (I6) Nr. 7409/41. Verpflegung disziplinarisch bestrafter Kr.Gef.
107 BA-MA RW 6/270, 11/3/42: OKW Az. 2 f 24. 22 a Kriegsgef. Allg (IVb) Nr. 1865/42.
108 BA-MA RW 6/270, 11/3/42: OKW Az. 2 f 24. 22 a Kriegsgef. Allg (IVb) Nr. 2-011/42.
109 BA-MA RH 49/52, 10/8/42: OKH (Ch Rüst u BdE) 62 f V 3 (V d) Nr 495/42.
110 This applied to non-British or American prisoners of war, as these two groups were not used, as a matter of policy, in the armaments industry.
111 BA-MA RH 49/66, 14/10/42: OKW 62 f V 3 (V d). Verpflegungssätze nichtsowjetischer Kriegsgefangener im Heimatkriegsgebiet.
112 BA-MA RH 53-17/188, 30/1/42: OKW Az. 2 f 24. 22a Kriegsgef.Allg. (IVb) Nr.1142/42.
113 BA-MA RW 6/270, 1/6/44: OKW Az. 2 f 24. 22 a Kriegsgef.Allg. (IVb) Nr. 03896/44. Versorgung der Kriegsgefangenen mit Bier.
114 BA-MA RW 6/270, 1/8/44: OKW Az. 2 f 24. 63 b Kriegsgef.Allg. (V) Nr. 04725/44. Wein und Fruchtsäfte in Liebesgaben und Postpaketen an britische Kriegsgefangene.
115 BA-MA RW 6/270, 26/10/42: OKW Az. 2 f 24. 82 k Kriegsgef. Org. (IVa) Nr. 5001/42 v.8.10.42. Behandlung der Konservendosen für Kriegsgef.
116 BA-MA RW 6/270, 17/8/43: OKW Az. 2 f 24. 21 e Kriegsgef.Allg. (IVa) Nr. 6994/43. Aufbewahrung von Lebensmitteln.
117 BA-MA RW 6/270, 1/7/44: OKW Az. 2 f 24. 76 Kriegsgef.Allg. (Ib) Nr. 2671/44. Behandlung der Konservenbüchsen für Kriegsgefangene.
118 BA-MA RW 6/270, 11/1/43: OKW Az. 2 f 24. 21 e Kriegsgef.Allg. (IVa) Nr. 14078/42. Zubereitung der Zusatzverpflegung der Kriegsgefangenen.
119 BA-MA RW 6/270, 1/5/44: OKW Az. 2 f 24. 22 a Kriegsgef.Allg. (IVb) Nr. 02807/44. Freibankfleisch für Lagerküchen.
120 BA-MA RW 6/270, 1/5/44: OKW Az. 2 f 24. 63 b Kriegsgef.Allg. (V) Nr. 02640/44. Anhäufung von Liebesgaben.
121 BA-MA RW 6/270, 1/6/44: OKW Az. 2 f 24. 63 b Kriegsgef.Allg. (V) Nr. 03887/44. Anhäufung von Liebesgaben. The "two-key" system simply required that the room or shed in which prisoner-of-war supplies were placed in storage be locked with two different locks, the key to one of which would be held by the Man of Confidence, and the other of which would be held by

the German staff. As both keys were needed to gain access to the supplies, the prisoners of war could be assured that their supplies were safe from possible pilfering by German guards, and the German staff were assured that the MOC did not remove any supplies on his own, without proper authority.
122 BA-MA RW 6/270, 15/10/44: OKW Az. 2 f 24. 22 a Kriegsgef.Allg. (IVb) Nr. 06599/44. Kürzung der deutschen Verpflegungsportionen für Kriegsgef.
123 BA-MA RHD 4/38/4, p. 20-21.
124 BA-MA RH 53-17/185, 20/8/40: OKW Az. 2 f 24. 23 Kriegsgef. -(II) Nr. 2780/40. Kriegsgefangenen-Bekleidung.
125 BA-MA RW 6/270, 8/4/42: OKW Az. 2 f 24. 23 a Kriegsgef. Allg. (IVb) Nr. 2701/42. Versorgung der Kriegsgefangenen mit Spinnstoffwaren aus dem zivilen Sektor.
126 Individual parcels were those sent to a specific prisoner, as from a family member, for example; "collective" parcels were those sent by aid organizations such as the various national Red Cross committees for use by a set number of prisoners of war of the designated Stalag or Oflag.
127 BA-MA RW 6/270, 1/2/43: OKW Az. 2 f 24. 23 a Kriegsgef. Allg. (IVb) Nr. 118/43. Anrechnung privater Bekleidungsstücke auf das Bekleidungssoll.
128 BA-MA RW 6/270, 18/9/43: OKW Az. 2 f 24. 23 a Kriegsgef.Allg. (IVb) Nr. 8167/43. Decken für Kriegsgefangene.
129 BA-MA RW 6/270, 1/2/43: OKW Az. 2 f 24. 23 a Kriegsgef. Allg. (IVb) Nr. 119/43. Haftung der Kr.Gef. bei Verlust und Beschädigung an Bekleidungsstücken aus Liebesgabensammelsendungen.
130 BA-MA RW 6/270, 4/7/43: OKW Az. 2 f 24. 23 a Kriegsgef.Allg. (IVb) Nr. 5446/43 I. Ang. Verlust von Kr.Gef.-Bekleidung durch Luftangriffe.
131 BA-MA RW 6/270, 21/7/43: OKW Az. 2 f 24. 23 a Kriegsgef.Allg. (IVb) Nr. 5535/43 I. Ang. Abnahme von Winterbekleidung in den Sommermonaten.
132 BA-MA RW 6/270, 21/7/43: OKW Az. 2 f 24. 82 u Kriegsgef.Org. (IVc) Nr. 1705/43. Wegnahme von Uniformen.
133 BA-MA RW 6/270, 15/1/44: OKW Az. 2 f 24. 82 k Kriegsgef.Org. (IV) Nr. 0389/43. Zivilkleidung kr.gef. Offiziere.
134 BA-MA RW 6/270, 15/1/44: OKW Az. 2 f 24. 21 a Kriegsgef.Allg. (IVa) Nr. 280/43. Wäschereinigung der Kriegsgefangenen.
135 BA-MA RW 6/270, 1/6/44: OKW Az. 2 f 24. 21 a Kriegsgef.Allg. (IVa) Nr. 02426/44. Wäschereinigung kriegsgefangener Offiziere und des geschützten Personals.
136 BA-MA RW 6/270, 1/4/44: OKW Az. 2 f 24. 21 e Kriegsgef.Allg. (IVa) Nr. 0602/44. Mangelware für Kriegsgefangene.
137 BA-MA RW 6/270, 1/7/44: OKW Az. 2 f 24. 23 a Kriegsgef.Allg. (IVb) Nr. 04332/44. Beschlagnahmte Zivilkleidung für Kriegsgefangene aus Individualpaketen. No mention was made of which refugees would be the beneficiaries of this order.
138 BA-MA RW 6/270, 15/7/44: OKW Az. 2 f 24. 82 k Kriegsgef.Org. (IV) Nr. 2711/44. Zivilkleider in den Kriegsgefangenen-Unterkünften.
139 BA-MA RHD 4/38/5, p. 22.
140 Ibid., p. 23.
141 BA-MA RHD 4/38/4, p. 24.
142 BA-MA RW 6/270, 10/10/41: OKW Az. 2 f 24. 19a Kriegsgef. (San) Nr. 6935/41. Behandlung von Artzneimitteln in Paketen der Kr.Gef.

143 BA-MA RW 6/270, 10/10/41: OKW Az. 2 f 24. 19a Kriegsgef. (San) Nr. 6936/41. Kr.Gef. mit abgeschlossener ärztlicher Behandlung.
144 BA-MA RW 6/270, 31/12/41: OKW Az. 2 f 24. 40 a Kriegsgef. (IV1/San.) Nr. 2951/41. Heimsendung von Weltkriegsbeschädigten Kr.Gef.
145 BA-MA RW 6/270, 8/4/42: OKW Az. 2 f 24. 82 u Kriegsgef. Allg. (Ia) Nr. 3311/42. Bärte der Kr.Gef.
146 BA-MA RW 6/270, 26/6/42: OKW Az. 2 f 24. 82 u Kriegsgef. Allg. (Ia) Nr. 4858/42. Bärte der Kriegsgefangenen.
147 BA-MA RW 6/270, 16/5/42: OKW Az. 2 f 24. 63 b Kriegsgef. Allg. (V) Nr. 3473/42. Liebesgaben- und Medikamentensendungen des Britischen Roten Kreuzes an mit Kr.Gef. belegte Lazarette.
148 BA-MA RW 6/270, 10/8/42: OKW Az. 2 f 24. 19 a Kriegsgef. Allg. (San) Nr. 8305/42. Kr.Gef. als Blutspender.
149 BA-MA RW 6/270, 22/9/42: OKW Az. 21 Kriegsgef. Org. (II) Nr. 2868/42. Erkrankungen, Beurlaubungen und Kommandierungen von Offizieren.
150 BA-MA RH 53-17/187, 25/9/42: OKW Az. 2 f 24. 17a Kriegsgef. Org. (IIIb) Nr. 4674/42.
151 BA-MA RW 6/270, 17/11/42: OKW Az. 2 f 24. 19 a Kriegsgef. / San Nr. 11040/42. Ärztliche Betreuung der Kr.Gef.-Arb.Kdos.
152 BA-MA RW 6/270, 17/8/43: OKW Az. 2 f 24. 19 a Kriegsgef. (San) Nr. 7457/43. Vortäuschung von Krankheiten durch Kr.Gef.
153 BA-MA RW 6/270, 16/10/43: OKW Az. 2 f 24. 19 a Kriegsgef. / San. Nr. 9762/43. Vortäuschung von Bindehautentzündung.
154 BA-MA RW 6/270, 15/1/44: OKW Az. 2 f 24. 19 a Chef Kriegsgef. / Chef W San Nr. 545/44. Unterbringung geisteskranker Kriegsgefangener bezw. Internierter.
155 BA-MA RW 6/270, 15/1/44: OKW Az. 2 f 24. 73 a Kriegsgef.Allg. (II) Nr. 0274/43. Brit. Kr.Gef. ohne Erinnerungsvermögen.
156 BA-MA RW 6/270, 15/8/44: OKW Az. 2 f 24. 63 c Kriegsgef.Allg. (V) Nr. 05318/44. Nachrichtenübermittlung über den Gesundheitszustand lazarettkranker britischer Kriegsgefangener.
157 BA-MA RH 49/111, 10/11/44: OKW Az. 2 f 24. Tgb.Nr. 1244/44. I Krankmeldung von Kgf., II Vortäuschen von Krankheiten bei Kgf., III Absonderung neuanfallender Kgf. in Lazaretten und Krankenrevieren, IV Abwehr in Kgf.-Laz.
158 BA-MA RW 6/270. 7/7/41: OKW Az. 2 f 24. 73 o Kgf. Ch 2 Nr. 4673/41. Stellung von kriegsgef. Ärtzen, Sanitätern und Feldgeistlichen.
159 BA-MA RW 6/270, 1/9/41: OKW Az. 2 f 24. 77e Kriegsgef. (Ch 2) Nr. 3151/41. Sonderbehandlung von Ärtzen, Sanitätspersonal und Feldgeistlichen in Kriegsgefangenenlagern.
160 BA-MA RW 6/270, 1/9/41: OKW Az. 2 f 24. 18a Kriegsgef. (I5/VI) Nr. 5198/41.
161 BA-MA RW 6/270, 31/12/41: OKW Az. 2 f 24. 40 a Kriegsgef. (IV1) Nr. 2856/41. Bezeichnung des Sanitätspersonals.
162 BA-MA RW 6/270, 16/5/42: OKW Az. 2 f 24. 45 b Kriegsgef. Allg. (IIe) Nr. 2876/42. Freiwillige Hilfsgesellschaft in der brit. u. nordamerikanischen Wehrmacht.
163 BA-MA RW 6/270, 18/9/43: OKW Az. 2 f 24. 45 b Kriegsgef.Allg. (VIe) Nr. 9503/43. Freiwillige Hilfsgesellschaft "American Field Service."

164 BA-MA RW 6/270, 1/5/44: OKW Az. 2 f 24. 45b/46b Kriegsgef.Allg.(VIe) Tgb.Nr. 2117/44. Anerkennung brit. und franz. Sanitätsangehöriger.
165 BA-MA RW 6/270, 1/6/44: OKW Az. 2 f 24. 19 a Allg. (Ia) / (IVa) Nr. 1392/44. Anerkanntes feindl. Sanitätspersonal.
166 BA-MA RHD 4/38/4, p. 26.
167 Ibid., p. 25.
168 BA-MA RH 53-17/188, 4/7/40: OKW Az. 2 f 24. 10e Kriegsgef. Ch 2(16) Nr. 1973/40.
169 BA-MA RW 6/270, 8/12/41: OKW Az.31 v AWA/J (Ia) v. 12.5.41 Nr. 2411/41. Gottesdienst der britischer Kr.Gef.
170 BA-MA RW 6/270, 1/2/43: OKW Az. 2 f 24. 73 Kriegsgef. Allg. (VI) Nr. 349/43. Überwachung der feindl. Feldgeistlichen und kr.gef. Geistlichen.
171 BA-MA RW 6/270, 21/7/43: OKW Az. 2 f 24. 72 f Kriegsgef.Allg. (VIb) Nr. 5148/43. Feiertage der Inder.
172 BA-MA RW 6/270, 1/8/44: OKW Az. 2 f 24. 73 a Kriegsgef.Allg. (Ia) Nr. 3673/44. Religiöse Feste der indischen Kriegsgefangenen im Jahre 1944.
173 BA-MA RW 6/270, 1/6/44: OKW Az. 2 f 24. 72 f Kriegsgef.Allg. (Ic) Nr. 1958/44. Schächtungserlaubnis für Mohammedaner.
174 BA-MA RH 49/35, 20/12/43: OKW Az. 2 f 24. 72 f Kriegsgef.Allg. (Ic) Nr. 0131/43. Ausgleich feindlicher Geistlicher.
175 BA-MA RW 6/270, 1/4/44: OKW Az. 2 f 24. 72 f Kriegsgef.Allg. (Ic) Nr. 637/44. Seelsorge für Kriegsgefangene in Wehrmachtgefängnissen.
176 BA-MA RW 6/270, 1/4/44: OKW Az. 2 f 24. 72 f Kriegsgef.Allg. (Ic) Nr. 564/44. Einzelanforderungen von feindl. Geistlichen für die Kr.Gef.-Lagern.
177 BA-MA RW 6/270, 1/9/44: OKW Az. 2 f 24. 72 f Kriegsgef.Allg. (Ic) Nr. 4244/44. Vornahme gottesdienstlicher Handlungen an Kriegsgefangenen.
178 BA-MA RW 6/270, 15/12/44: OKW Az. 2 f 24. 72 f AWA/Insp.Kriegsgef. (AIb) Nr. 5964/44. Verteilung von Predigten für protestantische britische (und amerikanische), französische, holländische und polnische Kriegsgefangene durch das Evangelische Hilfswerk für Internierte und Kriegsgefangene.
179 BA-MA RHD 4/38/5, p. 33.
180 BA-MA RH 53-17/188, 4/5/40: OKW Az. 2 f 24. 10e Kriegsgef. (Ch) Nr. 1281/40. Spaziergänge und Sport in den Kriegsgefangenenlagern.
181 BA-MA RH 53-17/192, 23/8/40: OKW Az. 2 f 24. 10 e Kriegsgef. Ch 2(6) Nr. 2827/40.
182 BA-MA RH 53-17/193, 7/5/40: OKW Az. 2 f 24. 10 e Kriegsgef. (Ch) Nr. 1328/40. Musik in den Kriegsgefangenenlagern.
183 BA-MA RW 6/270, 1/2/42: OKW Az. 2 f 24. 72 g Kriegsgef.Allg (Ia) Nr. 9085/42. Material für Kunsterzeugnisse.
184 BA-MA RW 6/270, 22/9/42: OKW Az. 2 f 24. 72 g Kriegsgef. Allg. (Ia) Nr. 9238/42. Ausstellung von kunstgewerblichen und künstlerischen Gegenständen sowie Spielsachen.
185 BA-MA RW 6/270, 11/1/43: OKW Az. 2 f 24. 17 a Kriegsgef. Org. (IIIb) Nr. 6532/42. Kriegsgefangene in Theater- und Musiktrupps.
186 BA-MA RW 6/270, 17/11/42: OKW Az. 2 f 24. 72 e Kriegsgef. Allg. (Ib) Nr. 12435/42. Sportwettkämpfe in den Kr.Gef.-Lagern.
187 BA-MA RW 6/270, 1/4/44: OKW Az. 2 f 24. 72 e Kriegsgef.Allg. (Ic) Nr. 709/44. YMCA-Sportabzeichen für Kriegsgefangene.

188 BA-MA RW 6/270, 1/6/44: OKW Az. 2 f 24. 17 a Kriegsgef.Org. (III) Nr. 1852/44. Anpassung von Lagerwerkstätten [außer Schuster- und Schneiderwerkstätten] an die Erfordernisse des totalen Krieges.
189 BA-MA RHD 4/38/5, p. 21.
190 BA-MA RW 6/270, 9/2/42: OKW Az. 2 f 24. 22 a Kriegsgef.Allg (IVb) Nr. 1196/42. Beschaffung von Waren für Kriegsgefangenen-Lager-Kantinen.
191 BA-MA RW 6/270, 15/8/44: OKW Az. 2 f 24. 22 Kriegsgef.Allg. (IVa) Nr. 05332/44. Umsatzsteuer für Kriegsgefangenen-Kantinen.
192 BA-MA RW 6/270, 15/8/44: OKW Az. 2 f 24. 22 Kriegsgef.Allg. (IVa) Nr. 03889/44. Rechnungsprüfung der Kriegsgefangenen-Kantinen.
193 BA-MA RW 6/270, 1/10/44: OKW Az. 2 f 24. 76 a Kriegsgef.Allg. (Ib) Nr. 4999/44. Verbot der Verwendung von Tintenstiften und Farbstiften durch Kriegsgefangene, Militär- und Zivilinternierte für Postzwecke.
194 BA-MA RHD 4/38/4, p. 16.
195 Ibid., pp. 14–15.
196 BA-MA RH 53-17/185, 25/11/39: OKW Az. 2 f 24. 11 a Kriegsgef. Ic Nr. 2275/39. Breyer, OKW Berlin.
197 BA-MA RW 6/270, 11/11/41: OKW Az. 2 f 24. 24 e Kriegsgef. (II,1) Nr. 7196/41. Übertragung der Kriegsgefangenen-Guthaben infolge Versetzung der Kriegsgefangenen.
198 BA-MA RW 6/270, 26/6/42: OKW Az. 2 f 24. 60 c Kriegsgef. Allg. (V) Nr. 6815/42. Nachsendung der Post verlegter Kriegsgefangener.
199 BA-MA RW 6/270, 31/12/41: OKW Az. 2 f 24. 10 qu Kriegsgef. (I1) Nr. 8373/41. Rechtzeitige Anmeldung von Kr.Gef.Transporten.
200 BA-MA RW 6/270, 10/8/42: OKW Az. 2 f 24. 10 q Kriegsgef. Org. (IIIc) Nr. 3676/42. Anmeldung von Kriegsgef.-Transporten.
201 BA-MA RW 6/270, 10/8/42: OKW Az. 2 f 24. 10 q Kriegsgef. Org. (IIIc) Nr. 3677/42. Übernachten von Kr.Gef.-Transporten in Berlin.
202 BA-MA RW 6/270, 11/1/43: OKW Az. 2 f 24. 62 n Chef Kriegsgef. Allg. (VI) Nr. 395/43. Transport wiederergriffener oder unzuverlässiger Kriegsgefangener.
203 BA-MA RW 6/270, 5/4/43: OKW Az. 2 f 24. 63 b Kriegsgef.Allg. (V) Nr. 1734/43. Liebesgabensendungen an westl. Kr.Gef. im Gen.Gouv.
204 BA-MA RW 6/270, 5/4/43: OKW Az. 2 f 24. 82 u Kriegsgef.Allg. (VIa) Nr. 2223/43. Mitgabe der Negative von Lichtbildern bei Versetzung von Kr.Gef.
205 BA-MA RW 6/270, 21/7/43: OKW Az. 2 f 24. 74 f Kriegsgef.Allg. (Ia) Nr. 5778/43. Verlegung von Kr.Gef. in das M.-Stammlager III D Berlin aus besonderen Gründen.
206 BA-MA RW 6/270, 21/7/43: OKW Az. 2 f 24. 83 b Kriegsgef.Org. (IVb) Nr. 2862/43. Verlegung von Kriegsgefangenen.
207 BA-MA RW 6/270, 16/10/43: OKW Az. 2 f 24. 83 b Kriegsgef.Org. (IVb) Nr. 5158/43. Identitätsprüfung bei Versetzungen Kriegsgefangener.
208 BA-MA RH 49/35, 24/5/44: OKW Az. 24. 82 a Kriegsgef.Org. (IVb) Nr. 2553/44. Verlegung von Kr.Gef.
209 BA-MA RW 6/270, 1/6/44: OKW Az. 2 f 24. 82 k Kriegsgef.Org. (IV) Nr. 2174/44. Kriegsgefangene auf Bürgersteigen.
210 BA-MA RW 6/270, 1/6/44: OKW Az. 2 f 24. 82 y Kriegsgef.Org. (Ib) Nr. 1929/44. Aufpflanzen des Seitengewehrs im Kr.Gef.- Wachdienst.

211 BA-MA RH 49/91, 8/8/44: OKW Az. 2f 24. 82x Ch Kriegsgef./ Org. (Ib) Nr. 3253/44. Verhalten von Wachmannschaften bei feindlichen Fliegerangriffen auf Kriegsgefangenen-Transporten.
212 BA-MA RW 6/270, 1/9/44: OKW Az. 2 f 24. 12 c Kriegsgef.Org. (Ic) Nr. 3966/44. Versetzung von kr.gef. San.-Personal.
213 BA-MA RW 6/270, 15/11/44: OKW Az. 2 f 24. 10 qu (Gr. III/3) Nr. 417/44. Transport abgeschossener Feindflieger bzw. kr.gef. Offiziere.
214 BA-MA RW 6/270, 15/11/44: OKW Az. 2 f 24. 10 qu (Gr. III/3) Nr. 418/44. Transportmeldungen.
215 BA-MA RH 3/378: 14/2/45: OKH /GenQu (Qu 4) Nr. röm.2/699/45 geheim.
216 BA-MA RH 49/29, 13/2/45: Anlage zu Ob.d.E./Chef Kriegsgef. Nr. 908/45. Merkblatt über Vorbereitung und Durchführung von Marschbewegungen (aus den Erfahrungen der Kdtrn. über Gebietsräumen und Ausweichbewegungen von Kriegsgefangenen).

Chapter 4: Crimes and Punishment of Prisoners of War

1 Article 45 of the 1929 Geneva Convention.
2 Article 46.
3 Article 47.
4 Article 48.
5 Article 49.
6 Article 53.
7 Article 55.
8 Article 56.
9 Article 57.
10 The following points are drawn from articles 48–52.
11 Article 58.
12 Article 59.
13 BA-MA RHD 4/38/4, p. 28.
14 Alfons Waltzog, *Recht der Landeskriegsführung* (Berlin: Verlag Franz Vahlen, 1942), pp. 158–9.
15 Ibid.
16 BA-MA RW 6/270, 26/10/42: OKW Az. 2 f 24. 82 u Kriegsgef. Allg. (VIa) Nr. 10505/42 Bedeutung des Begriffes "Flucht."
17 BA-MA RW 6/270, 17/5/43: OKW Az. 2 f 24. 82 u Kriegsgef.Allg (VIa) Nr. 4512/43. Bedeutung des Begriffs "Flucht."
18 BA-MA RW 6/272 [also RH 49/35], 27/8/43: OKW Az. 2f 24. 191 AWA/Kriegsgef.Allg.(R/I) Nr. 8595/43. Verfolgung von Nebentaten Kr.Gef. bei der Flucht.
19 BA-MA RHD 4/38/4, p. 28.
20 BA-MA RW 6/270, 16/6/41: OKW Az. 2 f 24. 12 a Kriegsgef. (I) Nr. 3712/41.
21 BA-MA RW 6/270, 10/10/41: OKW Az. 2 f 24. 83 b Kriegsgef. (I) Nr. 6925/41. Versetzung kgf.Offiziere nach Offiziere-Lager IV C, Colditz.
22 BA-MA RW 6/270, 15/1/45: OKW Az. 2 f 24. 36 b BdE / Chef Kriegsgef. (Gr. V) Nr. 122/45. Sonderkommandos für bestrafte Kriegsgefangene.
23 BA-MA RHD 4/38/4, p. 27.

24 BA-MA RW 6/270, 9/2/42: OKW Az. 2 f 24. 82 x Kriegsgef.Org. (Ib) Nr. 574/42. Disziplinarbefugnisse gegenüber Kriegsgefangenen.
25 BA-MA RW 6/270, 11/3/42: OKW Az. 2 f 24. 73 b Kriegsgef. Allg (Ia) Nr. 1262/42. Strafbefugnisse der Lagerältesten.
26 BA-MA RW 6/270, 26/6/42: OKW Az. 2 f 24. 19 Kriegsgef. Allg. (R) /Org. (Ia) Nr. 4333/42. Disziplinarbefugnisse gegenüber Kriegsgefangenen.
27 BA-MA RW 6/270, 15/12/44: OKW Az. 2 f 24. 82 y BdE / Chef Kgf. (Gr. I/2) Nr. 1160/44. Vorgesetzten-Eigenschaft der Hilfswachmänner.
28 BA-MA RW 6/270, 1/9/44: OKW Az. 2 f 24. 12 c Kriegsgef.Org. (Ic) Nr. 3965/44. Bestrafung von Kr.Gef., Dienststrafbefugnisse des Lagerkommandanten und Lagerarztes gegenüber kr.gef. San.-Personal.
29 BA-MA RW 6/270, 1/12/44: OKW Az. 2 f 24. 74 f Insp.Kriegsgef. (IIa) Nr. 5567/44. Verantwortung der Lagerkommandanten für Bekanntgabe von Befehlen an die Lagerinsassen.
30 BA-MA RW 6/270, 1/5/44: OKW Az. 2 f 24. 19 m Kriegsgef.Allg. (Id) Nr. 154/44. Auskunfterteilung über Verurteilungen von Kr.Gef.
31 BA-MA RW 6/270, 11/1/43: OKW Az. 2 f 24. 77s/63h Kriegsgef.Allg. (I/V/R) Nr. 14243/42. 1. Erschießung und ernstliche Verletzung von Kriegsgefangenen und Zivilinternierten; 2. Verluste von brit., franz., belg. und amerik. Kr.Gef. infolge feindlicher Fliegerangriffe.
32 BA-MA RHD 4/38/4, p. 27.
33 BA-MA RW 6/270, 1/2/43: OKW Az. 2 f 24. 19 l Kriegsgef. Allg. (R) Nr. 1250/43. Disziplinarstrafen gegen Kriegsgefangene.
34 BA-MA RW 6/270, 22/9/42: OKW Az. 2 f 24. 77 z Kriegsgef. Allg. (I) Nr. 8238/42. Arrestzellen in Kgf.-Lazaretten.
35 BA-MA RW 6/270, 26/10/42: OKW Az. 2 f 24. 19 l Kriegsgef. Allg. (R) Nr. 4037/42. Behelfsvollstreckung von Disziplinarstrafen.
36 BA-MA RHD 4/38/4, p. 27.
37 BA-MA RW 6/270, 11/1/43: OKW Az. 2 f 24. 19 p Kriegsgef. (VIb) Nr. 13641/42. Verkehr Kriegsgefangener mit deutschen Frauen.
38 BA-MA RW 6/270, 17/5/43: OKW Az. 2 f 24. 19 Kriegsgef.Allg (VIa/b) Nr. 4173/43. Bestrafung der Kr.Gef. bei Betrieb von Rundfunkgeräten und Abhören ausl. Sender.
39 BA-MA RHD 4/38/4, p. 28.
40 BA-MA RW 6/270, 16/6/41: OKW Az. 2 f 24. 12 a Kriegsgef. (I) Nr. 3712/41.
41 BA-MA RHD 4/38/4, p. 28.
42 BA-MA RW 6/270, 26/10/42: OKW Az. 2 f 24. 50 c Kriegsgef. Org. (IVa) Nr. 5035/42. Gepäck der Kriegsgefangenen in Wehrmachtgefängnissen und Zuchthäusern.
43 BA-MA RW 6/270, 15/8/44: OKW Az. 2 f 24. 19 l Chef Kriegsgef.Allg. (R/I) Nr. 3021/44. Arrestvollzug im Kriege.
44 BA-MA RHD 4/38/4, p. 28; RHD 4/38/5, p. 40.
45 BA-MA RW 6/270, 16/6/41: OKW Az. 2 f 24. 12 a Kriegsgef. (I) Nr. 3712/41.
46 BA-MA RHD 4/38/4, p. 28.
47 BA-MA RW 6/270, 15/1/44: OKW Az. 2 f 24. 82 u Kriegsgef.Org. (IVc) Nr. 0388/43. Vollstreckung von Disziplinarstrafen.
48 BA-MA RHD 4/38/4, p. 28.
49 Ibid.

50 BA-MA RH 53-17/185, 14/12/39. OKW Az. 2 f 24. 11 a Kriegsgef. I c Nr. 2794/39.
51 BA-MA RH 53-17/185, 19/12/39: OKW Az. 2 f 24. 11 a Kriegsgef. I c Nr. 2932/39.
52 BA-MA RW 6/270, 22/9/42: OKW Az. 2 f 24. 74 f Kriegsgef. Allg. (Ia) Nr. 9838/42. Grüssen der Kr.Gef.
53 BA-MA RW 6/270, 5/12/42: OKW Az. 2 f 24. 74 f Kriegsgef. Allg. (Ia) Nr. 13613/42. Ehrenbezeichnung der Kriegsgefangenen.
54 BA-MA RW 6/270, 26/10/42: OKW Az. 2 f 24. 82 k Kriegsgef. Org. (IVa) Nr. 5062/42. Tägliche Flaggenparade der Kriesgefangenenlager.
55 BA-MA RW 6/270, 1/9/41: OKW Az. 2 f 24. 16 a Kriegsgef. (I3) Nr. 5196/41. Spaziergänge kr.gef. britischer Offiziere.
56 BA-MA RW 6/270, 26/6/42: OKW Az. 2 f 24. 73 o Kriegsgef. Allg. (Ia) Nr. 2292/42.
57 BA-MA RW 6/270, 10/10/41: OKW Az. 2 f 24. 17 b Kriegsgef. (I5) Nr. 6949/41. Rauchen der Kriegsgefangenen.
58 BA-MA RW 6/270, 22/9/42: OKW Az. 2 f 24. 76 b Kriegsgef. Allg. (VIa) Nr. 9798/42. Jagdschutz. Wildernde Kr.Gef.
59 BA-MA RW 6/270, 11/1/43: OKW Az. 2 f 24. 82 u Kriegsgef.Allg. (VIa) Nr. 14488/42. Untersuchung der Kriegsgefangenen und ihrer Unterkünfte nach Fliegerangriffen.
60 BA-MA RW 6/270, 15/1/44: OKW Az. 2 f 24. 76 Kriegsgef.Allg. (Id) Nr. 18/44. Ablieferung feindlicher Flugblätter usw. im Besitz von Kriegsgefangenen.
61 BA-MA RW 6/270, 15/6/44: OKW Az. 2 f 24. 19 m Kriegsgef.Allg. (Id) Nr. 2445/44. Wildereien durch Kriegsgefangene.
62 BA-MA RW 6/270, 9/3/43: OKW Az. 2 f 24. 23 a Kriegsgef. Allg. (IV) Nr. 1950/43. Fluchten der Kriegsgef. in nachgemachten Uniformen.
63 BA-MA RW 6/270, 19/4/43: OKW Az. 2 f 24. 82 u Kriegsgef.Org. (IVc) Nr. 1432/43. Behandlung von Erkennungsmarken durch Kriegsgefangene.
64 BA-MA RW 6/270, 16/10/43: OKW Az. 2 f 24. 77 z Kriegsgef.Allg. (IIa) Nr. 7996/43. Ehrenwort bzw. Verpflichtungserklärung brit.Kr.Gef.
65 BA-MA RW 6/270, 15/6/44: OKW Az. 2 f 24. 72 e Kriegsgef.Allg. (Ic) Nr. 2660/44. Verpflichtungserklärung brit. Kriegsgefangener.
66 BA-MA RW 6/270, 15/1/44: OKW Az. 2 f 24. 76 Kriegsgef.Allg. (Ia) Nr. 322/44. Wucherischer Schwarzhandel zwischen Kriegsgefangenen und Zivilpersonen.
67 BA-MA RW 6/270, 15/6/44: OKW Az. 2 f 24. 76 a Kriegsgef.Allg. (Ib) Nr. 03846/44. Warndraht.
68 BA-MA RW 6/270, 1/2/43: OKW Az. 2 f 24. 77 s Kriegsgef. Allg. (Ic) Nr. 10544/42. Schmuckplakate brit. Eisenbahnen.
69 BA-MA RW 6/270, 1/10/44: OKW Az. 2 f 24. 76 a Kriegsgef.Allg. (Ib) Nr. 34483/44. Verbot der Herstellung von Segelflugzeugmodellen durch Kriegsgefangene.
70 BA-MA RW 6/270, 1/12/44: OKW Az. 2 f 24. 74 f Insp.Kriegsgef. (Ia) Nr. 5887/44. Singen der Kriegsgefangenen.
71 BA-MA RW 6/270, 15/12/44: OKW Az. 2 f 24. 72 f AWA/Insp.Kriegsgef. (AIb) Nr. 5333/44. Verbot der Veranstaltung von Geldlotterien unter Kriegsgefangener, Militär- und Zivilinternierten.

72 BA-MA RW 6/270, 16/5/42: OKW Az. 2 f 24. 60 c Kriegsgef. Allg. (V) Nr. 3538/42. Postverkehr der Kriegsgefangenen in Wehrmachtgefängnissen.
73 BA-MA RW 6/270, 26/6/42: OKW Az. 2 f 24. 19 p Kriegsgef. Allg. (VI) Nr. 4933/42. Bekanntgabe gerichtlicher Bestrafung Kriegsgefangener.
74 BA-MA RW 6/270, 1/6/44: OKW Az. 2 f 24. 23 a Kriegsgef.Allg. (IVb) Nr. 03271/44. Bekleidung von zur Strafverbüßung in Festungsgefängnissen zu überführenden Kriegsgefangenen.
75 For more detail, see the latter part of Chapter 5, on "External Relations."
76 Articles 60, 61, 65, 66, and 67.
77 Articles 61–7.
78 BA-MA RHD 4/38/5, p. 28.
79 Waltzog, p. 152.
80 See the section on disciplinary regulations, above. As was noted, the OKW adopted the policies approximately one year later.
81 BA-MA RH 26-172/9, 5/6/41: OKW 14. n 19 Mob WR (II/6a) Nr. 1163/41. Merkblatt für die Ausübung der Gerichtsbarkeit in Kriegsgefangenen-Angelegenheiten.
82 BA-MA RW 6/270, 18/9/43: OKW Az. 2 f 24. 19 l Kriegsgef.Allg. (R) Nr. 8140/43. Anrechnung von Untersuchungshaft bei Disziplinarstrafen Kriegsgefangener.
83 BA-MA RW 6/270, 1/1/45: OKW Az. 2 f 24. 30 a BdE / Chef Kriegsgef. (Ger.Offz.) Nr. 1647/44. Vollzug von geschärftem Stubenarrest und Untersuchungshaft bei Kriegsgefangenen einschl. kriegsgefangenen Offizieren.
84 BA-MA RW 6/270, 7/7/41: OKW Az. 2 f 24. 19 l Kgf.Ib Nr. 4213/41.
85 BA-MA RW 6/270, 17/5/43: OKW Az. 2 f 24. 19 l Kriegsgef. R / Allg (VIb) Nr. 2877/43. Verkehr Kr.Gef. mit ihren Verteidigern.
86 BA-MA RW 6/270, 15/1/44: OKW Az. 2 f 24. 74 f Kriegsgef.Allg. (IIb) Nr. 171/43. Vornahme richterlicher Handlungen durch Kr.Gef.
87 BA-MA RW 6/270, 15/11/44: OKW Az. 2 f 24. 24 k Kriegsgef.Allg. (IVa) Nr. 6544/44. Sold für kriegsgefangene Offiziere.
88 BA-MA RW 6/270, 1/1/45: OKW Az. 2 f 24. 24 k BdE / Chef Kriegsgef. (IVa) Nr. 1513/44. Sold für kriegsgefangene Offiziere.
89 BA-MA RW 6/270, 1/4/44: OKW Az. 2 f 24. 60 c Kriegsgef.Allg. (V) Nr. 01037/44. Brief- und Paketpost für bestrafte Kr.Gef. in Wehrmachtgefängnissen.
90 BA-MA RW 6/270, 1/8/44: OKW Az. 2 f 24. 50 c Kriegsgef.Org. (IV) Tgb. Nr. 3461/44. Kr.Gef. Offiziere und arbeitsunwillige Unteroffiziere in Wehrmachtgefängnissen.
91 BA-MA RW 6/270, 1/9/44: OKW Az. 2 f 24. 24 a Kriegsgef.Allg. (IVa) Nr. 05467/44. Kriegsgefangenen in Wehrmachtgefängnissen.
92 BA-MA RH 49/34, 21/1/42: OKW Az. 2 f 24. 19 a Chef Kriegsgef.Allg.(VI) Nr. 7365/41. Behandlung Kriegsgefangener, die einer vor der Gefangennahme oder einer während der Gefangenschaft begangenen Straftat verdächtig sind.
93 BA-MA RW 6/270, 1/8/44: OKW Az. 2 f 24. 19 l Chef Kriegsgef.Allg. (R) Nr. 3782/44. Sonderkompanien.
94 BA-MA RW 6/270, 15/1/44: OKW Az. 2 f 24. 82 u Kriegsgef.Allg. Id/Org. (IV) Nr. 0387/43. Abschreckung der kriegsgefangenen von Fluchten.

95 BA-MA RW 6/270, 5/4/43: OKW Az. 2 f 24. 82 u Kriegsgef.Allg. (VIa) Nr. 2227/43. Benutzung deutscher Uniformen und Zivilkleidung durch Kr.Gef.
96 BA-MA RW 6/270, 15/11/44: OKW Az. 2 f 24. 76 a Kriegsgef.Allg. (Ib) Nr. 5369/44. Prüfung der Personalien geflohener und wiederergriffener Kriegsgefangener.
97 BA-MA RW 6/270, 17/8/43: OKW Az. 2 f 24. 19 l Kriegsgef.Allg. (VIb) (R) Nr. 8606/42. Diebstähle aus fliegerbeschädigten Häusern.
98 BA-MA RH 49/54, 4/10/43: Kommandeur der Kriegsgefangenen im Wehrkreis XII, Az. 2 f 24. 9 Abt. I c.
99 BA-MA RH 49/91, 7/11/44: OKW Az. 2 f 24. 17a (Gr. III/3) Tgb.Nr. 251/44.
100 BA-MA RH 49/99, 10/10/40.
101 BA-MA RW 6/270, 11/1/43: OKW Az. 2 f 24. 82 x Kriegsgef. Org. (Ib) Nr. 183/43. Verkehr von Kr.Gef. mit der Bevölkerung.
102 BA-MA RW 6/270, 21/7/43: OKW Az. 2 f 24. 19 m Kriegsgef.Allg. (VIb) Nr. 6464/43. Feindliches Sanitätspersonal. The prohibition order for medical personnel referred to in this order is OKW Az. 2 f 24 AWA Kriegsgef. (I6) Nr. 4455/40.
103 The relevant section of the Geneva Convention on Prisoners of war makes no such mention. Article 12, para. 3, of the Geneva Convention for the Amelioration of the Condition of the Wounded and Sick in Armies in the Field, entered into force June 19, 1931 (LNTS 303, 118) states: "Pending their [captured enemy medical personnel] return they shall continue to carry out their duties under the direction of the enemy; they shall preferably be engaged in the care of the wounded and sick of the belligerent to which they belong." Therefore, it is unclear where the legal justification for this order comes from.
104 BA-MA RW 6/270, 11/11/41: OKW Az. 2 f 24. 77e Kriegsgef. (Ch 2) Nr. 7733/41. Feindliches Sanitätspersonal.
105 BA-MA RH 26-172/9, 5/6/41: OKW 14. n 19 Mob WR (II/6a) Nr. 1163/41. Bestrafung Kriegsgefangener wegen verbotenen Umgangs mit deutschen Frauen. Merkblatt für die Ausübung der Gerichtsbarkeit in Kriegsgefangenen-Angelegenheiten.
106 BA-MA RH 49/34, 21/1/42: OKW Az. 2 f 24. 19 a Chef Kriegsgef.Allg.(VI) Nr. 7365/41. Behandlung Kriegsgefangener, die einer vor der Gefangennahme oder einer während der Gefangenschaft begangenen Straftat verdächtig sind.
107 BA-MA RW 6/270, 10/8/42: OKW Az. 2 f 24. 19 m Kriegsgef. Allg. (VI) Nr. 7196/42. Behandlung Kriegsgefangener, gegen die ein Bau- und Arbeitsbataillon Tatbericht wegen Verstoßes gegen das Verbot vom 10.1.40 betr. "Verkehr mit deutschen Frauen" vorlegt.
108 BA-MA RW 6/270, 15/11/44: OKW Az. 2 f 24. 19 m Kriegsgef.Allg. (Id) Nr. 2819/44. Todesstrafe gegen Kriegsgefangene wegen verbotenen Verkehrs mit deutschen Frauen.
109 BA-MA RW 6/270, 8/4/42: OKW Az. 2 f 24. 19 m Kriegsgef. Allg. (VI) Nr. 2182/42. Wildereien durch Kriegsgefangene.
110 BA-MA RW 6/270, 18/9/43: OKW Az. 2 f 24. 19 m Kriegsgef.Allg. (Id) Nr. 7909/43. Wildereien durch Kriegsgefangene.
111 BA-MA RW 6/270, 26/6/42: OKW Az. 2 f 24. 75 c Kriegsgef. Allg. (Ia) Nr. 5874/42. Rauchen der Kriegsgefangenen.

112 BA-MA RH 53-7/724, 28/9/39: Abt. Wehrmachtverlust u. Kriegsgefangenenwesen, Az. 2 f 24 10 Abt. I. Nr. 296/39.
113 BA-MA RW 6/270, 15/1/44: OKW Az. 2 f 24. 73 c Kriegsgef.Allg. (Ia) Nr. 6471/43 II. Ang. Mißhandlung von Kr.Gef. durch Hilfswachmannschaften.
114 BA-MA RH 53-17/185, 25/11/39: OKW Az. 2 f 24. 11 a Kriegsgef. Ic Nr. 2275/39. Breyer, OKW Berlin.
115 BA-MA RH 49/66, 30/7/42: OKW Az. 2 f 24. 11 a AWA/Kriegsgef. Org. (I) Nr. 151/42 geheim. Besondere Massnahmen in der Kriegsgefangenenbewachung.
116 BA-MA RH 49/112, 22/9/42: OKW Az. 2 f 24. 12c Chef Kriegsgef/Allg (VIa) Nr. 3252/42 g. Fluchterlaß.
117 BA-MA RW 6/270, 1/2/43: OKW Az. 2 f 24. 82 u Kriegsef. Allg. (VIa) Nr. 348/43. Lockerung der verschärften Bewachung der in Arbeit eingesetzten franz. u. brit. Kriegsgef.
118 BA-MA RW 6/485, 1/1/43: OKW Az.2 f 24.74 Kriegsgef Allg (Ia) Nr. 3868/42 g. This order was reissued by the OKW later that same year, on July 17, 1943: OKW Az.2 f 24.74 Kriegsgef Allg (Ia) Nr. 1665/43 g.
119 BA-MA RW 6/487, 16/1/43: OKW AWA/Chef Kriegsgef. Merkblatt: Der Deutsche Soldat in der Kriegsgefangenenbewachung.
120 BA-MA RW 6/270, 5/4/43: OKW Az. 2 f 24. 71c/73o Kriegsgef.Allg. (I/VI) Nr. 2168/43. Britische Kriegsgefangene.
121 BA-MA RH 49/101, 8/5/43: OKW Az. 2 f 24. 82 u. Chef. Kriegsgef./Allg.(VIa) Nr. 4254/43. Mitwirkung der Gendarmerie zur Bewachung der Kriegsgef. auf dem Lande.
122 BA-MA RW 6/270, 17/5/43: OKW Az. 2 f 24. 76 Kriegsgef.Allg (VIa) Nr. 3715/43. Abstand der Wachmannschaften von den Kr.Gef.
123 BA-MA RW 6/270, 16/10/43: OKW Az. 2 f 24. 82 x Kriegsgef.Org. (Ib) Nr. 4942/43. Aufpflanzen des Seitengewehrs im Kgf.-Wachdienst.
124 BA-MA RW 6/270, 15/6/44: OKW AWA Az. 2 f 24. 19 m Kriegsgef. Allg.(Id)/Org.(Ib) Nr. 2270/44. Überfall auf Wachmannschaften.
125 BA-MA RW 6/270, 15/1/44: OKW Az. 2 f 24. 19 m Kriegsgef.Allg. (Id) Nr. 9927/43. Gebrauch der Schußwaffe gegen Kriegsgefangene.
126 BA-MA RH 49/116, 26/5/44: OKW Az. 2 f 24. 12 c AWA/Kriegsgef.Allg. (Ib) Nr.2500/44 geheim. Gebrauch der Schußwaffe bei Nacht.
127 BA-MA RW 6/270, 15/6/44: OKW Az. 2 f 24. 76 a Kriegsgef.Allg. (Ib) Nr. 03846/44. Warndraht.
128 BA-MA RH 49/91, 14/7/44: OKW Az. 2f 24.76a Chef Kriegsgef.Allg.(Ib) Nr. 3629/44. Gebrauch der Schußwaffe gegen Kriegsgefangene ohne Anruf; hier insbesondere Bekanntgabe dieser Vorschriften an die Kr. Gef.
129 BA-MA RH 49/112, 6/9/44: OKW Az. 2 f 24. 76 Chef Kriegsgef./Allg. (Ib) Nr. 1252/44. Widerstandsbewegung unter den Kriegsgefangenen.
130 BA-MA RW 6/270, 1/10/44: OKW Az. 2 f 24. 76 a Kriegsgef.Allg. (Ib) Nr. 4993/44. Abwehrmäßige Durchsuchung von Kr.Gef.-Unterkünften.
131 BA-MA RW 6/270, 1/1/45: OKW Az. 2 f 24. 82 x – BdE / Chef Kriegsgef. (Gr. I/2) Nr. 1699/44. Ausweiskontrolle bei Arbeitskommandos.
132 BA-MA RW 6/270, 1/1/45: OKW Az. 2 f 24. 82 x – BdE / Chef Kriegsgef. (Gr. I/2) Nr. 1655/44. Fluchten auf Transporten.
133 BA-MA RH 49/115, 16/1/45: Der Abwehroffizier des WKdos VI Bb. Nr. 6012/45 geh kgf. The precise references for these orders were, respectively:

OKW Tr.Abw. Nr. 01157/44 (Kgf); OKW Tr.Abw. Nr. 01338/44 (Kgf); OKW Tr.Abw. Nr. 01529/44 (Kgf); and OKW Tr.Abw. Nr. 0974/44 (Kgf).
134 BA-MA RW 49/66, 5/6/42: OKW Az. 2 f 24. 73 Kriegsgef.Allg. (II/IVb) Nr. 6325/42. Belohnungen.
135 BA-MA RW 6/270, 26/10/42: OKW Az. 2 f 24. 82 u Kriegsgef. Allg. (VIa) Nr. 10242/42. Geldbelohnung für Wiederergreifung entflohener [sic] Kr.Gef.
136 BA-MA RW 6/270, 1/5/44: OKW Az. 2 f 24. 24 a Kriegsgef.Allg. (IVa) Nr. 02206/44. Belohnung für Ergreifung geflohener Kriegsgefangener.
137 BA-MA RH 53-17/187, 31/5/40: OKW Az. 2 f 24. 20 Kriegsgef. -(II) Nr. 1661/40. Anfertigung von Lichtbildern für Kriegsgefangene.
138 BA-MA RW 6/270, 11/3/42: OKW Az. 2 f 24. 71 d Kriegsgef. Allg (Ia) Nr. 2169/42. Fotos von Kr.Gef. für die Kartothek.
139 BA-MA RH 49/66, 12/5/42: OKW Az. 2 f 24. 82 u Kriegsgef. Allg. (A) Nr. 5079/42. Fluchten von Kr. Gef.
140 BA-MA RW 6/270, 16/5/42: OKW Az. 2 f 24. 23 e Kriegsgef. Allg. (IVb) Nr. 3920/42. Zivilkleidung wiederergriffener Kriegsgef.
141 BA-MA RW 6/270, 17/8/43: OKW Az. 2 f 24. 82 u Kriegsgef.Org. (IVc) Nr. 3431/43. Fluchten in Zivilkleidung.
142 BA-MA RW 6/270, 5/12/42: OKW Az. 2 f 24. 82 u Kriegsgef. Org. (IVc) Nr. 5020/42. Schlüssel in Kr.Gef.-Lagern.
143 BA-MA RH 49/112, 22/9/42: OKW Az. 2 f 24. 12c Chef Kriegsgef/Allg (VIa) Nr. 3252/42 g. Fluchterlaß.
144 BA-MA RW 6/270, 22/9/42: OKW Az. 2 f 24. 82 u Abw III (Kgf)/Kriegsgef. Allg. (VIa) Nr. 4351/42. Fluchtverhinderung.
145 BA-MA RW 6/270, 11/1/43: OKW Az. 2 f 24. 82 k Kriegsgef. Org. (IVa) Nr. 5669/42. Sicherung der Kriegsgefangenenlager gegen Fluchtversuche.
146 BA-MA RW 6/270, 1/2/43: OKW Az. 2 f 24. 19 l Kriegsgef. Allg. (R) Nr. 424/43. Bestechlichkeit der Wachmannschaften.
147 BA-MA RW 6/270, 5/4/43: OKW Az. 2 f 24. 82 x Kriegsgef.Org. (Ib) Nr. 1539/43. Todesurteil gegen einen in der Kriegsgefangenen-bewachung verwendeten Landesschützen.
148 BA-MA RW 6/270, 4/7/43: OKW Az. 2 f 24. 82 u Kriegsgef.Org. (IVc) Nr. 2309/43. Feldurteil eines Gerichts.
149 BA-MA RW 6/270, 18/9/43: OKW Az. 2 f 24. 82 u Kriegsgef.Org. (IVc) Nr. 4687/43. Rechzeitiger Waffengebrauch zur Verhinderung von Kriegsgefangenenfluchten.
150 BA-MA RW 6/270, 9/3/43: OKW Az. 2 f 24. 82 k Kriegsgef.Org. (IVa) Nr. 562/43. Ausweiskontrolle am Lagereingang (Torkontrolle).
151 BA-MA RW 6/270, 19/4/43: OKW Az. 2 f 24. 82 u Kriegsgef.Org. (IVc) Nr. 1542/43. Verhinderung der Torfluchten in den Oflag.
152 BA-MA RW 6/270, 15/7/44: OKW Az. 2 f 24. 82 k Kriegsgef.Org. (IV) Nr. 1804/44. Ausweiskontrolle am Eingang zu Kr.Gef. -Lagern [Torkontrolle].
153 BA-MA RW 6/270, 1/6/44: OKW / Kriegsgef.Allg. (Ib)/(IV) Nr. 2244/44 v 4.5.44 Fluchtverhindernde Maßnahmen; hier: Ausstellung von Empfangsbescheinigungen über von Kr.Gef. in Verwahrung genommenen Wertsgegenstände usw.
154 BA-MA RW 6/270, 1/6/44: OKW Az. 2 f 24. 24 l Kriegsgef.Allg. (IVa) Nr. 03033/44. Lagergeld.

155 BA-MA RW 6/270, 15/8/44: OKW Az. 2 f 24. 76 a Kriegsgef.Allg. (Ib) Nr. 3834/44. Empfangsbescheinigungen und Ausweise für Kriegsgefangene, Militär- und Zivilinternierte.
156 BA-MA RH 49/116, 19/8/43: OKW Az. 2 f 24. 12 c AWA/Kriegsgef.Allg. (VIa) Nr. 3300/43 geheim. Zusammenarbeit von Wehrmacht und Sicherheitspolizei zur Verhinderung von Kr.Gef.-Fluchten.
157 BA-MA RW 6/270, 17/5/43: OKW Az. 2 f 24. 82 u Kriegsgef.Allg (VIa) Nr. 4581/43. Festsetzung des Begriffs Massenflucht. Meldung der Flucht von kriegsgef. Offizieren.
158 BA-MA RH 49/116, 25/5/44: OKW Az. 2 f 24 of 11f Chef Kriegsgef Org (Ib) Nr. 2399/44 g. [Transcribed verbatim with the OKW reference from WKdo VI Abt. Kr.Gef. IV Az. K 2 Nr. 751/44 geh.] Kriegsgefangenenbewachung.
159 BA-MA RH 49/116, 1/6/44: WKdo VI Abt. Kr.Gef. I Az. K 18/I Nr. 792/44 geheim. Bewachung der Kr. Gef., Verhinderung von Fluchten.
160 BA-MA RH 49/116, 6/6/44: WKdo VI Abt. Kr.Gef. I Az. K Nr. 821/44 geheim.
161 BA-MA RH 49/35, 14/6/44: OKW Az. 2 f 24. 74 f Chef Kriegsgef./Allg. (Ia) Nr. 2095/44. Beschiessung der deutschen Zivilbevölkerung durch feindliche Flieger. Verhalten der Zivilbevölkerung gegenüber Kr.Gef.
162 BA-MA RW 6/270, 1/1/45: OKW Az. 2 f 24. 30 a BdE / Chef Kriegsgef. (Ger. Offz.) Nr. 1643/44. Tatberichte bei Kgf.-Fluchten.
163 BA-MA RW 6/270, 15/1/45: OKW Az. 2 f 24. 23 BdE / Chef Kriegsgef. (Ger.Offz.) Nr. 151/45. Tatberichte gegen Lager-Kommandanten nach Massenfluchten usw.
164 BA-MA RW 6/12, 29/3/45: Chef des Kriegsgefangenenwesens – Gruppe I/1.
165 BA-MA RHD 4/38/5, p. 7.
166 BA-MA RHD 4/38/5, p. 33-36.
167 BA-MA RW 6/270, 8/12/41: OKW Az. 2 f 24. 82 e Kriegsgef. (I4) Nr. 7556/41. Sabotageversuche in Kriegsgefangenenlagern.
168 BA-MA RW 6/270, 8/4/42: OKW Az. 2 f 24. 19 a Kriegsgef. San Nr. 2668/42. Wärmekissen mit Chemikalienfüllung.
169 BA-MA RW 6/270, 11/1/43: OKW Az. 2 f 24. 72 c Kriegsgef.Allg. (Ib) Nr. 13458/42. Verbot des sogenannten Dartboard-Spieles.
170 BA-MA RH 49/66, 30/7/42: OKW Az. 2 f 24. 11 a AWA/Kriegsgef. Org. (I) Nr. 151/42 geheim. Besondere Massnahmen in der Kriegsgefangenenbewachung.
171 BA-MA RW 6/270, 16/5/42: OKW Az. 2 f 24. 77 s Kriegsgef. Allg. (Ia) Nr. 2574/42. Arbeitsverpflichtungserklärung brit. Uffz.
172 BA-MA RW 6/270, 5/4/43: OKW Az. 2 f 24. 73 o Kriegsgef.Allg. (Ia) Nr. 3019/43. Luftschutzmaßnahmen im Kriegsgefangenenwesen.
173 BA-MA RW 6/270, 15/6/44: OKW Az. 2 f 24. 82 u Kriegsgef. Org.(IV)/Allg.(I) Nr. 2704/44. Luftschutzmaßnahmen im Kr.Gef.-Wesen.
174 BA-MA RH 49/111, 10/11/44: OKW Az. 2 f 24. Tgb.Nr. 1244/44. I Krankmeldung von Kgf., II Vortäuschen von Krankheiten bei Kgf., III Absonderung neuanfallender Kgf. in Lazaretten und Krankenrevieren, IV Abwehr in Kgf.-Laz.
175 The order did not indicate what this object was, or what it could be used for.
176 BA-MA RW 6/270, 1/1/45: OKW Az. 2 f 24. 82 k BdE/Chef Kriegsgef. (Gr.V/2) Nr. 1352/44. Gepäcke britischer und amerikanischer Kriegsgefangener.

Chapter 5: Economics and External Relations of Prisoners of War

1. Article 27 of the 1929 Geneva Convention.
2. Articles 28–30. The potential conflict of these last two points would be a source of contention concerning Germany's treatment of Anglo-American prisoners during the war years, but one which the Allies (and the ICRC and Protecting Power delegates) generally felt powerless to resolve in their soldiers' favor.
3. Article 31.
4. Article 32.
5. Article 33.
6. Article 34.
7. BA-MA RHD 4/38/5, pp. 33–6.
8. BA-MA RHD 4/38/4, p. 22.
9. BA-MA RHD 4/38/5, p. 45.
10. Alfons Waltzog, *Recht der Landeskriegsführung* (Berlin: Verlag Franz Vahlen, 1942), p. 137.
11. Also, on May 16, 1942, the OKW decided that, for reasons of pragmatism, it was better to send noncommissioned officers who no longer wished to work back to their camps rather than make them work (BA-MA RW 6/270, 16/5/42: OKW Az. 2 f 24. 77 s Kriegsgef. Allg. (Ia) Nr. 2574/42. Arbeitsverpflichtungserklärung brit. Uffz.).
12. Waltzog, p. 138.
13. Ibid.
14. BA-MA RH 49/99, 28/11/41: Kdr.d.Kgf. im WK IV Az. 2 f St.Gru. Nr. 6607/41.
15. BA-MA RW 19/836, 20/4/42: OKW Az. 2 f 24. 77i/w Kriegsgef.Allg.(Ia) Org.(IIIb) Nr.4100/42. Freiwillige Arbeit kr.gef. Offiziere.
16. BA-MA RW 19/836, 15/11/40: OKW Az. 2 f 24. 17 a Kriegsgef. Ie Nr 5231/40. Arbeitseinsatz von kriegsgef. Uffz.
17. BA-MA RW 19/836: 11/3/41: OKW Az. 2 f 24. 17 a Kriegsgef. Ie Nr. 1443/41. Arbeitseinsatz kriegsgefangener Unteroffiziere.
18. BA-MA RW 6/270, 16/5/42: OKW Az. 2 f 24. 77 s Kriegsgef. Allg. (Ia) Nr. 2574/42. Arbeitsverpflichtungserklärung brit. Uffz.
19. BA-MA RW 6/270, 1/7/44: OKW Az. 2 f 24. 24 a Kriegsgef.Allg. (IVa) Nr. 04520/44. Geldsammlungen der Kriegsgefangenen.
20. BA-MA RW 19/836, 18/11/40: OKW Az. 2 f 24. 16 Kriegsgef. Ie Nr. 2204/40 geh. Einsatz von englischen Kriegsgefangenen bei Luftschutzbauten.
21. The order explained neither how the employment of prisoners of war in the munitions industry was "compatible" with article 31 of the Convention (which specifically prohibited any work in the munitions industry) nor, if it was compatible with the Convention, why it should be hidden from official reports. BA-MA RW 19/836, 19/3/41: OKW Az. 2 f 24. 17 f Kriegsgef. (Ie) Nr. 1585/41. Kriegsgefangeneneinsatz.
22. BA-MA RW 19/836, 29/5/41: OKW Az. 2 f 24. 16 Kriegsgef. (Ic) Nr. 1561/41. Einsatz von Kriegsgefangenen und ausländischen Zivilarbeitern in der Rüstungsindustrie.

232 *Notes*

23 BA-MA RW 6/270, 1/10/44: OKW Az. 2 f 24. 17 h Kriegsgef.Org. (IIIb) Nr. 4481/44. Scharfe Überprüfung des wehrmachteigenen Einsatzes.
24 BA-MA RW 19/836, 26/3/41: OKW Az. 2 f 24. 16 Kriegsgef. (Ie) Nr. 837/41. Steigerung der Arbeitsleistung der Kr.Gef. durch verschärfte Arbeitsaufsicht.
25 BA-MA RW 6/270, 16/6/41: OKW Az. 2 f 24. 12a Kriegsgef. (I) Nr. 3712/41. Anlage: Schnellbriefe der Reichsarbeitsminister an die Landesarbeitsämter und Arbeitsämter. V a 5135/565. Einsatz von Kriegsgefangenen.
26 BA-MA RH 53-17/195, 26/6/42: OKW Az. 2 f 24. 17 a Chef Kriegsgef.Allg. (I) Org. (IIIb) Nr. 2916/42. Hebung der Arbeitsleistung aller Kriegsgefangenen. Verhalten der Wachmannschaften.
27 BA-MA RW 19/836, 19/8/42: OKW Az. 2 f 24.17 a AWA/Kriegsgef.Org(IIIb) Nr. 3879/42. Verhalten der Wachmannschaften bei Nachlassen der Arbeitsleistung der Kriegsgefangenen.
28 BA-MA RW 6/270, 15/1/44: OKW Az. 2 f 24. 17 a Kriegsgef.Org. (IIIb) Nr. 537/44. Zurückführung wiedergenesener Kr.Gef. an ihre alten Arbeitsplätze.
29 BA-MA RW 6/270, 1/6/44: OKW Az. 2 f 24. 17 i Kriegsgef.Org. (IIIb) Nr. 2373/44. Leistungssteigerung der im Bergbau eingesetzten Kr.Gef.
30 BA-MA RW 6/270, 15/7/44: OKW Az. 2 f 24. 17 a Kriegsgef.Org. (IIIb) Nr. 3197/44. Steigerung der Arbeitsleistungen der Kriegsgefangenen; hier: Aufgaben der Arbeitseinsatz-Offiziere.
31 BA-MA RW 6/270, 15/7/44: OKW Az. 2 f 24. 17 a Kriegsgef.Org. (IIIb) Nr. 3267/44. Zusammenarbeit von Kr.Gef. mit K.Z.-Häftlingen.
32 BA-MA RH 49/101, 17/8/44: OKW Az. 2 f 24. 74 f AWA/Chef Kriegsgef./Allg.(Ia) Nr. 4440/44. Behandlung der Kriegsgefangenen: Leistungssteigerung.
33 BA-MA RW 6/272, 5/10/44: Nr. 2 f 24.72d AWA/Chef Kriegsgef.Allg. (Ic).
34 BA-MA RH 49/91, 3/12/44: OKW Az. 2 f 24. 17 a Nr. 96/44 (Gr.VI/1) (Gr. III/2).
35 BA-MA RH 49/91, 10/12/44: OKW Az. 2 f 24. 71 (Gr.VI/1) Tgb.Nr. 1279/44. Entmischung der Kriegsgefangenenlager und Arb.Kdos.
36 BA-MA RH 49/100, 13/6/41: OKW Az. 2 f 24.17 a Kriegsgef. (Ic) Nr. 2950/41.
37 BA-MA RW 6/270, 26/10/42: OKW Az. 2 f 24. 17 a Kriegsgef. Org. (IIIb) Nr. 4505/42. Bezahlung der Anmarschwege der Kriegsgef. zur Arbeitsstelle.
38 BA-MA RH 49/91, 15/9/44: Stab/Ia 2 Nr. 6870/44. Der Chef der Heeresrüstung und Befehlshaber des Ersatzheeres, based on a reference to a previous order [not found]: OKW Az. 2f 24.17a Kriegsgef. Org (IIIb) von 7.9.44.
39 BA-MA RW 6/270, 1/10/44: OKW Az. 2 f 24. 17 a Kriegsgef.Org. (IIIb) Nr. 4659/44. Tägliche Arbeitszeit der Kriegsgefangenen; hier: Sonntagsarbeit.
40 BA-MA RW 6/270, 10/10/41: OKW Az. 2 f 24. 17 a Kriegsgef. (I5) Nr. 6929/41. Zusammenhängende Ruhezeit der Kriegsgefangenen.
41 BA-MA RW 6/270, 26/10/42: OKW Az. 2 f 24. 82 u Kriegsgef. Allg. (VIa) Nr. 11163/42. Abnahme von Stiefeln und Hosen bei Kr.Gef.
42 BA-MA RW 6/270, 21/7/43: OKW Az. 2 f 24. 82 u Kriegsgef.Allg. (VIa) Nr. 6573/43. Fluchtverhinderung durch Abnahme von Hosen und Stiefeln.

43 BA-MA RW 6/270, 18/9/43: OKW Az. 2 f 24. 82 m Kriegsgef.Allg. (Id) Nr. 9171/43. Abnahme von Stiefeln und Hosen bei Kr. Gef. in luftgefahrdeten Gebieten.
44 BA-MA RW 6/270, 15/6/44: OKW Az. 2 f 24. 82 u Kriegsgef.Org. (IVc)/Allg.(I) Nr. 2703/44. Abnahme von Stiefeln und Hosen bei Kr.Gef. auf Arbkdos.
45 BA-MA RW 6/270, 15/9/44: OKW Az. 2 f 24. 76 a Kriegsgef.Allg. (Ib) Nr. 4353/44. Abnehmen der Stiefel und Hosen der auf Arb.-Kdo. befindlichen Kriegsgefangenen bei Nacht.
46 BA-MA RW 6/270, 21/7/43: OKW Az. 2 f 24. 73 o Kriegsgef.Allg. (Ia) Nr. 6471/43. Mißhandlung von Kriegsgefangenen.
47 BA-MA RW 6/270, 15/1/44: OKW Az. 2 f 24. 82 k Kriegsgef.Org. (IVa) Nr. 667/44. Austreten der Kriegsgefangenen während der Arbeit.
48 BA-MA RW 6/270, 1/4/44: OKW Az. 2 f 24. 73 Kriegsgef.Allg. (Ia) Nr. 658/44. Benutzung von Fahrrädern durch Kr.Gef.
49 BA-MA RH 53-17/195, 2/7/42: Kommandeur der Kriegsgefangenen im WK XVII Az. XIII MbV. Nr. 9762/42, referring to OKW Az. 2 f 24 77i AWA/Kriegsgef.Allg. (Ia) Nr. 196/42 of 18/2/42. Streiks, Arbeitsverweigerung von Kriegsgefangenen.
50 BA-MA RW 6/270, 10/8/42: OKW Az. 2 f 24. 82 d Kriegsgef. Org. (IVb) Nr. 3317/42. Versetzung von Kr.Gef. aus verwandtschaftlichen Gründen.
51 BA-MA RHD 4/38/4, p. 13.
52 BA-MA RH 49/57, 20/4/44: Kommandeur der Kriegsgefangenen im Wehrkreis XII Az. a f 24.12 Gr.III.
53 BA-MA RW 6/487, 1/5/42: Merkblatt: Verhalten gegenüber Kriegsgefangenen.
54 BA-MA RW 6/487, 9/5/42: W.Kdo. XVII IV a Az. 60n/III Kgf. Merkblatt: für die allgemeinen Bedingungen, die für den Arbeitseinsatz von Kgf.-Arbeitskräften in Geltung stehen.
55 BA-MA RH 49/35, 1/7/43: Merkblatt: Verhalten gegenüber Kriegsgefangenen.
56 BA-MA RW 19/836, 29/5/41: OKW Az. 2 f 24. 17 r Kriegsgef. (Ic) Nr. 3260/41. Anträge von Unternehmern auf Zuweisung namentlich bennanter Kriegsgefangener.
57 BA-MA RW 19/836, 7/7/41: OKW Az. 2 f 24. 17 a Kriegsgef. (Ie) Nr. 4167/41. Erfassung und Umsetzung von Facharbeitern unter den Kr.Gef.
58 BA-MA RW 6/270, 26/10/42: OKW Az. 2 f 24. 71 e Kriegsgef. Allg. (Ic) Nr. 8063/42. Wissenschaftliche Arbeiten Kriegsgefangener.
59 BA-MA RW 6/270, 15/6/44: OKW Az. 2 f 24. 82 x Kriegsgef.Org. (Ib) Nr. 2303/44. Kriegsgefangenen-Bewachung durch Fachkräfte zur Steigerung der Arbeitsleistung.
60 BA-MA RW 6/270, 1/4/44: OKW Az. 2 f 24. 17 r Kriegsgef.Org.(III)/Org.(IV) Nr. 938/44. Anträge auf Verlegung von Kriegsgefangenen.
61 BA-MA RW 6/270, 4/7/43: OKW Az. 2 f 24. 17 b Kriegsgef.Org. (IIIb) Nr. 871/43. Brit.Kr.Gef. als Treckerführer in landwirtschaftlichen Betrieben.
62 BA-MA RW 6/270, 1/5/44: OKW Az. 2 f 24. 72 f Kriegsgef.Allg. (Ic) Nr. 1253/44. Kriegsgräberfürsorge, Pflege der Kr.-Gef.-Gräber.
63 BA-MA RW 6/270, 18/9/43: OKW Az. 2 f 24. 82 k Kriegsgef.Org. (IVa) Nr. 3893/43. Sammelplätze für Kriegsgefangene nach Luftangriffen.

64 BA-MA RH 49/91, 8/6/44: OKW Az. 2f 24. 17 a Kriegsgef.Org.(IIIb)/Allg.(I) Nr. 2860/44.
65 BA-MA RW 6/270, 1/7/44: OKW Az. 2 f 24. 82 x Kriegsgef.Org. (Ib) Nr. 2882/44. Verhalten der Kr.Gef. bei Fliegeralarm. 1. Bewachung der Kr.Gef.-Arb.Kdos., and OKW Az. 2 f 24. 73 o Kriegsgef.Allg. (Ia) Nr. 3092/44. Verhalten der Kr.Gef. bei Fliegeralarm. 2. Aufsuchen öffentlicher und privater Luftschutzräume durch auf dem Marsche befindliche Kr.Gef.
66 BA-MA RW 6/270, 8/4/42: OKW Az. 2 f 24. 22 a Kriegsgef. Allg. (IVb) Nr. 2896/42. Verpflegung der Kriegsgefangenen auf Arbeitskommandos.
67 BA-MA RW 6/270, 26/10/42: OKW Az. 2 f 24. 63 b Kriegsgef. Allg. (V) Nr. 11508/42. Aufbewahrung und Ausgabe von Postpaketen und Liebesgaben.
68 BA-MA RW 6/270, 16/5/42: OKW Az. 2 f 24. 63 b Kriegsgef. Allg. (V) Nr. 3597/42. Liebesgaben.
69 BA-MA RW 6/270, 5/12/42: OKW Az. 2 f 24. 63 b Kriegsgef. Allg. (V) Nr. 3597/42. Schokolade und Kaffee aus Liebesgaben.
70 BA-MA RW 6/270, 10/8/42: OKW Az. 2 f 24. 23 a Kriegsgef. Allg. (IVb) Nr. 6781/42. Arbeits- u. Berufskleidung der Kr.Gef.
71 BA-MA RW 6/270, 19/4/43: OKW Az. 2 f 24. 21 Kriegsgef.Allg. (IVa) Nr. 1819/43. Wäschereinigung der Kriegsgefangenen im Arbeitseinsatz.
72 BA-MA RW 6/270, 1/12/44: OKW Az. 2 f 24. 17 a BdE / Chef Kgf. (Gr. III/2) Nr. 584/44. Verpflichtung der Unternehmer zur Gestellung von Arbeitsschutzbekleidung.
73 BA-MA RH 49/47, 26/10/39: Stellv. Generalkommando VI. A.K. (WKdo VI) Ib/Org. Nr. 1329/39.
74 BA-MA RW 19/836, 3/11/41: OKW Az. 2 f 24.17 b Kriegsgef. (15) Nr. 7544/41. Notstandsaktion für die Kartoffelernte.
75 BA-MA RW 19/836, 18/11/41: OKW Az. 2 f 24. 17 b Kriegsgef. (I 5) Nr. 7999/41. Notstandsaktion für die Zuckerrübenernte.
76 BA-MA RH 53-17/188, 21/8/42: OKW Az. 2 f 24. 17 b Kriegsgef.Org. (IIIb) Nr.3945/42. Notstandsmassnahmn für die bevorstehende Erntezeit.
77 BA-MA RW 6/270, 11/1/43: OKW Az. 2 f 24. 72 g Kriegsgef.Allg. (I) Nr. 13325/42. Kunstverfügung.
78 BA-MA RW 6/270, 9/3/43: OKW Az. 2 f 24. 22 a Kriegsgef. Allg. (IVb) Nr. 2013/43. Kaninchenhaltung in den Kriegsgefangenenlagern.
79 BA-MA RH 49/114, 20/7/44: Kdr.d.Krgf. i/Wkrs.VI Abt.Ia(G) Az. Nr. 1352/44 geh. Wetterberatung für Gasabwehr.
80 BA-MA RW 6/270, 4/7/43: OKW Az. 2 f 24. 24 Kriegsgef.Allg. (IVa) Nr. 4442/43. Lagergeld.
81 BA-MA RW 6/270, 1/4/44: OKW Az. 2 f 24. 24 l Kriegsgef.Allg. (IVa) Nr. 0721/44. Lagergeld.
82 BA-MA RW 6/270, 1/10/44: OKW Az. 2 f 24. 24 k Kriegsgef.Allg. (IVa) Nr. 03804/44. Soldzahlung an kriegsgefangene Offiziere außerhalb der Offizierlager.
83 BA-MA RH 53-17/185, 10/5/40: OKW Az. 2 f 24. Kriegsgef. (II) Nr. 1768/40. Neufestsetzung der Geldsätze für Verpflegung und Unterkunft für Kriegsgefangene.
84 BA-MA RH 53-17/185, 29/6/40: OKW Az. 2 f 24. 27 Kriegsgef. -(II) Nr. 1736/40. Abzüge vom Arbeitslohn der westl. Kr.Gef. für Bekleidung und Lagermittel.

85 BA-MA RW 6/270, 1/7/44: OKW Az. 2 f 24. 17 o Kriegsgef.Allg. (IVc) Nr. 04254/44. Abzug der Kosten für Unterkunft und Verpflegung für die ersten 3 Krankheitstage.
86 BA-MA RW 6/270, 8/12/41: OKW Az. 2 f 24. 24 Kriegsgef. (II,1) Nr. 8216/41. Abzüge von Geldern der Kriegsgefangenen.
87 BA-MA RW 6/270, 10/10/41: OKW Az. 2 f 24. 17 a Kriegsgef. (I5) Nr. 6934/41. Pauschalsteuer vom Arbeitsentgelt der Kriegsgefangener.
88 BA-MA RW 6/270, 15/1/44: OKW Az. 2 f 24. 17 o Kriegsgef.Allg. (IVc) Nr. 0212/44. Lohnsteuer für Kr.Gef.
89 BA-MA RW 6/270, 16/6/41: OKW Az. 2 f 24. 12 a Kriegsgef. (I) Nr. 3712/41.
90 BA-MA RW 19/836, 20/3/42: OKW Az. 2 f 24. 17 a AWA/Kriegsgef.Org. (IIIb) Nr. 1324/42.
91 BA-MA RH 53-17/187, 18/5/42: OKW Az. 2 f 24. 17 a Kriegsgef. Org. (IIIb) Nr. 1898/42. Freiwillige Leistungszulagen an Krieggef., die von Wehrmachtdienststellen in eigener Regie beschäftigt werden.
92 BA-MA RW 6/270, 11/11/41: OKW Az. 2 f 24. 24 k Kriegsgef. (II,1) Nr. 7632/41. Soldnachzahlung an Sanitätsdienstgrade.
93 BA-MA RW 6/270, 26/10/42: OKW Az. 2 f 24. 24 k Kriegsgef. Allg. (IVa) Nr. 10648/42. Soldzahlung an Sanitätspersonal.
94 BA-MA RW 6/270, 4/7/43: OKW Az. 2 f 24. 24 e Kriegsgef.Allg. (IVa) Nr. 4886/43. Sold an zur Entlassung kommende Kriegsgefangene.
95 BA-MA RW 6/270, 15/1/44: OKW Az. 2 f 24. 24 Kriegsgef.Allg. (IVa) Nr. 11019/43. Soldzahlung an britische Warrant-Officers.
96 BA-MA RW 6/270, 10/8/42: OKW Az. 2 f 24. Kriegsgef. Allg. (Ia) Nr. 6617/42. Einstufung und Besoldung der brit.Kr.Gef.
97 BA-MA RW 6/270, 17/5/43: OKW Az. 2 f 24. 74 i Kriegsgef.Allg (Ic) Nr. 3746/43. Warrant-Officers der USA-Wehrmacht.
98 BA-MA RW 6/270, 18/9/43: OKW Az. 2 f 24. 24 Kriegsgef.Allg. (IVa) Nr. 8370/43. Sold für ind. kriegsgef.Offiziere.
99 BA-MA RW 6/270, 15/1/44: OKW Az. 2 f 24. 24 k Kriegsgef.Allg. (IVa) Nr. 9946/43. Soldzahlung an amerikanische kriegsgef. Unteroffiziere und Mannschaften.
100 BA-MA RW 6/270, 1/6/44: OKW Az. 2 f 24. 24 k Kriegsgef.Allg. (IVa) Nr. 03400/44. Britische kgf. Warrant-Offiziere des Heeres.
101 BA-MA RH 49/91, 2/1/45: OKW Az. 2 f 24.30 a AWA/Insp.Kriegsgef. (AIIIc) Nr. 08383/44. Fernspr.: 933 App.178.
102 BA-MA RH 53-17/188, 5/7/40: OKW Az 2 f 24. 24 Kriegsgef.-(II) Nr. 1333/40. Behandlung der Geldmittel der Kriegsgefangenen in Res. Lazaretten und Res. Lazaretten (Kgf.); BA-MA RH 53-17/188, 11/7/40: OKW Az. 2 f 24. 24 Kriegsgef. -(II) Nr. 2188/40. Behandlung der Geldmittel der westlichen Kriegsgefangenen.
103 BA-MA RW 6/270, 19/4/43: OKW Az. 2 f 24. 24 Kriegsgef.Allg. (IVa) Nr. 3365/43. Ausländische Banknoten.
104 BA-MA RW 6/270, 1/6/44: OKW Az. 2 f 24. 24 e Kriegsgef.Allg. (IVa) Nr. 02756/44. RM-Ueberweisungen nach Groß-Britannien.
105 BA-MA RW 6/270, 15/6/44: OKW Az. 2 f 24. 24 b Kriegsgef.Allg. (IVa) Nr. 03989/44. Versendung von Devisen nach Amerika.
106 BA-MA RW 6/270, 23/7/41: OKW Az. 2 f 24. 24 Kriegsgef. (II, 1) Nr. 5163/41. Quittungserteilung bei Reichsmarktransfer.

236 *Notes*

107 BA-MA RW 6/270, 16/10/43: OKW Az. 2 f 24. 24 e Kriegsgef.Allg. (IVa) Nr. 10334/43. Überweisung von Reichsmarkbeträgen brit.Kr.Gef. in die Heimat.
108 BA-MA RW 6/270, 21/7/43: OKW Az. 2 f 24. 24 Kriegsgef.Allg. (IV) Nr. 3141/43. Behandlung der den kriegsgef.fliegern abgenommenen Geldbeträge.
109 BA-MA RW 6/270, 21/7/43: OKW Az. 2 f 24. 24 l Kriegsgef.Allg. (IVa) Nr. 5390/43. Gelder der Vertrauensleute usw.
110 BA-MA RW 6/270, 18/9/43: OKW Az. 2 f 24. 24 Kriegsgef.Allg. (IVa) Nr. 8127/43. Lagergeld.
111 BA-MA RH 49/66, 12/12/42: OKW Az. 2 f 24. 24 Kriegsgef.Allg. (IVa) Nr. 13 505/42.
112 BA-MA RW 6/270, 1/2/42: OKW Az. 2 f 24. 20 a Kriegsgef.Allg (IVb) Nr. 801/42. Schadensersatz für bei Fliegerangriffen zerstörtes und unbrauchbar gewordenes Privateigentum von Kr.Gef.
113 BA-MA RW 6/270: 8/4/42: OKW Az. 2 f 24. 24 c Kriegsgef. Allg. (IVa) Nr. 4412/42. Lagermittel.
114 BA-MA RW 6/270, 16/5/42: OKW Az. 2 f 24. 24 e Kriegsgef. Allg. (IVa) Nr. 3813/42. Behandlung von Geld- und Wertsachen geflohener Kriegsgefangener und Internierter.
115 BA-MA RW 6/270, 26/10/42: OKW Az. 2 f 24. 20 a Kriegsgef. Allg. (IVb) Nr. 7115/42. Schadensersatz bei Sachbeschädigungen.
116 BA-MA RW 6/270, 19/4/43: OKW Az. 2 f 24. 24 Kriegsgef.Allg. (IVa) Nr. 2912/43. Schadensersatz bei Sachbeschädigungen.
117 BA-MA RW 6/270, 1/4/44: OKW Az. 2 f 24. 24 c AWA Kriegsgef.Allg. (IVa) Nr. 0535/44. Finanzwirtschaft im Kriegsgefangenenwesen.
118 BA-MA RW 6/270, 1/2/42: OKW Az. 2 f 24. 77 b Kriegsgef.Allg (Ia) Nr. 627/42. Schutzmacht für Grossbritannien und die Vereinigten Staaten von Amerika.
119 Article 60.
120 Article 62.
121 Article 65.
122 Article 66.
123 BA-MA RHD 4/38/5, p. 28.
124 Waltzog, p. 149. Though not relevant to the American or British experience, Waltzog's argument in this regard was that the logical precondition for a representative of a warring state was the existence of a warring state. Therefore, if the state no longer existed, no Protecting Power could exist for the former state's soldiers in German captivity.
125 BA-MA RW 6/270, 11/11/41: OKW Az. 2 f 24. 77 c Kriegsgef. (Ch 2) Nr. 5756/41. Vorbereitung für den Besuch von Schutzmachtvertretern.
126 BA-MA RW 6/270, 11/1/43: OKW Az. 2 f 24. 77 b Kriegsgef.Allg. (Ia) Nr. 14474/42. Wünsche der Kr. Gef. bei Besuch Delegierter.
127 BA-MA RW 6/270, 1/2/43: OKW Az. 2 f 24. 75 d Kriegsgef. Allg. (Ia) Nr. 663/43. Beschwerden von Kr.Gef.
128 BA-MA RW 6/270, 4/7/43: OKW Az. 2 f 24. 75 d Kriegsgef.Allg. (Ia2) Nr. 5421/43. Beschwerden und Gesuche Kr.Gef.
129 BA-MA RW 6/270, 15/1/44: OKW Az. 2 f 24. 74 f Kriegsgef.Allg. (IIb) Nr. 551/44. Beschwerden von Kr.Gef.

130 BA-MA RH 53-17/185, 10/6/42: OKW Az. 2 f 24. 10 e (14) Kriegsgef.Ch 2 Nr. 1769/42.
131 BA-MA RW 6/270, 26/6/42: OKW Az. 2 f 24. 77 s Kriegsgef. Allg. (Ia) Nr. 6378/42. Unmittelbarer Schriftverkehr der britischen Kr.Gef. mit der Schutzmacht.
132 BA-MA RW 6/270, 26/6/42: OKW Az. 2 f 24. 77 s Kriegsgef. Allg. (Ib) Nr. 3733/42. Aufforderung der Schutzmacht an die Vertrauensmänner brit.Kr.Gef. zur Abgabe von Paketmeldungen und Briefverkehr zwischen Schutzmacht-Kr.Gef.-Vertrauensmann.
133 BA-MA RW 6/270, 10/8/42: OKW Az. 2 f 24. 77 s Chef Kriegsgef./Allg. (Ia/R) Nr. 6540/42. Erschiessung und ernstliche Verletzungen britischer Kr.Gef. oder Zivilinternierter. This order was replaced by one dated 11/1/43.
134 BA-MA RW 6/270, 9/3/43: OKW Az. 2 f 24. 73 o Kriegsgef. Allg. (Ia) Nr. 839/43. Lagerälteste in Oflags mit verschiedenen Nationalitäten.
135 BA-MA RW 6/270, 1/4/44: OKW Az. 2 f 24. 77 b Kriegsgef.Allg. (IIa) Nr. 557/44. Lagerbesuche durch ausl. Delegierte.
136 BA-MA RH 49/91, 22/8/44: OKW Az. 2f 24.74 i Kriegsgef.Allg.(IIc).
137 Article 78.
138 Ibid.
139 Article 43.
140 Described in article 77.
141 Article 79.
142 Article 87.
143 Article 88.
144 BA-MA RW 48/13, 22/7/40: letter from Carl J. Burckhardt, CICR Agence centrale des prisonniers de guerre, to OKW Abteilung für Kriegsgefangenenwesen.
145 BA-MA RW 48/13, 25/6/40: Ref. VIII, WASt. Bericht über Tätigkeit und Erfahrungen.
146 BA-MA RW 48/12: 6/2/41: OKW Az. 2 f 24. 11 a Kriegsgef.V/Ia Nr. 152/41.
147 BA-MA RW 6/270, 10/10/41: OKW Az. 2 f 24. 60 a Kriegsgef. (VI) Nr. 5935/41. Ärtzliche Auskünfte über den Gesundheitszustand der Kriegsgefangenen an das Internationale Komitee vom Roten Kreuz.
148 BA-MA RW 6/270, 11/3/42: OKW Az. 2 f 24. 63 b Kriegsgef. Allg (V) Nr. 2271/42. Versendung von Paketaufklebeadressen an das I.R.K.
149 BA-MA RW 6/271, 20/6/42: OKW Az. 2 f 24. 77 Chef Kriegsgef./Allg. (Ia) Nr 80/42 g. Anweisung über Besuche ausländischer Staatsangehöriger in den Kriegsgefangenenlagern.
150 BA-MA RW 6/270, 5/12/42: OKW Az. 2 f 24. 64 d Kriegsgef. Allg. (V) Nr. 12677/42. Mitteilung des Bestandes der brit.Kr.Gef. an IRK.
151 BA-MA RH 53-17/183, 16/12/42: OKW Az. 2 f 24. 72f Chef Kriegsgef./Allg. (Ia) Nr. 13780/42 -II Ang.-
152 BA-MA RW 6/270, 5/4/43: OKW Az. 2 f 24. 63 h Kriegsgef.Allg. (V) Nr. 1625/43. Rundschreiben des IRK an die Vertrauensleute.
153 BA-MA RW 6/270, 1/7/44: OKW Az. 2 f 24. 24 a Kriegsgef.Allg. (IVa) Nr. 04428/44. Sammlungen britischer Kriegsgefangener.
154 BA-MA RH 53-17/185, 21/8/40: OKW Az. 2 f 24. 10 e Kriegsgef. Ch 2 (20a) Nr. 2797/40. Liebesgaben für deutsche und englische Kriegsgefangene.

155 BA-MA RH 53-17/192, 19/6/40: OKW Az. 2 f 24. 10 e (7 g) Kriegsgef. Ch 2 Nr.: 1885/40.
156 BA-MA RW 6/270, 1/9/41: OKW Az. 2 f 24. 23 a Kriegsgef. (II, 2) Nr. 5028/41, with ref to OKW Az. 2 f 24. 23 Kriegsgef. (II) Nr. 4798/40 v. 27.11.1940. Bekleidung der Kr.Gef. aus Liebesgaben.
157 BA-MA RW 6/270: 10/10/41: OKW Az. 2 f 24. 18 a Kriegsgef. (I5) Nr. 6927/41. Ausgabe von Paketaufklebeadressen an kranke Kriegsgefangene.
158 BA-MA RW 6/270, 1/2/42: OKW Az. 2 f 24. 23 a Kriegsgef.Allg (IVb) Nr. 303/41. Bekleidungsstücke aus Liebesgaben-Sammelsendungen.
159 BA-MA RW 6/270, 8/4/42: OKW Az. 2 f 24. 20 a Kriegsgef. Allg. (IVb) Nr. 3182/42. Abgrenzung der Zuständigkeit für Bearbeitung der Liebesgaben-Sammelsendungen.
160 BA-MA RW 6/270, 26/6/42: OKW Az. 2 f 24. 63 b Kriegsgef. Allg. (V) Nr. 6234/42. Zustellung von Liebesgaben für die Bau- und Arb.Batl.
161 BA-MA RW 6/270, 26/10/42: OKW Az. 2 f 24. 63 b Kriegsgef. Allg. (V) Nr. 10501/42. Liebesgaben-Reserven in den Kr.Gef. -Lagern.
162 BA-MA RW 6/270, 11/1/43: OKW Az. 2 f 24. 63 b Kriegsgef.Allg. (V) Nr. 83/43. Meldungen des Kr.Gef.-Bestandes an das I.R.K. – Liebesgabenanforderung.
163 BA-MA RW 6/270, 11/1/43: OKW Az. 2 f 24. 63 b Kriegsgef.Allg. (V) Nr. 14808/42. Prüfung der Standardpakete des Britischen Roten Kreuzes.
164 BA-MA RW 6/270, 11/1/43: OKW Az. 2 f 24. 63 b Kriegsgef.Allg. (V) Nr. 13944/42. Versendung von Paketaufklebeadressen nach den U.S.A.
165 BA-MA RW 6/270, 5/4/43: OKW Az. 2 f 24. 63 b Kriegsgef.Allg. Nr. 2038/43. Liebesgabensendungen des Amerikanischen und Britischen Roten Kreuzes für Kr.Gef. anderer Nationalitäten.
166 BA-MA RW 6/270, 5/4/43: OKW Az. 2 f 24. 60 c Kriegsgef.Allg. (V) Nr. 2859/43. Postverkehr brit. und amer. Kr.Gef..
167 BA-MA RW 6/270, 5/4/43: OKW Az. 2 f 24. 50 c Kriegsgef.Org. (IVa) Nr. 1342/43. Verringerung des Kr.Gef.-Gepäcks in den Lagern.
168 BA-MA RW 6/270, 15/1/44: OKW Az. 2 f 24. 63 b Kriegsgef.Allg. (V) Nr. 0845/44. Liebesgaben.
169 BA-MA RW 6/270, 16/10/43: OKW Az. 2 f 24. 63 b Kriegsgef.Allg. (I/V) Nr. 1064/43. Zwei-Schlüssel-System bei Aufbewahrung von Postpaketen und Liebesgaben bei den Arb.Kdos.
170 BA-MA RW 6/270, 15/6/44: OKW Az. 2 f 24. 63 b Kriegsgef.Allg. (V) Nr. 04274/44. Zweischlüsselsystem.
171 BA-MA RW 6/270, 1/4/44: OKW Az. 2 f 24. 24 a Kriegsgef.Allg. (IVa) Nr. 0934/44. Schadenersatz für Verluste und Beschädigungen an Bekleidungsstücken aus Liebesgaben-Sammelsendungen.
172 BA-MA RW 6/270, 1/5/44: OKW Az. 2 f 24. 63 b Kriegsgef.Allg. (V) Nr. 1083/44. Beschlagnahme von Liebesgabensendungen des Amerikanischen Roten Kreuzes mit Propaganda-Aufdrucken.
173 BA-MA RW 6/270, 1/5/44: OKW Az. 2 f 24. 60 c Kriegsgef.Allg. (V) Nr. 02809/44. Behandlung der eingehenden Post für USA-Kr.Gef. und Zivilinternierte.
174 BA-MA RH 49/35, 2/6/44: OKW Az. 2 f 24. 12 a Chef Kriegsgef./Allg. (Ia) Nr. 2670/44. Richtlinien für das Vetrauenmännerwesens, Kgf.-Plannsoll

der für die Mannschafts- Stammlager beschäftigten Kr.Gef. hier insbesondere: Einsatz von kgf.Bezirks-Vertrauenmännern.
175 BA-MA RW 6/270, 15/7/44: OKW Az. 2 f 24. 63 b Kriegsgef.Allg. (V) Nr. 04426/44. Verwendung beschlagnahmter Liebesgaben.
176 BA-MA RW 6/270, 1/9/44: OKW Az. 2 f 24. 60 c Kriegsgef.Allg. (V) Nr. 05364/44. Unanbringliche Kriegsgefangenenpost.
177 BA-MA RW 6/270, 15/9/44: OKW Az. 2 f 24. 64 d Kriegsgef.Allg. (V) Nr. 06256/44. Anforderungen von Liebesgaben beim IRK durch die Vertrauensleute.
178 BA-MA RW 6/270, 26/10/42: OKW Az. 2 f 24. 74 f Kriegsgef. Allg. (Ia) Nr. 10675/42. Gifte in Händen von Kr.Gef.
179 BA-MA RW 6/270, 26/10/42: OKW Az. 2 f 24. 63 b Kriegsgef. Allg. (V) Nr. 11315/42. Ersatzteile für Uhren von Kr.Gef.
180 BA-MA RW 6/270, 1/12/44: OKW Az. 2 f 24. 63 b Insp.Kriegsgef. (V) Nr. 07395/44. Paketinhalt.
181 BA-MA RW 6/270, 17/8/43: OKW Az. 2 f 24. 82 u Kriegsgef.Allg. (VIa) Nr. 6721/43. Verkauf von Cellophanhüllen und Tusche in den Kr.Gef.-Lagerkantinen.
182 Articles 35 and 36.
183 Article 26.
184 Article 37.
185 Article 38.
186 Article 39.
187 Article 40.
188 Article 41.
189 Article 57.
190 BA-MA RHD 4/38/4, p. 35; BA-MA RHD 4/38/5, pp. 40–1.
191 Waltzog, pp. 145–7.
192 BA-MA RH 49/47, 1/10/39: A.O.Kr.Gef. Erläuterung zu einzelnen Artikeln im "Abkommen über die Behandlung der Kriegsgefangenen" vom 27.Juli 1929.
193 BA-MA RH 49/47, 1/10/39: A.O.Kr.Gef. Erläuterung zu einzelnen Artikeln im "Abkommen über die Behandlung der Kriegsgefangenen" vom 27.Juli 1929.
194 BA-MA RH 49/47, 1/10/39: A.O.Kr.Gef. Erläuterung zu einzelnen Artikeln im "Abkommen über die Behandlung der Kriegsgefangenen" vom 27.Juli 1929.
195 BA-MA RH 49/47, 1/10/39: A.O.Kr.Gef. Erläuterung zu einzelnen Artikeln im "Abkommen über die Behandlung der Kriegsgefangenen" vom 27.Juli 1929.
196 BA-MA RH 49/47, 10/10/39: OKW Az. 2 f 24. Abt.Kriegsgef. I f Nr. 953/39. Kriegsgefangenenpost.
197 BA-MA RH 49/47, 14/12/39: Amtsblatt des Reichspostministeriums Nr.136.
198 BA-MA RH 49/47, 30/12/39: Amtsblatt des Reichspostministeriums Nr.143.
199 BA-MA RW 48/12, 24/2/40: OKW Az. 2 f 24 18 a AWA/Kriegsgef. If
200 BA-MA RW 6/270, 16/6/41: OKW Az. 2 f 24. 12 a Kriegsgef. (I) Nr. 3712/41.
201 BA-MA RW 6/270, 1/9/41: OKW Az. 2 f 24. 20 a Kriegsgef. (II) Nr. 5268/41.
202 BA-MA RW 48/12, 22/9/41: OKW Az. 2 f 24. 18 a Kriegsgef. (I5) Nr. 6191/41.

203 BA-MA RW 6/270, 10/10/41: OKW Az. 2 f 24. 18 a Kriegsgef. (I5) Nr. 6930/41. Postverkehr Kriegsgefangener untereinander.
204 BA-MA RW 6/270, 8/12/41: OKW Az. 2 f 24. 77 m Kriegsgef. (Z) Nr. 8784/41. Schriftwechsel der Vertrauensleute.
205 BA-MA RW 6/270, 16/5/42: OKW Az. 2 f 24. 60 c Kriegsgef. Allg. (V) Nr. 4400/42. Rundschreiben des Internationalen Komitees v. Roten Kreuz an die britischen Vertrauensleute.
206 BA-MA RW 6/270, 26/6/42: OKW Az. 2 f 24. 60 c Kriegsgef. Allg. (V) Nr. 4358/42. Eingeschriebene Postsendungen.
207 BA-MA RW 6/270, 26/6/42: OKW Az. 2 f 24. 60 c Kriegsgef. Allg. (V) Nr. 6815/42. Nachsendung der Post verlegter Kriegsgefangener.
208 BA-MA RW 6/487, 20/7/42: OKW Az. 2 f 24. 60 c Kriegsgef. Allg. (V) Nr. 2763/42. Merkblatt: für den Postverkehr der Kr.Gef. u. Zivilinternierten.
209 BA-MA RW 6/270, 26/10/42: OKW Az. 2 f 24. 60 c Kriegsgef. Allg. (V) Nr. 8440/42. Briefwechsel der frz. sprechenden Kanadier.
210 BA-MA RW 6/270, 17/5/43: OKW Az. 2 f 24. 60 c Kriegsgef.Allg (V) Nr. 1672/43. Prüfung der Kr.Gef.-Post–hier von Briefen in einer Sprache, für die Dolmetscher nicht vorhanden sind.
211 BA-MA RW 6/270, 4/7/43: OKW Az. 2 f 24. 76 Kriegsgef.Allg. (VI/V) Nr. 4235/43. Behandlung der Kr.Gef. Post.
212 BA-MA RH 49/35, 7/8/43: OKW Az. 2 f 24. 60 c Kriegsgef.Allg. (V) Nr. 5466/43. Postverkehr der brit. und amerik. Kr.Gef.
213 Ibid.
214 Ibid.
215 Ibid.
216 BA-MA RW 6/270, 16/10/43: OKW Az. 2 f 24. 60 c Kriegsgef.Allg. (V) Nr. 9984/43. Verbot von Briefen mit Werbeaufdrucken.
217 BA-MA RW 6/270, 1/4/44: OKW Az. 2 f 24. 24 a Kriegsgef.Allg. (IVa) Nr. 01185/44. Postvordrücke der nichtsowjetischen Kriegsgefangenen.
218 BA-MARW 6/270, 1/5/44: OKW Az. 2 f 24. 60 a Kriegsgef.Allg. (V) Nr. 0265/44. Kr.Gef.-Post.
219 BA-MA RW 6/270, 15/6/44: OKW Az. 2 f 24. 74 f Kriegsgef.Allg. (IIa) Nr. 2445/44. Schriftstellerische Arbeiten Kr.Gef. [Büchermanuskripte, Gedichte usw.].
220 BA-MA RW 6/270, 15/6/44: OKW Az. 2 f 24. 71 d Kriegsgef.Allg. (Ic) Nr. 2626/44. Versand von Lichtbildern der Kr.Gef. an ihre Angehörigen.
221 BA-MA RW 6/270, 1/10/44: OKW Az. 2 f 24. 71 d Kriegsgef.Allg. (Ic) Nr. 4107/44. Versand von Lichtbildern brit. u. amerikan. Kr.Gef. an ihre Angehörigen.
222 BA-MA RW 6/270, 15/10/44: OKW Az. 2 f 24. 60 c Kriegsgef.Allg. (V) Nr. 06848/44. Friedensbotschaften des Australischen Roten Kreuzes.
223 BA-MA RW 6/270, 15/10/44: OKW Az. 2 f 24. 60 c Kriegsgef.Allg. (V) Nr. 03070/44. Korrespondenzsprache der Kriegsgefangenen und Zivilinternierten in deutschem Gewahrsam.
224 BA-MA RW 6/270, 1/12/44: OKW Az. 2 f 24. 60 c Insp.Kriegsgef. (V) Nr. 07562/44. Nachforschungen nach Postsendung amerikanischer Kriegsgefangener.
225 BA-MA RW 6/270, 1/12/44: OKW Az. 2 f 24. 60 c Insp.Kriegsgef. (V) Nr. 07563/44. Unanbringliche Kriegsgefangenenpost.

226 This did not occur between Germany and either the United States or any British Commonwealth governments during the Second World War.
227 BA-MA RHD 4/38/5, pp. 42–3.
228 Waltzog, pp. 173–5.
229 BA-MA RW 6/270, 23/7/41: OKW Az. 2 f 24. 24 e Kriegsgef. (II) Nr. 5024/41. Beurlaubung und Entlassung von Kriegsgefangenen.
230 BA-MA RW 6/270: 1/9/41: OKW Az. 2 f 24. 24 e Kriegsgef. (II, 1) Nr. 5010/41.
231 BA-MA RW 6/270, 11/11/41: OKW Az. 2 f 24. 24 c Kriegsgef. (II,1)S Nr. 7620/41. Geldzuwendungen an heimzusendende Kriegsgefangene.
232 BA-MA RW 6/270, 11/3/42: OKW Az. 2 f 24. 20 a Kriegsgef. Allg (IVb) Nr. 1959/42. Privateigentum von Kriegsgefangenen.
233 BA-MA RW 6/271, 20/6/42: OKW Az. 2 f 24. 77 Chef Kriegsgef./Allg. (Ia) Nr 80/42 g. Anweisung über Besuche ausländischer Staatsangehöriger in den Kriegsgefangenenlagern.
234 BA-MA RW 6/270, 26/6/42: OKW Az. 2 f 24. 24 Kriegsgef. Allg. (IVa) Nr. 6150/42. Abnahme von Lagergeld.
235 BA-MA RW 6/270, 17/11/42: OKW Az. 2 f 24. 63 b Kriegsgef. Allg. (V) Nr. 9066/42. Verwendung der Lebensmittel aus beschlagnahmten Individualpaketen.
236 BA-MA RW 6/270, 4/7/43: OKW Az. 2 f 24. 45 c Kriegsgef.Allg. (IIe) Nr. 4619/43. Abfertigung von Kriegsgefangenen, die unmittelbar aus Lazaretten mit Lazarettzug zur Entlassung kommen.
237 BA-MA RW 6/270, 15/7/44: OKW Az. 2 f 24. 24 l Kriegsgef.Allg. (IVa) Nr. 04678/44. Entlassungen von Kriegsgefangenen.
238 BA-MA RW 6/270, 17/8/43: OKW Az. 2 f 24. 46 c Kriegsgef.Allg. (IIe) Nr. 7924/43. Lagerbesuche der Gemischten Ärztekommission.
239 BA-MA RW 6/270, 1/4/44: OKW Az. 2 f 24. 45 c Kriegsgef.Allg. (VIe) Nr. 0201/44. Untersuchung durch Gemischte Ärztekommissionen.
240 BA-MA RW 6/270, 1/8/44: OKW Az. 2 f 24. 45 c Kriegsgef.Allg. (VI) Tgb.-Nr. 0428/44 vom 5.7.1944 Austausch britischer-nordamerikanischer Kriegsgefangener und überzählen Sanitätspersonals. [sic]
241 BA-MA RW 6/270, 15/1/44: OKW Az. 2 f 24. 45 c Kriegsgef.Allg. (VIe) Nr. 0381/44. Vorstellung brit. Kriegsgef. vor Gem. Ärztekommissionen.
242 BA-MA RH 49/111, 10/11/44: OKW Az. 2 f 24. Tgb.Nr. 1244/44. I Krankmeldung von Kgf, II Vortäuschen von Krankheiten bei Kgf., III Absonderung neuanfallender Kgf. in Lazaretten und Krankrevieren, IV Abwehr in Kgf.-Laz.
243 "britische und nordamerikanische Kriegsgefangenen," as opposed to "britische und amerikanische Kriegsgefangenen"; there is no apparent reason for the unusual phraseology, though one may speculate that the author of the order, a general of the German Medical Corps, was not well versed in the nomenclature used elsewhere in the prisoner-of-war administrative bureaucracy.
244 BA-MA RH 12-23/6, 23/2/45: OKW Az. 2 f 24 b Chef W San Tgb.Nr. 230/45. Untersuchung von Kriegsgefangenen bzw. Zivilinternierten durch Gemischte Ärztekommissionen.

245 BA-MA RW 6/270, 15/11/44: OKW Az. 2 f 24. 60 c Kriegsgef.Allg. (V) Nr. 07317/44. Behandlung der Post von heimgeschafften amerikanischen Kriegsgefangenen und Zivilinternierten.
246 BA-MA RH 12-23/6, 26/2/45: OKW Az. 2 f 24 b Tgb.Nr. 300/45. Untersuchung von Kriegsgefangenen durch die Gemischte Ärztekommissionen.
247 Article 76.
248 BA-MA RHD 4/38/5, p. 28.
249 Ibid., p. 26.
250 Waltzog, p. 138.
251 BA-MA RW 48/12, 2/4/40: OKW W.A.St. Nr. Ref.VIII. 802/40; BA-MA RW 48/12, 8/5/40: OKW W.A.St. Az. Ref. Verw. 6/8.5; BA-MA RW 48/12, 14/11/40: OKW WASt. Ref.VIII 811.16.40.
252 BA-MA RW 6/270, 23/7/41: OKW Az. 2 f 24. 62 a Kriegsgef. (VI) Nr. 135/41. Todesfall-Fragebogen bei Sterbefällen von Kriegsgefangenen.
253 BA-MA RW 6/270, 11/11/41: OKW Az. 2 f 24. 50 a Kriegsgef. (V) Nr. 7335/41. Listen verstorbener englischer Kriegsgefangener.
254 BA-MA RW 6/270: 11/11/41: OKW Az. 2 f 24. 71 d Kriegsgef. (Ch 2) Nr. 7728/41. Photographische Aufnahmen.
255 BA-MA RW 6/270, 9/2/42: OKW Az. 2 f 24. 71 d Kriegsgef.Allg (Ia) Nr. 597/42. Fotografische Aufnahmen von Begräbnissen Kr.Gef.
256 BA-MA RW 6/270, 1/9/44: OKW Az. 2 f 24. 71 d Kriegsgef.Allg. (II) Nr. 3729/44. Fotografische Aufnahme von Begräbnissen Kr.Gef.
257 BA-MA RW 6/270, 16/5/42: OKW Az. 2 f 24. 60 a Kriegsgef. Allg. (V) Nr. 3401/42. Meldung von Todesfällen britischer in deutschem Gewahrsam verstorbener Kriegsgefangener.
258 BA-MA RW 6/270, 17/8/43: OKW Az. 2 f 24. 63 e Kriegsgef.Allg. (V) Nr. 6860/43. Meldung von Todesfällen in deutschem Gewahrsam verstorbener brit. und amerik. Kr.Gef.
259 BA-MA RW 6/270, 9/3/43: OKW Az. 2 f 24. 72 f Kriegsgef. Allg. (VIb) Nr. 1639/43. Beerdigung gefallener oder verstorbener feindlicher Wehrmachtangehöriger.
260 BA-MA RW 6/270, 16/5/42: OKW Az. 2 f 24. 60 c Kriegsgef. Allg. (V) Nr. 3805/42. Rücksendung der Post für verstorbene Kriegsgefangene.
261 BA-MA RW 6/270, 1/10/44: OKW Az. 2 f 24. 60 c Kriegsgef.Allg. (V) Nr. 06585/44. Rücksendung der Post für verstorbene Kriegsgefangene.
262 BA-MA RW 6/270, 11/3/42: OKW Az. 2 f 24. 63 a Kriegsgef. Allg (Vb) Nr. 2276/42. Todesfälle bei Kriegsgefangenen.
263 BA-MA RW 6/270, 26/6/42: OKW Az. 2 f 24. 50 c Kriegsgef. Org. (IVa) Nr. 1748/42. Nachlässe von Kriegsgefangenen.
264 BA-MA RW 6/270, 18/9/43: OKW Az. 2 f 24. 24 e Kriegsgef.Allg. (IVa) Nr. 9311/43. Guthaben verstorbener brit. Kriegsgefangener.
265 BA-MA RW 6/270, 5/4/43: OKW Az. 2 f 24. 62 a Kriegsgef.Allg. (V) Nr. 2577/43. Todesfall-Fragebogen des I.R.K.
266 BA-MA RW 6/270, 1/4/44: OKW Az. 2 f 24. 62 a Kriegsgef.Allg. (V) Nr. 01742/44. Ausfüllung von Todesfall-Fragebogen für Kr.Gef.
267 BA-MA RW 6/270, 15/9/44: OKW Az. 2 f 24. 82 l Kriegsgef.Org. (IVc) Nr. 4330/44. Besondere Vorkommisse; hier: Verluste von Kriegsgefangenen durch Fliegerangriffe.

268 BA-MA RW 6/270, 15/11/44: OKW Az. 2 f 24. 74 f Kriegsgef.Allg. (IIb) / (V) Nr. 5704/44. 1. Tötung oder schwere Verletzung von Kriegsgefangenen und Zivilinternierten (außer Polen, Serben, und Russen). 2. Verluste von brit., franz., belg. u. amerik. Kr.Gef. infolge feindl. Fliegerangriffe.
269 Article 75.
270 BA-MA RHD 4/38/5, p. 43.
271 Waltzog, pp. 173–5.
272 Ibid., p. 110.
273 BA-MA RW 6/270, 10/10/41: OKW Az. 2 f 24. 74 f Kriegsgef. Ch 2 Nr. 1717/41 -3 Ang. Rettungstaten durch Kriegsgefangene. No indication appeared in any subsequent orders that a British or American prisoner of war received his freedom in this way.
274 BA-MA RW 6/270, 11/11/41: OKW/Kriegsgef. (IV 2) Nr. 2703/41. Freilassung von Kriegsgefangenen.
275 BA-MA RH 49/112, 26/2/43: Abt. Kr.Gef. VI Az K 8 Nr. 452/43 g, referring to OKW Az. 2 f 24. 76 Kgf.Allg. (VIa) Nr. 408/43 geheim of 10/2/43 [not present]. Zuweisung und Entlassung von Kriegsgefangenen aller Nationen für Abwehraufgaben.
276 BA-MA RW 6/270, 15/11/44: OKW Az. 2 f 24. 82 a (Gr. V) Nr. 562/44. Zur Waffen-SS (Freiwilligen-Verbände) gemusterte Kr.Gef.
277 BA-MA RH 49/116, 16/7/44: OKW Az. 2 f 24. 19 b Chef Kriegsgef./Allg. (Id) Nr.1998/44 geheim. Überstellung von Kriegsgefangenen an die Geheime Staatspolizei. In a short follow-up order dated July 27, 1944, the commander of military district VI stated that prisoners of war of any nationality were to be handed over to the Gestapo if ordered by either the OKW in Berlin or military district headquarters, or if they belonged to an illegal resistance organization.
278 BA-MA RH 12-23/6: 20/4/45: Berlin, den 20. April 1945. Aufzeichnung.

Chapter 6: Final Assessments

1 André Durand's *From Sarajevo to Hiroshima: History of the International Committee of the Red Cross* (Geneva: Henry Dunant Institute, 1984) provides a good overview of Red Cross activities, which are covered more extensively in the ICRC's own *Report of the International Committee of the Red Cross on its activities during the Second World War (September 1, 1939 – June 30, 1947)*. 3 vols.: vol. 1, "General Activities"; vol. 2, "The Central Agency for Prisoners of War"; vol. 3, "Relief Activities." Geneva: ICRC, 1948.
2 The reports used in this study were of every camp containing American or British prisoners of war which could be found in the national archives of the United States, Canada, and Great Britain (which carried copies of visits to all Commonwealth prisoners, not just those from the United Kingdom itself). Occasionally, work detachments located far from the main camp were the object of separate reports from the Protecting Power or ICRC delegates. All of these were examined for this study, but were included in the analyses which follow only if they indicated differing conditions than those found at the main camps to which they were administratively attached. In

some camps, such as Stalag III D, the main camp was merely an administrative center, and all the prisoners of war were located in largely autonomous work detachments; in these cases, the reports of each of the work detachments were considered separately from those of the main camp and were included in the study. In some such cases, reports contain the same date (i.e. "Stalag II D Kdos"); in these cases, each report should be taken to be for a separate work detachments visited on the same day by the inspector. The total number of reports used in this study was 967.

3 The sole exception found to this rule was the proposed visit of a Swiss delegate to the naval transit camp, Dulag Nord Westertimke, on August 16, 1944: the delegate was not allowed to visit the camp, and no explanation for the decision was given. NAC RG 24, vol. 8025, file 23-0, "Note received from the Swiss," 04/09/44. No explanation was found in the OKW's records for this event, but as there were no other reports of this sort of problem at either this camp or others, one may conjecture that the problem occured at a relatively low level of command and was rectified without difficulty.

4 Durand, pp. 448–51.

5 Even in the sections on general impressions, the information transmitted to the home governments of the prisoners of war was not always detailed: a visit to Oflag VII B by an ICRC delegate on March 10, 1942, for example, resulted only in a one-line report by telegram, stating that conditions were generally sufficient (NARA RG 59 Dec. File 1940-44 740.00114 A European War 1939/304, 10/03/42: Report of ICRC visit to Oflag VII B).

6 As mentioned earlier (in Chapter 3), protected personnel were captured enemy religious and medical personnel, including doctors. While they were not legally prisoners of war, they could be held by the Detaining Power to care for their compatriots, but were nonetheless supposed to be subject to greater privileges than prisoners of war. Bearing in mind the need for security, the privileges granted usually came in the form of mail benefits – protected personnel were allowed to write double the letters and cards per month normally granted to prisoners of their same rank, and often were permitted parole walks as well.

7 The decision to assess the reports made by Protecting Power and ICRC delegates to camps containing American and British/ Dominion prisoners of war by calendar season (Spring: March 22 to June 21; Summer: June 22 to Sept. 21; Autumn: Sept. 22 to Dec. 21; Winter: Dec. 22 to March 21), rather than by month, was made after reading the reports themselves for the first time. Many problems indicated by the inspectors were appropriate to seasons (such as "more blankets needed before the onset of winter," "provided the Autumn remains mild, the coal supply for heating the prisoners barracks should suffice") rather than specific dates, and they formed a more manageable base unit than the individual months of each year.

8 PRO FO 916/2574, 06/08/40: Report of ICRC visit to Oflag IX A.

9 NAC RG 24, vol. 8021, file 19-7-1-1, 31/10/43: Report of ICRC visit to BAB 21. NAC RG 24, vol. 8021, file 19-7-2-1, 31/10/43: Report of ICRC visit to BAB 20.

10 NAC RG 24, vol. 8023, file 19-2, 05/04/43: Reports of Protecting Power (Swiss) visit to Stalag IV A Kommandos.

11 NARA RG 389, E 460 A, Box 2144, 25/03/45: Report of Protecting Power (Swiss) visit to Oflag XIII B.
12 This was the claim of the camp staff; no order authorizing this sort of measure could be found.
13 NAC RG 24, vol. 8023, file 19-44, 14/09/44: Report of Protecting Power (Swiss) visit to Stalag VIII B. The next report of a visit to this camp indicated that while material conditions remained problematic, a new commandant (a one-time chief of police of a small town) was proving fairer to the prisoners than the old one regarding minor issues and vexations, and exercised firmer command over his own staff. PRO WO 224/27, 17/01/45: Report of Protecting Power (Swiss) visit to Stalag VIII B.
14 PRO WO 224/46, 23/10/41: Report of ICRC visit to Stalag XVIII D.
15 NARA RG 389, E 460A, Box 2150, File: Stalag 10B Sandbostel (020), 13/04/45: Report of ICRC visit to Stalag X B.
16 NARA RG 389, E 460A, Box 2150, File: Stalag 10B Sandbostel (020), 13/04/45: Report of Protecting Power (Swiss) visit to Stalag X B.
17 Many of the reports indicated more than only one problem; the total number of reports for the types of harassment indicated below will therefore total more than 107.
18 The issue of reciprocity and the interrelatedness of treatment of German and British/American prisoners of war will be discussed more fully later in this chapter. For general overviews of the politics surrounding this incident, see Jonathan Vance, *Objects of Concern: Canadian Prisoners of War through the Twentieth Century* (Vancouver: University of British Columbia Press, 1994), or S.P. MacKenzie, "The Shackling Crisis: Krieger in Ketten. Eine Fallstudie über die Dynamik der Kriegsgefangenenpolitik," in Günter Bischof and Rüdiger Overmans, eds., *Kriegsgefangenschaft im Zweiten Weltkrieg. Eine vergleichende Perspektive* (Vienna: Verlag Gerhard Höller, 1999), pp. 45–69.
19 The 20 reports which noted this incident were: NAC RG 24, vol. 8025, file 23-0, 28/06/43: Report of ICRC visit to Marlag / Milag; NARA RG 389, E 460 A, Box 2144, 05/04/43: Report of Protecting Power (Swiss) visit to Marlag M; NAC RG 24, vol. 8023, file 20-3, 02/11/42: Report of Protecting Power (Swiss) visit to Oflag VII B; PRO WO 224/74, 10/11/42: Report of ICRC visit to Oflag VII B; NAC RG 24, vol. 8023, file 20-3, 01/12/42: Report of ICRC visit to Oflag VII B; NAC RG 24, vol. 8023, file 20-3, 10/03/43: Report of ICRC visit to Oflag VII B. NAC RG 24, vol. 8023, file 20-3, 20/07/43: Report of ICRC visit to Oflag VII B; NAC RG 24, vol. 8023, file 20-3, 05/11/43: Report of Protecting Power (Swiss) visit to Oflag VII B; NAC RG 24, vol. 8024, file 20-10, 11/03/43: Report of ICRC visit to Stalag 383; NAC RG 24, vol. 8024, file 20-10, 22/06/43: Report of ICRC visit to Stalag 383; NAC RG 24, vol. 8024, file 20-10, 06/11/43: Report of Protecting Power (Swiss) visit to Stalag 383; NAC RG 24, vol. 8021, file 19-9, 19/10/42: Report of Protecting Power (Swiss) visit to Stalag IX C & Kdos; NAC RG 24, vol. 8021, file 19-7-1, 28/11/42: Report of Protecting Power (Swiss) visit to Stalag VIII B; NAC RG 24, vol. 8021, file 19-7-1, 12/02/43: Report of ICRC visit to Stalag VIII B; NAC RG 24, vol. 8021, file 19-7-1, 05/03/43: Report of Protecting Power (Swiss) visit to Stalag VIII B; NAC RG 24, vol. 8021, file 19-7-1, 29/06/43: Report of Protecting Power (Swiss)

visit to Stalag VIII B; NAC RG 24, vol. 8021, file 19-7-1, 30/10/43: Report of ICRC visit to Stalag VIII B; NAC RG 24, vol. 8025, file 23-0, 24/08/43: Report of Protecting Power (Swiss) visit to Marlag / Milag; NAC RG 24, vol. 8025, file 23-0, 04/05/43: Report of Protecting Power (Swiss) visit to Marlag / Milag.

20 PRO WO 224/74, 10/11/42: Report of ICRC visit to Oflag VII B.
21 NAC RG 24, vol. 8023, file 20-3, 05/11/43: Report of Protecting Power (Swiss) visit to Oflag VII B.
22 NAC RG 24, vol. 8023, file 20-3, 08/02/45: Report of Protecting Power (Swiss) visit to Oflag VII B; NAC RG 24, vol. 8022, file 19-20, 09/01/43: Report of Protecting Power (Swiss) visit to Stalag 319; PRO WO 224/74, 29/01/45: Report of ICRC visit to Oflag VII B; NAC RG 24, vol. 8023, file 19-47, 11/02/45: Report of ICRC visit to Stalag 357.
23 NAC RG 24, vol. 8022, file 19-13, 18/03/41: Report of Protecting Power (American) visit to Stalag XX A Fort 15.
24 There appears to be some disagreement in the reports about this point. The commandant initially claimed it was "a reprisal ordered by the O.K.W. because the Australian authorities are holding back all the mail addressed to German prisoners or civil internees in Australia." NAC RG 24, vol. 8021, file 19-5, 07/09/42: Report of Protecting Power (Swiss) visit to Stalag VII A. In a visit to the camp one month later, however, the ICRC delegate was told by the German staff that the delays were the result of "a lack of personnel in the Censorship Departments... . This situation is abnormal and contrary to the orders of superior authorities and a note on the subject has been sent to the German authorities." PRO WO 224/24, 10/10/42: Report of ICRC visit to Stalag VII A. During a visit by the Swiss one month after that, the mail situation was described as "adequate." PRO WO 224/24, 03/11/42: Report of Protecting Power (Swiss) visit to Stalag VII A.
25 PRO FO 916/17, 28/07/41: Report of Protecting Power (American) visit to Oflag V B; PRO WO 224/62, 07/10/41: Report of Protecting Power (American) visit to Stalag Luft; PRO WO 224/10, 07/10/41: Report of Protecting Power (American) visit to Stalag III E; NAC RG 24, vol. 8024, file 20-11, 26/11/42: Report of Protecting Power (Swiss) visit to Oflag IX A/H; NAC RG 24, vol. 8021, file 19-9, 28/07/43: Report of Protecting Power (Swiss) visit to Stalag IX C; NAC RG 24, vol. 8024, file 21-0, 13/01/44: Report of Protecting Power (Swiss) visit to Stalag Luft I; NAC Reel C-5339, file HQS 9050-24-1, vol. 10, 04/04/44: Report of Protecting Power (Swiss) visit to Stalag IX C Kdo; PRO WO 224/50, 17/08/42: Report of Protecting Power (Swiss) visit to Stalag XXI A; NAC Reel C-5339, file HQS 9050-24-1, vol. 8, 15/02/44: Report of Protecting Power (Swiss) visit to Stalag IV D Kdos; NAC RG 24, vol. 8023, file 20-0, 22/07/43: Report of Protecting Power (Swiss) visit to Oflag IV C; NAC Reel C-5339, file HQS 9050-24-1, vol. 11, 21/06/44: Report of Protecting Power (Swiss) visit to Stalag Luft VI; NAC RG 24, vol. 8022, file 19-11, 22/04/44: Report of Protecting Power (Swiss) visit to Stalag XVIII A Kdos.
26 With the exception of Dulag Luft's relocation to Frankfurt am Main (which was noted in two reports, and which will discussed in more detail below), the other five reports concerned Wehrkreis-level decisions leading

to the dangerous placements of working prisoners of war. For example, the major problem with the location of BAB 20 and BAB 21 during the late summer 1944 was their situation near the IG Farben industrial plant in Wehrkreis VIII. The work detachments were located within the German smokescreen and anti-aircraft defenses, and their slit-trenches were not of effective use against the ferocity of the bombings; several prisoners of war were killed during Allied air-raids in August 1944. When the German commander of Wehrkreis VIII, visiting BAB 20 in early August, was formally requested by the British MOC to remove the detachment outside the smokescreen area, the commander, General von Wolff, called the MOC a coward and refused. Formal protests lodged by the Swiss after visits to these two camps in September 1944, however, resulted in their removal to a safer location, away from the immediate bombing zone: NAC RG 24, vol. 8021, file 19-7-2-1, 09/09/44: Report of Protecting Power (Swiss) visit to BAB 21; NAC RG 24, vol. 8021, file 19-7-1-1, 19/09/44: Report of Protecting Power (Swiss) visit to BAB 20. The other three reports which indicated similar significant problems regarding location were: NAC Reel C-5339, file HQS 9050-24-1, vol. 10, 25/05/44: Report of Protecting Power (Swiss) visit to Oflag 79; NAC Reel C-5339, file HQS 9050-24-1, vol. 11, 01/06/44: Report of Protecting Power (Swiss) visit to Stalag IV C; NAC Reel C-5339, file HQS 9050-24-1, vol. 10, 24/05/44: Report of Protecting Power (Swiss) visit to Stalag IV G Kdo.

27   PRO WO 224/27, 27/01/42: Report of ICRC visit to Stalag VIII B; PRO WO 224/102, 09/05/42: Report of Protecting Power (Swiss) visit to BAB 20; NAC RG 24, vol. 8023, file 20-0, 22/07/43: Report of Protecting Power (Swiss) visit to Oflag IV C; NAC Reel C-5339, file HQS 9050-24-1, vol. 6, 13/10/43: Report of Protecting Power (Swiss) visit to Oflag IV C; NARA RG 389, E 460A, Box 2148, File: Stalag 2B, Hammerstein (003), 22/11/43: Report of Protecting Power (Swiss) visit to Stalag II B; NAC RG 24, vol. 8024, file 21-4, 28/11/43: Report of Protecting Power (Swiss) visit to Stalag Luft VI; NAC RG 24, vol. 8024, file 20-11, 21/01/44: Report of Protecting Power (Swiss) visit to Oflag IX A/H; NAC RG 24, vol. 8022, file 19-37, 01/02/44: Report of Protecting Power (Swiss) visit to Stalag IV G Kdos; NAC RG 24, vol. 8024, file 21-1, 22/02/44: Report of Protecting Power (Swiss) visit to Stalag Luft III; NAC Reel C-5339, file HQS 9050-24-1, vol. 11, 21/06/44: Report of Protecting Power (Swiss) visit to Stalag Luft VI; NAC RG 24, vol. 8023, file 19-3, 03/07/44: Report of ICRC visit to Stalag IV B.

28   PRO WO 224/45, 24/10/41: Report of ICRC visit to Stalag XVIII A; PRO WO 224/27, 27/01/42: Report of ICRC visit to Stalag VIII B; PRO WO 224/49, 20/05/42: Stalag XX B; PRO WO 224/22, 22/09/42: Report of ICRC visit to Stalag VI J; NAC RG 24, vol. 8021, file 19-7-1, 06/03/43: Report of Protecting Power (Swiss) visit to Stalag VIII B Kdos; NAC RG 24, vol. 8021, file 19-10, 20/07/43: Report of Protecting Power (Swiss) visit to Stalag XIII C; NARA RG 59 Dec. File 1940-44 711.62114 a I.R./40, 20/09/43: Report of Protecting Power (Swiss) visit to Oflag 64; NAC Reel C-5339, file HQS 9050-24-1, vol. 7, 18/01/44: Report of Protecting Power (Swiss) visit to Stalag XX B Kdos; NAC RG 24, vol. 8024, file 20-16, 26/01/44: Report of Protecting Power (Swiss) visit to Oflag V A; NARA RG 389, E 460A, Box 2148, File: Stalag 2B, Hammerstein (003), 06/03/44: Report of Protecting

Power (Swiss) visit to Stalag II B; NAC RG 24, vol. 8022, file 19-24, 18/03/44: Report of Protecting Power (Swiss) visit to Graudenz; NAC RG 24, vol. 8022, file 19-11, 22/04/44: Report of Protecting Power (Swiss) visit to Stalag XVIII A Kdos; NAC RG 24, vol. 8022, file 19-36, 02/05/44: Report of Protecting Power (Swiss) visit to Stalag II D; NAC Reel C-5339, file HQS 9050-24-1, vol. 10, 19/05/44: Report of Protecting Power (Swiss) visit to Stalag XII A; NARA RG 59 Dec. File 1940-44 Box 2223 711.62114 a I.R./6-3044, 31/05/44: Report of Protecting Power (Swiss) visit to Stalag XVII B; NAC Reel C-5339, file HQS 9050-24-1, vol. 12, 23/06/44: Report of Protecting Power (Swiss) visit to Stalag XX B; PRO WO 224/38, 25/07/44: Stalag XII F; NAC RG 24, vol. 8021, file 19-10, 11/09/44: Report of Protecting Power (Swiss) visit to Stalag XIII C; NARA RG 59 Dec. File 1940-44 711.62114 I.R./12-2644, 29/09/44: Report of ICRC visit to Stalag XIII D; NARA RG 389, E 460 A, Box 2149, 18/03/45: Report of Protecting Power (Swiss) visit to Stalag IV F Kdos.
29 NAC RG 24, vol. 8022, file 19-15, 24/08/42: Report of Protecting Power (Swiss) visit to Stalag XX B; NAC RG 24, vol. 8023, file 20-0, 20/10/42: Report of Protecting Power (Swiss) visit to Oflag IV C; NAC RG 24, vol. 8022, file 19-15, 18/11/42: Report of Protecting Power (Swiss) visit to Stalag XX B; NAC Reel C-5339, file HQS 9050-24-1, vol. 3, 29/06/43: Report of Protecting Power (Swiss) visit to Stalag XVIII B; NAC RG 24, vol. 8024, file 21-4, 01/09/43: Report of Protecting Power (Swiss) visit to Stalag Luft VI; NAC Reel C-5339, file HQS 9050-24-1, vol. 6, 13/10/43: Report of Protecting Power (Swiss) visit to Oflag IV C; NAC RG 24, vol. 8022, file 19-15, 13/03/44: Report of Protecting Power (Swiss) visit to Stalag XX B; NAC RG 24, vol. 8022, file 19-13, 18/03/44: Report of Protecting Power (Swiss) visit to Stalag XX A; NAC RG 24, vol. 8022, file 19-11, 22/04/44: Report of Protecting Power (Swiss) visit to Stalag XVIII A Kdos; NAC Reel C-5339, file HQS 9050-24-1, vol. 8, 01/05/44: Report of Protecting Power (Swiss) visit to Stalag III A; NAC RG 24, vol. 8022, file 19-27, 27/05/44: Report of ICRC visit to Stalag VIII A; NAC Reel C-5339, file HQS 9050-24-1, vol. 12, 23/06/44: Report of Protecting Power (Swiss) visit to Stalag XX B; NAC RG 24, vol. 8023, file 19-3, 03/07/44: Report of ICRC visit to Stalag IV B; NAC RG 24, vol. 8022, file 19-27, 27/07/44: Report of Protecting Power (Swiss) visit to Stalag VIII A; NAC RG 24, vol. 8022, file 19-36, 12/08/44: Report of ICRC visit to Stalag II D; NAC RG 24, vol. 8022, file 19-36, 21/08/44: Report of Protecting Power (Swiss) visit to Stalag II D.
30 NAC RG 24, vol. 8021, file 19-10, 14/09/44: Report of Protecting Power (Swiss) visit to Stalag XIII C; NARA RG 389, E 460A, Box 2149, File: Stalag 5A Ludwigsburg (007), 11/11/44: Report of ICRC visit to Stalag V A.
31 PRO WO 224/45, 24/10/41: Report of ICRC visit to Stalag XVIII A; NAC Reel C-5339, file HQS 9050-24-1, vol. 2, 29/06/43: Report of Protecting Power (Swiss) visit to Stalag VIII B Kdos; NAC RG 24, vol. 8022, file 19-37, 01/02/44: Report of Protecting Power (Swiss) visit to Stalag IV G Kdos; NARA RG 389, E 460A, Box 2148, File: Stalag 2B, Hammerstein (003), 06/03/44: Report of Protecting Power (Swiss) visit to Stalag II B; NAC RG 24, vol. 8023, file 19-48, 14/11/44: Report of ICRC visit to Stalag XI A Laz.
32 PRO FO 916/17, 28/07/41: Report of Protecting Power (American) visit to Oflag V B; NAC Reel C-5339, file HQS 9050-24-1, vol. 4, 22/07/43: Report

of ICRC visit to Oflag IV C; NAC RG 24, vol. 8024, file 21-4, 28/11/43: Report of Protecting Power (Swiss) visit to Stalag Luft VI; NARA RG 389, E 460 A, Box 2148, 20/05/44: Report of Protecting Power (Swiss) visit to Stalag III B; NAC RG 24, vol. 8023, file 19-49, 09/11/44: Report of ICRC visit to Stalag XI B; PRO WO 224/43, 17/01/45: Report of Protecting Power (Swiss) visit to Stalag XVII B.

33 PRO WO 224/27, 27/01/42: Report of ICRC visit to Stalag VIII B; NAC RG 24, vol. 8023, file 20-0, 20/10/42: Report of Protecting Power (Swiss) visit to Oflag IV C; NAC RG 24, vol. 8023, file 19-2, 23/01/43: Report of Protecting Power (Swiss) visit to Stalag IV A Kdo; NAC Reel C-5339, file HQS 9050-24-1, vol. 8, 15/02/44: Report of Protecting Power (Swiss) visit to Stalag IV D Kdos.

34 NAC Reel C-5339, file HQS 9050-24-1, vol. 10, 19/05/44: Report of Protecting Power (Swiss) visit to Stalag XII A; NAC RG 24, vol. 8022, file 19-15; FO 916/241, 01/05/42: Report of ICRC visit to Stalag XX B; NAC RG 24, vol. 8023, file 19-48, 06/12/44: Report of Protecting Power (Swiss) visit to Stalag XI A Kdos; PRO WO 224/38, 25/07/44: Stalag XII F; NAC RG 24, vol. 8022, file 19-37, 01/02/44: Report of Protecting Power (Swiss) visit to Stalag IV G Kdos; PRO WO 224/38, 08/02/45: Report of ICRC visit to Stalag XII F.

35 In the Kriegsmarine internment camp, the behavior of the German security officer, Lt. Gussifeld, personally accounted for complaints of harassment noted in four separate reports: NAC RG 24, vol. 8025, file 23-0, 04/05/43: Report of Protecting Power (Swiss) visit to Marlag / Milag; NARA RG 389, E 460 A, Box 2144, 24/08/43: Report of Protecting Power (Swiss) visit to Marlag M.; NAC RG 24, vol. 8025, file 23-0, 10/01/44: Report of Protecting Power (Swiss) visit to Marlag / Milag; NAC RG 24, vol. 8025, file 23-0, 24/04/44: Report of Protecting Power (Swiss) visit to Marlag / Milag.

36 PRO WO 224/49, 15/08/41: Stalag XX B; PRO WO 224/49, 19/09/41: Report of ICRC visit to Stalag XX B.

37 NAC RG 24, vol. 8024, file 21-1, 17/04/44: Report of Protecting Power (Swiss) visit to Stalag Luft III.

38 IMT (International Military Tribunal, *Trial of the Major War Criminals before the International Military Tribunal*, 42 vols., Nuremburg, 1947–9), vol. 8, pp. 489 ff; IMT Document UK-48; IMT vol. 11, p. 171, p. 192. Also: NAC Reel C-5339, file HQS 9050-24-1, vol. 9, "Summary of Proceedings of Court of Enquiry held to Investigate the shooting of Air Force Personnel at Stalag Luft III"; and NAC Reel C-5339, file HQS 9050-24-1, vol. 13, "MI9 Report of the shooting of 50 Officers during an escape Attempt from Stalag Luft III, March 1944."

39 NAC RG 24, vol. 8023, file 19-56, 26/05/44: Report of Protecting Power (Swiss) visit to Stalag V C.

40 NAC RG 24, vol. 8024, file 21-5, 05/10/44: Report of ICRC visit to Stalag Luft IV; NAC RG 24, vol. 8024, file 21-5, 10/10/44: Report of Protecting Power (Swiss) visit to Stalag Luft IV.

41 NAC RG 24, vol. 8022, file 19-29, 20/10/44: Report of Protecting Power (Swiss) visit to Stalag 317.

42 NARA RG 389, E 460A, Box 2148A, File: Stalag 4A, Hohenstein (080), 22/02/45: Report of ICRC visit to Stalag IV A.

43 Rudolf Absolon, *Die Wehrmacht im Dritten Reich* (Schriften des Bundesarchivs 16: Band V, VI, Boppard am Rhein: Boldt, 1988, 1995), lists the documentary trail which led to the reorganization of Kriegsgefangenenwesen in Germany over the course of the war years: p. 632 (the transfer of the leadership/responsibility of Kriegsgefangenenwesens to the newly formed Chef des Kriegsgefangenenwesens im Oberkommando der Wehrmacht (Chef Kriegsgef.) on 1/1/42); p. 725 (Hitler's Befehl über das Kriegsgefangenenwesen of 30/5/43); p. 830 (Hitler's order on Neuordnung des Kriegsgefangenenwesens 25/9/44); p. 836 (the appointment of Gen.d.Inf. Roettig as Generalinspekteur für das Kriegsgefangenenwesen der Wehrmacht on 31/10/44); p. 839 (the reorganization of prisoner-of-war administration, "Neue Organisation des Kriegsgefangenenwesens," announced by Himmler on 17/11/44).

44 Germany also employed Commandos in its operations against the Allies during the war. Italy chose not to follow the German lead: after capturing, on January 15, 1943, 15 sailors and 1 officer of a British torpedo boat which had sunk an Italian ship and damaged several other Italian and German vessels, the Italians refused to hand them over to the Germans for execution: "According to the Italian viewpoint this manner of using torpedo-boats comes under the heading of regular military action. Members of the Italian Navy taken prisoner in similar actions against Malta, Alexandria, Gibraltar and Algiers have also been treated by the enemy as prisoners of war and not as members of diversion units."(IMT, 505-PS) – the German government did not press the Italians on implementing the Commando Order after this. Szymon Datner, *Crimes against POWs, Responsibility of the Wehrmacht* (Warsaw: Zachodnia Agencja Prasowa, 1964), pp. 140 ff.

45 IMT vol. 5, p. 279; Datner provides the best summary of complaints raised at Nuremberg and elsewhere against the Wehrmacht, including direct references to IMT documents.

46 Datner, p. 145; IMT Document 1265-PS, Canaris to Wehrmachtführungsstab, Oct. 13, 1942.

47 The Chief of the SD and and Secret Police Mueller complained in a letter to the OKW, dated 20/6/44, that the Armed Forces were avoiding their responsibility, under the Hitler order, of slaughtering captured Commandos. Mueller wanted the Armed Forces to kill them, even after SD participated in interrogations; the SD was to be given the commandos for execution only if they were captured by local police, but not if they were captured by the Army. (IMT Document 1276-PS.) However, Richard Raiber, "Generalfeldmarschall Albert Kesselring, Via Rasella, and the 'Ginny Mission,'" *Militärgeschichtliche Mitteilungen* 56 (1997), pp. 69–107, provides a thorough exposition of the depth to which the Commando Order permeated even supposedly "honorable" regular military officers' commands. See also Datner (pp. 158–9, p. 162) for other examples of German Navy and Army complicity.

48 Numerous examples of the actual implementation of the Commando Order against British and American soldiers are listed in Datner, pp. 139ff.

49 IMT vol. 22, p. 587, presents the finding of the Tribunal: "Bormann is responsible for the lynching of Allied airmen."

50 IMT vol. 22, p. 587; Datner, p. 189.
51 Datner, p. 191; IMT Document 731-PS.
52 Datner, p. 193.
53 IMT Document 057-PS.
54 IMT vol. 9, pp. 357–8.
55 IMT Document 735-PS.
56 Datner, p. 195; IMT vol. 35, p. 522 (Document 786-D).
57 Datner p. 198; IMT Document NOKW-3060.
58 Just how many Allied airmen were lynched is difficult to ascertain. Datner's examination of the issue (Datner, pp. 188–206) provides examples listing thirty-nine lynched airmen. The Chief Historian at the Directorate of History of the Canadian Armed Forces, Dr. Stephen Harris, stated in an interview with the author (March 4, 2000) that he was unaware of any complete list ever being compiled; Dr. Harris wrote the portion of the *The Official History of Royal Canadian Air Force*, vol. 3: *Crucible of War* (Toronto: University of Toronto Press / Department of National Defense, 1980), pp. 801–2, based on the Canadian War Crimes Investigation Unit on Miscellaneous War Crimes Against Members of the Canadian Armed Forces in the European Theater of Operations, Sept. 9, 1939 to May 8, 1945. No summary total of the number of Allied airmen lynched was found in official histories of the United States or Great Britain, journal articles, other published works on the Nuremberg Trials, or any other work on the Second World War consulted for this study, including in the testimony and evidence entered at the International Military Tribunal. At Nuremberg, the American prosecutors presented two examples of German civilians who had been sentenced to death for their roles in lynching American airmen, and stated that, "We could cite further orders of American and other Allied military commissions sentencing German civilians to death for the lynching and murdering of Allied airmen who bailed out and landed without means of defense on German territory. We think our point is made by taking the time of the tribunal to cite those two orders." IMT vol. 5, p. 330.
59 Gordon Risius and Michael M. Meyer, "The Protection of Prisoners of War Against Insults and Public Curiosity," *International Review of the Red-Cross* 7–8 (1993), pp. 288–99; Datner, pp. 198ff, catalogs a list of such attacks which were noted in the Nuremberg trials.
60 IMT vol. 6, pp. 185–6, 234–6.
61 Yoav Gelber, "Palestinian POWs in German Captivity," *Yad Vashem Studies on the European Jewish Catastrophe and Resistance* 14 (1981), pp. 91–3.
62 Ibid., pp. 95–100. Of more concern were the Palestinian volunteers who had once been citizens of Germany or Austria but who had fled those countries before the onset of hostilities; these prisoners apparently suffered some forms of abuse by their captors, though no mention is made of physical abuse, and an investigation into possibly trying them as traitors by the German Attorney of the Twelfth Army concluded that they could not be tried as such. Despite this favorable outcome, the British decided as a precaution to henceforth delete the nationality and place of birth from the identification certificates of all the Palestinian volunteers. Gelber, p. 101.

63 Gelber, p. 105.
64 Ibid., pp. 107–8. The decision not to have Jewish prisoners of war wear the Jewish star, was formally announced in OKW orders on March 11, 1942.
65 Gelber, p. 111. In the only instance in which Jewish prisoners were allegedly denied prisoner-of-war status, Gelber notes, on p. 119, that, "Palestinian [regular prisoners of war] met with a group of Jewish prisoners who had been brought from Auschwitz ... Among them they found some of their comrades, originally from Salonica, who had escaped from captivity in Greece, returned to their home town, and had been deported to Auschwitz together with Salonica's Jews. Despite representations to the Red Cross, they were held as civilians and not as POWs until 1945."
66 Leonard Winograd, "Double Jeopardy: What an American Army Officer, a Jew, Remembers of Prison Life in Germany," *American Jewish Archives* 28(1) (1976), pp. 3–17. Winograd recalls that the interrogators, in a crude attempt at intimidation, tried to pry information from him by saying that unless he cooperated, he would handed over to the Gestapo as a potential bandit; Winograd refused, and suffered no other forms of discrimination because of his religion during his captivity.
67 Robert W. Kesting, "Forgotten Victims: Blacks in the Holocaust," *Journal of Negro History* 77(1) 1992, p. 31. Kesting does not indicate if this order was made by the commander of this battalion alone or if it came down the SS chain of command.
68 See the examples and references to investigations made after the war, offered by Kesting, pp. 30–6.
69 Article 2 required, in part, that prisoners of war "shall at all times be humanely treated and protected, particularly against acts of violence, from insults and from public curiosity."
70 Ellipses in original. Risius and Meyer, p. 295.
71 Mitchell Bard, *Forgotten Victims: The Abandonment of Americans in Hitler's Camps* (Oxford: Westview Press, 1994), pp. 43–56.
72 David Foy, "'For You The War is Over':The Treatment and Life of United States Army and Army Air Corps Personnel Interned in POW Camps in German," Ph.D. dissertation, University of Akansas, 1981, p. 66, describes the case of an advance-reconnaissance American infantryman who was placed to work with Polish and Soviet laborers digging anti-aircraft emplacements for one month until his status was finally clarified.
73 Datner, pp. 35–46; IMT vol. 1, 53-54; IMT vol. 4, p. 222, Document 2997-PS; James M. Whalen, "The Face of the Enemy: Kurt Meyer: Normandy to Dorchester," *Beaver* 74 (1994), pp. 20–3.
74 IMT Documents 2309-PS, L-051, 2997-PS; IMT vol. 4, pp. 276, 384–5; vol. 6, pp. 185–6, 234, 236.
75 Datner, p. 365–6.
76 Ibid., p. 366.
77 Ibid., referring to IMT vol. 35, p. 182, Document 602-D.
78 Foy, pp. 69–80, provides several examples of travel to the Dulags under difficult conditions; Gelber, p. 107.
79 According to Gerald H. Davis, "Prisoners of War in Twentieth-Century War Economies," *Journal of Contemporary History* 12 (1977), p. 624, "British military intelligence occasionally uncovered extremely important infor-

mation through prisoner interrogations, as in the case of German rocket construction at Peenemünde. The American Psychological Warfare Division interrogated several hundred German prisoners each week during the latter stages of the war to develop a more effective propaganda." Arnold Krammer, "American Treatment of German Generals during World War II," *Journal of Military History* 54(1) (1990), pp. 28–9, describes the British practice of housing captured German generals in stately homes near London, occasionally taking them on sightseeing tours and shows in the city, as part of a subtle but successful campaign to extract important information from them; Krammer's conclusion was that the United States failed to capitalize in the same manner as the British, due to confusing directives from Washington DC on the German generals' treatment.

80 Foy, pp. 83–90; corroborating accounts of Foy's narrative on the issue of interrogations and Dulags can be found in both Hasselbring's and A. A. Durand's dissertations.

81 Gelber, pp. 110–11, reports that approximately 100 did join; the remainder were returned to Lamsdorf.

82 Datner, pp. 245–6: Göring formally proposed to the OKW that allied airmen POWs be moved into urban areas as human shields on Aug. 18, 1943, and began negotiations with the municipal authorities of Frankfurt/Main; on Sept. 3, 1943, the OKW agreed. Bormann had opposed this option in an earlier letter dated 16 June 1943, afraid of reprisals against Germans held even as far away as Canada.

83 NAC RG 24, vol. 8025, file 22-0, 01/11/43: Report of Protecting Power (Swiss) visit to Dulag Luft.

84 NAC RG 24, vol. 8025, file 22-0, 15/11/43: Report of ICRC visit to Dulag Luft.

85 NAC RG 24, vol. 8025, file 22-0, 24/1/44: Report of Protecting Power (Swiss) visit to Dulag Luft. The Canadian notation is dated May 9, 1944.

86 The delegate here is, in effect, passing along a warning from the Luftwaffe to the USAAF and RAF not to bomb the camp again; this use of a commandant and Protecting Power delegate to pass along an official notification to the US and British Governments, rather than the German Foreign Office, was unusual.

87 NAC RG 24, vol. 8025, file 22-0, 22/05/44: Report of Protecting Power (Swiss) visit to Dulag Luft.

88 Gelber, pp. 122–3.

89 Hasselbring, p 159.

90 Durand, pp. 590–1, notes that by Jan. 1945, with the German railway system "virtually unusable, or being used primarily for military purposes," several hundred trucks were borrowed by the ICRC from the US Army, the American Red Cross, the YMCA, French and Swiss authorities, and other private bodies to transport food and clothing to prisoners of war in Germany.

91 Noted by the ICRC inspector during his visit to Stalag 317. PRO WO 224/47, 22/02/45: Report of ICRC visit to Stalag 317.

92 Examples of the 39 camp reports indicating such material conditions include: NAC RG 24, vol. 8023, file 19-46, 08/02/45: Report of ICRC visit to Stalag III A; PRO WO 224/29, 18/01/45: Report of Protecting Power

(Swiss) visit to Stalag IX A; NARA RG 389, E 460 A, Box 2150 A, 23/03/45: Report of Protecting Power (Swiss) visit to Stalag IX B; NAC RG 24, vol. 8023, file 19-46, 16/02/45: Report of Protecting Power (Swiss) visit to Stalag III A , "Oflag III A".
93 NAC RG 24, vol. 8021, file 19-10, 18/02/44: Report of Protecting Power (Swiss) visit to Stalag XIII C; NARA RG 389, E 460 A, Box 2148, 29/07/44: Report of Protecting Power (Swiss) visit to Stalag III B; NARA RG 389, E 460 A, Box 2144, 23/01/45: Report of Protecting Power (Swiss) visit to Oflag XIII B.
94 Hasselbring, p. 179.
95 Ibid., p. 197.
96 David Rolf, "The Education of British [Commonwealth] Prisoners of War in German Captivity, 1939–1945," *History of Education* 18/3 (1989), pp. 258.
97 Ibid., p. 259.
98 Ibid., p. 263.
99 Hasselbring, p. 260.
100 Gelber, pp. 130–3.
101 Durand, pp. 625–6.
102 Datner, p. 209; IMT Document 3786-PS.
103 Hasselbring, p. 133.
104 Durand, pp. 461ff.
105 Gelber, p. 136.
106 Ibid., p. 113.
107 Ibid., pp. 117–19.
108 NAC Reel C-5339, file HQS 9050-24-1, vol. 13, "MI9 Report of the shooting of 50 Officers during an escape Attempt from Stalag Luft III, March 1944"; Datner, pp. 271–81, provides a summary of both the testimony and the evidence in the IMT volumes for the numerous references to the Sagan killings; Aidan Crawley, *Escape from Germany: A History of R.A.F. Escapes During the War* (London: Collins, 1956).
109 IMT vol. 10, pp. 565–6.
110 IMT Document EC-488.
111 IMT vol. 5, p. 477.
112 IMT 232-PS; Speer testified that only Russian PWs and Italian internees were used in labor directly related to war production: IMT vol. 16, p. 522.
113 J. Billig, "Le role des prisonnniers de guerre dans l'économie du IIIe Reich," *Histoire de la deuxième guerre mondiale* 37 (1960), p. 63.
114 For example, Billig, p. 74: "Il y a a la catégorie des P.G. engagés dans l'économie allemande selon le statut normal de la captivité de guerre – les Anglais, les Belges, les Américains, les Balkaniques. Ils subissent dans l'ensemble le poids sévère, main normal de leur sort de P.G."; and Klaus Drobisch and Dietrich Eichholtz, "Die Zwangsarbeit ausländischer Arbeitskräfte in Deutschland während des zweiten Weltkrieges," *Zeitschrift fur Geschichtswissenschaft* 18(5) (1970), p. 631, who argue that non-Polish and non-Soviet foreigners (including Western prisoners of war) were "die mit der jenigen der deutschen Arbeiter vergleichbar war oder sein sollte."
115 Davis, p. 628.
116 Ibid., p. 629.

117 Absolon, vol. 6, p. 741.
118 Billig, p. 55.
119 Billig, p. 58.
120 Durand, pp. 455ff.
121 Davis, p. 625: "The director of the American Prisoner of War Operations Division in the second world war believed that fair treatment of German POWs in the United States protected Americans in German hands." Perhaps the best treatment of the over-all issue of reciprocity is S. P. Mackenzie, "The Treatment of Prisoners of War in World War II," *Journal of Modern History* 66(3) (1994), pp. 487–520.
122 The Protecting Power and ICRC reports noting the reprisals taken for these actions at this and other camps were noted earlier, in the section describing "harassment." Gelber, pp. 115–16, corroborates the information found in the reports.
123 Gelber, p. 116.
124 Durand, pp. 466ff.
125 Alfred De Zayas, *The Wehrmacht War Crimes Bureau, 1939–1945* (Lincoln: University of Nebraska Press, 1989), pp. 107ff.
126 Ibid., p. 108.
127 Durand, p. 454.
128 Ibid., p. 448.
129 As was seen in the case of Dulag Luft, whose impending movement to Frankfurt was noted by an ICRC delegate in Nov. 1943, noted earlier; confirmed at Nuremberg, this was a calculated attempt to use American and British airmen as human shields, in direct contravention of article 9 of the Convention.
130 IMT vol. 1, p. 363.

Bibliography

Archives

Bundesarchiv-Militärarchiv (BA-MA), Freiburg im Bresgau
MSg 1 – Nachlaßsplitter in der Abteilung Militärarchiv
MSg 200 – Spezialsammlungen zur Militärgeschichte
RH 2 – OKH / Generalstab des Heeres
RH 3 – OKH / Generalquartiermeister
RH 7 – OKH / Heerespersonalamt
RH 12 – Inspektionen
RH 18 – Chef der Heeresarchive
RH 20 – Oberkommandos vom Armeen und Armeeabteilungen
RH 22 – Befehlshaber der rückwärtigen Heeresgebiete
RH 26 – Infanteriedivisionen
RH 31 – Verbindungskommandos und -stäbe
RH 49 – Kriegsgefangenenlager, Arbeits- und Baueinheiten der Kriegsgefangenen
RH 53 – Wehrkreiskommandos
RH 56 – Versorgungs- und Verwaltungsdienststellen außerhalb des Feldheeres
RH 58 – Osttruppen und frendländische Verbände
RHD 4 – Heer Druckerei
RL 23 – Kriegsgefangenenlager der Luftwaffe
RW 4 – OKW / Wehrmachtführungsstab
RW 6 – OKW / Allgemeines Wehrmachtamt
RW 19 – OKW / Wehrwirtschafts- und Rüstungsamt
RW 30 – Rüstungsdienststellen in den Reichskommissariaten Ostland und Ukraine
RW 48 – Wehrmachtauskunftstelle für Kriegsverluste und Kriegsgefangene
RW 49 – Dienststellen und Einheiten der Abwehr

Public Record Office (PRO), Kew, London
ADM 1 code 79 – Admiralty and Secretariat Papers: Prisoners of War and Internment Files
AIR 2 code B 89 – Air Ministry Correspondence
DEFE – Combined Operations Headquarters, and Ministry of Defence, Records
FO 371 – Foreign Office General Correspondence
FO 916 – Foreign Office Consular (War) Department
WO 32 code 91 – War Office Registered Files
WO 163 – Imperial Prisoners of War Committee
WO 319 – Directorate of Military Operations Collation Files
WO 224 – War Office: International Red Cross and Protecting Power Reports

National Archives and Record Administration (NARA), Washington DC and College Park, MD
RG 59 – General Records of the State Department

RG 200 – National Archives Gift Collection – American Red Cross
RG 389 – Office of the Provost Marshal General

National Archives of Canada (NAC), Ottawa
Reel C-5339 – Official Reports on Prisoner of War Camps, Germany, 1942–1945
RG 24 – Office of the Provost Marshal General

Air Force Historical Research Agency (AFHRA), Maxwell Air Force Base, Alabama
142.704-2 – Assistant Chief of Air Staff, Intelligence

Government Documents/Official Publications

American National Red Cross. *Historical Background of International Agreements Relating to Prisoners of War* (revised Feb. 15, 1944). Washington DC: ARC 313, 1944.Canada, Privy Council. *Regulations Governing the Maintenance of Discipline among and Treatment of Prisoners of War.* Ottawa: King's Printer, 1939.

Canada, Department of National Defence. *The Official History of Royal Canadian Air Force. Volume 3: Crucible of War.* Toronto: University of Toronto Press/Department of National Defence, 1980.

"Convention on the Treatment of Prisoners of War." *League of Nations Treaty Series* 118, no. 2734.

"Convention for the Amelioration of the Condition of the Wounded and Sick in Armies in the Field." *League of Nations Treaty Series* 118, 303.

Germany, Oberkommando der Wehrmacht. *Vorschrift für das Kriegsgefangenenwesen Teil 2: I Abkommen über die Behandlung der Kriegsgefangenen vom 27. Juli 1929, II Genfer Abkommen zur Verbesserung des Loses der Verwundeten und Kranken der Heere im Feld vom 27. Juli 1929.* Berlin: Reichsdruckerei, 1939.

Great Britain, War Office. *Handbook of the German Army.* London: Imperial War Museum, Dept. of Printed Books, 1996.

Great Britain, War Office. *Regulations for Maintenance of Discipline among Prisoners of War.* London, 1939.

Hall, David Oswald William. *Prisoners of Germany.* Wellington, NZ: War History Branch, Department of Internal Affairs, 1949.

International Committee of the Red Cross. *Report of the International Committee of the Red Cross on its activities during the Second World War, September 1, 1939–June 30, 1945.* Vol. 2: "The Central Agency for Prisoners of War." Geneva: 1948.

International Committee of the Red Cross. *Revue Internationale de la Croix-Rouge.* Geneva: published monthly, 1939–1945 issues.

International Military Tribunal. *Trial of the Major War Criminals before the International Military Tribunal.* 42 vols. Nuremberg: 1947–9.

Lewis, Colonel George C., and Mewha, Captain John. *Department of the Army Pamphlet no. 20-213: History of Prisoner of War Utilization by the United States Army 1776–1945.* Washington DC: Government Printing Office, 1955.

Mason, W. Wyne. *Official History of New Zealand in the Second World War, 1939–1945. Prisoners of War.* Wellington, 1954.

Mellor, W. Franklin, ed. *Official Medical History of the Second World War: Casualties and Medical Statistics.* London: HMSO, 1972.

Stacey, C. P. *The Canadian Army, 1939–1945.* Ottawa: E. Cloutier, King's Printer, 1948.
United States, Department of the Army. *United States Army in World War II.* Washington, DC: Government Printing Office, 1948–85.
United States, Judge Advocate General of the Army. *Manual for Courts-Martial, U.S. Army.* Washington: Government Printing Office, 1936 (with 1941 update insert).
United States, Office of Chief of Counsel for the Prosecution of Axis Criminality. *Nazi conspiracy and aggression.* 9 volumes. Washington DC: Government Printing Office, 1946–7; Supplements A-B. Washington DC: Government Printing Office, 1947–8.
United States, War Department. *Rules of Land Warfare. Basic Field Manual FM-27-10.* Washington, DC: Government Printing Office, 1940.
United States, War Department. *Mobilization Regulations (MR) no. 1-11.* Washington, DC: Goverment Printing Office, 1940.

Dissertations

Brandt, Wilhelm. "Das Recht der Kriegsgefangenen im Landkriege." Ph.D. dissertation: Universität zu Greifswald, 1919.
Durand, Arthur. "Stalag Luft III: An American Experience in a World War II German Prisoner of War Camp." Ph.D. thesis, Louisiana State University, 1976.
Foy, David Alden. " "For You the War is Over": The Treatment and Life of United States Army and Army Air Corps Personnel Interned in POW Camps in Germany." Ph.D. dissertation: University of Arkansas, 1981.
Frey, Hans K. "Die disziplinarische und gerichtliche Bestrafung von Kriegsgefangenen." Ph.D. dissertation: Universität Bern, 1948.
Hasselbring, Andrew S. "American Prisoners of War in the Third Reich." Ph.D. dissertation: Temple University, 1990.
Locker, Max. "Die Kriegsgefangenschaft insbesondere nach römischen un heutigem Recht." Ph.D. dissertation: Universität Breslau, 1913.
Wunderlich, Wolfgang. "Das Kriegsgefangenenrecht im Deutschen Reich vom 16. Jahrhundert bis 1785." Ph.D. dissertation: Universität zu Köln, 1968.

Journal Articles

Absalom, Roger. "'Another Crack at Jerry?' Australian prisoners of war in Italy, 1941–1945." *Journal of the Australian War Memorial* 1989, 14: pp. 24–32.
Allen, Louis. "To be a prisoner." *Journal of European Studies* 1986: pp. 233–248.
August, Jochen. "Die Entwicklung des Arbeitsmarktes in Deutschland in den 30er Jahren und der Masseneinsats ausländischer Arbeitskräfte während des Zweiten Weltkrieges." *Archiv für Sozialgeschichte* 1984, 150: pp. 17–20.
Buecker, Thomas R. "Nazi influence at the Fort Robinson prisoner of war camp during World War II." *Nebraska History* 1992, 73(1): pp. 32–41.
Billig, J. "Le role des prisonniers dans l'économie du IIIe Reich." *Revue d'Histoire de la Deuxieme Guerre Mondiale* 1960 (37): pp. 53–76.
Billinger, Robert D., Jr. "Behind the wire: German prisoners of war at Camp Sutton, 1944–1946." *North Carolina Historical Review* 1984, 61(4): pp. 481–509.
Boll, Bernd. "Zwangsarbeiter in Baden 1939–1945." *Geschichte in Wissenschaft und Unterricht* 1992 43(9): pp. 523–65.

Braudel, Fernand. "La captivité devant l'histoire." *Revue d'histoire de la deuxième guerre mondiale* 25, pp. 3–6.

Brown, Gary D. "Prisoner of war parole: ancient concept, modern utility." *Military Law Review* 156, June 1998: pp. 200–23

d'Hoop, Jean-Marie. "Lübeck, Oflag X C." *Revue d'histoire de la deuxième guerre mondiale* no. 10, pp. 15–29.

d'Hoop, Jean-Marie. "Propagande et Attitudes Politiques dans les camps des prisonniers: le cas des Oflags." *Revue d'histoire de la deuxième guerre mondiale* 31(122): pp. 3–26.

d'Hoop, Jean-Marie. "Notes sur les évasions." *Revue d'histoire de la deuxième guerre mondiale.* no. 25: pp. 66–77.

Davis, Gerald H. "Prisoners of war in twentieth-century war economies." *Journal of Contemporary History* 1977 12(4): pp. 623–34.

Drobisch, Klaus and Eichholtz, Dietrich. "Die zwangsarbeit auslandischer arbeitskrafte in Deutschland wahrend des zweiten weltkrieges." *Zeitschrift fur Geschichtswissenschaft* 1970 18(5): pp. 626–39.

Dunn, Joe. "The POW chronicles: a bibliographic review." *Armed Forces & Society* 1983, 9(3): pp. 495–514.

Eide, Asbjorn. "Humanitet I Vaepnet Kamp? Krigens Folkrett under Revisjon." *Internasjonal Politikk* [Norway]. 1973 (2): pp. 341–58.

Fedorowich, Kent and Moore, Bob. "Co-belligerency and prisoners of war: Britain and Italy, 1943–1945." *International History Review* 1996 18(1): pp. 28–47.

Flament, Pierre. "La vie religieuse d'un Oflag." *Revue d'histoire de la deuxième guerre mondiale* 25: pp. 47–65.

Fleming, Gerald and Beller, Steven. "Kurt Waldheim and the Allied commandos." *The Times Literary Supplement* 4431, March 4–10 1988: pp. 239–42.

Forwick, Helmuth. "Zur Behandlung alliierter Kriegsgefangener im Zweiten Weltkrieg." *Militärgeschichtliche Mitteilungen* 1967: pp. 119–34.

Fruman,-Norman, "Last days at Stalag 7A," *The Times Literary Supplement* 4805, May 5 1995: p. 6.

Gelber, Yoav. "Palestinian POWs in German captivity." *Yad Vashem Studies on the European Jewish Catastrophe and Resistance* 1981, 14: pp. 89–138.

Hantecler, G. "L'origine et le nombre des prisonniers de Guerre Belges 1940–1945." *Revue internationale d'histoire militaire* [Belgium] 1970 (29): pp. 949–61.

Heaps, Jennifer Davis. "World War II prisoner-of-war records." *Prologue* 1991 23(3): pp. 324–8.

Jones, Priscilla Dale. "Nazi atrocities against Allied airmen: Stalag Luft II and the end of British War Crimes trials." *Historical Journal* 1998 41(2): pp. 543–65.

Kesting, Robert W. "Forgotten victims: Blacks in the Holocaust." *Journal of Negro History* 1992 77(1): pp. 30–6.

Knight, Maxwell S. "The Employment of Prisoners of War in the United States." *International Labour Review* 50 (1944): pp. 47–64.

Krammer, Arnold. "American treatment of German generals during World War II." *Journal of Military History* 1990, 54(1): pp. 27–46.

Krammer, Arnold P. "When the Afrika Korps came to Texas." *Southwestern Historical Quarterly.* 1977, 80(3): pp. 247–82.

Krammer, Arnold. "German prisoners of war in the United States." *Military Affairs* 1976, 40 (2): pp. 68–73.

Kelly, John Joseph. "Intelligence and counter-intelligence in German prisoner of war camps in Canada during World War II." *Dalhousie Review* 1978 58(2): pp. 285–94.
Langdon-Ford, Jean. "Prisoners of war as library users." *Canadian Military History* 1997, 6(1): pp. 92–6.
Laurie, Clayton D. "The 'Sauerkrauts': German prisoners of war as OSS agents, 1944–45." *Prologue* 1994 26(1): pp. 49–61.
Lador-Lederer, Joseph. "World War II: Jews as prisoners of war." *Israel Yearbook on Human Rights* 10 (1980): pp. 70–89.
Lehmann, Hans G. "Gefangenen-Vernehmung nach St. Nazaire und Dieppe." *Marine Rundschau* 1973, 70(3): 153–67.
Levie, Howard S. "Prisoners of war and the Protecting Power." *American Journal of International Law* 1961, 55(2): pp. 374–97.
Levie, Howard S. "Penal sanctions for maltreatment of prisoners of war." *American Journal of International Law* 1962, 56(2): pp. 433–68.
MacKenzie, S. P. "The treatment of prisoners of war in World War II." *Journal of Modern History* 66 (1994): 487–520.
MacKenzie, S. P. "The Shackling Crisis: a case-study in the dynamics of prisoner-of-war diplomacy in the Second World War.". *International History Review* 1995 17(1): pp. 78–98.
Madsen, Chris. "Victims of circumstance: the execution of German deserters by surrendered German troops under Canadian control in Amsterdam, May 1945." *Canadian Military History* 1993, 2(1): pp. 93–113.
Mcnight, Major Maxwell S. "The employment of prisoners of war in the United States." *International Labour Review* 50, 1944: pp. 47–64.
Moore, Bob. "Turning liabilities into assets: British government policy toward German and Italian prisoners of war during the Second World War." *Journal of Contemporary History* 1997 32(1): pp. 117–36.
Moore, John Hammond. "Hitler's Wehrmacht in Virginia, 1943–1946." *Virginia Magazine of History and Biography* 1977, 85(3): pp. 259–73.
Moret-Bailly, Jean. "Le camp de base du Stalag XVII B." *Revue d'histoire de la deuxième guerre mondiale* 25: pp. 7–46.
Overmans, Rüdiger. "Die Rheinwiesenlager 1945." *Dokumentationsarchiv des österreichischen Widerstandes – Jahrbuch* 1997, pp. 118–34.
Raiber, Richard. "Generalfeldmarschall Albert Kesselring, Via Rasella, and the 'Ginny Mission.'" *Militärgeschichtliche Mitteilungen* 56 (1997): pp. 69–107.
Risius, Gordon and Meyer, Michael M. "The protection of prisoners of war against insults and public curiosity." *International Review of the Red Cross* 1993 (7–8); pp. 288–99.
Rolf, David. "The education of British prisoners of war in German captivity, 1939–1945." *History of Education* 1989, 18(3): pp. 257–65.
Scheidl, Franz. *Die Kriegsgefangenschaft von den ältesten Zeiten bis zur Gegenwart.* Berlin: Verlag Ebering, 1943.
Spidle, Jake W. Jr. "Axis Prisoners of War in the United States, 1942–1946: A Bibliographical Essay." *Military Affairs* 39 (1975): pp. 61–6.
Szefer, Andrzej. "Die Ausbeutung der Kriegsgefangenen in der industrie und landwirtschaft 1939–1945 am beispiel Oberschlesiens." *Studia Historiae Oeconomicae* 14: pp. 283–93.

Vance, Jonathan F. "The war behind the wire: the battle to escape from a German prison camp." *Journal of Contemporary History* 1993 28(4): pp. 675–93.
Vance, Jonathan F. "Men in manacles: the shackling of prisoners of war, 1942–1943." *Journal of Military History* 1995, 59(3): pp. 483–504.
Vance, Jonathan F. "The politics of camp life: the bargaining process in two German prison camps." *War & Society* 1992, 10(1): pp. 109–26.
Vance, Jonathan F. "Canadian Relief Agencies and POWs." *Journal of Canadian Studies* 31 (1996): pp. 133–47.
Whalen, James M. "The face of the enemy: Kurt Meyer: Normandy to Dorchester." *Beaver* 1994, 74(2): pp. 20–3.
Wiggers, Richard. "The United States and the Denial of Prisoner of War (POW) Status at the End of the Second World War." *Militärgeschichtliche Mitteilungen* 1/1993: pp. 91–104.
Winograd, Leonard. "Double Jeopardy: what an American army officer, a Jew, remembers of prison life in Germany." *American Jewish Archives* 1976 28(1): pp. 3–17.
Zelt, Johannes. "Kriegsgefangenen in Deutschland." *Zeitschrift für Geschichtswissenschaft* 1967 15(4): pp. 621–38.

Books

Absolon, Rudolf. *Die Wehrmacht im Dritten Reich.* Boppard am Rhein: Boldt (Schriften des Bundesarchivs 16), vols. V and VI, 1988, 1995.
Adams, D. Guy. *Backwater: Oflag IX A/H Lower Camp.* New York, 1944.
Adam-Smith, Patsy. *Prisoners of War, From Gallipoli to Korea.* Victoria, Australia: Viking Penguin Books, 1992.
Althusser, Louis. *Journal de captivité: Stalag X A.* Paris: IMEC, 1992.
Aquinas, Saint Thomas. *Summa Theologica,* vol. II. Tr. Fathers of the English Dominican Province. Chicago: Encyclopedia Britannica, 1953.
Bacque, James. *Other Losses.* Toronto: Stoddart Publishing, 1989.
Bard, Mitchell. *Forgotten victims. The Abandonment of Americans in Hitler's Camps.* Oxford: Westview Press, 1994.
Barker, A. J. *Behind Barbed Wire.* London: Batsford, 1974.
Bartusis, Mark C. *The Late Byzantine Army: Arms and Society, 1204–1453.* Philadelphia: University of Pennsylvania Press, 1992.
Bischof, Günter and Ambrose, Stephen, eds. *Eisenhower and the POWs: Facts against Falsehood.* Louisiana State Universtiy Press, 1992.
Bischof, Günter and Overmans, Rüdiger, eds. *Kriegsgefangenschaft im Zweiten Weltkrieg. Ein vergleichende Perspektive.* Ternitz-Pottschach: Verlag Gerhard Höller, 1999.
Böhme, Kurt W. *Geist und Kultur der deutschen Kriegsgefangenen in Westen* München: Verlag Ernst und Werner Gieseking, 1968 [Band XIV of the Maschke Series].
Borgsen, Werner. *Stalag X B Sanbostel: zur Geschichte eines Kriegsgefangenen- und KZ-Auffanglagers in Norddeutschland, 1939–1945.* Bremen: Edition Temmen, 1991.
Carter, David J. *Behind Canadian Barbed Wire: Alien, Refugee and Prisoner of War Camps in Canada 1914–1946.* Calgary: Tumbleweed Press, 1980.

Contamine, Philippe. *War in the Middle Ages*. Tr. Michael Jones. Oxford: Blackwell Publishers, 1984.
Crawley, Aidan. *Escape from Germany: A History of R.A.F. Escapes During the War*. London: Collins, 1956.
Dancocks, Daniel G. *In Enemy Hands*. Edmonton: Hurtig, 1983.
Datner, Szymon. *Crimes against POWs. Responsibility of the Wehrmacht*. Warsaw: Zachodnia Agencia Prasowa, 1964.
Dib, Djamel. *L'archipel du Stalag*. Algiers: Enteprises nationale du livre, 1989.
Diether Cartellieri, Diether. "Erinnerungsveränderungen und Zeitabstand – Ein Beitrag zum Problem der Erinnerungsleistungen in Abhangigkeit vom Behaltensintervall." Erich Maschke, ed., *Die deutschen Kriegsgefangenen des Zweiten Weltkriegs: Eine Zusammenfassung* (Munich: Verlag Ernst und Werner Gieseking, 1974) [Band XV of the Maschke Series].
Durand, Arthur A. *Stalag Luft III: The Secret Story* Baton Rouge, La.: Lousiana State University Press, 1988.
Durand, André. *From Sarajevo to Hiroshima; History of the International Committee of the Red Cross*. Geneva: Henry Dunant Institute, 1984.
Durand, Yves. *La Captivité, Histoire des Prisonniers de Guerre Français, 1939–1945*. Paris: Fédération Nationale des Combattants Prisonniers de Guerre et Combattants d'Algérie, Tunisie, Maroc, 1982.
Durand, Yves. *Les Prisonniers de guerre dans les Stalags, les Oflags et les Kommandos 1939–1945*. Paris: Hachette, 1994.
Eisermann, Frank, ed. *Main-Kinzig-Kreis: Dokumentation zum Schicksal der Zwangsarbeiter und Kriegsgefangenen, der Flüchtlinge und Vertriebenen im Main-Kinzig-Kreis*. Hanau: Main-Kinzig-Kreis, 1993.
Ellis, John. *World War II: A Statistical Survey*. New York: Facts on File, Inc., 1993.
Elton, Hugh. *Warfare in Roman Europe, AD 350–425*. Oxford: Clarendon Press, 1996.
Faulk, Henry. *Die deutschen Kriegsgefangenen in Großbritannien. Re-education*. München: Verlag Ernst und Werner Gieseking, 1970 [Band XI/2 of the Maschke Series].
Foot, M. R. D. and Langley, J. M. *MI9: the British Secret Service that Fostered Escape and Evasion, 1939–1945, and its American Counterpart*. London: Bodley Head, 1979.
Foy, David. *For You the War is Over: American Prisoners of War in Nazi Germany*. New York: Stein and Day, 1984.
Flory, William. *Prisoners of War: A Study in the Development of International Law*. Washington, DC: American Council on Public Affairs, 1942.
Gansberg, Judit. *Stalag USA*. New York, 1977.
Garrett, Richard. *P.O.W.* London: David and Charles Publishers, 1981.
Grotius, Hugo. *The Law of War and Peace*. Tr. Louise R. Loomis. Roslyn, NY: Walter J. Black, 1949.
Gurlt, Ernst. *Zur Geschichte der Internationalen und Freiwilligen Krankenpflege im Kriege*. Leipzig: Vogel, 1873.
Herbert, Ulrich, ed. *Europa und der "Reichseinsatz": ausländische Zivilarbeiter, Kriegsgefangene und KZ-Häftlinge in Deutschland 1938–1945*. Essen: Klartext, 1991.
Hirschfeld, Gerhard, ed. *The Policies of Genocide: Jews and Soviet Prisoners of War in Nazi Germany*. Boston: Allen and Unwin, 1986.

Hume, David. *An Enquiry Concerning the Principle of Morals*. Edited by L. A. Selby-Bigge and P. H. Nidditch. Oxford: Clarendon Press, 1975.
Jackson, Robert. *The Prisoners, 1914–18*. London: Routledge, 1989.
Jung, Hermann. *Die deutschen Kriegsgefangenen in amerikanischer Hand. USA*. München: Verlag Ernst und Werner Gieseking, 1972 [Band X/1 of the Maschke Series].
Kierman, Frank, and Fairbank, John, eds. *Chinese Ways in Warfare*. Cambridge, MA: Harvard University Press, 1974.
Keen, M.H. *The Laws of War in the Late Middle Ages*. Toronto: University of Toronto Press, 1965.
Kern, Erich and Balzer, Karl. *Alliierte Verbrechen an Deutschen: Die verschwiegenen Opfer*. Preußisch Oldendorf: Verlag K.W. Schütz KG, 1980.
Kierman, Frank. "Phases and Modes of Combat in Early China." In Kierman, Frank, and Fairbank, John, eds., *Chinese Ways in Warfare*. Cambridge, MA: Harvard University Press, 1974.
Kosthorst, Erich. *Konzentrations- und Strafgefangenenlager im Dritten Reich: Beispiel Emslang: Zusatzteil, Kriegsgefangenenlager: Dokumentation und Analyse zum Verhältnis von NS-Regime und Justiz*. 3 volumes. Düsseldorf: Droste, 1983.
Krammer, Arnold. *Nazi prisoners of war in America*. New York: Stein and Day, 1979.
Longson, Jim, and and Taylor, Christine. *An Arnhem Odyssey: "Market Garden" to Stalag IV B*. Barnsley: Leo Cooper, 1991.
Loewe, Michael. "The Campaigns of Han Wu-ti." In Kierman, Frank, and Fairbank, John, eds., *Chinese Ways in Warfare*. Cambridge, MA: Harvard University Press, 1974.
Mattiello, G., and Vogt, W. *Deutsche Kriegsgefangenen- und Internierten- einrichtungen 1939–1945*. Bd. 1: Stalag, Bd. 2: Oflag, Dulag. Koblenz, 1986 [Bd. 1], 1987 [Bd. 2].
Maschke, Erich, ed., *Zur Geschichte der deutschen Kriegsgefangenen des Zweiten Weltkrieg*.20 volumes. Munich: Verlag Ernst und Werner Gieseking, 1962–1974 [referred to as the Maschke Series].
McCarthy, Daniel J. *The Prisoners of War in Germany*. New York: Moffat, Yard and Co., 1918.
Montesquieu, Charles de Secondat. *De l'esprit des lois*. Paris: Librairies Barnier Frères, n.d.
Moore, Bob and Fedorowich, Kent, eds. *Prisoners of War and their Captors in World War II*. Washington, DC: Berg, 1996.
Morrison, Walter. *Flak and Ferrets*. London: Sentinel, 1995.
Morton, Desmond. *Silent Battle: Canadian Prisoners of War in Germany 1914–1919*. Toronto: Lester Publishing, 1992.
Müller, K-D., Nikischkin, K., and Wagenlehner, G., eds. *Die Tragödie der Gefangenschaft in Deutschland und in der Sowjetunion 1941–1956*. Köln; Weimar: Böhlau, 1998.
Pfahlmann, Hans. *Fremdarbeiter und Kriegsgefangene in der deutschen Kriegswirtschaft, 1939–1945*. Darstadt, 1968.
Plato. *Republic*. Tr. G. M. A. Grube. Indianapolis: Hackett Publishing, 1974.
Pringle, Jack. *Colditz Last Stop*. Sussex, UK: Temple House Books, 1995.
Reid, P. R. *Colditz: the full story*. London: Macmillan, 1984.
Reiss, Rodolphe Archibald. *Le Traitement des prisonniers et des blessés par les Germano-Bulgares*. Paris: Librairie Bernard Grasset, 1919.

Robel, Hergard. "Vergleichender Überblick." Erich Maschke, ed., *Die deutschen Kriegsgefangenen des Zweiten Weltkriegs: Eine Zusammenfassung*. Munich: Verlag Ernst und Werner Gieseking, 1974 [Band XV of the Maschke Series].

Rolf, David. *Prisoners of the Reich*. London: Cooper, 1988.

Romilly, Giles and Alexander, Michael. *The Privileged Nightmare*. London: Weidenfeld and Nicolson, 1954.

Rousseau, J. J. *The Social Contract*. Tr. Christopher Betts. Oxford: Oxford University Press, 1994.

Roxburgh, Ronald F. *The Prisoners of War Information Bureau in London*. London: Longmans, Green and Co., 1915.

Schönborn, Siegfried. *Kriegsgefangene und Fremdarbeiter in unserer Heimat 1939–1945*. Freigericht: Naumann, 1990.

Streim, Alfred. *Die Behandlung sowjetischer Kriegsgefangener im "Fall Barbarosa"*. Heidelberg: Müller Verlag, 1981.

Streit, Christian. *Keine Kameraden: die Wehrmacht und die sowjetischen Kriegsgefangenen 1941–1945*. Bonn: Verlag J. H. W. Dietz Nachf., 1997.

Thucydides. *The Peloponnesian War*. Translated by Rex Warner. Middlesex, England: Penguin Press, 1954.

Tzu, Sun. *The Art of War*. Tr. Samuel B. Griffith. Oxford: Oxford University Press, 1963.

Vance, Jonathan. *Objects of Concern: Canadian Prisoners of War through the Twentieth Century*. Vancouver: University of British Columbia Press, 1994.

Waltzog, Alfons. *Recht der Landeskriegsführung*. Berlin: Verlag Franz Vahlen, 1942.

Ward, Robert. *An Enquiry into the Foundation and History of the Law of Nations in Europe from the Time of the Greeks and Romans to the Age of Grotius*. 2 vols. New York: Garland Publishing, 1973 (repr. of 1795 London ed.).

Wells, David. *The Laws of Land Warfare: A Guide to the U.S. Army Manuals*. Westport, CN: Greenport Press, 1992.

Wolff, Helmut. *Die deutschen Kriegsgefangenen in britischer Hand. Ein Überblick*. München: Verlag Ernst und Werner Gieseking, 1974 [Band XI/1 of the Maschke Series].

Wheaton, Henry. *History of the Law of Nations in Europe and America from the Earliest Times to the Treaty of Washington, 1842*. New York: Garland Publishing, 1973; repr. of 1845 edition.

De Zayas, Alfred. *Die Wehrmacht-Untersuchungsstelle: Deutsche Ermittlungen über alliierte Völkerrechtsverletungen im Zweiten Weltkrieg*. München: Universitas-Verlag/Langen Müller, 1979; published in English as *The Wehrmacht War Crimes Bureau, 1939–1945*. Lincoln: University of Nebraska Press, 1989.

Index

BAB 20/21 169–70

Capture and early captivity of prisoners: 43–8, 193
Commando Order ["Kommandobefehl"]: cross-examination of Keitel regarding xi, 44–5, 186–7
Crimes and punishments: 75–6. *See also* Disciplinary issues, Judicial issues, Security issues

Disciplinary issues: 76ff.
 conclusions 197–8
 disciplinary authority 80–1
 equality of punishment 82
 escape 77–80, 198; *see also* Security issues: escapes
 German clarifications and local disciplinary rules 83–7
 promulgation of orders 81–2
Dulags: 29, 44
Dulag Luft 29, 193

Ends of captivity
 death 158–61
 liberation 162–4
 wounded repatriation/Mixed Medical Commission (MMC) 153–8
External relations:
 Collective Parcels 140–3
 International Committee of the Red Cross (ICRC) 5, 7, 8ff., 137–40, reports 165–85
 Mail/Post 144–53
 Protecting Power 6, 7, 8ff., 133–7, reports 165–85

Finance: general issues 109–13, 131, foreign currencies and transfers 131–3

Geneva Convention of 1929: 25–6
 copies available in the camps 47–8
 violations of: *see* Harrassment
 For the Convention on specific subtopics, see the beginning of each relevant section in Chapters 3, 4, and 5
Germany
 distribution and opening dates of camps 31ff.
 prisoner-of-war policy in 1939, 28–9
 structure of prisoner of war affairs 29ff.
Great Britain/Commonwealth prisoner-of-war policy in 1939, 26ff.

Harrassment and serious violations of the Geneva Convention 178–83, 201
Historical background 11ff.
 First World War 23–5
 Hague Conventions 22
 Henri Dunant 21
 Lieber Code 20–1
 modern era 16ff.
 treaties 18ff.
 See also Geneva Convention
Historiography: 2ff.

Identification and status of prisoners (rank, nationality, partisans, etc.) 37–43, 186–93
International Committee of the Red Cross (ICRC) *see* External relations

Judicial issues 87ff.
 fraternization 92–3
 new judicial rules 91–2
 poaching 93–4
 trials 88–91

265

Labor
    conclusions 198–200
    forbidden labor 113–14
    general directives 121–7
    general issues 109–13
    improving labor efficiency 114–19
    officers and noncommissioned
        officers 112–13
    rest period 119; boots and pants
        120–1
    wages and deductions 127–30
Lynching of Allied airmen 188–9

Material conditions in prisoner-of-war
    camps 165–77
Minorities among prisoners 189–91

Numbers of prisoners of war 34ff.
Nuremburg Trials 10

Oflags 30; *see also*: Germany,
    distribution and opening dates of
    camps
    Oflag IV C 79
    Oflag IX A 167–9
    Oflag XIII B 171–2

Prisoner-of-war camps – general:
    clothing 58–60
    conclusions 194–6
    food 55–8
    health issues/protected personnel
        (doctors, clergy) 61–5
    infrastructure, location, air-raid
        shelters 48–53
    interior accommodations 53–4
    recreation/canteens 67–70
    religion 65–7
    transportation and transfers 70–4
Protecting Power: *see* External
    relations

Security issues 94ff.
    cooperation with the SS 104–5
    escapes 101–4, *see also* Disciplinary
        issues, escape
    guarding the prisoners 94–101
    Normandy 105–7
    sabotage 107–8
Stalags 30; *see also* Germany,
    distribution and opening dates of
    camps
    Stalag IV A 170–1, 182
    Stalag V C 181–2
    Stalag VIII B 172–3
    Stalag X B 4, 29, 175–6
    Stalag XVIII D 173–5
    Stalag XX B 181
    Stalag 317 182
    Stalag Luft III Great Escape 4, 181
    Stalag Luft VI and IV transfer of
        prisoners 182

United States prisoner-of-war policy
    in 1939, 27ff.

Waltzog, Dr. Alfons, 1942 update to
    German policy, 210 (n. 96). *For
    specific topics, see the beginning of
    each relevant section in Chapters 3,
    4, and 5*
Wehrkreis map p. x, 30; *see also*:
    Germany, distribution and
    opening dates of camps